MR/MRS G.A.LENNOX
7670-18TH AVENUE
BURNABY,B.C.
V3N 1H9

THE INSPIRAT

Benjamin Breckinridge Warfield

# THE INSPIRATION AND AUTHORITY OF THE BIBLE

BY

## BENJAMIN BRECKINRIDGE WARFIELD

*Professor of Didactic and Polemic Theology*
*in the Theological Seminary of Princeton*
*New Jersey, 1887–1921*

*Edited by*

## SAMUEL G. CRAIG

*With an Introduction by*

## CORNELIUS VAN TIL

*"The Scripture cannot be broken"*

*Published by*

THE PRESBYTERIAN AND REFORMED PUBLISHING COMPANY

ISBN 0-87552-527X

Library of Congress Catalog Card Number 53-12862

PRINTED IN THE UNITED STATES OF AMERICA

# FOREWORD

THIS volume contains the principal articles by the late Benjamin Breckinridge Warfield having to do with the nature and authority of the Bible. A distinctly biblical theologian, fully abreast of the critical scholarship of the day, and a foe of irrationalism in all its forms—faith for him was conviction grounded on evidence—it is not surprising that he devoted such exceptional attention to this theme. Written from time to time and printed in various publications during his lifetime, these articles were included in the volume *Revelation and Inspiration* published by the Oxford University Press subsequent to his death. Unfortunately the sponsors of that volume—of which a limited edition was printed—underestimated the interest it would attract with the result that it has not been obtainable for several years. These articles have been reprinted by the Presbyterian and Reformed Publishing Company—in response to a widespread demand—under a different title because the content of this volume, even apart from its Introduction, is not exactly the same as the content of the volume published under the auspices of the Oxford University Press. We are of the opinion that in choosing the title *The Inspiration and Authority of the Bible* it has chosen a title more indicative than the previous one of the main thesis Warfield sought to establish in these articles.

That the view of the inspiration and authority of the Bible expounded and defended in these articles is essentially that which has been held by the Christian Church in all its main branches throughout its entire history, at least until recent times, is generally admitted. It is somewhat different, however, as regards the claim that the doctrine of the Bible held and taught by the Church is the doctrine of the Bible not only held and taught by the writers of the New Testament but by Jesus himself as reported in the Gospels. To the exegetical establishment of this claim, so frequently ignored and even denied, Warfield brings the resources of his immense scholarship. The evidence in its support is marshalled comprehensively in chapter three and with, perhaps, unexampled thoroughness as regards the meaning of certain crucial words and phrases as employed in the New Testament in chapters six, seven and eight. The practical and apologetical significance of this fact—for fact we believe he has abundantly proven it to be—is emphasized throughout these articles but especially in chapters two and four.

The major difference between this volume and its predecessor is its Introduction by Cornelius Van Til, Ph.D., Professor of Apologetics in Westminster Theological Seminary of Philadelphia. If the articles included in this volume had been published in book form during Warfield's lifetime it is safe to say that he himself would have written some such introduction. Even if he had done so Dr. Van Til's introduction would not be superfluous in view of the developments in philosophy and theology since Warfield's death in 1921. For instance the most important cleavage within Protestantism today as regards the inspiration and authority of the Bible—that between the Theology of Crisis, or so-called Neo-orthodoxy, and the historic Protestant position—had not yet made its appearance. We count ourselves fortunate, therefore, in being able to preface these articles by Warfield by so extensive an article written by one who is as fully abreast of the thought-movements of today as Warfield was of his day and who nevertheless shares his view of the inspiration and authority of the Bible. An outstanding feature of Dr. Van Til's contribution is its challenge of the modern theory of knowledge insofar as it has significance for the question of the infallibility of the Bible as it came from the hands of its writers. While many influential scholars under the influence of that theory deny not only the actuality but the very possibility of an infallible Bible, Dr. Van Til maintains not only the actuality of such a Bible but its vital importance not only for theology but for science and philosophy.

Evangelicals, other than Reformed, who hold that "Scripture cannot be broken" will take exception to the representation that only the followers of Calvin have a theology in which this conception of Scripture fully fits. It is not to be supposed, however, that this will keep such evangelicals from welcoming this volume with its scholarly defense of that view of the nature and authority of the Bible that they profess in common with their Reformed brethren. At the same time they will no doubt agree that in order to justify their objection they must be able to show that this conception of Scripture fits into, finds a more natural and logical a place in their system of theological thought, whether Lutheran or Arminian, than in the Reformed.

S. G. C.

# CONTENTS

# OTHER ARTICLES ON INSPIRATION AND THE BIBLE

# I
# INTRODUCTION

# INTRODUCTION

In the present volume there is offered to the public a reproduction of the major writings of the late Benjamin Breckinridge Warfield on the doctrine of Scripture. In his day Dr. Warfield was perhaps the greatest defender of what is frequently called "the high Protestant doctrine of the Bible." More particularly as one of the outstanding Reformed theologians of his day he was deeply concerned to defend the view of Scripture set forth in the Westminster Confession of Faith. He was not concerned to defend the classical Reformed view of Scripture merely because it was found in the Confession to which, perhaps for other reasons, he had subscribed.[1] For him the classical doctrine of the infallible inspiration of Scripture was involved in the doctrine of divine sovereignty. God could not be sovereign in his disposition of rational human beings if he were not also sovereign in his revelation of himself to them. If God is sovereign in the realm of being, he is surely also sovereign in the realm of knowledge. Scripture is a factor in the redeeming work of God, a component part of the series of his redeeming acts, without which that series would be incomplete and so far inoperative for its main end.[2] As one deeply interested in the progress of the doctrine of God's sovereign grace, Warfield put all his erudition to work for the vindication of an infallible Bible.

In his writings there is a discussion on the general problem of Scripture. There is also a very detailed and painstaking analysis of questions pertaining to textual and higher criticism. Through it all there is the contention that the Bible is, in its autographa, the infallible Word of God.

It is not our purpose here to analyze or recapitulate that argument. The reader can see at a glance with what care and

[1] *Cf.* p. 419.
[2] *Cf.* p. 80.

acumen it proceeds. It is our purpose rather to ask whether it is true, as is frequently asserted, that the day for such an argument has passed. There will always be room, it is said, for a critical analysis of the text of Scripture as there will always be room for a critical analysis of the text of *The Critique of Pure Reason.* But who today thinks that the original manuscripts of Scripture will ever be found? And who today thinks that, if they could be found, we should be in actual possession of the infallible Word of God? In any case, does not God come to man by free and living personal encounter even when he uses the words of the past? With such rhetorical questions many would dismiss Warfield's argument as wholly irrelevant to our present situation. It is perhaps not too much to say that, for many professing Christian theologians, the idea of a final and finished revelation from God to man about himself and his place in the universe has no serious significance today.

No doubt the first thing that those who still profess adherence to the traditional view of the Bible should do is to ask whether in stating the argument for their view they have done it in such a way as to challenge the best thought of our age. To challenge that thought requires of us that we should enter sympathetically into the problems of the modern theory of knowledge. Modern man asks how knowledge is possible. In answering this question he wants to be *critical* rather than *dogmatic.* He says he seeks to test all assumptions, not excluding his own.

Those who believe the Bible in the traditional sense have no cavil with this manner of stating the matter. Certainly Warfield would not have had. He was a profound as well as an erudite theologian. His many contributions in the field of doctrine and apologetics show him to have been a man fully abreast of the thought of his time. He was aware of the developments in post-Kantian philosophy as well as post-Kantian theology. Nor was he unmindful of the philosophical assumptions that underlie the factual studies of modern biblical research.

———————

Since Warfield's day the matter of the philosophical presuppositions that underlie the factual discussion of the data of knowledge has come to stand in the foreground of interest. Great emphasis is being placed upon the subject's contribution in the knowledge situation. Every fact, we are told, is *taken* as much as *given*. It is as useless to speak of facts by themselves as it is to speak of a noise in the woods a hundred miles from the woodman's house. In consequence the distinction so commonly made by Ritschlian theologians between judgments about pure facts and judgments about values is not so common as it was a generation ago. In a recent analysis of the question of religious knowledge in our day Alan Richardson says:

"The consequences of this false distinction between judgments of fact and judgments of value have proved a veritable *hereditas damnosa* in subsequent theological discussion. From it springs directly the false contrast between the 'simple Gospel' of Jesus and the 'theology' of the apostolic Church. The true Gospel is regarded as consisting in the simple facts about and teachings of the historical Jesus, who can thus be objectively portrayed by modern historical research, while the interpretations of St. Paul and the other apostles may be discarded as representing values for them which are no longer values for us." [3]

The Ritschlians were seeking to safeguard or reinstate the rightful place of objectivity in the gospel message. "They were trying to safeguard the objectivity of the facts themselves, as existing independently of the wishes of the believer. They thus placed great emphasis upon the historical character of the revelation, and they held that historical research, being scientific and independent of all value-judgments, could put an end to subjective speculation and free us from all the 'accretions' of traditional dogma." [4] Yet the Ritschlians themselves knew that "many able and well-disposed minds have looked at the historical facts and have found no revelation in them . . ." [5] Thus "the illusion of 'objective' or uninterpreted history is finally swept away. The facts of history cannot be disentangled from the principles of interpretation by which alone they can

[3] *Christian Apologetics*, p. 148. London: The S. C. M. Press, 1947; New York: Harper & Brothers, 1948.
[4] *Idem*, p. 149.          [5] *Idem*, p. 150.

be presented to us *as history,* that is, as a coherent and connected series or order of events. Christian faith supplies the necessary principle of interpretation by which the facts of the biblical and Christian history can be rationally seen and understood." [6]

It is this principle of the inseparability of the facts from the principle of interpretation by which they are observed that has been greatly stressed since Warfield's time. We shall call this the new, the current, or modern principle. In contending for the relevance of Warfield's argument for our day it is with this principle that we shall primarily need to be concerned. In it lies embedded the current form of the problem of objectivity in religious knowledge.

---

It is claimed that it is only by means of this principle that true objective knowledge of God and of his Christ can be obtained. For in it, the subjective itself has been taken into the objective. In the traditional view, we are told, the subject stood hostile over against the object. The object of knowledge itself was conceived in a static sort of way. In consequence the subject's activity in relation to the object was discounted or disparaged. When the subject rebelled against this artificial and dictatorial sort of treatment its only recourse was to cut itself loose from all connection with the objective aspect of the gospel. The result was rationalism, materialism and secularism.

The contention is further made that only by the use of the principle of the interdependence of fact and interpretation can the uniqueness of the Christian revelation be maintained. Christianity is an historical religion. It stands or falls with the facts of the life, death and resurrection of Jesus of Nazareth. But the categories of orthodoxy could do no justice to the uniqueness of historical facts. According to the tenets of traditional belief, we are told, the facts of history are handled as roughly as Procrustes was accustomed to handling his guests. According to orthodoxy the whole of history is said to be but the expres-

[6] *Idem,* p. 150.

sion in time of a static, changeless plan of God. God himself was conceived statically. He was eternally the same. There was no increment of being or wisdom in him. He was all-glorious. How then could anything that should take place in the course of history really add to his glory? Man's chief end was said to be to glorify God while all that man might have done in the course of fulfilling this task had already been done, or could not be done. God was thought of as the first cause of man and his world, thus making all things in the world, including man, mechanically dependent upon him. Man was endowed with certain static qualities such as rationality and will which together were called the image of God. These qualities man could neither gain nor lose. Even though he was said to have fallen, and thus to have lost original knowledge, righteousness and holiness, this fall was pre-determined. And among those that had thus "fallen" there were some that were pre-determined to a changeless eternal life and others who were pre-determined to a changeless eternal death. Thus the whole of history, including even its purported miracles, was reduced to something static.

The form of revelation that went with this static conception of reality as a whole was naturally that of conveying to man in the form of intellectual propositions the content of this eternally changeless plan. The mind of man was not given any significant function in the realization of this plan. All man could do was to accept passively the set of propositions, together forming a system of doctrine, that was laid before him. No difference was made in orthodox theology between the revelation that took place in the events of history and the recording of that revelation in the Scripture. Even the minds of the prophets, who were called the special media of revelation, were thought of as being primarily passive in their reception of revelation.

But with the acceptance of the notion of the interdependence of the facts of history and their principle of interpretation, we are told, all that has changed. Revelation is now seen to be historical or eventual. The events are genuinely significant for it is their very individuality and reality that is presupposed even for the making of a "system of truth." It is no longer some abstract static deity, who stands back of history from whom in some mysterious, wholly unintelligible way a set number of propositions drop till he decides it is enough, but it is the living God who gives himself in his revelation. When God thus actively gives himself then man spontaneously responds. He responds with love and adoration because it is through God giving himself that man is able to respond. Revelation thus becomes a process of interaction between God giving himself to man and man by God's grace in return giving himself to God. *God is what he is for man and man is what he is for God.* It is this divine-human encounter in constant living form that is said to overcome the meaningless and artificial staticism of the traditional concept of Scripture.

In claiming true objectivity and uniqueness for itself the modern principle also claims certain other advantages. It claims to have solved the problem of authority and reason. Those who stress the need for authority and those who stress the need for reason are both in search of objectivity.

Those who advocate the idea of authority hold that reason cannot give objective certainty in knowledge. In particular it cannot give objective certainty in the religious field. Reason may assert things about God and about things beyond the experience of man but what it thus asserts cannot be said to be a part of knowledge by experience. By reason man cannot reach into the field of the divine. At least he cannot there speak with the same assurance that he is wont to employ with respect to the empirical realm.

Therefore if there is to be any certainty with respect to the unique historical facts of Christianity and, in particular, if there is to be any assurance with respect to the miraculous element in Scripture, this, it is often said, will have to be accepted on purely non-rational grounds. Now this is precisely, it is said, what the traditional view wanted men to do. Men were required to believe the utterly non-rational and even the irrational, or meaningless. They were asked to believe in the

self-existent and self-contained God. This God was said to be
eternal and unchangeable. And then they were asked to believe
in the causal creation of the universe at a certain time. This
is to say they were asked to hold that this world and all that it
contains were rationalistically related to and dependent upon
God and at the same time they were asked to believe that this
rational dependence of the universe upon God was effectuated
by means of the arbitrary action of God's will. Thus they were
asked to be both rationalists and irrationalists at the same time.
But fundamentally it was irrationalism that prevailed. The
believer was to accept blindly what was offered by absolute
authority.

It is true that the Roman Catholics tried hard to soften
down the bald antithesis between authority and reason by
their doctrine of analogy of being. They did not have the
courage of their conviction and therefore did not start with the
Creator-creature distinction as basic to all their interpretation
of doctrine. They started with the idea of being as such and
introduced the distinction of Creator and creature as a secondary something. This did at first seem to produce the necessary rational connection between God and man. For it posited
a principle of unity that reduced the Creator-creature distinction to a matter of gradation within one general being. And
then corresponding to the principle of continuity thus brought
into Christian thought from Plato and Aristotle, they did also
hold to a measure of real individuality in history. They attributed a measure of freedom to man in independence of the
plan of God. They even gave God a measure of freedom so that
by his will he did not always need to follow the dictates of a
rational eternally unchangeable nature.

"The distinction between the inner necessity of the very
being of God and the free determination of His will is in
Thomism a distinction of opposites. The element of necessity
is understood as inherent to the relations within the Godhead.
The causation of created being, on the other hand, is attributed
to the will of God, who does not create of necessity (Qu. XIX,
a.3). In this latter sense God exercises 'liberum arbitrium'

(a.10). 'The will of God has no cause' (a.5). This arbitrary nature of divine freewill must needs be extended to the Ideas in God."[7]

It is also true that Lutheran and Arminian theology to some extent followed Rome in both of these respects. But neither Lutheranism nor Arminianism had the courage of its convictions. They always fell back on the Scriptures as an infallible external authority. And this is also, though to a lesser degree, true of Rome.

So it remained true, we are told, that by and large orthodox Christians continued to believe in a non-rational concept of authority. The early Reformers seemed to have a more modern or dialectical view but then they were soon followed by those who made the belief in an infallible book the test of orthodoxy. But how can such a view of authority expect to yield the objectivity of which it was in search? Such an authority can, in the nature of the case, speak only of that which is beyond the reach of man. It must speak of that which has no intelligible relation to man. It speaks of a God who exists in such a form as to be wholly out of touch with the categories of man's own existence. It therefore speaks of what must be inherently meaningless for man.

In particular it must be noted that the traditional view of authority led to self-frustration. Nowhere is this more clearly the case than when it sought to deal with the facts of history. The notion of absolutely authoritative revelation with respect to the facts of history is a contradiction in terms.

But, we are told, now all that is changed. With the new principle we are no longer asked to talk about the inherently meaningless. When we are asked to believe the Word of the prophets we are not asked to think of some blank of which they are first supposed to have thought. We can now think of the facts of revelation as they appeared in history. Then we may use the insights of the prophets for the interpretation of these events. " Christians believe that the perspective of biblical faith enables us to see very clearly and without distortion

[7] Evgueny Lampert, *The Divine Realm*, London, 1944, p. 37.

the biblical facts as they really are: they see the facts clearly because they see their true meaning. On the other hand, when once the Christian meaning of the facts is denied, the facts themselves begin to disappear into the mists of doubt and vagueness." [8]

In short we are asked to accept the expert authority of a great personality, not that of abstract system. We stand face to face with the great personality of Jesus Christ as the central figure of the category of revelation. We trust in him. The traditional view could not deal with genuine history because it reduced historical fact to mere logical connection in a timeless system. On the other hand, the system that was presented by the traditional view was, because of the very destruction of history it required, totally aloof from those whose experience is time-conditioned (*Cf.* Dorothy M. Emmet, *Philosophy and Faith,* London, 1936; William Temple, *Nature, Man and God,* London, 1935).

The problem of reason too is said to be solved by the modern principle. Our reason is no longer asked to abdicate. It is not asked to accept blindly an abstract system of truth. Neither is our reason even required to admit that there is an area about which it has nothing to say. According to the traditional view there were two sources of revelation quite distinct from one another. "Natural theology, as distinct from revealed theology, consisted of those truths about the divine Being which could be discovered by the unaided powers of human reason. This kind of knowledge of God, it was held, was accessible to pagans as well as to Christians, and indeed, after the days of Albertus Magnus and St. Thomas Aquinas, it was generally conceded that Aristotle was the great master of this type of knowledge of God. But this natural knowledge of God, it was held, does not give to man all that he needs to know; it is not *saving* knowledge, and it cannot satisfy the craving of the human soul for that measure of truth which is beyond the natural capacity of the human mind. The full Christian knowledge of God and of His redemptive activity on man's behalf, as expressed in

[8] Alan Richardson: *Op. cit.,* p. 105.

such doctrines as those of the Incarnation and the Trinity, can be learnt only from revelation and is not ascertainable by the natural reason. Man is an *ens incompletum* and therefore stands in need of the divine grace." [9] Against this orthodox conception of the relation of faith to reason, says Richardson, the old liberal view argued that in revelation we had little more than the republication of what is essentially discoverable by reason. But this view "finds few supporters amongst theologians of the front rank today." [10] It is only with the full recognition of the value of the new principle that we have found the harmony between the "natural knowledge of man" and "special revelation." It is no longer necessary to distinguish between the natural and the supernatural in revelation. There is rather general and special revelation. "The only kind of theory of the knowledge of God which will adequately embrace all the facts of man's experience will be one which recognizes that there are two kinds of revelation or divine disclosure of truth. There is first *general* revelation, which pertains to the universal religious consciousness of mankind; and there is also *special* revelation, which is mediated through particular episodes at definite times and places in history. The broad distinction between general and special revelation is that the former is non-historical, in that its content is not communicated to mankind through particular historical situations but is quite independent of the accidents of time and place, whereas the latter is historical, that is, bound up with a certain series of historical persons and happenings through which it is communicated to mankind." [11]

It is true of course that in matters of historical communication we cannot attain unto impartial and impersonal knowledge of facts. "The illusion of having attained an impartial scientific viewpoint is the inevitable penalty of embracing the rationalist theory of the nature of historical research; there are no such things as 'absolute perspectives' in existential matters; we see facts not as they are in themselves, but in the

[9] *Idem*, pp. 110-111.
[10] *Idem*, p. 113.
[11] *Idem*, p. 117.

light of our own personal categories of belief and interpretation." [12]

At last then there has come to us what is essentially a solution of the age-old problem of authority and reason. Authority no longer speaks of an abstraction; reason no longer refuses to accept the expert assertions about the "beyond." The faith principle must be freely accepted in the interpretation of the whole of history. Christianity deals with the supernatural and the miraculous. It is in vain to follow the rationalists in their efforts to expunge all of the miraculous from the earliest documents of Christianity. Nor is it necessary to do so. In fact it is precisely the supernatural and the unique that we desire. History would not be history without it. But to hold to the historical element in religion and with it to true uniqueness, yes even to hold to the miraculous character of Christianity, is not to hold to what is out of relation with general human experience. "We must never deny to the philosophical activity of the mind its proper function of elucidating and unifying all our experience." [13] Our experience of religious truth, as of truth of historical fact in general, may indeed be doubted from a strict historical point of view. Christianity stands or falls with the idea of the resurrection of Christ under Pontius Pilate. "A Christianity without the belief in the resurrection of Christ as an historical event would be another Christianity than that which the world has hitherto known; . . ." [14] But it is quite possible for historical research as such to doubt the fact of the resurrection. "What we find in the accounts of the resurrection of Jesus is obviously, from the modern historian's point of view, full of difficulties, which there is no probability that any further investigation at this distance of time could entirely remove." [15] "But the strictly religious interest in these events does not demand that the historian's curiosity should be fully

[12] *Idem*, p. 107.
[13] Clement C. J. Webb, *The Historical Element in Religion*, London, 1935; p. 93.
[14] *Idem*, p. 100.
[15] *Idem*, p. 103.

satisfied before faith is accorded to them." [16] Only a genuine experience of intercourse with a living historical person victorious over death can lie behind the creation of the Christian church. In this way we have not left the safe ground of experience in talking about the resurrection of Christ. We have used it as a "fact" that is required as a limit without which our experience of the church community is unintelligible.

---

If there is anything that is clearly implied in the preceding discussion, it is that the rejection of the Bible as the infallible Word of God is connected with the rejection of that of which the Bible claims to give infallible revelation. The rejection of the traditional view of Scripture involves the rejection of Christianity as orthodoxy holds to it. The argument about the Bible and its claim to infallibility is certainly no longer, if it ever was, exclusively an argument about "facts." Nor is it characterized on the part of those who reject biblical infallibility by the older deistic and rationalistic effort to reduce the whole of life to an illustration of the law of non-contradiction. Pure factuality, that is pure non-rationality, is freely allowed a place in the philosophical principles of those who are engaged in biblical criticism.

To be sure, it is taken for granted that not much can be said today from the point of view of factual defense for the orthodox point of view. It is also customary to assert that the benefits of old liberalism must be conserved. Old liberalism is said to have been right in its rejection of orthodoxy and its literalism. But, it is argued, we must now go beyond old liberalism. It was rationalistic. It claimed to be able to give what was tantamount to an exhaustive explanation of reality. It too did not allow for genuine historical fact. It did not permit of newness in science or miracle in religion. We must now make room for both. We must substitute for a philosophy of static being the transcendental philosophy of pure act. Then we shall

[16] *Idem*, p. 103.

be able to save the insights of orthodoxy. For orthodoxy was not wholly wrong. Luther and Calvin knew that Christianity was unique, that it was historical and that it required the Holy Spirit's testimony for men to accept it. They knew that it was not rationally defensible in the strict sense of the term. But all these insights were burdened down with the incompatible ideas of an infallible Bible and a fixed system of truth as revealed in that Bible. The salvation of men was made to depend upon their accidental acquaintance or non-acquaintance with, and their acceptance or non-acceptance of, a set of propositions about the nature of reality found in a certain book. Thus the Reformers were rationalists in their teaching of salvation by system and irrationalists in their willingness to permit this supposedly indispensable system of truth to be distributed by the winds of chance.

Rejecting both this rationalism and this irrationalism of orthodoxy, and rejecting also the remnants of rationalism found in old liberalism, we now at last have reached a category of revelation that is not mechanical but personal. In the Bible we now confront God as personal Creator — our Creator, not the cause of the universe.

Orthodoxy left the question as to how God and his world might be brought together unsolved. Its conception of causation led logically to his identification with the world. " To see in God the cause of the world or its prime mover means either to substitute the idea of causality for its opposite and utterly deform it, or to make an attempt on God (*and* on the world!), by making Him wholly immanent in the world and dragging them both into a single monistic being — *vide* Aristotelianism! " [17] "The existence of God is known by an act of madness, daring, and love: it is to throw the thread of life into the heavens in the certainty that it will take hold there without any guarantees of causality; it is a dumb, beseeching act; it is a prayer. *Sursum* corda, sursum, sursum, sursum!" [18]

[17] Evgueny Lampert: *The Divine Realm*, p. 42.
[18] *Idem*, p. 43.

Creation, then, is a mystery. But its mystery is "positively implied in the depths of our very existence: as such it becomes accessible to us; it illuminates and gives impetus to our thought and knowledge . . . Created life, then, must be regarded as the *other-being* of this world in the relative. In creation divine life becomes other to its divine subject. In it take place, as it were, God's mysterious self-alienation and return to Himself through His object which was still Himself, a losing of His self-sameness, self-negation and re-appropriation of Himself in the other. The very act of creation is an activity whereby this world exists, is 'planned-out' as a being other than the Creator. Creation is therefore the establishment of other existence or existence in the other." [19]

Still further, as orthodoxy interpreted the problem of origins in terms of impersonal physical causation so it interpreted the problem of sin in impersonal biological terms of inheritance. By the new principle every man virtually stands where orthodoxy claims that Adam and Eve stood, face to face with the claims of the personal God. Better than that, in terms of the new principle every man comes directly face to face with Christ and the necessity of choosing for or against him. The last vestiges of impersonalism have disappeared.

In view of all these claims it is apparent that the orthodox apologist cannot pacify the adherents of the new principle by making certain concessions. There are otherwise orthodox believers who are willing to concede that Scripture was not infallibly inspired. They seek to preserve the general historical trustworthiness of the Bible without maintaining its infallibility. Those who make such "minor concessions" will find, however, that the same objections that are raised against an infallible Bible will hold in large degree against a Bible that is essentially trustworthy in some more or less orthodox sense of the word. Those who recede from the high claim of Scriptural infallibility as maintained by Warfield to the position of maintaining the general trustworthiness of Scripture, do not in the least thereby shield themselves against the attack of the mod-

[19] *Idem*, p. 50.

ern principle as outlined above. That principle attacks the very possibility of the existence in history of an existential system. And the orthodox advocates of the general trustworthiness of Scripture cannot afford to give up the claim of Scripture to provide such a system.

---

It is of importance to note that the current principle of Scripture is of a piece with modern philosophical and scientific procedure in general. The history of recent philosophy has been in the direction of "phenomenalism." We are not now concerned about the internal differences among modern philosophers. What is of significance in the present discussion is that, by and large, the methodology of modern philosophy and science involves the idea of the wholly unique or the purely factual. Since Kant the idea of pure fact ordinarily stands for pure existential possibility. On this question German philosophy has gone its course till it has reached a position fitly exemplified by Heidegger's notion of reality temporalizing itself. The British-American point of view is expressed by Samuel Alexander's *Space Time and Deity* and by the works of John Dewey or Alfred North Whitehead. In France the philosophy of Bergson is typical. There is a general assumption that reality has an utterly non-rational aspect. Moreover, what is true of modern philosophy is, generally speaking, also true of modern science. Current scientific methodology also assumes absolute contingency in the sphere of fact.

So then the whole emphasis of the modern principle with respect to the Bible, insofar as that is expressed in willingness to accept the "supernatural" and the "miraculous" is in accord with the idea of general philosophy and science. Philosophy and science also accept the "miraculous" and the "unique," but they mean by the supernatural and the unique that which men have not yet rationalized, or that which may be forever unrationalizable, that is, the purely contingent. In fact emphasis should be laid upon the latter idea. Reality is assumed to have something ultimately mysterious in it. The God of modern thought is no less surrounded by mystery than is man. Events in history are therefore in part determined by that within them which is made up of the ultimately irrational.

On this assumption of modern thought there could be no infallible interpretation of historical fact, no existential system of truth in the orthodox sense of the term. The orthodox principle of continuity is taken to be impossible by an assumed doctrine of chance.

Corresponding to this general concept of factuality as ultimately non-rational is the idea of rational coherence as being merely a matter of perspective. If factuality is non-rational, it is to be expected that rationality will be merely "practical." That is to say rationality will not be that which the "rationalists" before Kant thought it was. Post-Kantian rationality is, broadly speaking, correlative to non-rational factuality. It does not pretend to reduce factuality itself to relations within an exhaustively rational system. If there is to be no individuation by complete description there can be no claim to a system that is exhaustive. A non-rational principle of individuation allows only for a *de facto* system.

---

We are now prepared to state the issue between the basic principle of interpretation of human life and experience that thus comes to expression in modern theology, philosophy and science and that which comes to expression in the idea of an infallible Bible as set forth by Warfield. That issue may be stated simply and comprehensively by saying that in the Christian view of things it is the self-contained God who is the final point of reference while in the case of the modern view it is the would-be self-contained man who is the final point of reference in all interpretation.

For the Christian, facts are what they are, in the last analysis, by virtue of the place they take in the plan of God. Idealist logicians have frequently stressed the idea that if facts are to be intelligible they must be integrally related to system. But idealist philosophers do not have any such system as their negative argument against the adherents of the "open universe" requires them to have. Together with the pragmatists they assume an utterly non-rational concept of pure fact. Thus there is in their view no individuation by complete description. There is a kernel of thingness in every concrete fact that utterly escapes all possibility of expression. "There always are, and always will be, loose ends, 'bare' conjunctions not understood, in all our actual natural knowledge, just because it all starts from and refers to the historical and individual, which analysis cannot exhaust."[20] Taylor does not mean to say merely that God does and man does not have the ability to exhaust the meaning of individual facts. He is making an assertion about reality which, he assumes, is true for God as well as for man. Both God and man are, for Taylor, confronted with non-rational material.

So then only the orthodox Christians actually hold to that which idealist philosophers cannot hold while yet they recognize it to be the minimal requirement even for the distinguishing of facts from one another. And among orthodox Christians it is only they who hold with Warfield to the comprehensiveness of God's plan who do full justice to the Christian principle.

This does not mean that the orthodox position is tantamount to a return to pre-Kantian rationalism. Not even those rationalists were able to do altogether without "truths of fact" which, to the precise extent that they existed, detracted from the "rational" interpretation of the whole of reality that was the aim of a Leibniz or a Wolff. They did not make the God-man distinction fundamental in their thought. The orthodox Christian does. He claims for God complete control over all the facts and forces of the universe. Hence he claims for God exhaustive knowledge of all things. All the light of men is in relation to him who is *the* Light as candlelight is in relation to the sun. All interpretation on the part of man must, to be true, be reinterpretation of the interpretation of God by which facts are what they are.

[20] A. E. Taylor: *The Faith of a Moralist*, London, 1931, Series II, p. 172.

That this is the case has never been so clear as it is now. All too frequently Christian theology and apologetics has not been consistent with its own principles. It has sought to prove the existence of God and the propriety or necessity of believing in the Bible as the Word of God by arguments that assumed the possibility of sound and true interpretation without God and without the Bible. Following the example of Aquinas such men as Bishop Butler and his many followers assumed that by "reason," quite apart from any reference to the Bible, it was possible to establish theism. Fearing to offend the unbeliever they thus failed to challenge his basic approach. Thus the full claim of Scripture about itself was not even presented. Virtually assuming that the candle of human reason derived its light exclusively from itself they set out to prove that there was another, an even greater light than the candle, namely, the sun.

The Aquinas-Butler type of argument assumed that there is an area of "fact" on the interpretation of which Christians and non-Christians agree. It virtually assumes a non-rational principle of individuation. It therefore concedes that since historical facts are "unique" nothing certain can be asserted of them. But this assumption, always untrue, has never before appeared so clearly false as today.

To be sure, there is a sense in which it must be said that all men have the facts "in common." Saint and sinner alike are face to face with God and the universe of God. But the sinner is like the man with colored glasses on his nose. Assuming the truth of Scripture we must hold that the facts speak plainly of God (Romans 1:20; Romans 2:14-15, etc.). But *all* is yellow to the jaundiced eye. As he speaks of the facts the sinner reports them to himself and others as yellow every one. There are no exceptions to this. And it is the facts as reported to himself, that is as distorted by his own subjective condition, which he assumes to be the facts as they really are.

Failing to keep these things in mind, Thomas and Butler appeal to the sinner as though there were in his repertoire of "facts" some that he did not "see yellow." Nor was this done merely for the sake of the argument. Thomas and Butler actually placed themselves on a common position with their opponents on certain "questions of fact."

The compromising character of this position is obvious. It is compromising, in the first place with respect to the objective clarity of the evidence for the truth of Christian theism. The psalmist does not say that the heavens *probably* declare the glory of God, they surely and clearly do. Probability is not, or at least should not be, the guide of life. He who runs may read. Men ought, says Calvin following Paul, to believe in God, for each one is surrounded with a superabundance of evidence with respect to him. The whole universe is lit up by God. Scripture requires men to accept its interpretation of history as true without doubt. Doubt of this is as unreasonable as doubt with respect to the primacy of the light of the sun in relation to the light bulbs in our homes.

But according to Thomas and Butler men have done full justice by the evidence if they conclude that God *probably* exists. Worse than that, according to this position they are assumed to have done full justice by the evidence if they conclude that *a* God exists. And *a* God is a finite God, is *no* God, is an idol. How then can the Bible speak to men of the God on whom all things depend?

In presupposing a non-Christian philosophy of fact the Thomas-Butler type of argument naturally also presupposes a non-Christian principle of coherence, or rationality. The two go hand in hand. The law of non-contradiction employed positively or negatively is made the standard of what is possible or impossible. On this basis the Bible could not speak to man of any God whose revelation and whose very nature is not essentially penetrable to the intellect of man.

In the second place, the Thomas-Butler type of argument is compromising on the subjective side. It allows that the natural man has the plenary ability to interpret certain facts correctly even though he wears the colored spectacles of the covenant-breaker. As though covenant-breakers had no axe to grind. As though they were not anxious to keep from seeing the facts for what they really are.

The traditional argument of Thomas and of Butler was, moreover, not only compromising but also self-frustrative. More than ever before, men frankly assert that "facts" are taken as much as *given*. Thus they admit that they wear glasses. But these glasses are said to help rather than to hinder vision. Modern man assumes that seeing facts through the glasses of himself as ultimate he can really see these facts for what they are. For him it is the orthodox believer who wears the colored glasses of prejudice. Thus the Christian walks in the valley of those who more than ever before identify their false interpretations of the facts with the facts themselves.

The argument of Thomas or of Butler does not challenge men on this point. It virtually grants that they are right. But then, if men are virtually told that they are right in thus identifying their false interpretations of the facts with the facts themselves in certain instances, why should such men accept the Christian interpretation of other facts? Are not all facts within one universe? If men are virtually told that they are quite right in interpreting certain facts without God they have every logical right to continue their interpretation of all other facts without God.

From the side of the believer in the infallible Word of God the claim should be made that there are not because there cannot be other facts than God-interpreted facts. In practice, this means that, since sin has come into the world, God's interpretation of the facts must come in finished, written form and be comprehensive in character. God continues to reveal himself in the facts of the created world but the sinner needs to interpret every one of them in the light of Scripture. Every thought on every subject must become obedient to the requiremen of God as he speaks in his Word. The Thomas-Butler argument fails to make this requirement and thus fatally compromises the claims of Scripture.

It has frequently been argued that this view of Scripture is impracticable. Christians differ among themselves in their interpretation of Scripture. And even Christ, says A. E. Taylor, if we grant his genuine humanity, would himself introduce a subjective element into the picture. Or, assuming he did not, and assuming we knew his words without doubt, those who would live by his words would in each instance insinuate a subjective element.

These objections, however, are not to the point. No one denies a subjective element in a restricted sense. The real issue is whether God exists as self-contained, whether therefore the world runs according to his plan, and whether God has confronted those who would frustrate the realization of that plan with a self-contained interpretation of that plan. The fact that Christians individually and collectively can never do more than restate the given self-contained interpretation of that plan approximately does not correlativize that plan itself or the interpretation of that plan.

The self-contained circle of the ontological trinity is not broken up by the fact that there is an economical relation of this triune God with respect to man. No more is the self-contained character of Scripture broken up by the fact that there is an economy of transmission and acceptance of the word of God it contains. Such at least is, or ought to be, the contention of Christians if they would really challenge the modern principle. The Christian principle must present the full force and breadth of its claim. It is compelled to engage in an all-out war.

---

But if the Christian position has not always been consistent with itself the same holds true of the non-Christian position.

It has not been brought out clearly in the history of non-Christian philosophy till recent times that, from its point of view, all predication that is to be meaningful must have its reference point in man as ultimate. But that this is actually the case is now more plain than ever. This is the significance of Kant's "Copernican Revolution." It is only in our day that there can therefore be anything like a fully consistent presentation of one system of interpretation over against the other. For the first time in history the stage is set for a head-on collision. There is now a clear-cut antithesis between the two positions. It is of the utmost significance that we see what is meant by this antithesis. It does not mean that any one person fully exemplifies either system perfectly. But it does mean that to the extent that the two systems of interpretation are self-consistently expressed it will be an all-out global war between them. To illustrate this point we may refer to Paul's teaching on the new man and the old man in the Christian. It is the new man in Christ Jesus who is the true man. But this new man in every concrete instance finds that he has an old man within him which wars within his members and represses the working out of the principles of his true new man. Similarly it may be said that the non-believer has his new man. It is that man which in the fall declared independence of God, seeking to be his own reference point. As such this new man is a covenant breaker. He is a covenant breaker always and everywhere. He is as much a covenant breaker when he is engaged in the work of the laboratory as he is when he is engaged in worshiping gods of wood or stone. But as in the new man of the Christian the new man of the unbeliever finds within himself an old man warring in his members against his will. It is the sense of deity, the knowledge of creaturehood and of responsibility to his Creator and Judge which, as did *Conscience* in Bunyan's *Holy War,* keeps speaking of King Shaddai to whom man really belongs. Now the covenant breaker never fully succeeds in this life in suppressing the old man that he has within him. He is never a finished product. That is the reason for his doing the relatively good though in his heart, in his new man, he is wholly evil. So then the situation is always mixed. In any one's statement of personal philosophy there will be remnants of his old man. In the case of the Christian this keeps him from being consistently Christian in his philosophy of life and in his practice. In the case of the non-believer this keeps him from being fully Satanic in his opposition to God.

But however true it is that non-Christians are always much better in their statements of philosophy and in their lives than their own principle would lead us to expect and however true it is that Christians are always much worse in the statement of their philosophy and in their lives than their principle would lead us to expect, it is none the less also true that in principle there are two mutually exclusive systems, based upon two mutually exclusive principles of interpretation. And in our day the non-Christian principle of interpretation has come to a quite consistent form of expression. It has done so most of all by stressing the relativity of all knowledge in any field to man as its ultimate reference point. It would seem to follow from this that Christians ought not to be behind in stressing the fact that in their thinking all depends upon making God the final reference point in human predication. The Thomas-Butler type of argument confuses this basic issue.

Secondly, the issue at the present time is not whether man is himself involved in all that he knows, whether facts are taken as much as given. That man as the subject of his knowledge is to some extent taking as well as giving facts may be taken for granted by all. As such it is a quite formal matter. The question is whether in his taking of facts man assumes himself to be ultimate or to be created. Both Descartes and Calvin believed in some form of innateness of ideas, yet the former made man and the latter made God the final reference point in human thought.

The issue about the Bible is thus seen to involve the issue about the sovereign God of the Bible. It involves the idea of an existential system. The opposition between the two points of view is all comprehensive. There is no question of agreeing on an area or dimension of reality. Reason employed by a Christian always comes to other conclusions than reason employed by a non-Christian. There is no agreement on the faith principle that is employed. Each has his own conception of reason and his own conception of faith. The non-Christian conception of reason and the non-Christian principle of faith stand or fall together. The same is true of the relation between the Christian principles of reason and of faith. The one will always be in analogy with the other. If one starts with man as ultimate and therefore with his reason as virtually legislative for reality then the faith principle that is added to this in order to fill out the interpretation of man's religious as well as his scientific interests will be of such a sort as to allow only for such facts and such rationality as are also allowed by his reason. There will be occasion to develop this point more fully when we are dealing more directly with the Romanist view of tradition. Romanism makes the effort to attach a Christian faith principle to a non-Christian principle of reason. The result is compromise with the non-Christian principle of the autonomous man.

On the surface it might seem that there is on the modern principle a great difference if not a contrast between the procedure of faith and that of reason. It will be said that in the field of science and philosophy man is merely following a method that involves no personal relationships at all. Science and philosophy is said to deal with the impersonalist factors of the material universe. It is said to deal merely with the subject-object relationships in a non-personal way. It is said to be non-existential. Then it is added — and in this the modern view is joined by those who claim to be critical of it in the realm of religion, the Romanists and the dialecticists in theology — that of course in natural things the impersonal method of human reason must be allowed to have full sway. Certainly no man is to be asked to make a *sacrificium intellectus.* Only orthodoxy requires us to make that. The "absurdity of Christianity" has no bearing on the facts of chemistry and biology.

Frequently, and in particular in the case of the Romanist, it may then be added that God will not require man to believe on faith something that is contrary to what he has already learned to know by his God-given reason. Appeal is made to the idea of man's creation in the image of God. In doing so men virtually assert that the faith principle that is to be accepted must be adjusted to the principle of reason that is already at work in the so-called lower dimensions of life. Man is said to be created in the image of God, but the explanation is made that this does not mean that he has been causally produced by God. In other words the image idea is itself interpreted in terms that are out of accord with orthodox theology. In the case of Thomas Aquinas this takes the form of saying that as far as reason is concerned it is not possible to disprove that Aristotle was right about his conception of eternity for the world. That means that if creation is to be accepted it must be accepted by a non-rational principle of faith. Thus the faith principle is made to fit the non-Christian principle of reason used in the first place. The faith principle must then be made non-rational. It must be identified with the idea of accepting as an aspect of reality that which is non-rational.

Then if the harmony of the two is to be effected it can be done and is done by the notion of correlativity. The principle of faith then stands for belief in the unique as that comes to us in the facts of history. The principle of reason then stands for the notion of coherence as that comes to us primarily in science. The two may be combined and that which is believed in faith will be analogous to what is believed in science and in philosophy. There will be the same principle of continuity and the same principle of discontinuity in both faith and reason. The only difference will be one of degree. In the realm of faith there is more of discontinuity and less of continuity while in science there is more of continuity and less of discontinuity. Then too the seemingly sharp difference between the impersonal realm of science and the personal confrontation of religion will virtually disappear. The impersonal realm is not ultimately impersonal at all. How could it be if in science we also have "selective subjectivism?" It is true that those who hold to the modern principle continue to speak of the non-biased historian as imitating the method of science in its impersonalism. But there is no unbiased historian and there is no unbiased scientist. Both have the same fundamental bias. Both have the same fundamental bias of making man ultimate. Therefore science is as personalist as is religion.

On the other hand the two of them are equally impersonal.

A point of great importance to the modern approach is its claim that it for the first time has done full justice to religion as personal confrontation. The effort at this point is the same as that of personalist philosophy in general. (*Cf.* the writings of Borden P. Bowne, Knudson, E. S. Brightman and Flewelling.) But all non-orthodox personalisms are virtually impersonalist. This too is not difficult to perceive. They all want to start with man as ultimate in the realm of science and philosophy. They argue that if our beliefs are to be affirmed without reasons then there is no difference between Nazism and Christianity and no settlement but by force. If God himself put propositions into our minds he would have to appeal to our reason or we could not tell his truth from the devil's falsehood. But the assumption of this manner of putting things is that man himself as such must be the standard between the truth of God and the devil's falsehood. And unless he is willing to assert that he is himself directly the source and standard of law as an individual he must appeal to some abstract law above himself and other individuals. He must with Socrates demand a definition of holiness in itself apart from what gods or men have said about it. In the rational realm he will appeal to the law of non-contradiction. He will not accept as revelation from God that which he cannot order by means of the law of non-contradiction. But then he ought really to do away with the idea of speaking of God as personal and with speaking of Christ as his Lord whom he would obey. He can then listen to God if God can show him that what he says is in accord with the non-personal law of contradiction or the impersonal law of the good as man himself in any given situation interprets this.

The conclusion then is that both in religion and in science the modern temper is impersonalist in its conception of some abstract super-personal law and personalist in that in practice even this impersonal law is interpreted in terms of the standards that are within man himself apart from God. Thus there is no personal confrontation of man with either God or Christ. Both of these become impersonal ideals that man has set before himself. These depersonalizations may be hypostatized and then anew personalized. It is only then that they meet the demands of modern man and answer to the requirements that man has set for himself as his own ultimate standard of right and wrong, of truth and falsehood.

---

It will now be apparent in what way the argument between those who hold to the infallible Bible and those who hold to man as the final reference point will have to be carried on. It cannot be carried on in the traditional way that has been set for both the Romanist and the Protestant by Thomas Aquinas and his school. This method does indeed fit into a Romanist scheme of things. Of this more in the sequel. But, as already pointed out, it does not fit in with the Protestant view of Scripture and of theology.

---

We have now cleared the ground by pointing out that both the position of those who believe and that of those who do not believe in the ultimate authority of Scripture have to be brought to a measure of internal self-consistency if the argument between them is to be really fruitful.

There can be then no way of avoiding the fact that it is in the theology of Warfield, the Reformed Faith, that we have the most consistent defense of the idea of the infallibility of Scripture. This is not to lack appreciation of the Evangelicals or non-Reformed Protestants who hold *con amore* to the Bible as the infallible Word of God. But it is only in a theology such as that of Warfield, a theology in which the doctrine of salvation by the grace of the sovereign God has come to something like adequate expression that the doctrine of the Bible as the infallible Word of God can, with full consistency, be maintained. It is only on this basis that the modern idea of revelation as event without being at the same time in part man's own interpretation of event can be opposed at every point. If God is really self-contained and if he has really causally created this world and if he really controls it by his providence then the revelation of himself and about this world must be that of

fully *interpreted fact*. All facts in the whole of created reality
are then God-interpreted.

This is true no less of the things of nature than of the things
of Scripture. Accordingly when man is confronted with the
facts of nature and is called upon to give them a scientific interpretation he is no less engaged in the re-interpretation of
that which has already been fully interpreted by God to himself than when he reads his Bible. This does not mean that God
has exhaustively revealed the meaning of these facts to man.
Man would not even be able to receive into his mind a full
revelation of all that God has in his mind. Moreover it is true
that the revelation of God in nature is "factual," rather than
propositional. This is partly true even of Scripture. Just the
same it is also true, and this is basic, that as man studies any
of the factual revelation of either nature or Scripture he is
required to do so in subordination to and in conformity with
the propositional revelation given him in the way of direct
communication by God. This was true even before the Fall.
The revelation of God in the facts of nature has always required
and been accompanied by revelation in propositional form
given by supernatural positive communication. Natural and
supernatural revelation are limiting concepts the one of the
other.

Thus the work of scientists and philosophers is no less a
re-interpretative enterprise than is that of theology. And only
thus can a genuine unity of outlook be obtained. Then and
then only is there an intelligible, and at the same time a consistently Christian, connection between general and special
revelation. From the formal point of view it is to be appre-
ciated that the modern principle has worked out what it believes so consistently as to have a unified concept of both the
natural and the supernatural. We have seen how it is maintained that general and special revelation are of a piece with
one another. This is no doubt true. Orthodox Christianity ought
to maintain the same thing from its own point of view. But
then in its case this unity of outlook comes from the fact that

of Scripture is once again the limiting concept that is required as supplementation to the idea of fact revelation given to us in word revelation. The issue here is not at all a question of the use of man's natural abilities. The orthodox view does not hold that in receiving revelation from God man's abilities need to be suppressed. Warfield points out that God could and did freely use the various gifts of intellect and heart that he himself had given to men who were the special instruments of his revelation. The issue is therefore whether those who were called upon to be prophets or apostles needed the direction and illumination of the Spirit so as to guide them and keep them from error. And the answer is that only God can reveal God.

Thus we have the objective situation before us. If sinful man is to be saved he must be saved against his will. He hates God. God's work of salvation must be a work into territory that belongs to him by right but that has been usurped by King Diabolus. And the government illegitimately in control of man's soul controls all the means of entrance, through eye gate, ear gate and nose gate. So an entrance has to be forced. Concrete has to be built under water. And when God by grace makes friends within the enemy country these friends are still but creatures. They are as much as was Adam in need of supernatural word revelation. And they are, even so, often and always to an extent under the influence of the old man within them and so would even when redeemed never be able to interpret mere revelational facts correctly and fully. Hence the necessity of Scripture.

Protestants also claim that Scripture is perspicuous. This does not mean that it is exhaustively penetrable to men. When the Christian restates the content of Scriptural revelation in the form of a "system" such a system is based upon and therefore analogous to the "existential system" that God himself possesses. Being based upon God's revelation it is on the one hand, fully true and, on the other hand, at no point identical with the content of God's mind. Scripture is therefore perspicuous in the way that all of God's revelation of himself as the self-contained God is perspicuous. All things in the universe are perspicuous in that they can be nothing but speakers of God. The very essence of things is exhausted ultimately in what they are in relation to God. And God is wholly light, in him is no darkness at all. So in Scripture God's purpose for man in his relation to his environment in this world and in his relation to God who controls both him and his environment is so clear that he who runs may read it.

Scripture is further said to be sufficient. It is a finished revelation of God. It does not stand in a relation of correlativity to its acceptance as the word of God by man. It may be compared to the internal completeness of the ontological trinity. This trinity requires within itself the idea of the inter-correlativity of the three persons of the Godhead and the correlativity of the diversity represented by these three persons to the essence of God. As important therefore as it is to keep a clear distinction between the ontological and the economical trinity in the field of theology so important is it to make clear that the facts of God's revelation in general and of his special revelation are mutually dependent upon one another for their intelligibility and again the facts of Scripture are related by way of interdependence upon the work of the Holy Spirit in inspiration.

It is only if this interdependence is maintained that it is possible to indicate clearly that the work of the Church in collecting the canon or the acceptance of the revelation of Scripture as the word of God stands in a relation of one way dependence upon it. It is true that as far as the whole plan of God with history, and, in particular, with redemption, is concerned the revelation in Scripture requires the acceptance of that revelation by the Church and the individual for what it is. It is true further that for the acceptance of that revelation it is again upon the testimony of the Spirit that we must depend. And this testimony brings no direct personal information to the individual. It works within the mind and heart of the individual the conviction that the Scriptures are the objective Word in the sense described. Still further it is of the utmost importance to stress that this testimony of the Spirit is in the heart of the believer as supernatural as is the work of inspiration of Scripture itself. If this were not the case the main point of our argument to the effect that in Christianity God is the final reference point of man would not be true. Even as the internal completeness of Scriptural revelation may be compared to the internal completeness of the ontological trinity, so the acceptance of this revelation as the part of man under the influence of the Holy Spirit may be compared to the work of the economical trinity. On the one hand creation and providence must be maintained as being an expression of the plan of God. Yet this work is not an emanation of the being but an expression of the will of God. And these two are not to be contrasted with one another in the way that we have seen Thomas Aquinas contrast them. And not being contrasted to one another they cannot be made correlative of one another. The ontological trinity is wholly complete within itself. The works of God within do not require the works of God without. The revelation of God in creation and providence is wholly voluntary. In the same way also the acceptance or the rejection of the revelation of God on the part of man must be kept distinct from revelation itself. To be sure, even the acceptance of revelation is itself revelational of God in the more comprehensive sense that all that happens in the universe happens in accord with the will of God. In this sense even the rejection of the will of God by man is revelational of God. For Satan is not some sort of principle of non-being that is somehow given some sort of power independent of God. He is a creature of God that has fallen into sin. And the entrance of sin is within the plan of God. It is on this basis only that one can maintain the sovereignty of grace. It is the God who is truly sovereign in all things who alone can be sovereign in giving or withholding grace.

On this basis alone is it possible to distinguish the orthodox position of the relation of objective revelation and subjective acceptance of this revelation from the modern view in which the two have become correlative to one another and even made into aspects of one process. It is said in the modern view that revelation and discovery are like the convex and the concave sides of the same disc. And there is not much that the Romanist or the Arminian views can offer in opposition to this. The modern view has substituted for the ontological trinity and the free creation of the world the idea of reality as a process. In this process God and man are aspects of the same reality. But the consistently orthodox position keeps God and the universe apart. The laws of the universe depend on God and do the bidding of God but they are not laws of the being of God. So the activity of the mind of created man depends upon God. It can function only in connection with a universe that is itself wholly dependent upon God. The two together must be revelational of the same God. Man must re-think God's revelation. So man is responsible for the revelation of God in the universe about him and within him. He is again responsible for the revelation of grace as it comes to him. His rejection of the original revelation of God did not take place except within the counsel of God; his renewed rejection of the revelation of the grace of God does not happen independently of his counsel. But in each case it is a genuine action on his part. The acceptance or the rejection of God's revelation is no more identical with revelation than are the laws of the created universe identical with the internal procession of the Son from the Father.

Finally a word must be said about the authority of Scripture. Here again our start may be made from the idea of the ontological trinity. The self-contained God is self-determinate. He cannot refer to anything outside that which has proceeded from himself for corroboration of his words. Once more the conservative view stands squarely over against the modern view when this conservative view is set forth according to the principles of the Reformed Faith. For on this basis, as already emphasized a moment ago, the mind of man is itself in all of its activities dependent upon and functional within revelation. So also it is, as already made clear, with respect to the material that confronts it anywhere. All the facts are through and through revelational of the same God that has made the mind of man. If then appeal is made from the Bible to the facts of history or of nature outside the Bible recorded in some documents totally independent of the Bible it must be remembered that these facts themselves can be seen for what they are only if they are regarded in the light of the Bible. It is by the light of the flashlight that has derived its energy from the sun that we may in this way seek for an answer to the question whether there be a sun. This is not to disparage the light of reason. It is only to indicate its total dependence upon God. Nor is it to disparage the usefulness of arguments for the corroboration of the Scripture that comes from archaeology. It is only to say that such corroboration is not of independent power. It is not a testimony that has its source anywhere but in God himself. Here the facts and the principle of their interpretation are again seen to be involved in one another. Thus the modern and the orthodox positions stand directly over against one another ready for a head-on collision.

It is now apparent in what manner we would contend in our day for the philosophical relevance of Scripture. Such philosophical relevance cannot be established unless it be shown that all human predication is intelligible only on the presupposition of the truth of what the Bible teaches about God, man and the universe. If it be first granted that man can correctly interpret an aspect or dimension of reality while making man the final reference point then there is no justification for denying him the same competence in the field of religion. If the necessity for the belief in Scripture is established in terms of "experience" which is not itself interpreted in terms of Scripture it is not the necessity of Scripture that is established. The Scripture offers itself as the sun by which alone men can see their experience in its true setting. The facts of nature and history corroborate the Bible when it is made clear that they fit into no frame but that which Scripture offers.

If the non-believer works according to the principles of the new man within him and the Christian works according to the principles of the new man within him then there is no interpretative content of any sort on which they can agree. Then both maintain that their position is reasonable. Both maintain that it is according to reason and according to fact. Both bring the whole of reality in connection with their main principle of interpretation and their final reference points.

It might seem then that there can be no argument between them. It might seem that the orthodox view of authority is to be spread only by testimony and by prayer, not by argument. But this would militate directly against the very foundation of all Christian revelation, namely, to the effect that all things in the universe are nothing if not revelational of God. Christianity must claim that it alone is rational. It must not be satisfied to claim that God probably exists. The Bible does not say that God probably exists. Nor does it say that Christ probably rose from the dead. The Christian is bound to believe and hold that his system of doctrine is certainly true and that other systems are certainly false. And he must say this about a system of doctrine which involves the existence and sovereign action of a self-contained God whose ways are past finding out.

The method of argument that alone will fit these conditions may be compared to preaching. Romanist and Arminian theologians contend that since according to the Reformed Faith man is dead in trespasses and sin there is no use in appealing to him to repent. They contend that since the Bible does appeal to the natural man it implies that he has a certain ability to accept the revelation of God. They contend further that Scripture attributes a measure of true knowledge of God to the natural man. To all this the Reformed theologian answers by saying that the Bible nowhere makes appeal to the natural man as able to accept or as already to some extent having given a true, though not comprehensive and fully adequate, interpretation to the revelation of God. To be sure, the natural man knows God. He does not merely know that a god or that probably a god exists. By virtue of his old man within him he knows that he is a creature of God and responsible to God. But as far as his new man is concerned he does not know this. He will not own this. He represses it. His ethical hostility will never permit him to recognize the facts to be true which, deep down in his heart, he knows in spite of himself to be true. It is this new man of the natural man that we must be concerned to oppose. And it is to his old man that we must make our appeal. Not as though there are after all certain good tendencies within this old man which, if sufficiently played upon, will assert themselves and reach the ascendency. Not as though we can, after the fashion of a liberating army, appeal to the underground army of true patriots who really love their country. The true appeal may be compared to Christ's speaking to Lazarus. There was not some little life left in some part of his body to which Christ could make his appeal. Yet he made his appeal to Lazarus, not to a stone. So the natural man is made in the image of God. He has the knowledge of God. The appeal is made to what is suppressed. And then as it is the grace of God that must give man the ability to see the truth in preaching so it is also the Spirit of God that must give man the ability to accept the truth as it is presented to him in apologetical reasoning.

---

This reasoning will accordingly have to be by way of presupposition. Since there is no fact and no law on which the two parties to the argument agree they will have to place themselves upon one another's positions for the sake of argument. This does not mean that we are thus after all granting to the natural man the ability to reason correctly. He can follow a process of reasoning intellectually. He may even have a superior intellect. But of himself he always makes the wrong use of it. A saw may be ever so shiny and sharp, but if its set is wrong it will always cut on a slant. Hence, following Paul's example when he asks, "Hath not God made foolish the wisdom of this world," we also place ourselves on the ground of the opponent. We may first ask him to place himself on our ground. We can then show that if there is to be rationality at any point there must be rationality at the basis of all. But on his own basis he will understand this to mean that there can be nothing temporal and unique. He will claim that this is determinism.

We may then ask him to show how on his position there is genuine significance in the individual facts of history. He will answer that this is the case because his principle of coherence by which he unites these facts is not determinist but is itself correlative to the facts in their individuality. He will say that he begins by presupposing the genuine individuality of these facts and that this is a basic ingredient in his thought.

At this point it will be necessary to point out that on this basis individuality consists of non-rationality. By definition the individuality and reality of temporal things must then have nothing to do with an all-controlling plan of God. Creation is set over against causation by God. In similar fashion the orthodox idea of providence is denied. The principle of discontinuity is not found within the plan but in opposition to the idea of a plan of God. To be sure, a plan of God may be accepted but then it will be accepted as a limiting concept in the modern critical sense of the term. And this limiting concept is the opposite of the idea of a plan as a constitutive concept. It is of the essence of the modern principle to say that the thingness of the thing, to the extent that this may be spoken of at all outside its relation to the human knower of that thing, is independent of any divine knowledge or activity. In other words all antecedent being is rigorously excluded from the idea of individuality.

This involves the view that all reality, as far as can ever be known by man, is of a piece. But even this cannot really be said. It can only be said that all the reality that man will know must be of one piece. At least reality must not be distinguished into uncreated and created reality in the way that orthodoxy does. But as far as there may be any sort of reality that is beyond the knowledge of the human mind it must have no qualities at all. It must be interchangeable with the idea of pure possibility. The only alternative to making God the source of the possible in the universe is to make pure possibility or chance ultimate and therefore the mother of all being.

The point just made should be stressed. The modern approach requires the notion of pure non-being. At least it needs the notion of being in which there is no rationality at all. Then this pure being must, as far as the world of power is concerned, be identified with creativity. This sort of view has found expression in the works of Alexander, Bergson, Whitehead and Dewey. But it is important for us to know that it is precisely from this same point that all modern theology must also begin if it is to be true to its principle. Fundamental to the idea of uniqueness in history or in any other dimension on this basis is the notion of pure Chance. When theologians speak of this they call it the *Father*.

This is only to say that for modern thought time is ultimate. If God is said to have consciousness it must be consciousness in time. He must himself be subject to the same conditions to which man is subject. But then it must be remembered that on this basis the idea of God is a personalization of a non-rational force. All non-orthodox views are essentially non-personalist. This is usually admitted in the field of science. But it is no less true in theology. There could be no harmony between science and theology on this basis if both did not share an ultimate impersonalism with respect to man's environment. Theology then becomes a matter of hypostatizing and personalizing forces that in reality are non-personal. Gilson says with respect to Aristotle that so far as he has a god that exists this god is plural and that so far as he has a god that is known this god is a principle. The same may be said for all non-Christian philosophy.

So then we may distinguish between two aspects of the idea of individuality on the non-orthodox basis. There is first this notion of pure possibility or force as hypostatized and personalized. But as such it is a limiting concept and out of reach of the actual knowledge of man. It is but a projection into the void of personal ideals that man has formed individually or collectively. From the orthodox point of view such a God is but an idol since he has proceeded from the mind of sinful man that is opposed to God.

This God then is as unknown to man and as unreachable by man as was the God of Plotinus. As it is the projection of an ideal on the part of man so the only way it can be reached by man is by way of his identification with it. And this is in reality the aim that is back of the method of non-orthodox theology and non-Christian philosophy or science. The whole of the ethical struggle on this basis becomes one of lifting man into the same high idealized realm of being into which he has put his God. This is virtually how A. E. Taylor puts it when he says that the Greek and the Christian views of the ethical problem are the same, namely, that of escaping the limitations of finitude.

In the second place individuality is that which is such *for man*. That is, so much of this chance reality as has been brought within the categories of human logic must conform to the laws of this logic. It may be said that space and time are not categories of logic but institutions that precede all logical manipulation. But at some point in the activity of the mind of man the miracle of contact must take place between the logical function of the human mind and non-logical or non-rational existence. Every handling of factual material such as counting is in reality the making of a judgment about the nature of the whole of being.

Between these two individuals—the one that is wholly by itself and unknown and the one that is *for man*—there is therefore a wide difference. If Christ were to be thought of as the individual that is *for us* and therefore *known* he would have nothing unique about him. In fact on that basis there is nothing unique about human personality in general. It is then woven into the patterns of relationships that are impersonal. On the other hand if Christ is to be identified with the individual that is in itself and prior to all relationships with human knowledge then *he* is or *it* is wholly meaningless.

This then is the dilemma. If the individual is to be really individual it is unknown; if it is known it is no longer individual but an instance of a law.

One can see that it is this dilemma that faces the modern principle when it seeks to combine its concepts of science and of religion. In the former all is said to be impersonal and in the latter all is personal. Yet if there is to be any harmony between the two outlooks they must either be both personal or both impersonal. Both are personal in that both presuppose the human person as ultimate and both are impersonal as both surround this human person with an ultimate impersonal environment.

But for the moment our main point is to stress that the rejection of the orthodox principle of continuity requires the acceptance of a non-Christian principle of discontinuity. And this is a notion of individuality as wholly non-rational taken as a limit.

So Christ according to the modern principle becomes an ideal that man has set for himself.

Corresponding to this non-Christian principle of discontinuity is that of continuity. The rejection of the Christian principle of discontinuity between God and man requires the acceptance of a rationalistic principle of continuity. It cannot be stressed too much that the most irrationalist positions today are still rationalist. They are rationalist in the sense that negatively nothing can be accepted by them but what man can himself see through by means of the principle of non-contradiction. No matter how much men stress the fact that rationalism is out of date and however much they laugh at old Parmenides, it remains true that they do the same thing that he did and that Procrustes did before him. The only difference is that they use the principle of non-contradiction negatively while Parmenides used it positively as well as negatively. In consequence Christ stands for ideal rationality which is said to be present to but not fully expressed in the process of reality.

But perhaps we should say that as interpreted by the modern principle Christ is in part free and in part rational. He is then an hypostatization and impersonation of what man is himself, namely, a combination of pure irrational factuality and formal rationality.

When this principle of pure rationality is allowed to function freely all individuality disappears. But lest this should happen pure rationality is made correlative to pure irrationality. Neither is ever allowed to function by itself. The result is that there is an appearance of real freedom, or transcendence and also an appearance of coherence while in reality there is neither.

The dilemma that faces modern theology with respect to the person of Christ must also be applied to its conception of revelation. There has been a great movement away from rationalism of the pre-Kantian sort. This seems to make room for revelation. But it is the sort of revelation that is allowed also in modern science. It is the wholly different. As wholly different it is also wholly irrational. Then when it seems that the wholly irrational would control all things there appears an influx of the principle of rationality and this rationality would kill all miracle and all newness of any sort.

The net result is that there is nothing by way of revelation that is added to what man knows or can know by himself. Revelation is not higher than the highest in man and the coherence of that which is higher and is given by revelation to man is in reality but an extension of the coherence that is already in man.

It should be added that the problem here is the same as that which may be found throughout the whole field of science and philosophy. The problem is everywhere that of methodology. And the dilemma is always that of pure single thingness without meaning and abstract rationality without content.

---

So then it appears that the modern principle has neither uniqueness nor coherence to offer. It may speak of objective connection of contents between observed experiences. It may reject the orthodox idea of authority because there is then said to be no test between various claimants to authority. But it can itself point to no objective connections between any one fact and any other fact. It cannot show how one fact can be differentiated from any other fact. It cannot find any application for the law of contradiction. It cannot even furnish a footing on the basis of which it might make an intelligent negation of the Christian position. Yet it is required to do so if it is to live up to its standard of being critical. But then it is not critical. There is no real reflective inquiry here. There is no real analysis of the basic concepts underlying knowledge. There is a dogmatic exclusion of a certain position without having shown how there is a foundation for excluding anything. There is a rejection of the Christian position as involving us in meaningless mystery. But there is instead an acceptance of that which is empty of all content. If the Christian notion of mystery is rejected because it is not penetrable to the mind of man, it ought to be possible for man to penetrate the whole of reality. And if he cannot penetrate the whole of reality he ought to be able to give an intelligible reason as to why it is that he cannot. But this he cannot do. He merely appeals to the use of the law of non-contradiction. But he himself has to maintain, unless he is a rationalist in the Leibnitzian sense of the term, that by this means it is not possible to establish the nature of reality. He must maintain that reality is prior to logic. But when he does this, then he has no reason to think that what he says in terms of logic will answer to what he himself says must be there in terms of fact. This is especially true inasmuch as he has by logic, by the law of contradiction, first excluded as impossible the idea that things should have any logical relation in them apart from what is put in them for the first time by their connection with the human mind.

So then it appears that the only position that has any connection between rationality and factuality is the position that works in terms of the self-contained God. It is true that there is mystery between this God and his creature. But it is also true that the only alternative to this mystery is mystery that is behind and before and around all forms of rationality. The Christian concept of mystery is that which is involved in the idea of God as the self-contained being and his plan for the whole of the created universe. The non-Christian concept of mystery, as implied in the modern principle, is that which is involved in assuming that all reality is flux and that factuality is more basic than logic or plan. The Christian concept of mystery is rejected as involving that which is meaningless. It is said to be meaningless on no better basis than that man cannot see through it clearly. Then the non-Christian concept of mystery is accepted though it involves the acceptance of the idea of complete separation of being and knowledge. But on this basis the process of learning cannot be explained at all.

There are then two positions with respect to reality and knowledge. Applied to the question of the Bible it now appears that the infallible Bible is required if man is to have any knowledge and if his process of learning is to be intelligible. This does not mean that on the basis of Scripture it is exhaustively intelligible to man. Nothing is. And the all or nothing demand that underlies the modern principle is the source of the debâcle that has come about. But man does not need to know all. He needs only to know that all reality is rationally controlled. It does not kill his spontaneity and his reason if he has to think God's thoughts after him. It does kill all this if it has to function in a vacuum. And this, precisely, is what the modern principle asks man to do.

Christians need not be worried about the fact that the autographa are lost.[22] On the other hand they must be deeply

[22] It is well known that Emil Brunner regards the orthodox view of the infallibility of the autographa of Scripture as not only useless but as idolatrous. In addition to that he thinks that textual criticism has made it utterly untenable. How completely meaningless it is, to speak with Warfield of a sort of " Bible-X " of which nothing can be really known and of which we must, none the less, assert that it is virtually the same as the Bible we now possess (*Revelation and Reason*, p. 274).

But is the orthodox view so useless? We have shown that unless it is true men are lost in the boundless and bottomless ocean of chance. Is it idolatrous? Without it men must make and do make themselves the source and goal of all intellectual and moral effort; the true God if he revealed himself at all could not but reveal himself infallibly. Are the known facts of textual criticism out of accord with the idea of an original perfect text? On the contrary the whole process of this criticism gets its meaning from the presupposition of such a text. Without this presupposition there is no more point to turning to Scripture than to the Upanishads for the Word of God. The existence of a perfect original text of Scripture is the presupposition of the possibility of the process of human learning. Without it there would be no criterion for man's knowledge.

Orthodox scholars therefore pursue the search for this text with enthusiasm. Each step they take in dealing with existing manuscripts removes some " difficulty." And should a few errors of detail remain unsolved in time to come this does not discourage them. They have every right to believe that they are on the right road and that the end of their concerned to maintain that an infallible revelation has actually entered into history. This is precisely as necessary as is the idea of the sovereignty of God in theology. The existence of all things in the world are what they are by the plan of God. The knowledge of anything is by way of understanding the connection that it has with the plan of God. The sin of man is within the plan of God. Its removal is within the plan of God. The facts of redemption, the explanation of those facts, are together a part of the plan of God. Man's acceptance is within this plan of God. On the current principle one thing can be exactly identical with the other in the realm of pure blankness. Hence anything as well as any other thing might happen. And if one thing rather than another does happen they are again reduced to virtual identity, by being placed as interchangeable parts in a timeless system. Or rather they are made to differ by means of complete description by the mind of man. That is, they could be made to differ only if there were such minute description. But there cannot be and so there will always be substitution of one for the other. This itself expresses the idea that in matters of history one cannot be too absolutely sure. We may feel that there is enough certainty at the bottom of things but we cannot be sure of any particular thing. We cannot be sure of the identity of Christ. In fact, as Brunner says, the identity of Christ is theoretically subject to question in the field of pure history. According to the rationalist position of the modern principle there should be individuation by minute description and therefore identity of indiscernibles in Leibnitz' sense of the term. Yet according to the irrationalism of the same principle real individuality must be due to the non-rational. Therefore there must be real difference in that which is indiscernible. But then the principle of individuation practically employed is a combination of these two principles. Hence it is that *Urgeschichte* is said to be related to present history while yet it is also said not to be related. It is wholly

way is near at hand. For those who do not hold to the orthodox view are at the mercy of a purely pragmatic and humanistic view of reality and truth.

other. Nothing can be said about it. Yet it becomes wholly identical ideally.

———————

With this we might conclude this introduction to the biblical writings of Warfield. The whole issue may be further clarified, however, if note is taken of two forms of theological thought current in our day, namely, Romanism and dialecticism, which claim to have rejected the modern view without accepting the traditional Protestant position. Both of these viewpoints claim to have solved the problem of the relation of authority and reason. Is there then, after all, we ask, another alternative? Have we been too hasty in our insistence that one must either return to the infallible Bible or else forfeit the claim even to explain the possibility of science?

## LUTHERANISM

Before turning to Romanism and dialecticism a word must be said in passing about orthodox Lutheranism. Its position on the relation of Scripture to reason is unique. It would challenge our main contention. It argues that it is in Lutheranism rather than in Calvinism that the Protestant doctrine of Scripture has found adequate expression and adherence. So far from really bowing to the infallible authority of Scripture the typically Reformed theologian, we are told, constructs his system of theology according to the requirements of reason. " Reformed theology is, in its distinctive characteristics, a philosophical system. Reason could not ask for more." [23] " Reformed theology insists that the Bible must be interpreted according to human reason, or according to rationalistic axioms." [24] These charges against the Reformed Faith center on the latter's effort to show the presence of coherent relationships between the various teachings of Scripture. " Calvin tells us, in his *Institutes*, that whatever does not agree, logically, with this central thought, is absurd and therefore false." [25] Calvinism is said at all costs

[23] Th. Engelder: *Reason or Revelation?* St. Louis, 1941, p. 74.
[24] John Theodore Mueller: *Christian Dogmatics*. St. Louis, 1934, p. 20.
[25] Engelder: *Op. Cit.*, p. 74.

to seek for a "logically harmonious whole" while Lutheranism is primarily concerned to ask what Scripture teaches.

What is forgotten in this criticism of Reformed thinking is that the latter, when true to itself, does not seek for "system" in the way that a non-Christian does. Its contention is that a "system" in the Christian sense of the terms rests upon the presupposition that whatever Scripture teaches is true because Scripture teaches it. With every thought captive to the obedience of Christ the Reformed theologian seeks to order, as far as he can, the content of God's special revelation. The Calvinist philosopher or scientist seeks to order the content of God's general revelation in self-conscious subordination to the infallible authority of Scripture. Nothing could be more unacceptable from the point of view of reason as taken by Engelder and Mueller.

Moreover it is only if the Christian "system" be set over against the non-Christian system that unbelief can be effectively challenged. Reformed thinking claims that Christianity is reasonable. To make good its claim it shows that reason itself must be interpreted in terms of the truths of Scripture about it. It is reasonable for a creature of God to believe in God. It is unreasonable for a creature of God to set up itself as God requiring a system of interpretation in which man stands as the ultimate point of reference. Not having a *system* of theology and philosophy in which reason itself is interpreted in terms of exclusively biblical principles, Romanism and Arminianism cannot effectively challenge the reason of the natural man.

It is here too that orthodox Lutheranism fails. In spite of specific Scripture teaching to the contrary it assumes, as does Arminianism, that man can initiate action apart from the plan of God. This is a basic concession to the non-Christian conception of reason. For the essence of this conception is its autonomy.

It is this basic concession to the non-Christian assumption of human autonomy that makes it impossible for orthodox Lutheranism to appreciate fully the difference between the Christian and the non-Christian ideas of *system*. On the one hand it will therefore decry *system* and *reason* wherever it sees these — in John Calvin as well as in John Dewey. In doing so it virtually presents Christianity as being irrational giving foothold, unwittingly, to the idea of autonomy that lurks underneath all irrationalism. On the other hand when it undertakes, in spite of this, to speak of "the absolute unity of the whole body of truth" and of "the perfect coherency of its elemental parts" [26] it appeals to reason in the non-Christian sense of the term. As though Christianity may be thought rational, at least to some extent, by the "paramour of Satan." "As the rational study of the book of nature points to its divine Creator, so the rational study of the book of revelation suggests that it is the work of a divine Author and that therefore it is more reasonable to believe than to disbelieve its claims (the scientific proof for the divine authority of Scripture)." [27] Failing to work out a truly biblical view of human reason orthodox Lutheranism is largely at the mercy of the cross currents of irrationalism and rationalism that constitute modern thought. Unable to put full biblical content into its own distinction between the ministerial and the magisterial use of reason orthodox Lutheranism fails to distinguish between what is objectively true and reasonable and what is subjectively acceptable to the natural man. The net result is that, for all its praiseworthy emphasis upon the fact that "Scripture cannot be broken" orthodox Lutheranism is subject to the criticism that has earlier been made on general evangelical or Arminian Protestantism, to the effect that it is insufficiently Protestant and therefore unable adequately to challenge the modern principle of interpretation that we have discussed.

---

The two positions to which we must now turn are those of the Roman Catholic church and of the Theology of Crisis. Each in its own way, these two positions oppose both the classical Protestant and the modern views of Scripture. Generally speaking, the Roman view stands closer to the traditional

[26] Mueller, *Op. Cit.*, p. 80.
[27] *Idem*, p. 123.

Protestant one and the dialectical view stands closer to the modern one. In fact, there is a deep antagonism between these two positions. One would surmise this antagonism to hinge on the question of antecedent being. Romanism claims to teach an existential system; Karl Barth and Emil Brunner, the two outstanding protagonists of the Theology of Crisis, are adherents of a modern critical epistemology and therefore abhor the idea of such a system. But the issue is not thus clearly drawn between them. Nor could it be. The reason is that Romanism itself suffers from the virus of the modern principle whose evil consequences it seeks to oppose.

## ROMANISM

The church of Rome claims to be the true defender of authority. Its argument is that the traditional Protestant view of the right of "private judgment" as introduced by the early Reformers reaps its mature fruitage in the modern Protestant view of "religion without God." But the issue between "the Church" and the fathers of the Reformation was not limited to a question of interpretation of the Scripture. Back of the difference with respect to private or church interpretation of the Scripture lay the difference on the doctrine of Scripture itself.

This difference can be signalized briefly by calling to mind again the gulf that separates a theology that does, and a theology that does not, take the distinction between the ontological and the economical trinity seriously. The former thinks in terms of an inner correlativity of personality and action within the Godhead. It makes this inner self-complete activity its controlling concept. It therefore employs a consistently Christian principle of continuity; it teaches an existential system. It therefore also employs a consistently Christian principle of discontinuity; it teaches man to think analogically. In contrast, the latter breaks up the internal completeness of the ontological trinity. It does so by positing man's ability to make ultimate decisions. Therewith the idea of an existential system is set aside. The God of Romanism does not determine whatsoever comes to pass. Space-time eventuation is set over against the plan of God. If the two are then to be brought together it must be by way of correlativity. Rationality and factuality are then abstractions unless joined in a process of correlativity.

It is in this way that Romanist theology, in positing man's "freedom" over against God, virtually throws overboard the biblical principles of continuity and of discontinuity and substitutes for them the non-Christian principles of continuity and of discontinuity. True, Romanism does not assert man's total independence of God. Accordingly its position is not consistently non-Christian. It seeks to build its theology in terms of two mutually exclusive principles. In practice this results in compromise. To the extent that it employs the Christian principle Rome should hold to the internal completeness of the ontological trinity, to an existential system and therefore also to an internally complete and self-authenticating revelation of God to sinful man in Scripture. To the extent that it employs a non-Christian principle it denies all these. Using both at the same time Romanism is like a Janus. It is like a Janus in its use of the principle of continuity. Against modern irrationalism it openly avows allegiance to the idea of transcendent being, the mystery of the trinity and a revelation of God that is not correlative to man. But then when going in this direction Rome seems to go much farther than does traditional Protestantism. It virtually holds to a principle of continuity that precedes or supersedes the Creator-creature distinction. In the clearest possible way Arthur O. Lovejoy points this out. He first quotes the following words from Thomas Aquinas: "'Everyone desires the perfection of that which for its own sake he wills and loves: for the things we love for their own sakes, we wish . . . to be multiplied as much as possible. But God wills and loves His essence for its own sake. Now that essence is not augmentable or multipliable in itself but can be multiplied only in its likeness, which is shared by many. God therefore wills things to be multiplied, inasmuch as he wills and loves his own perfection . . . Moreover, God in willing himself wills all the things which are in himself; but all things in a certain manner pre-exist in God by their types (*rationes*). God, therefore, in willing himself wills other things. . . . Again, the will follows the understanding. But God in primarily understanding himself, understands all other things; therefore, once more, in willing himself primarily, he wills all other things.'"[28] Then in reply to the argument of a Roman apologist who denies that Thomas really meant to teach the necessary creation of all possibles he adds: "Not only might the passage mean this; it can, in consistency with assumptions which Aquinas elsewhere accepts, mean nothing else. *All* possibles 'fall under an infinite understanding,' in Spinoza's phrase, and, indeed, belong to its essence; and therefore nothing less than the sum of all genuine possibles could be the object of the divine will, i.e., of the creative act."[29]

According to the Thomistic principle of continuity then there should be not merely a theistic existential system but a Parmenidean type of changeless reality. But to save Christianity from modern irrationalism with a principle of continuity that is essentially Greek rather than Christian is to kill that which one seeks to save. Continuity in history is saved by reducing the facts of history to foci in a timeless logic. Thus to save is also to kill. In this respect, therefore, the Romanist argument against irrationalism is in the same position as is the idealist philosophy of such men as Bradley and Bosanquet.

But then Rome is well aware of the monistic character of its principle of continuity or coherence. It therefore blames it on others, on Plato, on Descartes, or especially on Calvin. It hopes to escape the complete identification of man with God that is inherent in its concept of univocism by means of its principle of equivocism. It refers the creation of the world to the *will* of God. It speaks of the *mystery* of the trinity. It stresses the *genuineness* of historical fact and of the *freedom* of man. It does all this against the "rationalism" and "necessitarianism" of pantheistic philosophers and Calvinistic the-

[28] Arthur O. Lovejoy, *The Great Chain of Being*, Cambridge, 1942, p. 73.

[29] *Idem*, p. 74.

ologians. But as in its principle of continuity Romanism leads directly into monism, so, in its principle of discontinuity or equivocism, Romanism leads directly into modern existentialism and irrationalism. In noting this fact Lovejoy quotes from Thomas the following words: "'Since good, understood to be such, is the proper object of the will, the will may fasten on any object conceived by the intellect in which the notion of good is fulfilled. Hence, though the being of anything, as such, is good, and its not-being is evil; still, the very not-being of a thing may become an object to the will, though not of necessity, by reason of some good which is attached to it; for it is good for a thing to be, even at the cost of the non-existence of something else. The only good, then, which the will by its constitution cannot wish not to be is the good whose non-existence would destroy the notion of good altogether. Such a good is none other than God. The will, then, by its constitution can will the non-existence of anything except God. But in God there is will according to the fullness of the power of willing, for in Him all things without exception exist in a perfect manner. He therefore can will the non-existence of any being except himself, and consequently does not of necessity will other things than himself.'"[30] Then he adds, "But the argument by which the great Schoolman seeks to evade the dangerous consequences of his other, and equally definitely affirmed, premise is plainly at variance with itself as well as with some of the most fundamental principles of his system. It asserts that the existence of anything, in so far as it is possible, is intrinsically a good; that the divine will always chooses the good; and yet that its perfection permits (or requires) it to will the non-existence of some possible, and therefore good, things."[31]

Summing up then it must be maintained that the Thomistic principle of continuity is largely rationalistic and its principle of discontinuity is largely irrationalistic. When it defends the idea of the Bible as giving God's interpretation to man it is defending what any non-Christian idealist philosopher might

[30] Arthur O. Lovejoy, *Op. Cit.*, pp. 74, 75.
[31] *Idem*, p. 75.

for the most part agree with, namely, the need of unity if man is to appreciate diversity. On the other hand when it defends the idea of the concrete historical character of God's revelation through the living church in its authoritative teaching function it is defending what any non-Christian pragmatic philosopher might for the most part agree with, namely, a non-rational principle of individuation. The result of defending both principles at the same time as correlative of one another is the idea of a growing system enveloping both God and man, a system in which God grows less than man and man grows more than God.

There is, then, no fundamental difference between the Roman and the modern principle of interpretation. The opposition of Rome to the modern principle springs from the elements of Christianity that are retained.

Turning more directly now to the Romanist view of Scripture it is convenient to look at two points. The one pertains to the question of the attributes of Scripture and the other pertains to the place of tradition and that of the church.

Roman dogmaticians are wont to think of the attributes of Scripture as these are set forth by Protestants as clearly exhibiting the rationalist character of traditional Protestantism. The argument at this point is virtually identical in nature with that employed by modern Protestantism. Christianity, it is said, is not the religion of a book.[32] The point is that if we think of Scripture as being *the book* of Christianity we think of it as an abstraction, as some sort of abstract universal. As such it would be purely formal. We cannot apply the attributes of necessity, clarity, sufficiency and authority to an abstraction. We can use such adjectives only if we supplement the Scriptures with the idea of tradition and with that of the living church.

The assumption of this argument is that God cannot give a finished, clear, self-authenticating revelation about the course of history as a whole. The "unwritten traditions" are said to

[32] Bernhard Bartmann: *Lehrbuch der Dogmatik*, Freiburg in Breisgau, 1923, Erster Band, p. 28.

have been "received by the Apostles from the mouth of Christ himself, or from the Apostles themselves, the Holy Ghost dictating . . ."[33] A great deal of research has been expended on the question of the meaning of these traditions.[34] The points of greatest importance for our purpose are as follows:

There is a distinction made between declarative and constitutive tradition. As the terms indicate it is only in the latter that we meet the idea of revelational content given by God *in addition to* Scripture. Bartmann contends that it is not so much the former as the latter to which Protestants object.[35] This is scarcely correct. The idea of constitutive tradition militates against the Protestant doctrine of Scripture's sufficiency. But Rome does far more than maintain that there have been preserved some teachings of Christ or the Apostles not recorded in Scripture. For these by themselves might, on the Romanist principle, become a dead letter. It is in the claim of declarative tradition that the activistic character of Rome's concept of revelation is most clearly expressed.

Bartmann himself speaks of an objective content and an activity as equally contained in the idea of tradition *("tr. activa simul et obiectiva")*.[36] It is this present declarative activity that is of greatest importance. The Protestant is glad to make use of the works of great Bible expositors. He believes in the guidance of the Spirit in the church's work of interpretation of Scripture. Protestant churches formulate their creeds and these creeds are said to give the best brief systematic exposition of Scripture. But only Rome, in its concept of the active and finally authoritative teaching function of the church virtually identifies its interpretation of revelation with revelation itself.

Scripture and tradition objectively considered are said to be

[33] *Cf.* Philip Schaff, *The Creeds of Christendom, The Canons and Decrees of the Council of Trent*, Vol. II, p. 80.

[34] *Cf.* August Deneffe, S. J., *Der Traditionsbegriff*, Münster, 1931; Joseph Ranft, *Der Ursprung des katholischen Traditionsprinzips*, Würzburg, 1931.

[35] *Op. Cit.*, p. 34.

[36] *Op. Cit.*, p. 28.

the *regula fidei remota*, the church is the *regula fidei proxima*.[37] The church received the Bible from God. According to its God-given charisma it explains this Scripture authoritatively. Scripture has its authority *in se* but the church has authority *quoad nos*. In its teaching function the church is infallible.[38] The church does not give authority to Scripture. That she has in herself through inspiration. But the church represents Scripture and its authority with men. When Calvin argues that the church is built upon the authority of the Bible rather than the Bible upon the authority of the church this is right, says Bartmann, when we speak of *auctoritas in se*, but not when we speak of *auctoritas quoad nos*.[39]

It is now no longer difficult to see that the Roman view of Scripture is the fruitage and expression of its general principle of interpretation. The reasons Rome gives for rejecting the idea of the sufficiency and direct authority of Scripture are, to all intents and purposes, the same as those given by the modern principle. The idea of a self-authenticating Scripture implies the idea of an exhaustive interpretation by God, in finished form, of the whole course of history. But for Rome no less than for the modern Protestant theologian such an interpretation is an abstraction and needs in practice to be made intelligible to man by means of the teaching function of the living church. Rome stands no doubt near to the top of the incline and modern Protestantism lies near to the bottom of the incline. Yet it is the same decline on which both are found.

## THEOLOGY OF CRISIS

Turning now to the Theology of Crisis we seem at first to be in an atmosphere of genuine Protestantism. Barth's consistent polemic against the Roman idea of *analogia entis* is well known. Both Barth and Brunner claim to teach a theology of the Word.

[37] Bartmann, *Op. Cit.*, p. 37.
[38] *Idem*, p. 38.
[39] *Idem*, p. 37.

This claim is directed against the Roman conception of tradition and the Church.[40] And the acceptance of the Word is said to be due to the internal testimony of the Holy Spirit.

Moreover, the *Theology of the Word* sets itself in opposition to modern Protestantism. Turning away from Schleiermacher and Ritschl it stresses the *transcendence* of God. God is said to be *wholly other* than man. Brunner would speak of Revelation and Reason rather than of Reason and Revelation. We are asked to accept a theology of Luther and Calvin.

Yet even a cursory reading of the Crisis theologians reveals that Luther and Calvin are seen through the glasses of a modern critical epistemology. Accordingly we are asked to drop all *metaphysics* once and for all. When speaking of God's transcendence we are not to think of some being existing in self-contained form prior to his relation to man. God is identical with His revelation.[41] As identical with His revelation God is Lord. And "Lordship is freedom." [42] God has freedom to become wholly divorced from himself and then to return into himself. In the incarnation God is free *for us*. Christ is God for man and man for God. He stands for the process of revelation, or atonement that brings man into unity of being with God.

Without going into further details it is at once apparent that it is Luther and Calvin rather than Schleiermacher and Ritschl that really constitute the foe of the Crisis theologians. The very heart of a true Protestant theology is the self-contained character of God. But it is this heart that has been cut out of theology by both Barth and Brunner. For the internal correlativity of the three persons of the trinity as taught by orthodox theology they have substituted the correlativity between God and man.

In every major respect, then, the dialectical principle of interpretation is identical with that of the modern principle

[40] Emil Brunner: *Revelation and Reason*, tr. by Olive Wyon, Philadelphia, 1946, pp. 127, 146.

[41] Barth: *Kirchliche Dogmatik*, I, 1, p. 313.

[42] *Idem*, I, 1, p. 323.

discussed above. There is the same assumption of the autonomous man as the ultimate reference point for predication. Hence there is the same sort of principle of discontinuity and the same sort of principle of continuity. There is, consequently, in effect, the same denial of all the affirmations of orthodoxy. We say *in effect* there is the same denial. For verbally the reverse is often true.

In noting the bearing of the general dialectical principle upon the problem of Scripture we may consider Brunner's latest and fullest discussion of the subject in his work on *Revelation and Reason*. It is clear throughout this book that the ramshackle dwelling of orthodoxy must be completely demolished if the new and permanent edifice of dialecticism is to stand. A Scripture that claims to speak of an antecedent God, a metaphysical Christ, requires us to make a *sacrificium intellectus* and therefore cannot be accepted. "Faith is aware of the higher rationality and the higher actuality of the truth of revelation, and is ready to maintain this; but it is also aware of the impossibility of asserting its validity within the sphere which the autonomous human reason has delimited for itself . . . The truth of revelation is not in opposition to any truth of reason, nor to any fact that has been discovered by the use of reason. Genuine truths of faith are never in conflict with logic or with the sciences; they conflict only with the rationalistic or positivistic metaphysics, that is, with a reason that arrogates to itself the right to define the whole range of truth from the standpoint of *man*." [43] And this means in practice for Brunner that the Bible cannot teach anything about the "phenomenal world." According to the critical principles adopted in earlier works and assumed in the present one the phenomenal world is the world of impersonal forces. And revelation is said to deal with the world of "personal encounter." But orthodox theology speaks of God as creating the "phenomenal world." By creating orthodoxy means causing it to come into existence. It does not realize that the impersonal mechanical conception

[43] Emil Brunner: *Revelation and Reason*, p. 213.

of causality within the universe can tell us nothing about a personal God beyond the universe.[44] Further, orthodoxy speaks of certain all-determining events that took place at the beginning of the history of the "phenomenal" world. It thinks of God's creation of man in his image, of man's breaking the covenant that God had made with him, as being determinative of his own present personal relation to God. The Apostle Paul apparently thought that through one man, representing all his descendents, sin came into the world and passed upon all men.

But all this, Brunner argues or assumes, is but imaginary impersonation in a world of impersonal forces. If man is really to know himself as standing in persohal relation to God, he must be rid of this attempt on the part of orthodox theology to reduce personalistic relations to impersonal physical and biological categories.

Moreover, what holds for the past holds, of course, also for the present and the future. How could the uniqueness of Christ and his work be maintained if he were identified with a man called Jesus of Nazareth? If the incarnation really meant the eternal Son's entrance into, and even partial identification with, some individual man in his physico-biological existence as orthodoxy maintains, this would again be the reduction of the personal to the impersonal. Then as to the future, orthodoxy speaks of a judgment day, a last day. But how could a personal God mediate his judgments by way of impersonal forces in an impersonal environment?

The entire idea of thinking of Scriptural revelation as confronting man with an existential system must be cast aside. The ideas of system and that of personal encounter are mutually exclusive of one another.

Brunner thinks of the idea of system as being, in the nature of the case, non-historical. The orthodox view cannot, he says, do justice to the uniqueness of the historical. Thus orthodoxy kills the very idea of prophetic prediction. "Thus where, as in the orthodox view, revelation is identified with supernaturally communicated doctrinal truth, the difference between that

[44] *Idem*, p. 286.

which was foretold and its fulfillment can well be ignored. It is timeless; that is, it is a doctrine perfectly communicated in one form of revelation and imperfectly in another. This point of view leaves out of account the decisive element in the Biblical revelation, namely, its historical character." [45]

In presenting a non-historical system orthodoxy does despite to the freedom of the Holy Spirit. [46] It leads to "a breach of the Second Commandment; it is the deification of a creature, bibliolatry." [47] It "lacks a sense of community" and "does not allow for the necessary mediation between the word of the Bible and the modern man through the *viva vox ecclesiae.*" [48] With its "fatal confusion of revelation with the communication of theological truths in doctrinal form" orthodoxy tends toward moralism and legalism. [49] In its direct identification of the words of the Bible with the Word of God orthodoxy interposes a curtain between the believer and his Christ. [50] It does not permit the believer to become genuinely contemporary with Christ. [51]

Substituting the idea of revelation as personal encounter for the orthodox one of system I may as a believer become as contemporary with Christ as was Peter. [52] "No longer must I first of all ask the Apostle whether Jesus is really Lord. I know it as well as the Apostle himself, and indeed I know it exactly as the Apostle knew it; namely, from the Lord Himself, who reveals it to me." [53] Being thus contemporaneous with Christ the believer now shares in the grace and glory of God. [54] Being face to face with Christ as his contemporary also means having the true content of revelation. "We must say quite *clearly*: Christ is the Truth. *He* is the content; He is the "point" of all

[45] Emil Brunner: *Revelation and Reason*, p. 98.
[46] *Idem*, p. 145.
[47] *Idem*, p. 120.
[48] *Idem*, p. 145.
[49] *Idem*, p. 154.
[50] *Idem*, p. 145
[51] *Idem*, p. 170.
[52] *Ibid.*
[53] *Idem*, p. 171.
[54] *Idem*, p. 117.

preaching of the Church; but He is also really its *content.*" [55]
The Scriptures want to point to him. They want to be as a
telescope through which the Christ is drawn near to us and we
to him.

In addition to killing the true conception of revelation as
personal encounter, orthodoxy, says Brunner, has done almost
irreparable damage to the very idea of faith. "All Christian
faith is based, according to this theory, upon faith in the trustworthiness of the Biblical writers. The whole edifice of faith is
built upon them, upon their absolute and complete inspiration.
What a fearful caricature of what the Bible itself means by
faith. And on what a quaking ground has the Church of the
Reformation, in its 'orthodox' perversion, placed both itself
and its message! We owe a profound debt of gratitude to the
historical criticism that has made it quite impossible to maintain this position. This mistaken faith in the Bible has turned
everything topsy-turvy! It bases our faith-relation to Jesus
Christ upon our faith in the Apostles. It is impossible to describe the amount of harm and confusion that has been caused
by this fatal perversion of the foundations of faith, both in the
Church as a whole and in the hearts of individuals." [56]

Over against this orthodox idea of a "closed Bible" Brunner advocates the idea of the "open Bible." "It is not faith on
an assumption based on an authoritarian pre-conception, but
it is faith founded upon our relation to the content of that
which is proclaimed in the Scriptures, or rather to the Person
Himself, God manifest in the flesh, who speaks to me, personally, in the Scriptures." [57]

Enough has now been said to indicate that Brunner shares
with the modern principle its non-rational principle of individuation. Revelational events must be separated from anything like propositional revelation. The correlativity between
being and interpretation within the Godhead as maintained by
orthodox theology is rejected.

[55] *Idem,* p. 151.
[56] *Idem,* p. 168.
[57] *Idem,* p. 169.

It is to be expected then that Brunner will also share the modern rationalistic conception of coherence. One who rejects the internal correlativity between revelational fact and revelational word by implication asserts the correlativity between non-rational factuality and abstract non-personal logic.

Looking at Brunner's principle of coherence or continuity what strikes us most is its pure formality. This is strictly in accord with a critical epistemology. And it is the only thing that fits in with the completely non-rational principle of individuality. Brunner says that the form and the content of revelation are fitted to one another. Now the content of revelation, as Brunner views the matter, is anything but systematic. Orthodoxy sought to harmonize the various teachings of the separate parts of Scripture in the interest of unity. But true unity includes all varieties of teaching. A true unity is such as not to kill the true uniqueness of history. And by uniqueness Brunner means, as we have seen, the non-rational. "Where the main concern is with unity of doctrine, historical differences continually cause painful embarrassment; but where the main concern is the unity of the divine purpose in saving history, historical differences are not only not embarrassing; they are necessary." [58]

Having been liberated from the orthodox doctrine of an infallible Bible by higher criticism, Brunner feels that he is also liberated from all concern for internal consistency of the Bible's testimony to Christ. "For at some points the variety of the Apostolic doctrine, regarded purely from the theological and intellectual point of view, is an irreconcilable contradiction." [59]

The real unity of revelation lies beyond and above the unifying efforts of logic. "It is precisely the most contradictory elements that belong to one another, because only thus can the truth of the Christ, which lies beyond all these doctrines, be plainly perceived." [60]

All this, however, seems to be purely negative. But this very

[58] *Idem*, p. 197.
[59] *Idem*, p. 290.
[60] *Ibid.*

negativity clearly brings out the pure formality of the principle of continuity employed. And being thus purely formal it is, in practice, correlative to the idea of pure contingency. The result is a form of transcendentalism. Accordingly, there can be no knowledge of anything transcendent. All reference to that which is transcendent must be in the way of ideals rather than in concepts.

All religious concepts are merely regulative not constitutive. Thus the whole of the realm of personal encounter between man and God is in the realm of the practical rather than the theoretical.

Yet we are not to think that there is no positive intellectual content in this theology of dialecticism. Since it so vigorously negates the orthodox view of reality which is based upon the Creator-creature distinction it naturally advocates a position which leads to man's absorption in God. Brunner's principle of continuity presupposes the virtual identity of man with God. It also self-consciously aims at the complete envelopment of the human subject by the divine Subject. Revelation and knowledge in this world, says Brunner, is always imperfect.[61] But we aim to reach the perfect revelation, when we shall know as we are known. "Knowledge and revelation are then one; moreover, we are drawn into the inner being of God, and it is He alone who moves us inwardly to know Him . . . What is meant is that I am so drawn toward God that I have 'utterly passed over into God,' I am 'poured over into the will of God,' so that I have a share in His innermost creative movement; but, we must note, it is *I* who share in this movement."[62]

Of course, when Brunner's principle of continuity thus leads him to complete absorption of man in God he quickly brings in the correlative principle of discontinuity by saying: "*I* do not disappear; my living movement, even though it is derived from God alone, is still *my* movement. I have nothing of my own to say, yet through God's perfect revelation I have a share

[61] *Idem*, p. 185.
[62] *Idem*, p. 192.

is what *He* is saying, and what He says is Reality. Thus I am what God says, what God thinks, and what He wills. The contrast between subject and object will completely disappear, but the fact of personal encounter, and thus of the nonidentity of God and myself, will remain. For I am in the truth and the truth is in me, as truth which is given to me and received by me, and this truth will be my very being, and my life." [63]

This then is Brunner's Christ. "This truth will be no other than the God-man, Jesus Christ." [64] No Bible, in the orthodox sense, could possibly speak of such a Christ. The kind of Bible that fits with the dialectical principle is virtually the same as that which, as we have noted, fits with the modern principle. It is a Bible that "does not add to my knowledge." [65] It is a Bible that bears witness to a God who "does not 'instruct' or 'lecture' His people." [66] It is a Bible that contains high prophetic and apostolic perspectives from which, if we wish, we too may view reality.

If we accept the high perspective of prophets and apostles we too are prophets and apostles; we know precisely in the way they know. And though according to all our principles of knowledge the world of force is controlled by impersonal law yet we believe that somehow our ideal, our Christ, our virtual identification with God will be realized. "The personal truth of revelation, faith, and love includes within itself the impersonal truth connected with 'things,' and the impersonal truth connected with abstractions, but not vice versa. God Himself thinks, but He is not a thought. God has ideas, but He is not an idea. God has a plan, and He creates an order, but He is not a world order. God's Logos includes all the logos of reason within Himself, but He Himself is Person, the eternal Son." [67]

The impasse that faces Brunner when he seeks somehow to combine his wholly impersonal realm of the phenomenal and

[63] *Ibid.*
[64] *Ibid.*
[65] *Ibid.*, p. 27.
[66] *Ibid.*, p. 87.
[67] *Ibid.*, p. 373.

his wholly personal realm of the noumenal is the same as that of the modern principle. We believe it is obvious that it is only in orthodoxy that there is really personal confrontation of God and man. God meets man in nature. God meets man in the Old Testament. God, the triune God, meets man everywhere. In introducing the idea of an impersonal environment for man in nature, in the Old Testament and even in the propositional revelation of the New Testament while yet maintaining that only in the dialectical principle does religion mean personal confrontation of man with God, Brunner is compelled to make the person of man the final reference point. In the last analysis every theology or philosophy is personalistic. Everything "impersonal" must be brought into relationship with an ultimate personal point of reference. Orthodoxy takes the self-contained ontological trinity to be this point of reference. The only alternative to this is to make man himself the final point of reference. Thus dialectical theology is not a theology of the Word; it knows of no God who could speak a word. The God and the Christ of dialectical theology, like the God and the Christ of the modern principle is a projection of man himself. Feuerbach has every right to smile at this transcendence theology which is but undercover anthropology. It appears then that the Theology of Crisis works on the basis of a critical epistemology similar to that of Schleiermacher and his spiritual descendents and that it therefore holds a view of revelation and Scripture that is also similar to theirs.

----

The total picture that results from our brief general analysis then is as follows: The view of Scripture as so ably presented and defended by Warfield is held by orthodox Protestants alone. And among these orthodox Protestants it is only the followers of Calvin who have a theology that fully fits in with this idea of Scripture. Only a God who controls whatsoever comes to pass can offer to man His interpretation of the course of history in the form of an existential system. An evangelical, that is a virtually Arminian, theology makes concessions to the principle that controls a "theology of experience." In admitting and even maintaining a measure of autonomy for man, such evangelicalism is bound to admit that the non-Christian principles of continuity and of discontinuity have a measure of truth in them. And to the precise extent that evangelicalism makes these concessions in its theology does it weaken its own defense of the infallible Bible. Such evangelicals have done and are doing excellent detail work in the defense of Scripture but they lack the theology that can give coherence to their effort. Therefore they also lack the general apologetic methodology that can make their detail-work stand out in its real challenge against the principle of experience.

The Roman Catholic position goes much further along the road of Evangelicalism in the direction of an experience theology. It breaks openly with the idea of the Bible as a self-contained revelation. Its conception of tradition and the church leads directly in the direction of the modern view.

As for the theology of Experience we have seen that it is today divided into two main camps. Of these two it is the Theology of-Crisis that seems to stand nearer to the orthodox view than does the other. Yet this is only appearance. In the case of both camps it is the experience of man himself, individually or collectively, that is the final reference point of all meaning.

This theology of Experience, as has been shown, now faces the abyss of the utterly meaningless. The principle of discontinuity is frankly irrational. It is embraced in the interest of the *uniqueness* of historical fact and revelation. But this uniqueness is purchased at the price of utter darkness. Then as to its principle of continuity this is purely formal and, therefore, without ability to come into contact with reality. It is embraced in the interest of flexibility. And indeed it is flexible. It comports with and even requires the idea of the utterly irrational for its correlative.

And in all this the theology of Experience is of a piece with modern science and modern philosophy. The prodigal is at the swine-trough but finds that he cannot as a rational creature feed himself with the husks that non-rational creatures eat.

It is in this situation that the present volume goes out, beseeching the prodigal to return to the father's house. In the father's house are many mansions. In it alone will the "son" find refuge and food. The presupposition of all intelligible meaning for man in the intellectual, the moral and the aesthetic spheres is the existence of the God of the Bible who, if he speaks at all in grace cannot, without denying himself, but speak in a self-contained infallible fashion. Only in a return to the Bible as infallibly inspired in its autography is there hope for science, for philosophy and for theology. Without returning to this Bible science and philosophy may flourish with borrowed capital as the prodigal flourished for a while with his father's substance. But the prodigal had no self-sustaining principle. No man has till he accepts the Scripture that Warfield presents.

CORNELIUS VAN TIL.

# I
# THE BIBLICAL IDEA OF REVELATION

# THE BIBLICAL IDEA OF REVELATION[1]

## I. The Nature of Revelation

The religion of the Bible is a frankly supernatural religion. By this is not meant merely that, according to it, all men, as creatures, live, move and have their being in God. It is meant that, according to it, God has intervened extraordinarily, in the course of the sinful world's development, for the salvation of men otherwise lost. In Eden the Lord God had been present with sinless man in such a sense as to form a distinct element in his social environment (Gen. iii. 8). This intimate association was broken up by the Fall. But God did not therefore withdraw Himself from concernment with men. Rather, He began at once a series of interventions in human history by means of which man might be rescued from his sin and, despite it, brought to the end destined for him. These interventions involved the segregation of a people for Himself, by whom God should be known, and whose distinction should be that God should be "nigh unto them" as He was not to other nations (Deut. iv. 7; Ps. cxlv. 18). But this people was not permitted to imagine that it owed its segregation to anything in itself fitted to attract or determine the Divine preference; no consciousness was more poignant in Israel than that Jehovah had chosen it, not it Him, and that Jehovah's choice of it rested solely on His gracious will. Nor was this people permitted to imagine that it was for its own sake alone that it had been singled out to be the sole recipient of the knowledge of Jehovah; it was made clear from the beginning that God's mysteriously gracious dealing with it had as its ultimate end the blessing of the whole world (Gen. xii. 2.3; xvii. 4.5.6.16; xviii. 18; xxii. 18; cf. Rom. iv. 13), the bringing together again

[1] Article " Revelation," from *The International Standard Bible Encyclopaedia*, James Orr, General Editor, v. 4, pp. 2573–2582. Pub. Chicago, 1915, by The Howard-Severance Co.

of the divided families of the earth under the glorious reign of Jehovah, and the reversal of the curse under which the whole world lay for its sin (Gen. xii. 3). Meanwhile, however, Jehovah was known only in Israel. To Israel God showed His word and made known His statutes and judgments, and after this fashion He dealt with no other nation; and therefore none other knew His judgments (Ps. cxlvii. 19 f.). Accordingly, when the hope of Israel (who was also the desire of all nations) came, His own lips unhesitatingly declared that the salvation He brought, though of universal application, was "from the Jews" (Jn. iv. 22). And the nations to which this salvation had not been made known are declared by the chief agent in its proclamation to them to be, meanwhile, "far off," "having no hope" and "without God in the world" (Eph. ii. 12), because they were aliens from the commonwealth of Israel and strangers from the covenant of the promise.

The religion of the Bible thus announces itself, not as the product of men's search after God, if haply they may feel after Him and find Him, but as the creation in men of the gracious God, forming a people for Himself, that they may show forth His praise. In other words, the religion of the Bible presents itself as distinctively a revealed religion. Or rather, to speak more exactly, it announces itself as the revealed religion, as the only revealed religion; and sets itself as such over against all other religions, which are represented as all products, in a sense in which it is not, of the art and device of man.

It is not, however, implied in this exclusive claim to revelation — which is made by the religion of the Bible in all the stages of its history — that the living God, who made the heaven and the earth and the sea and all that in them is, has left Himself without witness among the peoples of the world (Acts xiv. 17). It is asserted indeed, that in the process of His redemptive work, God suffered for a season all the nations to walk in their own ways; but it is added that to none of them has He failed to do good, and to give from heaven rains and fruitful seasons, filling their hearts with food and gladness. And not only is He represented as thus constantly showing

Himself in His providence not far from any one of them, thus wooing them to seek Him if haply they might feel after Him and find Him (Acts xvii. 27), but as from the foundation of the world openly manifesting Himself to them in the works of His hands, in which His everlasting power and Divinity are clearly seen (Rom. i. 20). That men at large have not retained Him in their knowledge, or served Him as they ought, is not due therefore to failure on His part to keep open the way to knowledge of Him, but to the darkening of their senseless hearts by sin and to the vanity of their sin-deflected reasonings (Rom. i. 21 ff.), by means of which they have supplanted the truth of God by a lie and have come to worship and serve the creature rather than the ever-blessed Creator. It is, indeed, precisely because in their sin they have thus held down the truth in unrighteousness and have refused to have God in their knowledge (so it is intimated); and because, moreover, in their sin, the revelation God gives of Himself in His works of creation and providence no longer suffices for men's needs, that God has intervened supernaturally in the course of history to form a people for Himself, through whom at length all the world should be blessed.

It is quite obvious that there are brought before us in these several representations two species or stages of revelation, which should be discriminated to avoid confusion. There is the revelation which God continuously makes to all men: by it His power and Divinity are made known. And there is the revelation which He makes exclusively to His chosen people: through it His saving grace is made known. Both species or stages of revelation are insisted upon throughout the Scriptures. They are, for example, brought significantly together in such a declaration as we find in Ps. xix: "The heavens declare the glory of God . . . their line is gone out through all the earth" (vers. 1.4); "The law of Jehovah is perfect, restoring the soul" (ver. 7). The Psalmist takes his beginning here from the praise of the glory of God, the Creator of all that is, which has been written upon the very heavens, that none may fail to see it. From this he rises, however, quickly to the more full-throated praise of the mercy of Jehovah, the covenant God, who has visited His people with saving instruction. Upon this higher revelation there is finally based a prayer for salvation from sin, which ends in a great threefold acclamation, instinct with adoring gratitude: "O Jehovah, my rock, and my redeemer" (ver. 14). "The heavens," comments Lord Bacon, "indeed tell of the glory of God, but not of His will according to which the poet prays to be pardoned and sanctified." In so commenting, Lord Bacon touches the exact point of distinction between the two species or stages of revelation. The one is adapted to man as man; the other to man as sinner; and since man, on becoming sinner, has not ceased to be man, but has only acquired new needs requiring additional provisions to bring him to the end of his existence, so the revelation directed to man as sinner does not supersede that given to man as man, but supplements it with these new provisions for his attainment, in his new condition of blindness, helplessness and guilt induced by sin, of the end of his being.

These two species or stages of revelation have been commonly distinguished from one another by the distinctive names of natural and supernatural revelation, or general and special revelation, or natural and soteriological revelation. Each of these modes of discriminating them has its particular fitness and describes a real difference between the two in nature, reach or purpose. The one is communicated through the media of natural phenomena, occurring in the course of Nature or of history; the other implies an intervention in the natural course of things and is not merely in source but in mode supernatural. The one is addressed generally to all intelligent creatures, and is therefore accessible to all men; the other is addressed to a special class of sinners, to whom God would make known His salvation. The one has in view to meet and supply the natural need of creatures for knowledge of their God; the other to rescue broken and deformed sinners from their sin and its consequences. But, though thus distinguished from one another, it is important that the two species or stages of revelation should not be set in opposition to one another, or the closeness of their mutual relations or the constancy of their interaction be obscured. They constitute together a unitary whole, and each is incomplete without the other. In its most general idea, revelation is rooted in creation and the relations with His intelligent creatures into which God has brought Himself by giving them being. Its object is to realize the end of man's creation, to be attained only through knowledge of God and perfect and unbroken communion with Him. On the entrance of sin into the world, destroying this communion with God and obscuring the knowledge of Him derived from Nature, another mode of revelation was necessitated, having also another content, adapted to the new relation to God and the new conditions of intellect, heart and will brought about by sin. It must not be supposed, however, that this new mode of revelation was an *ex post facto* expedient, introduced to meet an unforeseen contingency. The actual course of human development was in the nature of the case the expected and the intended course of human development, for which man was created; and revelation, therefore, in its double form was the Divine purpose for man from the beginning, and constitutes a unitary provision for the realization of the end of his creation in the actual circumstances in which he exists. We may distinguish in this unitary revelation the two elements by the coöperation of which the effect is produced; but we should bear in mind that only by their coöperation is the effect produced. Without special revelation, general revelation would be for sinful men incomplete and ineffective, and could issue, as in point of fact it has issued wherever it alone has been accessible, only in leaving them without excuse (Rom. i. 20). Without general revelation, special revelation would lack that basis in the fundamental knowledge of God as the mighty and wise, righteous and good, maker and ruler of all things, apart from which the further revelation of this great God's interventions in the world for the salvation of sinners could not be either intelligible, credible or operative.

Only in Eden has general revelation been adequate to the needs of man. Not being a sinner, man in Eden had no need of that grace of God itself by which sinners are restored to communion with Him, or of the special revelation of this grace of God to sinners to enable them to live with God. And not being a sinner, man in Eden, as he contemplated the works of God, saw God in the unclouded mirror of his mind with a clarity of vision, and lived with Him in the untroubled depths of his heart with a trustful intimacy of association, inconceivable to sinners. Nevertheless, the revelation of God in Eden was not merely "natural." Not only does the prohibition of the forbidden fruit involve a positive commandment (Gen. ii. 16), but the whole history implies an immediacy of intercourse with God which cannot easily be set to the credit of the picturesque art of the narrative, or be fully accounted for by the vividness of the perception of God in His works proper to sinless creatures. The impression is strong that what is meant to be conveyed to us is that man dwelt with God in Eden, and enjoyed with Him immediate and not merely mediate communion. In that case, we may understand that if man had not fallen, he would have continued to enjoy immediate intercourse with God, and that the cessation of this immediate intercourse is due to sin. It is not then the supernaturalness of special revelation which is rooted in sin, but, if we may be allowed the expression, the specialness of supernatural revelation. Had man not fallen, heaven would have continued to lie about him through all his history, as it lay about his infancy; every man would have enjoyed direct vision of God and immediate speech with Him. Man having fallen, the cherubim and the flame of a sword, turning every way, keep the path: and God breaks His way in a round-about fashion into man's darkened heart to reveal there His redemptive love. By slow steps and gradual stages He at once works out His saving purpose and molds the world for its reception, choosing a people for Himself and training it through long and weary ages, until at last when the fulness of time has come, He bares His arm and sends out the proclamation of His great salvation to all the earth.

Certainly, from the gate of Eden onward, God's general revelation ceased to be, in the strict sense, supernatural. It is, of course, not meant that God deserted His world and left it to fester in its iniquity. His providence still ruled over all, leading steadily onward to the goal for which man had been created, and of the attainment of which in God's own good time and way the very continuance of men's existence, under God's providential government, was a pledge. And His Spirit still everywhere wrought upon the hearts of men, stirring up all their powers (though created in the image of God, marred and impaired by sin) to their best activities, and to such splendid effect in every department of human achievement as to command the admiration of all ages, and in the highest region of all, that of conduct, to call out from an apostle the encomium that though they had no law they did by nature (observe the word "nature") the things of the law. All this, however, remains within the limits of Nature, that is to say, within the sphere of operation of Divinely directed and assisted second causes. It illustrates merely the heights to which the powers of man may attain under the guidance of providence and the influences of what we have learned to call God's "common grace." Nowhere, throughout the whole ethnic domain, are the conceptions of God and His ways put within the reach of man, through God's revelation of Himself in the works of creation and providence, transcended; nowhere is the slightest knowledge betrayed of anything concerning God and His purposes, which could be known only by its being supernaturally told to men. Of the entire body of "saving truth," for example, which is the burden of what we call "special revelation," the whole heathen world remained in total ignorance. And even its hold on the general truths of religion, not being vitalized by supernatural enforcements, grew weak, and its knowledge of the very nature of God decayed, until it ran out to the dreadful issue which Paul sketches for us in that inspired philosophy of religion which he incorporates in the latter part of the first chapter of the Epistle to the Romans.

Behind even the ethnic development, there lay, of course, the supernatural intercourse of man with God which had obtained before the entrance of sin into the world, and the supernatural revelations at the gate of Eden (Gen. iii. 8), and at the second origin of the human race, the Flood (Gen. viii. 21.22; ix. 1–17). How long the tradition of this primitive revelation lingered in nooks and corners of the heathen world, conditioning and vitalizing the natural revelation of God always accessible, we have no means of estimating. Neither is it easy to measure the effect of God's special revelation of Himself to His people upon men outside the bounds of, indeed, but coming into contact with, this chosen people, or sharing with them a common natural inheritance. Lot and Ishmael and Esau can scarcely have been wholly ignorant of the word of God which came to Abraham and Isaac and Jacob; nor could the Egyptians from whose hands God wrested His people with a mighty arm fail to learn something of Jehovah, any more than the mixed multitudes who witnessed the ministry of Christ could fail to infer something from His gracious walk and mighty works. It is natural to infer that no nation which was intimately associated with Israel's life could remain entirely unaffected by Israel's revelation. But whatever impressions were thus conveyed reached apparently individuals only: the heathen which surrounded Israel, even those most closely affiliated with Israel, remained heathen; they had no revelation. In the sporadic instances when God visited an alien with a supernatural communication — such as the dreams sent to Abimelech (Gen. xx.) and to Pharaoh (Gen. xl. xli.) and to Nebuchadnezzar (Dan. ii. 1 ff.) and to the soldier in the camp of Midian (Jgs. vii. 13) — it was in the interests, not of the heathen world, but of the chosen people that they were sent; and these instances derive their significance wholly from this fact. There remain, no doubt, the mysterious figure of Melchizedek, perhaps also of Jethro, and the strange apparition of Balaam, who also, however, appear in the sacred narrative only in connection with the history of God's dealings with His people and in their interest. Their unexplained appearance cannot in any event avail to modify the general fact that the life of the heathen peoples lay outside the supernatural revelation of God. The heathen were suffered to walk in their own ways (Acts xiv. 16).

## II. THE PROCESS OF REVELATION

Meanwhile, however, God had not forgotten them, but was preparing salvation for them also through the supernatural revelation of His grace that He was making to His people. According to the Biblical representation, in the midst of and working confluently with the revelation which He has always been giving of Himself on the plane of Nature, God was making also from the very fall of man a further revelation of Himself on the plane of grace. In contrast with His general, natural revelation, in which all men by virtue of their very nature as men share, this special, supernatural revelation was granted at first only to individuals, then progressively to a family, a tribe, a nation, a race, until, when the fulness of time was come, it was made the possession of the whole world. It may be difficult to obtain from Scripture a clear account of why God chose thus to give this revelation of His grace only progressively; or, to be more explicit, through the process of a historical development. Such is, however, the ordinary mode of the Divine working: it is so that God made the worlds, it is so that He creates the human race itself, the recipient of this revelation, it is so that He builds up His kingdom in the world and in the individual soul, which only gradually comes whether to the knowledge of God or to the fruition of His salvation. As to the fact, the Scriptures are explicit, tracing for us, or rather embodying in their own growth, the record of the steady advance of this gracious revelation through definite stages from its first faint beginnings to its glorious completion in Jesus Christ.

So express is its relation to the development of the kingdom of God itself, or rather to that great series of Divine operations which are directed to the building up of the kingdom of God in the world, that it is sometimes confounded with them, or thought of as simply their reflection in the contemplating mind of man. Thus it is not infrequently said that revelation, meaning this special redemptive revelation, has been communicated in deeds, not in words; and it is occasionally elaborately argued that the sole manner in which God has revealed

Himself as the Saviour of sinners is just by performing those mighty acts by which sinners are saved. This is not, however, the Biblical representation. Revelation is, of course, often made through the instrumentality of deeds; and the series of His great redemptive acts by which He saves the world constitutes the preëminent revelation of the grace of God — so far as these redemptive acts are open to observation and are perceived in their significance. But revelation, after all, is the correlate of understanding and has as its proximate end just the production of knowledge, though not, of course, knowledge for its own sake, but for the sake of salvation. The series of the redemptive acts of God, accordingly, can properly be designated "revelation" only when and so far as they are contemplated as adapted and designed to produce knowledge of God and His purpose and methods of grace. No bare series of unexplained acts can be thought, however, adapted to produce knowledge, especially if these acts be, as in this case, of a highly transcendental character. Nor can this particular series of acts be thought to have as its main design the production of knowledge; its main design is rather to save man. No doubt the production of knowledge of the Divine grace is one of the means by which this main design of the redemptive acts of God is attained. But this only renders it the more necessary that the proximate result of producing knowledge should not fail; and it is doubtless for this reason that the series of redemptive acts of God has not been left to explain itself, but the explanatory word has been added to it. Revelation thus appears, however, not as the mere reflection of the redeeming acts of God in the minds of men, but as a factor in the redeeming work of God, a component part of the series of His redeeming acts, without which that series would be incomplete and so far inoperative for its main end. Thus the Scriptures represent it, not confounding revelation with the series of the redemptive acts of God, but placing it among the redemptive acts of God and giving it a function as a substantive element in the operations by which the merciful God saves sinful men. It is therefore not made even a mere constant accompaniment of the redemptive acts of God, giving their explanation that they may be understood. It occupies a far more independent place among them than this, and as frequently precedes them to prepare their way as it accompanies or follows them to interpret their meaning. It is, in one word, itself a redemptive act of God and by no means the least important in the series of His redemptive acts.

This might, indeed, have been inferred from its very nature, and from the nature of the salvation which was being wrought out by these redemptive acts of God. One of the most grievous of the effects of sin is the deformation of the image of God reflected in the human mind, and there can be no recovery from sin which does not bring with it the correction of this deformation and the reflection in the soul of man of the whole glory of the Lord God Almighty. Man is an intelligent being; his superiority over the brute is found, among other things, precisely in the direction of all his life by his intelligence; and his blessedness is rooted in the true knowledge of his God— for this is life eternal, that we should know the only true God and Him whom He has sent. Dealing with man as an intelligent being, God the Lord has saved him by means of a revelation, by which he has been brought into an ever more and more adequate knowledge of God, and been led ever more and more to do his part in working out his own salvation with fear and trembling as he perceived with ever more and more clearness how God is working it out for him through mighty deeds of grace.

This is not the place to trace, even in outline, from the material point of view, the development of God's redemptive revelation from its first beginnings, in the promise given to Abraham — or rather in what has been called the Protevangelium at the gate of Eden — to its completion in the advent and work of Christ and the teaching of His apostles; a steadily advancing development, which, as it lies spread out to view in the pages of Scripture, takes to those who look at it from the consummation backward, the appearance of the shadow cast athwart preceding ages by the great figure of Christ. Even from the formal point of view, however, there has been pointed out a progressive advance in the method of revelation, consonant with its advance in content, or rather with the advancing stages of the building up of the kingdom of God, to subserve which is the whole object of revelation. Three distinct steps in revelation have been discriminated from this point of view. They are distinguished precisely by the increasing independence of revelation of the deeds constituting the series of the redemptive acts of God, in which, nevertheless, all revelation is a substantial element. Discriminations like this must not be taken too absolutely; and in the present instance the chronological sequence cannot be pressed. But, with much interlacing, three generally successive stages of revelation may be recognized, producing periods at least characteristically of what we may somewhat conventionally call theophany, prophecy and inspiration. What may be somewhat indefinitely marked off as the Patriarchal age is characteristically "the period of Outward Manifestations, and Symbols, and Theophanies": during it "God spoke to men through their senses, in physical phenomena, as the burning bush, the cloudy pillar, or in sensuous forms, as men, angels, etc. . . . In the Prophetic age, on the contrary, the prevailing mode of revelation was by means of inward prophetic inspiration": God spoke to men characteristically by the movements of the Holy Spirit in their hearts. "Prevailingly, at any rate from Samuel downwards, the supernatural revelation was a revelation in the hearts of the foremost thinkers of the people, or, as we call it, prophetic inspiration, without the aid of external sensuous symbols of God" (A. B. Davidson, *OT Prophecy*, 1903, p. 148; cf. pp. 12–14, 145 ff.). This internal method of revelation reaches its culmination in the New Testament period, which is preëminently the age of the Spirit. What is especially characteristic of this age is revelation through the medium of the written word, what may be called apostolic as distinguished from prophetic inspiration. The revealing Spirit speaks through chosen men as His organs, but through these organs in such a fashion that the most intimate processes of their souls become the instruments by means of which He speaks His mind. Thus at all events there are brought clearly before us three well-marked modes of revelation, which we may perhaps designate respectively, not with perfect discrimination, it is true, but not misleadingly, (1) external manifestations, (2) internal suggestion, and (3) concursive operation.

### III. Modes of Revelation

Theophany may be taken as the typical form of "external manifestation"; but by its side may be ranged all of those mighty works by which God makes Himself known, including express miracles, no doubt, but along with them every supernatural intervention in the affairs of men, by means of which a better understanding is communicated of what God is or what are His purposes of grace to a sinful race. Under "internal suggestion" may be subsumed all the characteristic phenomena of what is most properly spoken of as "prophecy": visions and dreams, which, according to a fundamental passage (Num. xii. 6), constitute the typical forms of prophecy, and with them the whole "prophetic word," which shares its essential characteristic with visions and dreams, since it comes not by the will of man but from God. By "concursive operation" may be meant that form of revelation illustrated in an inspired psalm or epistle or history, in which no human activity — not even the control of the will — is superseded, but the Holy Spirit works in, with and through them all in such a manner as to communicate to the product qualities distinctly superhuman. There is no age in the history of the religion of the Bible, from that of Moses to that of Christ and His apostles, in which all these modes of revelation do not find place. One or another may seem particularly characteristic of this age or of that; but they all occur in every age. And they occur side by side, broadly speaking, on the same level. No discrimination is drawn between them in point of worthiness as modes of revelation, and much less in point of purity in the revelations communicated through them. The circumstance that God spoke to Moses, not by dream or vision but mouth to mouth, is, indeed, adverted to (Num. xii. 8) as a proof of the peculiar favor shown to Moses

and even of the superior dignity of Moses above other organs
of revelation: God admitted him to an intimacy of intercourse
which He did not accord to others. But though Moses was thus
distinguished above all others in the dealings of God with him,
no distinction is drawn between the revelations given through
him and those given through other organs of revelation in point
either of Divinity or of authority. And beyond this we have no
Scriptural warrant to go on in contrasting one mode of revelation with another. Dreams may seem to us little fitted to serve
as vehicles of Divine communications. But there is no suggestion in Scripture that revelations through dreams stand
on a lower plane than any others; and we should not fail to
remember that the essential characteristics of revelations
through dreams are shared by all forms of revelation in which
(whether we should call them visions or not) the images or
ideas which fill, or pass in procession through, the consciousness are determined by some other power than the recipient's
own will. It may seem natural to suppose that revelations rise
in rank in proportion to the fulness of the engagement of the
mental activity of the recipient in their reception. But we
should bear in mind that the intellectual or spiritual quality of
a revelation is not derived from the recipient but from its Divine Giver. The fundamental fact in all revelation is that it is
from God. This is what gives unity to the whole process of
revelation, given though it may be in divers portions and in
divers manners and distributed though it may be through the
ages in accordance with the mere will of God, or as it may have
suited His developing purpose — this and its unitary end,
which is ever the building up of the kingdom of God. In whatever diversity of forms, by means of whatever variety of modes,
in whatever distinguishable stages it is given, it is ever the
revelation of the One God, and it is ever the one consistently
developing redemptive revelation of God.

On a *prima facie* view it may indeed seem likely that a difference in the quality of their supernaturalness would inevitably obtain between revelations given through such divergent
modes. The completely supernatural character of revelations

given in theophanies is obvious. He who will not allow that God speaks to man, to make known His gracious purposes toward him, has no other recourse here than to pronounce the stories legendary. The objectivity of the mode of communication which is adopted is intense, and it is thrown up to observation with the greatest emphasis. Into the natural life of man God intrudes in a purely supernatural manner, bearing a purely supernatural communication. In these communications we are given accordingly just a series of "naked messages of God." But not even in the Patriarchal age were all revelations given in theophanies or objective appearances. There were dreams, and visions, and revelations without explicit intimation in the narrative of how they were communicated. And when we pass on in the history, we do not, indeed, leave behind us theophanies and objective appearances. It is not only made the very characteristic of Moses, the greatest figure in the whole history of revelation except only that of Christ, that he knew God face to face (Deut. xxxiv. 10), and God spoke to him mouth to mouth, even manifestly, and not in dark speeches (Num. xii. 8); but throughout the whole history of revelation down to the appearance of Jesus to Paul on the road to Damascus, God has shown Himself visibly to His servants whenever it has seemed good to Him to do so and has spoken with them in objective speech. Nevertheless, it is expressly made the characteristic of the Prophetic age that God makes Himself known to His Servants "in a vision," "in a dream" (Num. xii. 6). And although, throughout its entire duration, God, in fulfilment of His promise (Deut. xviii. 18), put His words in the mouths of His prophets and gave them His commandments to speak, yet it would seem inherent in the very employment of men as instruments of revelation that the words of God given through them are spoken by human mouths; and the purity of their supernaturalness may seem so far obscured. And when it is not merely the mouths of men with which God thus serves Himself in the delivery of His messages, but their minds and hearts as well — the play of their religious feelings, or the processes of their logical reasoning, or the tenacity of their memories, as, say, in a psalm or in an epistle, or a history — the supernatural element in the communication may easily seem to retire still farther into the background. It can scarcely be a matter of surprise, therefore, that question has been raised as to the relation of the natural and the supernatural in such revelations and, in many current manners of thinking and speaking of them, the completeness of their supernaturalness has been limited and curtailed in the interests of the natural instrumentalities employed. The plausibility of such reasoning renders it the more necessary that we should observe the unvarying emphasis which the Scriptures place upon the absolute supernaturalness of revelation in all its modes alike. In the view of the Scriptures, the completely supernatural character of revelation is in no way lessened by the circumstance that it has been given through the instrumentality of men. They affirm, indeed, with the greatest possible emphasis that the Divine word delivered through men is the pure word of God, diluted with no human admixture whatever.

We have already been led to note that even on the occasion when Moses is exalted above all other organs of revelation (Num. xii. 6 ff.), in point of dignity and favor, no suggestion whatever is made of any inferiority, in either the directness or the purity of their supernaturalness, attaching to other organs of revelation. There might never afterward arise a prophet in Israel like unto Moses, whom the Lord knew face to face (Deut. xxxiv. 10). But each of the whole series of prophets raised up by Jehovah that the people might always know His will was to be like Moses in speaking to the people only what Jehovah commanded them (Deut. xviii. 15.18.20). In this great promise, securing to Israel the succession of prophets, there is also included a declaration of precisely how Jehovah would communicate His messages not so much to them as through them. "I will raise them up a prophet from among their brethren, like unto thee," we read (Deut. xviii. 18), "*and I will put my words in his mouth,* and he shall speak unto them all that I shall command him." The process of revelation through the prophets was a process by which Jehovah put His words in the mouths of the prophets, and the prophets spoke precisely these words and no others. So the prophets themselves ever asserted. "Then Jehovah put forth his hand, and touched my mouth," explains Jeremiah in his account of how he received his prophecies, "and Jehovah said unto me, Behold, I have put my words in thy mouth" (Jer. i. 9; cf. v. 14; Isa. li. 16; lix. 21; Num. xxii. 35; xxiii. 5.12.16). Accordingly, the words "with which" they spoke were not their own but the Lord's: "And he said unto me," records Ezekiel, "Son of man, go, get thee unto the house of Israel, and speak with my words unto them" (Ezk. iii. 4). It is a process of nothing other than "dictation" which is thus described (2 S. xiv. 3.19), though, of course, the question may remain open of the exact processes by which this dictation is accomplished. The fundamental passage which brings the central fact before us in the most vivid manner is, no doubt, the account of the commissioning of Moses and Aaron given in Ex. iv. 10–17; vii. 1–7. Here, in the most express words, Jehovah declares that He who made the mouth can be with it to teach it what to speak, and announces the precise function of a prophet to be that he is "a mouth of God," who speaks not his own but God's words. Accordingly, the Hebrew name for "prophet" (nābhī'), whatever may be its etymology, means throughout the Scriptures just "spokesman," though not "spokesman" in general, but spokesman by way of eminence, that is, God's spokesman; and the characteristic formula by which a prophetic declaration is announced is: "The word of Jehovah came to me," or the brief "saith Jehovah" ( נְאָם יהוה, ne'eum Yahweh). In no case does a prophet put his words forward as his own words. That he is a prophet at all is due not to choice on his own part, but to a call of God, obeyed often with reluctance; and he prophesies or forbears to prophesy, not according to his own will but as the Lord opens and shuts his mouth (Ezk. iii. 26 f.) and creates for him the fruit of the lips (Isa. lvii. 19; cf. vi. 7; l. 4). In contrast with the false prophets, he strenuously asserts that he does not speak out of his own heart ("heart" in Biblical language includes the whole inner man), but all that he proclaims is the pure word of Jehovah.

The fundamental passage does not quite leave the matter, however, with this general declaration. It describes the characteristic manner in which Jehovah communicates His messages to His prophets as through the medium of visions and dreams. Neither visions in the technical sense of that word, nor dreams, appear, however, to have been the customary mode of revelation to the prophets, the record of whose revelations has come down to us. But, on the other hand, there are numerous indications in the record that the universal mode of revelation to them was one which was in some sense a vision, and can be classed only in the category distinctively so called.

The whole nomenclature of prophecy presupposes, indeed, its vision-form. Prophecy is distinctively a word, and what is delivered by the prophets is proclaimed as the "word of Jehovah." That it should be announced by the formula, "Thus saith the Lord," is, therefore, only what we expect; and we are prepared for such a description of its process as: "The Lord Jehovah . . . wakeneth mine ear to hear." He "hath opened mine ear" (Isa. 1.4.5). But this is not the way of speaking of their messages which is most usual in the prophets. Rather is the whole body of prophecy cursorily presented as a thing seen. Isaiah places at the head of his book: "The vision of Isaiah . . . which he saw" (cf. Isa. xxix. 10.11; Ob. ver. 1); and then proceeds to set at the head of subordinate sections the remarkable words, "The word that Isaiah . . . saw" (ii. 1); "the burden [margin "oracle"] . . . which Isaiah . . . did see" (xiii. 1). Similarly there stand at the head of other prophecies: "the words of Amos . . . which he saw" (Am. i. 1); "the word of Jehovah that came to Micah . . . which he saw" (Mic. i. 1); "the oracle which Habakkuk the prophet did see" (Hab. i. 1 margin); and elsewhere such language occurs as this: "the word that Jehovah hath showed me" (Jer. xxxviii. 21); "the prophets have seen . . . oracles" (Lam. ii. 14); "the word of Jehovah came . . . and I looked, and, behold" (Ezk. i. 3.4); "Woe unto the foolish prophets, that fol-

low their own spirit, and have seen nothing" (Ezk. xiii. 3);
"I . . . will look forth to see what he will speak with me, . . .
Jehovah . . . said, Write the vision" (Hab. ii. 1 f.). It is an
inadequate explanation of such language to suppose it merely
a relic of a time when vision was more predominantly the form
of revelation. There is no proof that vision in the technical
sense ever was more predominantly the form of revelation than
in the days of the great writing prophets; and such language
as we have quoted too obviously represents the living point of
view of the prophets to admit of the supposition that it was
merely conventional on their lips. The prophets, in a word,
represent the Divine communications which they received as
given to them in some sense in visions.

It is possible, no doubt, to exaggerate the significance of
this. It is an exaggeration, for example, to insist that therefore
all the Divine communications made to the prophets must
have come to them in external appearances and objective
speech, addressed to and received by means of the bodily eye
and ear. This would be to break down the distinction between
manifestation and revelation, and to assimilate the mode of
prophetic revelation to that granted to Moses, though these
are expressly distinguished (Num. xii. 6–8). It is also an exaggeration to insist that therefore the prophetic state must be
conceived as that of strict ecstasy, involving the complete
abeyance of all mental life on the part of the prophet (*amen-
tia*), and possibly also accompanying physical effects. It is
quite clear from the records which the prophets themselves
give us of their revelations that their intelligence was alert in
all stages of their reception of them. The purpose of both these
extreme views is the good one of doing full justice to the objectivity of the revelations vouchsafed to the prophets. If these
revelations took place entirely externally to the prophet, who
merely stood off and contemplated them, or if they were im-
planted in the prophets by a process so violent as not only to
supersede their mental activity but, for the time being, to an-
nihilate it, it would be quite clear that they came from a source
other than the prophets' own minds. It is undoubtedly the fun-

damental contention of the prophets that the revelations given through them are not their own but wholly God's. The significant language we have just quoted from Ezk. xiii. 3: "Woe unto the foolish prophets, that follow their own spirit, and have seen nothing," is a typical utterance of their sense of the complete objectivity of their messages. What distinguishes the false prophets is precisely that they "prophesy out of their own heart" (Ezk. xiii. 2–17), or, to draw the antithesis sharply, that "they speak a vision of their own heart, and not out of the mouth of Jehovah" (Jer. xxiii. 16.26; xiv. 14). But these extreme views fail to do justice, the one to the equally important fact that the word of God, given through the prophets, comes as the pure and unmixed word of God not merely to, but from, the prophets; and the other to the equally obvious fact that the intelligence of the prophets is alert throughout the whole process of the reception and delivery of the revelation made through them.

That which gives to prophecy as a mode of revelation its place in the category of visions, strictly so called, and dreams, is that it shares with them the distinguishing characteristic which determines the class. In them all alike the movements of the mind are determined by something extraneous to the subject's will, or rather, since we are speaking of supernaturally given dreams and visions, extraneous to the totality of the subject's own psychoses. A power not himself takes possession of his consciousness and determines it according to its will. That power, in the case of the prophets, was fully recognized and energetically asserted to be Jehovah Himself or, to be more specific, the Spirit of Jehovah (1S. x. 6.10; Neh. ix. 30; Zec. vii. 12; Joel ii. 28.29). The prophets were therefore 'men of the Spirit' (Hos. ix. 7). What constituted them prophets was that the Spirit was put upon them (Isa. xlii. 1) or poured out on them (Joel ii. 28.29), and they were consequently filled with the Spirit (Mic. iii. 8), or, in another but equivalent locution, that "the hand" of the Lord, or "the power of the hand" of the Lord, was upon them (2 K. iii. 15; Ezk. i. 3; iii. 14.22; xxxiii. 22; xxxvii. 1; xl. 1), that is to say, they were under the divine control. This control is represented as complete and compelling, so that, under it, the prophet becomes not the " mover," but the "moved" in the formation of his message. The apostle Peter very purely reflects the prophetic consciousness in his well-known declaration: 'No prophecy of scripture comes of private interpretation; for prophecy was never brought by the will of man; but it was as borne by the Holy Spirit that men spoke from God' (2 Pet. i. 20.21).

What this language of Peter emphasizes — and what is emphasized in the whole account which the prophets give of their own consciousness — is, to speak plainly, the passivity of the prophets with respect to the revelation given through them. This is the significance of the phrase: 'it was as borne by the Holy Spirit that men spoke from God.' To be "borne" ( $\phi\epsilon\rho\epsilon\iota\nu$, *phérein*) is not the same as to be led ( $\check{\alpha}\gamma\epsilon\iota\nu$, *ágein*), much less to be guided or directed ( $\dot{o}\delta\eta\gamma\epsilon\hat{\iota}\nu$, *hodēgeín*): he that is "borne" contributes nothing to the movement induced, but is the object to be moved. The term "passivity" is, perhaps, however, liable to some misapprehension, and should not be overstrained. It is not intended to deny that the intelligence of the prophets was active in the reception of their message; it was by means of their active intelligence that their message was received: their intelligence was the instrument of revelation. It is intended to deny only that their intelligence was active in the production of their message: that it was creatively as distinguished from receptively active. For reception itself is a kind of activity. What the prophets are solicitous that their readers shall understand is that they are in no sense co-authors with God of their messages. Their messages are given them, given them entire, and given them precisely as they are given out by them. God speaks through them: they are not merely His messengers, but "His mouth." But at the same time their intelligence is active in the reception, retention and announcing of their messages, contributing nothing to them but presenting fit instruments for the communication of them — instruments capable of understanding, responding profoundly to and zealously proclaiming them.

There is, no doubt, a not unnatural hesitancy abroad in thinking of the prophets as exhibiting only such merely receptive activities. In the interests of their personalities, we are asked not to represent God as dealing mechanically with them, pouring His revelations into their souls to be simply received as in so many buckets, or violently wresting their minds from their own proper action that He may do His own thinking with them. Must we not rather suppose, we are asked, that all revelations must be "psychologically mediated," must be given "after the mode of moral mediation," and must be made first of all their recipients' "own spiritual possession"? and is not, in point of fact, the personality of each prophet clearly traceable in his message, and that to such an extent as to compel us to recognize him as in a true sense its real author? The plausibility of such questionings should not be permitted to obscure the fact that the mode of the communication of the prophetic messages which is suggested by them is directly contradicted by the prophets' own representations of their relations to the revealing Spirit. In the prophets' own view they were just instruments through whom God gave revelations which came from them, not as their own product, but as the pure word of Jehovah. Neither should the plausibility of such questionings blind us to their speciousness. They exploit subordinate considerations, which are not without their validity in their own place and under their own limiting conditions, as if they were the determining or even the sole considerations in the case, and in neglect of the really determining considerations. God is Himself the author of the instruments He employs for the communication of His messages to men and has framed them into precisely the instruments He desired for the exact communication of His message. There is just ground for the expectation that He will use all the instruments He employs according to their natures; intelligent beings therefore as intelligent beings, moral agents as moral agents. But there is no just ground for asserting that God is incapable of employing the intelligent beings He has Himself created and formed to His will, to proclaim His messages purely as He gives them to them; or of making truly the possession of rational minds conceptions which they have themselves had no part in creating. And there is no ground for imagining that God is unable to frame His own message in the language of the organs of His revelation without its thereby ceasing to be, because expressed in a fashion natural to these organs, therefore purely His message. One would suppose it to lie in the very nature of the case that if the Lord makes any revelation to men, He would do it in the language of men; or, to individualize more explicitly, in the language of the man He employs as the organ of His revelation; and that naturally means, not the language of his nation or circle merely, but his own particular language, inclusive of all that gives individuality to his self-expression. We may speak of this, if we will, as " the accommodation of the revealing God to the several prophetic individualities." But we should avoid thinking of it externally and therefore mechanically, as if the revealing Spirit artificially phrased the message which He gives through each prophet in the particular forms of speech proper to the individuality of each, so as to create the illusion that the message comes out of the heart of the prophet himself. Precisely what the prophets affirm is that their messages do not come out of their own hearts and do not represent the workings of their own spirits. Nor is there any illusion in the phenomenon we are contemplating; and it is a much more intimate, and, we may add, a much more interesting phenomenon than an external "accommodation" of speech to individual habitudes. It includes, on the one hand, the " accommodation " of the prophet, through his total preparation, to the speech in which the revelation to be given through him is to be clothed; and on the other involves little more than the consistent carrying into detail of the broad principle that God uses the instruments He employs in accordance with their natures.

No doubt, on adequate occasion, the very stones might cry out by the power of God, and dumb beasts speak, and mysterious voices sound forth from the void; and there have not been lacking instances in which men have been compelled by the same power to speak what they would not, and in languages whose very sounds were strange to their ears. But ordinarily when God the Lord would speak to men He avails Himself of the services of a human tongue with which to speak, and He employs this tongue according to its nature as a tongue and according to the particular nature of the tongue which He employs. It is vain to say that the message delivered through the instrumentality of this tongue is conditioned at least in its form by the tongue by which it is spoken, if not, indeed, limited, curtailed, in some degree determined even in its matter, by it. Not only was it God the Lord who made the tongue, and who made this particular tongue with all its peculiarities, not without regard to the message He would deliver through it; but His control of it is perfect and complete, and it is as absurd to say that He cannot speak His message by it purely without that message suffering change from the peculiarities of its tone and modes of enunciation, as it would be to say that no new truth can be announced in any language because the elements of speech by the combination of which the truth in question is announced are already in existence with their fixed range of connotation. The marks of the several individualities imprinted on the messages of the prophets, in other words, are only a part of the general fact that these messages are couched in human language, and in no way beyond that general fact affect their purity as direct communications from God.

A new set of problems is raised by the mode of revelation which we have called "concursive operation." This mode of revelation differs from prophecy, properly so called, precisely by the employment in it, as is not done in prophecy, of the total personality of the organ of revelation, as a factor. It has been common to speak of the mode of the Spirit's action in this form of revelation, therefore, as an assistance, a superintendence, a direction, a control, the meaning being that the effect aimed at — the discovery and enunciation of Divine truth — is attained through the action of the human powers — historical research, logical reasoning, ethical thought, religious aspiration — acting not by themselves, however, but under the prevailing assistance, superintendence, direction, control of the Divine Spirit. This manner of speaking has the advantage of setting this mode of revelation sharply in contrast with prophetic revelation, as involving merely a determining, and not, as in prophetic revelation, a supercessive action of the revealing Spirit. We are warned, however, against pressing this discrimination too far by the inclusion of the whole body of Scripture in such passages as 2 Pet. i. 20 f. in the category of prophecy, and the assignment of their origin not to a mere "leading" but to the "bearing" of the Holy Spirit. In any event such terms as assistance, superintendence, direction, control, inadequately express the nature of the Spirit's action in revelation by "concursive operation." The Spirit is not to be conceived as standing outside of the human powers employed for the effect in view, ready to supplement any inadequacies they may show and to supply any defects they may manifest, but as working confluently in, with and by them, elevating them, directing them, controlling them, energizing them, so that, as His instruments, they rise above themselves and under His inspiration do His work and reach His aim. The product, therefore, which is attained by their means is His product through them. It is this fact which gives to the process the right to be called actively, and to the product the right to be called passively, a revelation. Although the circumstance that what is done is done by and through the action of human powers keeps the product in form and quality in a true sense human, yet the confluent operation of the Holy Spirit throughout the whole process raises the result above what could by any possibility be achieved by mere human powers and constitutes it expressly a supernatural product. The human traits are traceable throughout its whole extent, but at bottom it is a Divine gift, and the language of Paul is the most proper mode of speech that could be applied to it: "Which things also we speak, not in words which man's wisdom teacheth, but which the Spirit teacheth "

(1 Cor. ii. 13); "The things which I write unto you . . . are the commandment of the Lord" (1 Cor. xiv. 37).

It is supposed that all the forms of special or redemptive revelation which underlie and give its content to the religion of the Bible may without violence be subsumed under one or another of these three modes — external manifestation, internal suggestion, and concursive operation. All, that is, except the culminating revelation, not through, but in, Jesus Christ. As in His person, in which dwells all the fulness of the Godhead bodily, He rises above all classification and is *sui generis;* so the revelation accumulated in Him stands outside all the divers portions and divers manners in which otherwise revelation has been given and sums up in itself all that has been or can be made known of God and of His redemption. He does not so much make a revelation of God as Himself is the revelation of God; He does not merely disclose God's purpose of redemption, He is unto us wisdom from God, and righteousness and sanctification and redemption. The theophanies are but faint shadows in comparison with His manifestation of God in the flesh. The prophets could prophesy only as the Spirit of Christ which was in them testified, revealing to them as to servants one or another of the secrets of the Lord Jehovah; from Him as His Son, Jehovah has no secrets, but whatsoever the Father knows that the Son knows also. Whatever truth men have been made partakers of by the Spirit of truth is His (for all things whatsoever the Father hath are His) and is taken by the Spirit of truth and declared to men that He may be glorified. Nevertheless, though all revelation is thus summed up in Him, we should not fail to note very carefully that it would also be all sealed up in Him — so little is revelation conveyed by fact alone, without the word — had it not been thus taken by the Spirit of truth and declared unto men. The entirety of the New Testament is but the explanatory word accompanying and giving its effect to the fact of Christ. And when this fact was in all its meaning made the possession of men, revelation was completed and in that sense ceased. Jesus Christ is no less the end of revelation than He is the end of the law.

## IV. Biblical Terminology

There is not much additional to be learned concerning the nature and processes of revelation, from the terms currently employed in Scripture to express the idea. These terms are ordinarily the common words for disclosing, making known, making manifest, applied with more or less heightened significance to supernatural acts or effects in kind. In the English Bible (AV) the verb "reveal" occurs about fifty-one times, of which twenty-two are in the Old Testament and twenty-nine in the New Testament. In the Old Testament the word is always the rendering of a Hebrew term גָּלָה, galāh, or its Aramaic equivalent גְּלָה, gᵉlāh, the root meaning of which appears to be "nakedness." When applied to revelation, it seems to hint at the removal of obstacles to perception or the uncovering of objects to perception. In the New Testament the word "reveal" is always (with the single exception of Lk. ii. 35) the rendering of a Greek term ἀποκαλύπτω, apokalúptō (but in 2 Thess. i. 7; 1 Pet. iv. 13 the corresponding noun ἀποκάλυψις, apokálupsis), which has a very similar basal significance with its Hebrew parallel. As this Hebrew word formed no substantive in this sense, the noun "revelation" does not occur in the English Old Testament, the idea being expressed, however, by other Hebrew terms variously rendered. It occurs in the English New Testament, on the other hand, about a dozen times, and always as the rendering of the substantive corresponding to the verb rendered "reveal" (apokálupsis). On the face of the English Bible, the terms "reveal," "revelation" bear therefore uniformly the general sense of "disclose," "disclosure." The idea is found in the Bible, however, much more frequently than the terms "reveal," "revelation" in English versions. Indeed, the Hebrew and Greek terms exclusively so rendered occur more frequently in this sense than in this rendering in the English Bible. And by their side there stand various other terms which express in one way or another the general conception.

In the New Testament the verb φανερόω, phaneróō, with the general sense of making manifest, manifesting, is the most common of these. It differs from *apokalúptō* as the more general and external term from the more special and inward. Other terms also are occasionally used: ἐπιφάνεια, *epipháneia*, "manifestation" (2 Thess. ii. 8; 1 Tim. vi. 14; 2 Tim. i. 10; iv. 1; Tit. ii. 13; cf. ἐπιφαίνω, *epiphaínō*, Tit. ii. 11; iii. 4); δεικνύω, *deiknúō* (Rev. i. 1; xvii. 1; xxii. 1.6.8; cf. Acts ix. 16; 1 Tim. iv. 15); ἐξηγέομαι, *exēgéomai* (Jn. i. 18), of which, however, only one perhaps — χρηματίζω, *chrēmatízō* (Mt. ii. 12.22; Lk. ii. 26; Acts x. 22; Heb. viii. 5; xi. 7; xii. 25); χρηματισμός, *chrēmatismós* (Rom. xi. 4) — calls for particular notice as in a special way, according to its usage, expressing the idea of a Divine communication.

In the Old Testament, the common Hebrew verb for "seeing" (רָאָה, *rā'āh*) is used in its appropriate stems, with God as the subject, for "appearing," "showing": "the Lord appeared unto . . ."; "the word which the Lord showed me." And from this verb not only is an active substantive formed which supplied the more ancient designation of the official organ or revelation: רֹאֶה, *rō'eh*, "seer"; but also objective substantives, מַרְאָה, *mar'āh*, and מַרְאֶה, *mar'eh* which were used to designate the thing seen in a revelation — the "vision." By the side of these terms there were others in use, derived from a root which supplies to the Aramaic its common word for "seeing," but in Hebrew has a somewhat more pregnant meaning, חָזָה, *hāzāh*. Its active derivative, חֹזֶה, *hōzeh*, was a designation of a prophet which remained in occasional use, alternating with the more customary נָבִיא, *nābhī*, long after רֹאֶה, *rō'eh*, had become practically obsolete; and its passive derivatives *hāzōn*, *hizzāyōn*, *hāzūth*, *mahăzeh* provided the ordinary terms for the substance of the revelation or "vision." The distinction between the two sets of terms, derived respectively from *rā'āh* and *hāzāh*, while not to be unduly pressed, seems to lie in the direction that the former suggests external manifestations and the latter internal revelations. The *rō'eh* is he to whom Divine manifestations, the *hōzeh* he to whom Divine communications, have been vouchsafed; the *mar'eh* is an appearance, the *hāzōn* and its companions a vision. It may be of interest to observe that *mar'āh* is the term employed in Num. xii. 6, while it is *hāzōn* which commonly occurs in the headings of the written prophecies to indicate their revelatory character. From this it may possibly be inferred that in the former passage it is the mode, in the latter the contents of the revelation that is emphasized. Perhaps a like distinction may be traced between the *hāzōn* of Dan. viii. 15 and the *mar'eh* of the next verse. The ordinary verb for "knowing," יָדַע, *yādha',* expressing in its causative stems the idea of making known, informing, is also very naturally employed, with God as its subject, in the sense of revealing, and that, in accordance with the natural sense of the word, with a tendency to pregnancy of implication, of revealing effectively, of not merely uncovering to observation, but making to know. Accordingly, it is paralleled not merely with גָּלָה, *gālāh* (Ps. xcviii. 2: ' The Lord hath *made known* his salvation; his righteousness hath he *displayed* in the sight of the nation '), but also with such terms as לָמַד, *lāmadh* (Ps. xxv. 4: ' *Make known* to me thy ways, O Lord: *teach* me thy paths '). This verb *yādha'* forms no substantive in the sense of "revelation" (cf. דַּעַת, *da'ath,* Num. xxiv. 16; Ps. xix. 3).

The most common vehicles of the idea of "revelation" in the Old Testament are, however, two expressions which are yet to be mentioned. These are the phrase, "word of Jehovah," and the term commonly but inadequately rendered in the English versions by "law." The former (*dᵉbhar Yahweh,* varied to *dᵉbhar 'Ĕlōhīm* or *dᵉbhar hā-'Elōhīm; cf. nᵉ'um Yahweh, massā, Yahweh*) occurs scores of times and is at once the simplest and the most colorless designation of a Divine communication. By the latter (*tōrāh*), the proper meaning of which is "instruction," a strong implication of authoritativeness is conveyed; and, in this sense, it becomes what may be called the technical designation of a specifically Divine communication. The two are not infrequently brought together, as in Isa. i. 10: "Hear the word of Jehovah, ye rulers of Sodom; give ear unto the law [margin "teaching"] of our God, ye people of Gomorrah"; or Isa. ii. 3; Mic. iv. 2; "For out of Zion shall go forth the law [margin "instruction"], and the word of Jehovah from Jerusalem." Both terms are used for any Divine communication of whatever extent; and both came to be employed to express the entire body of Divine revelation, conceived as a unitary whole. In this comprehensive usage, the emphasis of the one came to fall more on the graciousness, and of the other more on the authoritativeness of this body of Divine revelation; and both passed into the New Testament with these implications. "The word of God," or simply "the word," comes thus to mean in the New Testament just the gospel, "the word of the proclamation of redemption, that is, all that which God has to say to man, and causes to be said" looking to his salvation. It expresses, in a word, precisely what we technically speak of as God's redemptive revelation. "The law," on the other hand, means in this New Testament use, just the whole body of the authoritative instruction which God has given men. It expresses, in other words, what we commonly speak of as God's supernatural revelation. The two things, of course, are the same: God's authoritative revelation is His gracious revelation; God's redemptive revelation is His supernatural revelation. The two terms merely look at the one aggregate of revelation from two aspects, and each emphasizes its own aspect of this one aggregated revelation.

Now, this aggregated revelation lay before the men of the New Testament in a written form, and it was impossible to speak freely of it without consciousness of and at least occasional reference to its written form. Accordingly we hear of a Word of God that is written (Jn. xv. 25; 1 Cor. xv. 54), and the Divine Word is naturally contrasted with mere tradition, as if its written form were of its very idea (Mk. vii. 10); indeed, the written body of revelation — with an emphasis on its written form — is designated expressly 'the prophetic word' (2 Pet. i. 19). More distinctly still, "the Law" comes to be thought of as a written, not exactly, code, but body of Divinely authoritative instructions. The phrase, "It is written in your law" (Jn. x. 34; xv. 25; Rom. iii. 19; 1 Cor. xiv. 21), acquires the precise sense of, "It is set forth in your authoritative Scriptures, all the content of which is 'law,' that is, Divine instruction." Thus "the Word of God," "the Law," came to mean just the written body of revelation, what we call, and what the New Testament writers called, in the same high sense which we give the term, "the Scriptures." These "Scriptures" are thus identified with the revelation of God, conceived as a well-defined *corpus,* and two conceptions rise before us which have had a determining part to play in the history of Christianity — the conception of an authoritative Canon of Scripture, and the conception of this Canon of Scripture as just the Word of God written. The former conception was thrown into prominence in opposition to the gnostic heresies in the earliest age of the church, and gave rise to a richly varied mode of speech concerning the Scriptures, emphasizing their authority in legal language, which goes back to and rests on the Biblical usage of "Law." The latter it was left to the Reformation to do justice to in its struggle against, on the one side, the Romish depression of the Scriptures in favor of the traditions of the church, and on the other side the Enthusiasts' supercession of them in the interests of the "inner Word." When Tertullian, on the one hand, speaks of the Scriptures as an "Instrument," a legal document, his terminology has an express warrant in the Scriptures' own usage of *tōrāh,* "law," to designate their entire content. And when John Gerhard argues that "between the Word of God and Sacred Scripture, taken in a material sense, there is no real difference," he is only declaring plainly what is definitely implied in the New Testament use of "the Word of God" with the written revelation in mind. What is important to recognize is that the Scriptures themselves represent the Scriptures as not merely containing here and there the record of revelations — "words of God," *tōrōth* — given by God, but as themselves, in all their extent, a revelation, an authoritative body of gracious instructions from God; or, since they alone, of all the revelations which God may have given, are extant — rather as the Revelation, the only "Word of God" accessible to men, in all their parts "law," that is, authoritative instruction from God.

LITERATURE. — Herman Witsius, " De Prophetis et Prophetia " in *Miscell. Sacr.*, I, Leiden, 1736, 1–318; G. F. Oehler, *Theology of the OT*, ET, Edinburgh, 1874, I, part I (and the appropriate sections in other Bib. Theologies) ; H. Bavinck, *Gereformeerde Dogmatiek*[2], I, Kampen, 1906, 290–406 (and the appropriate sections in other dogmatic treatises) ; H. Voigt, *Fundamentaldogmatik*, Gotha, 1874, 173 ff; A. Kuyper, *Encyclopaedia of Sacred Theology*, ET, New York, 1898, div. III, ch. 11; A. E. Krauss, *Die Lehre von der Offenbarung*, Gotha, 1868; C. F. Fritzsche, *De revelationis notione biblica*, Leipzig, 1828; E. W. Hengstenberg, *The Christology of the OT*, ET[2], Edinburgh, 1868, IV, Appendix 6, pp. 396–444; E. König, *Der Offenbarungsbegriff des AT*, Leipzig, 1882; A. B. Davidson, *OT Prophecy*, 1903; W. J. Beecher, *The Prophets and the Promise*, New York, 1905; James Orr, *The Christian View of God and the World*, 1893, as per Index, " Revelation," and *Revelation and Inspiration*, London and New York, 1910. Also: T. Christlieb, *Modern Doubt and Christian Belief*, ET, New York, 1874; G. P. Fisher, *The Nature and Method of Revelation*, New York, 1890; C. M. Mead, *Supernatural Revelation*, 1889; J. Quirmbach, *Die Lehre des h. Paulus von der natürlichen Gotteserkenntnis*, etc., Freiburg, 1906.

# II

# THE CHURCH DOCTRINE OF INSPIRATION

# THE CHURCH DOCTRINE OF INSPIRATION[1]

THE subject of the Inspiration of the Bible is one which has been much confused in recent discussion. He who, seeking to learn the truth, should gather about him the latest treatises, bearing such titles as, "Inspiration, and other Lectures," "Inspiration and the Bible," "What is Inspiration?" "How did God inspire the Bible?" "The Oracles of God?"[2]—would find himself led by them in every conceivable direction at once. No wonder if he should stand stock-still in the midst of his would-be guides, confounded by the Babel of voices. The old formula, *quot homines tot sententiæ*, seems no longer adequate. Wherever five "advanced thinkers" assemble, at least six theories as to inspiration are likely to be ventilated. They differ in every conceivable point, or in every conceivable point save one. They agree that inspiration is less pervasive and less determinative than has heretofore been thought, or than is still thought in less enlightened circles. They agree that there is less of the truth of God and more of the error of man in the Bible than Christians have been wont to believe. They agree accordingly that the teaching of the Bible may be, in this, that, or the other,—here, there, or elsewhere,—safely neglected or openly repudiated. So soon as we turn to the constructive side, however, and ask wherein the inspiration of the Bible consists; how far it guarantees the trustworthiness of the Bible's teaching; in what of its elements is the Bible a divinely safeguarded guide to truth: the concurrence ends and hopeless dissension sets in. They agree only in their common destructive attitude towards some higher view of the inspiration of the Bible, of the presence of which each one seems supremely conscious.

It is upon this fact that we need first of all to fix our atten-

---

[1] From "Bibliotheca Sacra," v. 51, 1894, pp. 614–640. Pub. in "Revelation and Inspiration" under the title, "The Inspiration of the Bible."

[2] Titles of recent treatises by Rooke, Horton, DeWitt, Smyth, and Sanday respectively.

tion. It is not of the variegated hypotheses of his fellow-the-orizers, but of some high doctrine of inspiration, the common object of attack of them all, that each new theorizer on the subject of inspiration is especially conscious, as standing over against him, with reference to which he is to orient himself, and against the claims of which he is to defend his new hypothesis. Thus they themselves introduce us to the fact that over against the numberless discordant theories of inspiration which vex our time, there stands a well-defined church-doctrine of inspiration. This church-doctrine of inspiration differs from the theories that would fain supplant it, in that it is not the invention nor the property of an individual, but the settled faith of the universal church of God; in that it is not the growth of yesterday, but the assured persuasion of the people of God from the first planting of the church until to-day; in that it is not a protean shape, varying its affirmations to fit every new change in the ever-shifting thought of men, but from the beginning has been the church's constant and abiding conviction as to the divinity of the Scriptures committed to her keeping. It is certainly a most impressive fact, — this well-defined, aboriginal, stable doctrine of the church as to the nature and trustworthiness of the Scriptures of God, which confronts with its gentle but steady persistence of affirmation all the theories of inspiration which the restless energy of unbelieving and half-believing speculation has been able to invent in this agitated nineteenth century of ours. Surely the seeker after the truth in the matter of the inspiration of the Bible may well take this church-doctrine as his starting-point.

What this church-doctrine is, it is scarcely necessary minutely to describe. It will suffice to remind ourselves that it looks upon the Bible as an oracular book, — as the Word of God in such a sense that whatever it says God says, — not a book, then, in which one may, by searching, find some word of God, but a book which may be frankly appealed to at any point with the assurance that whatever it may be found to say, that is the Word of God. We are all of us members in particular of the body of Christ which we call the church: and the life of the church, and the faith of the church, and the thought of the church are our natural heritage. We know how, as Christian men, we approach this Holy Book, — how unquestioningly we receive its statements of fact, bow before its enunciations of duty, tremble before its threatenings, and rest upon its promises. Or, if the subtle spirit of modern doubt has seeped somewhat into our hearts, our memory will easily recall those happier days when we stood a child at our Christian mother's knee, with lisping lips following the words which her slow finger traced upon this open page, — words which were her support in every trial and, as she fondly trusted, were to be our guide throughout life. Mother church was speaking to us in that maternal voice, commending to us her vital faith in the Word of God. How often since then has it been our own lot, in our turn, to speak to others all the words of this life! As we sit in the midst of our pupils in the Sabbath-school, or in the centre of our circle at home, or perchance at some bedside of sickness or of death; or as we meet our fellow-man amid the busy work of the world, hemmed in by temptation or weighed down with care, and would fain put beneath him some firm support and stay: in what spirit do we turn to this Bible then? with what confidence do we commend its every word to those whom we would make partakers of its comfort or of its strength? In such scenes as these is revealed the vital faith of the people of God in the surety and trustworthiness of the Word of God.

Nor do we need to do more than remind ourselves that this attitude of entire trust in every word of the Scriptures has been characteristic of the people of God from the very foundation of the church. Christendom has always reposed upon the belief that the utterances of this book are properly oracles of God. The whole body of Christian literature bears witness to this fact. We may trace its stream to its source, and everywhere it is vocal with a living faith in the divine trustworthiness of the Scriptures of God in every one of their affirmations. This is the murmur of the little rills of Christian speech which find their tenuous way through the parched heathen land of the early

second century. And this is the mighty voice of the great river
of Christian thought which sweeps through the ages, freighted
with blessings for men. Dr. Sanday, in his recent Bampton
Lectures on "Inspiration"—in which, unfortunately, he does
not teach the church-doctrine—is driven to admit that not
only may "testimonies to the general doctrine of inspiration"
from the earliest Fathers, "be multiplied to almost any extent; but [that] there are some which go further and point to
an inspiration which might be described as 'verbal'"; "nor
does this idea," he adds, "come in tentatively and by degrees,
but almost from the very first."[3] He might have spared the ad-
verb "almost." The earliest writers know no other doctrine. If
Origen asserts that the Holy Spirit was co-worker with the
Evangelists in the composition of the Gospel, and that, therefore, lapse of memory, error or falsehood was impossible to
them,[4] and if Irenæus, the pupil of Polycarp, claims for Christians a clear knowledge that "the Scriptures are perfect, seeing
that they are spoken by God's Word and his Spirit";[5] no less
does Polycarp, the pupil of John, consider the Scriptures the
very voice of the Most High, and pronounce him the first-born
of Satan, "whosoever perverts these oracles of the Lord."[6] Nor
do the later Fathers know a different doctrine. Augustine, for
example, affirms that he defers to the canonical Scriptures
alone among books with such reverence and honor that he most
"firmly believes that no one of their authors has erred in anything, in writing."[7] To precisely the same effect did the Reformers believe and teach. Luther adopts these words of Augustine's as his own, and declares that the whole of the Scriptures
are to be ascribed to the Holy Ghost, and therefore cannot err.[8]
Calvin demands that whatever is propounded in Scripture,
"without exception," shall be humbly received by us, — that

[3] Sanday, "Inspiration," p. 34.
[4] On Matt. xvi. 12 and Jno. vi. 18.
[5] Adv. Haer, ii. 28.
[6] Ep. ad Phil., cap. vii.
[7] Ep. ad Hier. lxxxii. 3.
[8] "Works" (St. Louis ed.), xix. 305; (Erlangen ed.), xxxvii. 11
and xxxviii. 33.

the Scriptures as a whole shall be received by us with the same reverence which we give to God, "because they have emanated from him alone, and are mixed with nothing human."[9] The saintly Rutherford, who speaks of the Scriptures as a more sure word than a direct oracle from heaven,[10] and Baxter, who affirms that "all that the holy writers have recorded is true (and no falsehood in the Scriptures but what is from the errors of scribes and translators),"[11] hand down this supreme trust in the Scripture word to our own day — to our own Charles Hodge and Henry B. Smith, the one of whom asserts that the Bible "gives us truth without error,"[12] and the other, that "all the books of the Scripture are equally inspired ; . . . all alike are infallible in what they teach ; . . . their assertions must be free from error."[13] Such testimonies are simply the formulation by the theologians of each age of the constant faith of Christians throughout all ages.

If we would estimate at its full meaning the depth of this trust in the Scripture word, we should observe Christian men at work upon the text of Scripture. There is but one view-point which will account for or justify the minute and loving pains which have been expended upon the text of Scripture, by the long line of commentators that has extended unbrokenly from the first Christian ages to our own. The allegorical interpretation which rioted in the early days of the church was the daughter of reverence for the biblical word ; a spurious daughter you may think, but none the less undeniably a direct offspring of the awe with which the sacred text was regarded as the utterances of God, and, as such, pregnant with inexhaustible significance. The patient and anxious care with which the Bible text is scrutinized today by scholars, of a different spirit no doubt from those old allegorizers, but of equal reverence for

[9] "Institutes," i. 18; "Commentary on Romans," xv. 4, and on 2 Tim. iii. 16.

[10] "Free Disputation against Pretended Liberty of Conscience," p. 373.

[11] "Works," xv. 65.

[12] Henry B. Smith, "Sermon on Inspiration" (Cincinnati ed.), p. 19.

[13] Charles Hodge, "Syst. Theol.," i. 163.

the text of Scripture, betrays the same fundamental view-point, — to which the Bible is the Word of God, every detail of the meaning of which is of inestimable preciousness. No doubt there have been men who have busied themselves with the interpretation of Scripture, who have not approached it in such a spirit or with such expectations. But it is not the Jowetts, with their supercilious doubts whether Paul meant very much by what he said, who represent the spirit of Christian exposition. This is represented rather by the Bengels, who count no labor wasted, in their efforts to distill from the very words of Holy Writ the honey which the Spirit has hidden in them for the comfort and the delight of the saints. It is represented rather by the Westcotts, who bear witness to their own experience of the "sense of rest and confidence which grows firmer with increasing knowledge," as their patient investigation has dug deeper and deeper for the treasures hid in the words and clauses and sentences of the Epistles of John,[14] — to the sure conviction which forty years of study of the Epistle to the Hebrews has brought them that "we come nearer to the meaning of Scripture by the closest attention to the subtleties and minute variations of words and order." It was a just remark of one of the wisest men I ever knew, Dr. Wistar Hodge, that this is "a high testimony to verbal inspiration."[15]

Of course the church has not failed to bring this, her vital faith in the divine trustworthiness of the Scripture word, to formal expression in her solemn creeds. The simple faith of the Christian people is also the confessional doctrine of the Christian churches. The assumption of the divine authority of the scriptural teaching underlies all the credal statements of the church ; all of which are formally based upon the Scriptures. And from the beginning, it finds more or less full expression in them. Already, in some of the formulas of faith which underlie the Apostles' Creed itself, we meet with the phrase "according to the Scriptures" as validating the items of belief ; while in the Niceno-Constantinopolitan Creed, amid the meagre clauses

[14] B. F. Westcott, " The Epistles of St. John," p. vi.
[15] C. Wistar Hodge, " Presbyterian and Reformed Review," ii. 330.

outlining only what is essential to the doctrine of the Holy Spirit, place is given to the declaration that He is to be found speaking in the prophets— "who spake by the prophets." It was in conscious dependence upon the immemorial teaching of the church that the Council of Trent defined it as of faith in the Church of Rome, that God is the author of Scripture,—a declaration which has been repeated in our own day by the Vatican Council, with such full explanations as are included in these rich words: "The church holds" the books of the Old and New Testaments, "to be sacred and canonical, not because, having been carefully composed by mere human industry, they were afterwards approved by her authority ; nor merely because they contain revelation with no admixture of error ; but because, having been written by the inspiration of the Holy Ghost, they have God for their author." Needless to say that a no less firm conviction of the absolute authority of Scripture underlies all the Protestant creeds. Before all else, Protestantism is, in its very essence, an appeal from all other authority to the divine authority of Holy Scripture. The Augsburg Confession, the first Protestant creed, is, therefore, commended to consideration, only on the ground that it is "drawn from the Holy Scriptures and the pure word of God." The later Lutheran creeds, and especially the Reformed creeds, grow progressively more explicit. It is our special felicity, that as Reformed Christians, and heirs of the richest and fullest formulation of Reformed thought, we possess in that precious heritage, the Westminster Confession, the most complete, the most admirable, the most perfect statement of the essential Christian doctrine of Holy Scripture which has ever been formed by man. Here the vital faith of the church is brought to full expression; the Scriptures are declared to be the word of God in such a sense that God is their author, and they, because immediately inspired by God, are of infallible truth and divine authority, and are to be believed to be true by the Christian man, in whatsoever is revealed in them, for the authority of God himself speaking therein.

Thus, in every way possible, the church has borne her testimony from the beginning, and still in our day, to her faith in the divine trustworthiness of her Scriptures, in all their affirmations of whatever kind. At no age has it been possible for men to express without rebuke the faintest doubt as to the absolute trustworthiness of their least declaration. Tertullian, writing at the opening of the third century, suggests, with evident hesitation and timidity, that Paul's language in the seventh chapter of First Corinthians may be intended to distinguish, in his remarks on marriage and divorce, between matters of divine commandment and of human arrangement. Dr. Sanday is obliged to comment on his language: "Any seeming depreciation of Scripture was as unpopular even then as it is now."[16] The church has always believed her Scriptures to be the book of God, of which God was in such a sense the author that every one of its affirmations of whatever kind is to be esteemed as the utterance of God, of infallible truth and authority.

In the whole history of the church there have been but two movements of thought, tending to a lower conception of the inspiration and authority of Scripture, which have attained sufficient proportions to bring them into view in an historical sketch.

(1) The first of these may be called the Rationalistic view. Its characteristic feature is an effort to distinguish between inspired and uninspired elements within the Scriptures. With forerunners among the Humanists, this mode of thought was introduced by the Socinians, and taken up by the Syncretists in Germany, the Remonstrants in Holland, and the Jesuits in the Church of Rome. In the great life-and-death struggle of the eighteenth century it obtained great vogue among the defenders of supernatural religion, in their desperate efforts to save what was of even more importance, — just as a hard-pressed army may yield to the foe many an outpost which justly belongs to it, in the effort to save the citadel. In the nineteenth century it has retained a strong hold, especially upon apologetical writers, chiefly in the three forms which affirm re-

[16] Sanday, "Inspiration," p. 42 (note).

spectively that only the *mysteries* of the faith are inspired, i. e. things undiscoverable by unaided reason, — that the Bible is inspired only in *matters of faith and practice*, — and that the Bible is inspired only in its *thoughts or concepts*, not in its words. But although this legacy from the rationalism of an evil time still makes its appearance in the pages of many theological writers, and has no doubt affected the faith of a considerable number of Christians, it has failed to supplant in either the creeds of the church or the hearts of the people the church-doctrine of the plenary inspiration of the Bible, i. e. the doctrine that the Bible is inspired not *in part* but *fully*, in all its elements alike, — things discoverable by reason as well as mysteries, matters of history and science as well as of faith and practice, words as well as thoughts.

(2) The second of the lowered views of inspiration may be called the Mystical view. Its characteristic conception is that the Christian man has something within himself, — call it enlightened reason, spiritual insight, the Christian consciousness, the witness of the Spirit, or call it what you will, — to the test of which every "external revelation" is to be subjected, and according to the decision of which are the contents of the Bible to be valued. Very varied forms have been taken by this conception ; and more or less expression has been given to it, in one form or another, in every age. In its extremer manifestations, it has formerly tended to sever itself from the main stream of Christian thought and even to form separated sects. But in our own century, through the great genius of Schleiermacher it has broken in upon the church like a flood, and washed into every corner of the Protestant world. As a consequence, we find men everywhere who desire to acknowledge as from God only such Scripture as "finds them," — who cast the clear objective enunciation of God's will to the mercy of the currents of thought and feeling which sweep up and down in their own souls, — who "persist" sometimes, to use a sharp but sadly true phrase of Robert Alfred Vaughan's, "in their conceited rejection of the light without until they have turned into darkness their light within." We grieve over the inroads

which this essentially naturalistic mode of thought has made in the Christian thinking of the day. But great and deplorable as they have been, they have not been so extensive as to supplant the church-doctrine of the absolute authority of the objective revelation of God in his Word, in either the creeds of the church, or the hearts of the people. Despite these attempts to introduce lowered conceptions, the doctrine of the plenary inspiration of the Scriptures, which looks upon them as an oracular book, in all its parts and elements, alike, of God, trustworthy in all its affirmations of every kind, remains to-day, as it has always been, the vital faith of the people of God, and the formal teaching of the organized church.

The more we contemplate this church-doctrine, the more pressing becomes the question of what account we are to give of it, — its origin and persistence. How shall we account for the immediate adoption of so developed a doctrine of inspiration in the very infancy of the church, and for the tenacious hold which the church has kept upon it through so many ages? The account is simple enough, and capable of inclusion in a single sentence: this is the doctrine of inspiration which was held by the writers of the New Testament and by Jesus as reported in the Gospels. It is this simple fact that has commended it to the church of all ages as the true doctrine; and in it we may surely recognize an even more impressive fact than that of the existence of a stable, abiding church-doctrine standing over against the many theories of the day, — the fact, namely, that this church-doctrine of inspiration was the Bible doctrine before it was the church-doctrine, and is the church-doctrine only because it is the Bible doctrine. It is upon this fact that we should now fix our attention.

In the limited space at our disposal we need not attempt anything like a detailed proof that the church-doctrine of the plenary inspiration of the Bible is the Bible's own doctrine of inspiration. And this especially for three very obvious reasons :

*First,* because it cannot be necessary to prove this to ourselves. We have the Bible in our hands, and we are accustomed to read it. It is enough for us to ask ourselves how the apostles and our Lord, as represented in its pages, conceived of what they called "the Scriptures," for the answer to come at once to our minds. As readers of the New Testament, we know that to the men of the New Testament "the Scriptures" were the Word of God which could not be broken, i. e. whose every word was trustworthy; and that a simple "It is written" was therefore to them the end of all strife. The proof of this is pervasive and level to the apprehension of every reader. It would be an insult to our intelligence were we to presume that we had not observed it, or could not apprehend its meaning.

*Secondly*, it is not necessary to prove that the New Testament regards "Scripture" as the mere Word of God, in the highest and most rigid sense, to modern biblical scholarship. Among untrammelled students of the Bible, it is practically a matter of common consent that the writers of the New Testament books looked upon what they called "Scripture" as divinely safeguarded in even its verbal expression, and as divinely trustworthy in all its parts, in all its elements, and in all its affirmations of whatever kind. This is, of course, the judgment of all those who have adopted this doctrine as their own, because they apprehend it to be the biblical doctrine. It is also the judgment of all those who can bring themselves to refuse a doctrine which they yet perceive to be a biblical doctrine. Whether we appeal, among men of this class, to such students of a more evangelical tendency, as Tholuck, Rothe, Farrar, Sanday, or to such extremer writers as Riehm, Reuss, Pfleiderer, Keunen, they will agree in telling us that the high doctrine of inspiration which we have called the church-doctrine was held by the writers of the New Testament. This is common ground between believing and unbelieving students of the Bible, and needs, therefore, no new demonstration in the forum of scholarship. Let us pause here, therefore, only long enough to allow Hermann Schultz, surely a fair example of the "advanced" school, to tell us what is the conclusion in this matter of the strictest and coldest exegetical science. "The

Book of the Law," he tells us, "seemed already to the later poets of the Old Testament, the 'Word of God.' The post-canonical books of Israel regard the Law and the Prophets in this manner. And for the men of the New Testament, the Holy Scriptures of their people are already God's word in which God himself speaks." This view, which looked upon the scriptural books as verbally inspired, he adds, was the ruling one in the time of Christ, was shared by all the New Testament men, and by Christ himself, as a pious conception, and was expressly taught by the more scholastic writers among them.[17] It is hardly necessary to prove what is so frankly confessed.

The *third* reason why it is not necessary to occupy our time with a formal proof that the Bible does teach this doctrine, arises from the circumstance that even those who seek to rid themselves of the pressure of this fact upon them, are observed to be unable to prosecute their argument without an implied admission of it as a fact. This is true, for example, of Dr. Sanday's endeavors to meet the appeal of the church to our Lord's authority in defence of the doctrine of plenary inspiration.[18] He admits that the one support which has been sought by the church of all ages for its high doctrine has been the "extent to which it was recognized in the sayings of Christ himself." As over against this he begins by suggesting "that, whatever view our Lord himself entertained as to the Scriptures of the Old Testament, the record of his words has certainly come down to us through the medium of persons who shared the current view on the subject." This surely amounts to a full admission that the writers of the New Testament at least, held and taught the obnoxious doctrine. He ends with the remark that "when deductions have been made . . . there still remains evidence enough that our Lord, while on earth *did* use the common language of his contemporaries in regard to the Old Testament." This surely amounts to a full admission that Christ as well as his reporters taught the obnoxious doctrine.

This will be found to be a typical case. Every attempt to

[17] Hermann Schultz, "Grundriss d. Evang. Dogmatik," p. 7.
[18] "Inspiration," p. 393 *seq.*

escape from the authority of the New Testament enunciation of the doctrine of plenary inspiration, in the nature of the case begins by admitting that this is, in very fact, the New Testament doctrine. Shall we follow Dr. Sanday, and appeal from the apostles to Christ, and then call in the idea of *kenosis,* and affirm that in the days of his flesh, Christ did not speak out of the fulness and purity of his divine knowledge, but on becoming man had shrunk to man's capacity, and in such matters as this was limited in his conceptions by the knowledge and opinions current in his day and generation? In so saying, we admit, as has already been pointed out, not only that the apostles taught this high doctrine of inspiration, but also that Christ too, in whatever humiliation he did it, yet actually taught the same. Shall we then take refuge in the idea of *accommodation,* and explain that, in so speaking of the Scriptures, Christ and his apostles did not intend to teach the doctrine of inspiration implicated, but merely adopted, as a matter of convenience, the current language, as to Scripture, of the time? In so speaking, also, we admit that the actual language of Christ and his apostles expresses that high view of inspiration which was confessedly the current view of the day — whether as a matter of convenience or as a matter of truth, the Christian consciousness may be safely left to decide. Shall we then remind ourselves that Jesus himself committed nothing to writing, and appeal to the uncertainties which are accustomed to attend the record of teaching at second-hand? Thus, too, we allow that the words of Christ as transmitted to us do teach the obnoxious doctrine. Are we, then, to fall back upon the observation that the doctrine of plenary inspiration is not taught with equal plainness in every part of the Bible, but becomes clear only in the later Old Testament books, and is not explicitly enunciated except in the more scholastic of the New Testament books? In this, too, we admit that it is taught in the Scriptures ; while the fact that it is taught not all at once, but with progressive clearness and fulness, is accordant with the nature of the Bible as a book written in the process of the ages and progressively developing the truth. Then, shall we affirm that our doctrine of inspiration is not to be derived solely from the teachings of the Bible, but from its teachings and phenomena in conjunction; and so call in what we deem the phenomena of the Bible to modify its teaching? Do we not see that the very suggestion of this process admits that the teaching of the Bible, when taken alone, i.e., in its purity and just as it is, gives us the unwelcome doctrine? Shall we, then, take counsel of desperation and assert that all appeal to the teaching of the Scriptures themselves in testimony to their own inspiration is an argument in a circle, appealing to their inspiration to validate their inspiration? Even this desperately illogical shift to be rid of the scriptural doctrine of inspiration, obviously involves the confession that this is the scriptural doctrine. No, the issue is not, What does the Bible teach? but, Is what the Bible teaches true? And it is amazing that any or all of such expedients can blind the eyes of any one to the stringency of this issue.

Even a detailed attempt to explain away the texts which teach the doctrine of the plenary inspiration and unvarying truth of Scripture, involves the admission that in their obvious meaning such texts teach the doctrine which it is sought to explain away. And think of explaining away the texts which inculcate the doctrine of the plenary inspiration of the Scriptures! The effort to do so is founded upon an inexplicably odd misapprehension — the misapprehension that the Bible witnesses to its plenary inspiration only in a text here and there: texts of exceptional clearness alone probably being in mind, — such as our Saviour's declaration that the Scriptures cannot be broken; or Paul's, that every scripture is inspired of God; or Peter's, that the men of God spake as they were moved by the Holy Ghost. Such texts, no doubt, do teach the doctrine of plenary inspiration, and are sadly in need of explaining away at the hands of those who will not believe this doctrine. As, indeed, we may learn from Dr. Sanday's treatment of one of them, that in which our Lord declares that the Scriptures cannot be broken. Dr. Sanday can only speak of this as "a passage of peculiar strangeness and difficulty"; "because," he tells us,

trustworthiness of the Scriptures lies at the foundation of trust in the Christian system of doctrine, and is therefore fundamental to the Christian hope and life. It is due to the church's instinct that the validity of her teaching of doctrine as the truth of God, — to the Christian's instinct that the validity of his hope in the several promises of the gospel, — rests on the trustworthiness of the Bible as a record of God's dealings and purposes with men.

Individuals may call in question the soundness of these instinctive judgments. And, indeed, there is a sense in which it would not be true to say that the truth of Christian teaching and the foundations of faith are suspended upon the doctrine of plenary inspiration, or upon any doctrine of inspiration whatever. They rest rather upon the previous fact of revelation: and it is important to keep ourselves reminded that the supernatural origin and contents of Christianity, not only may be vindicated apart from any question of the inspiration of the record, but, in point of fact, always are vindicated prior to any question of the inspiration of the record. We cannot raise the question whether God has given us an absolutely trustworthy record of the supernatural facts and teachings of Christianity, before we are assured that there are supernatural facts and teachings to be recorded. The fact that Christianity is a supernatural religion and the nature of Christianity as a supernatural religion, are matters of history; and are independent of any, and of every, theory of inspiration.

But this line of remark is of more importance to the Christian apologist than to the Christian believer, as such; and the instinct of the church that the validity of her teaching, and the instinct of the Christian that the validity of his hope, are bound up with the trustworthiness of the Bible, is a perfectly sound one. This for three reasons:

*First*, because the average Christian man is not and cannot be a fully furnished historical scholar. If faith in Christ is to be always and only the product of a thorough historical investigation into the origins of Christianity, there would certainly be few who could venture to preach Christ and him crucified with entire confidence; there would certainly be few who would be able to trust their all to him with entire security. The Christian scholar desires, and, thank God, is able to supply, a thoroughly trustworthy historical vindication of supernatural Christianity. But the Christian teacher desires, and, thank God, is able to lay his hands upon, a thoroughly trustworthy record of supernatural Christianity; and the Christian man requires, and, thank God, has, a thoroughly trustworthy Bible to which he can go directly and at once in every time of need. Though, then, in the abstract, we may say that the condition of the validity of the Christian teaching and of the Christian hope, is no more than the fact of the supernaturalism of Christianity, historically vindicated; practically we must say that the condition of the persistence of Christianity as a religion for the people, is the entire trustworthiness of the Scriptures as the record of the supernatural revelation which Christianity is.

*Secondly,* the merely historical vindication of the supernatural origin and contents of Christianity, while thorough and complete for Christianity as a whole, and for all the main facts and doctrines which enter into it, does not by itself supply a firm basis of trust for all the details of teaching and all the items of promise upon which the Christian man would fain lean. Christianity would be given to us; but it would be given to us, not in the exact form or in all the fulness with which God gave it to his needy children through his servants, the prophets, and through his Son and his apostles; but with the marks of human misapprehension, exaggeration, and minimizing upon it, and of whatever attrition may have been wrought upon it by its passage to us through the ages. That the church may have unsullied assurance in the details of its teaching, — that the Christian man may have unshaken confidence in the details of the promises to which he trusts, — they need, and they know that they need, a thoroughly trustworthy Word of God in which God himself speaks directly to them all the words of this life.

*Thirdly,* in the circumstances of the present case, we cannot fall back from trust in the Bible upon trust in the historical vindication of Christianity as a revelation from God, inasmuch as, since Christ and his apostles are historically shown to have taught the plenary inspiration of the Bible, the credit of the previous fact of revelation — even of the supreme revelation in Christ Jesus — is implicated in the truth of the doctrine of plenary inspiration. The historical vindication of Christianity as a revelation from God, vindicates as the truth of God all the contents of that revelation; and, among these contents, vindicates, as divinely true, the teaching of Christ and his apostles, that the Scriptures are the very Word of God, to be trusted as such in all the details of their teaching and promises. The instinct of the church is perfectly sound, therefore, when she clings to the trustworthiness of the Bible, as lying at the foundation of her teaching and her faith.

Much less can she be shaken from this instinctive conviction by the representations of individual thinkers who go yet a step further, and, refusing to pin their faith either to the Bible or to history, affirm that "the essence of Christianity" is securely intrenched in the subjective feelings of man, either as such, or as Christian man taught by the Holy Ghost; and therefore that there is by no means needed an infallible objective rule of faith in order to propagate or preserve Christian truth in the world. It is unnecessary to say that "the essence of Christianity" as conceived by these individuals, includes little that is characteristic of Christian doctrine, life, or hope, as distinct from what is taught by other religions or philosophies. And it is perhaps equally unnecessary to remind ourselves that such individuals, having gone so far, tend to take a further step still, and to discard the records which they thus judge to be unnecessary. Thus, there may be found even men still professing historical Christianity, who reason themselves into the conclusion that "in the nature of the case, no external authority can possibly be absolute in regard to spiritual truth"; [19] just as men have been known to reason themselves into the conclusion that the external world has no objective reality and is naught but the projection of their own faculties.

[19] Professor W. F. Adeney, "Faith and Criticism," p. 90.

But as in the one case, so in the other, the common sense of men recoils from such subtleties; and it remains the profound persuasion of the Christian heart that without such an " external authority " as a thoroughly trustworthy Bible, the soul is left without sure ground for a proper knowledge of itself, its condition, and its need, or for a proper knowledge of God's provisions of mercy for it and his promises of grace to it, — without sure ground, in a word, for its faith and hope. Adolphe Monod gives voice to no more than the common Christian conviction, when he declares that, " If faith has not for its basis a testimony of God to which we must submit, as to an authority exterior to our personal judgment, and independent of it, then faith is no faith." [20] " The more I study the Scriptures, the example of Christ, and of the apostles, and the history of my own heart," he adds, " the more I am convinced, that a testimony of God, placed without us and above us, exempt from all intermixture of sin and error which belong to a fallen race, and received with submission on the sole authority of God, is the true basis of faith." [21]

It is doubtless the profound and ineradicable conviction, so expressed, of the need of an infallible Bible, if men are to seek and find salvation in God's announced purpose of grace, and peace and comfort in his past dealings with his people, that has operated to keep the formulas of the churches and the hearts of the people of God, through so many ages, true to the Bible doctrine of plenary inspiration. In that doctrine men have found what their hearts have told them was the indispensable safeguard of a sure word of God to them, — a word of God to which they could resort with confidence in every time of need, to which they could appeal for guidance in every difficulty, for comfort in every sorrow, for instruction in every perplexity; on whose " Thus saith the Lord " they could safely rest all their aspirations and all their hopes. Such a Word of God, each one of us knows he needs, — not a Word of God that speaks to us only through the medium of our fellow-men, men of like passions and weaknesses with ourselves, so that we have to feel

[20] " Life of Adolphe Monod," p. 224.     [21] Ibid., p. 357.

our way back to God's word through the church, through tradition, or through the apostles, standing between us and God; but a Word of God in which God speaks directly to each of our souls. Such a Word of God, Christ and his apostles offer us, when they give us the Scriptures, not as man's report to us of what God says, but as the very Word of God itself, spoken by God himself through human lips and pens. Of such a precious possession, given to her by such hands, the church will not lightly permit herself to be deprived. Thus the church's sense of her need of an absolutely infallible Bible, has co-operated with her reverence for the teaching of the Bible to keep her true, in all ages, to the Bible doctrine of plenary inspiration.

What, indeed, would the church be — what would we, as Christian men, be — without our inspired Bible? Many of us have, no doubt, read Jean Paul Richter's vision of a dead Christ, and have shuddered at his pictures of the woe of a world from which its Christ has been stolen away. It would be a theme worthy of some like genius to portray for us the vision of a dead Bible, — the vision of what this world of ours would be, had there been no living Word of God cast into its troubled waters with its voice of power, crying, "Peace! Be still!" What does this Christian world of ours not owe to this Bible! And to this Bible conceived, not as a part of the world's literature, — the literary product of the earliest years of the church; not as a book in which, by searching, we may find God and perchance somewhat of God's will: but as the very Word of God, instinct with divine life from the "In the beginning" of Genesis to the "Amen" of the Apocalypse, — breathed into by God, and breathing out God to every devout reader. It is because men have so thought of it that it has proved a leaven to leaven the whole lump of the world. We do not half realize what we owe to this book, thus trusted by men. We can never fully realize it. For we can never even in thought unravel from this complex web of modern civilization, all the threads from the Bible which have been woven into it, throughout the whole past, and now enter into its very fabric. And, thank God, much less can we ever untwine them in fact, and separate our modern life from all those Bible influences by which alone it is blessed, and sweetened, and made a life which men may live. Dr. Gardiner Spring published, years ago, a series of lectures in which he sought to take some account of the world's obligations to the Bible, — tracing in turn the services it has rendered to religion, to morals, to social institutions, to civil and religious liberty, to the freedom of slaves, to the emancipation of woman and the sweetening of domestic life, to public and private beneficence, to literary and scientific progress, and the like.[22] And Adolphe Monod, in his own inimitable style, has done something to awaken us as individuals to what we owe to a fully trusted Bible, in the development of our character and religious life.[23] In such matters, however, we can trust our imaginations better than our words, to remind us of the immensity of our debt.

Let it suffice to say that to a plenarily inspired Bible, humbly trusted as such, we actually, and as a matter of fact, owe all that has blessed our lives with hopes of an immortality of bliss, and with the present fruition of the love of God in Christ. This is not an exaggeration. We may say that without a Bible we might have had Christ and all that he stands for to our souls. Let us not say that this might not have been possible. But neither let us forget that, in point of fact, it is to the Bible that we owe it that we know Christ and are found in him. And may it not be fairly doubted whether you and I, — however it may have been with others, — would have had Christ had there been no Bible? We must not at any rate forget those nineteen Christian centuries which stretch between us and Christ, whose Christian light we would do much to blot out and sink in a dreadful darkness if we could blot out the Bible. Even with the Bible, and all that had come from the Bible to form Christian lives and inform a Christian literature, after a millennium and a half the darkness had grown so deep that a Reformation was necessary if Christian truth was to persist, — a Luther was necessary, raised up by God to rediscover the Bible and give it

[22] Gardiner Spring, " Obligations of the World to the Bible." (New York: M. W. Dodd. 1855.)

[23] Adolphe Monod, " L'Inspiration prouvée par ses Œuvres."

back to man. Suppose there had been no Bible for Luther to rediscover, and on the lines of which to refound the church, — and no Bible in the hearts of God's saints and in the pages of Christian literature, persisting through those darker ages to prepare a Luther to rediscover it? Though Christ had come into the world and had lived and died for us, might it not be to us, — you and me, I mean, who are not learned historians but simple men and women, — might it not be to us as though he had not been? Or, if some faint echo of a Son of God offering salvation to men could still be faintly heard even by such dull ears as ours, sounding down the ages, who would have ears to catch the fulness of the message of free grace which he brought into the world? who could assure our doubting souls that it was not all a pleasant dream? who could cleanse the message from the ever-gathering corruptions of the multiplying years? No: whatever might possibly have been had there been no Bible, it is actually to the Bible that you and I owe it that we have a Christ, — a Christ to love, to trust and to follow, a Christ without us the ground of our salvation, a Christ within us the hope of glory.

Our effort has been to bring clearly out what seem to be three very impressive facts regarding the plenary inspiration of the Scriptures, — the facts, namely, that this doctrine has always been, and is still, the church-doctrine of inspiration, as well the vital faith of the people of God as the formulated teaching of the official creeds; that it is undeniably the doctrine of inspiration held by Christ and his apostles, and commended to us as true by all the authority which we will allow to attach to their teaching; and that it is the foundation of our Christian thought and life, without which we could not, or could only with difficulty, maintain the confidence of our faith and the surety of our hope. On such grounds as these is not this doctrine commended to us as true?

But, it may be said, there are difficulties in the way. Of course there are. There are difficulties in the way of believing anything. There are difficulties in the way of believing that God is, or that Jesus Christ is God's Son who came into the world to save sinners. There are difficulties in the way of believing that we ourselves really exist, or that anything has real existence besides ourselves. When men give their undivided attention to these difficulties, they may become, and they have become, so perplexed in mind, that they have felt unable to believe that God is, or that they themselves exist, or that there is any external world without themselves. It would be a strange thing if it might not so fare with plenary inspiration also. Difficulties? Of course there are difficulties. It is nothing to the purpose to point out this fact. Dr. J. Oswald Dykes says with admirable truth: "If men must have a reconciliation for all conflicting truths before they will believe any; if they must see how the promises of God are to be fulfilled before they will obey his commands; if duty is to hang upon the satisfying of the understanding, instead of the submission of the will, — then the greater number of us will find the road of faith and the road of duty blocked at the outset."[24] These wise words have their application also to our present subject. The question is not, whether the doctrine of plenary inspiration has difficulties to face. The question is, whether these difficulties are greater than the difficulty of believing that the whole church of God from the beginning has been deceived in her estimate of the Scriptures committed to her charge — are greater than the difficulty of believing that the whole college of the apostles, yes and Christ himself at their head, were themselves deceived as to the nature of those Scriptures which they gave the church as its precious possession, and have deceived with them twenty Christian centuries, and are likely to deceive twenty more before our boasted advancing light has corrected their error, — are greater than the difficulty of believing that we have no sure foundation for our faith and no certain warrant for our trust in Christ for salvation. We believe this doctrine of the plenary inspiration of the Scriptures primarily because it is the doctrine which Christ and his apostles believed, and which they have taught us. It may sometimes seem difficult to take our stand frankly by the side of Christ and his apostles. It will always be found safe.

[24] J. Oswald Dykes, " Abraham," etc. (1877), p. 257.

# III
# THE BIBLICAL IDEA OF INSPIRATION

# THE BIBLICAL IDEA OF INSPIRATION[1]

THE word "inspire" and its derivatives seem to have come into Middle English from the French, and have been employed from the first (early in the fourteenth century) in a considerable number of significations, physical and metaphorical, secular and religious. The derivatives have been multiplied and their applications extended during the procession of the years, until they have acquired a very wide and varied use. Underlying all their use, however, is the constant implication of an influence from without, producing in its object movements and effects beyond its native, or at least its ordinary powers. The noun "inspiration," although already in use in the fourteenth century, seems not to occur in any but a theological sense until late in the sixteenth century. The specifically theological sense of all these terms is governed, of course, by their usage in Latin theology; and this rests ultimately on their employment in the Latin Bible. In the Vulgate Latin Bible the verb *inspiro* (Gen. ii. 7; Wisd. xv. 11; Ecclus. iv. 12; 2 Tim. iii. 16; 2 Pet. i. 21) and the noun *inspiratio* (2 Sam. xxii. 16; Job xxxii. 8; Ps. xvii. 16; Acts xvii. 25) both occur four or five times in somewhat diverse applications. In the development of a theological nomenclature, however, they have acquired (along with other less frequent applications) a technical sense with reference to the Biblical writers or the Biblical books. The Biblical books are called inspired as the Divinely determined products of inspired men; the Biblical writers are called inspired as breathed into by the Holy Spirit, so that the product of their activities transcends human powers and becomes Divinely authoritative. Inspiration is, therefore, usually defined as a supernatural influence exerted on the sacred writers by the Spirit of God, by virtue of which their writings are given Divine trustworthiness.

[1] Article " Inspiration," from *The International Standard Bible Encyclopaedia*, James Orr General Editor, v. 3, pp. 1473–1483. Pub. Chicago, 1915, by The Howard-Severance Co.

Meanwhile, for English-speaking men, these terms have virtually ceased to be Biblical terms. They naturally passed from the Latin Vulgate into the English versions made from it (most fully into the Rheims-Douay: Job xxxii. 8; Wisd. xv. 11; Ecclus. iv. 12; 2 Tim. iii. 16; 2 Pet. i. 21). But in the development of the English Bible they have found ever-decreasing place. In the English versions of the Apocrypha (both Authorized Version and Revised Version) "inspired" is retained in Wisd. xv. 11; but in the canonical books the nominal form alone occurs in the Authorized Version and that only twice: Job xxxii. 8, "But there is a spirit in man: and the inspiration of the Almighty giveth them understanding"; and 2 Tim. iii. 16, "All scripture is given by inspiration of God, and is profitable for doctrine, for reproof, for correction, for instruction in righteousness." The Revised Version removes the former of these instances, substituting "breath" for "inspiration"; and alters the latter so as to read: "Every scripture inspired of God is also profitable for teaching, for reproof, for correction, for instruction which is in righteousness," with a marginal alternative in the form of, "Every scripture is inspired of God and profitable," etc. The word "inspiration" thus disappears from the English Bible, and the word "inspired" is left in it only once, and then, let it be added, by a distinct and even misleading mistranslation.

For the Greek word in this passage — θεόπνευστος, *theópneustos* — very distinctly does not mean "inspired of God." This phrase is rather the rendering of the Latin, *divinitus inspirata*, restored from the Wyclif ("Al Scripture of God ynspyrid is . . .") and Rhemish ("All Scripture inspired of God is . . .") versions of the Vulgate. The Greek word does not even mean, as the Authorized Version translates it, "given by inspiration of God," although that rendering (inherited from Tindale: "All Scripture given by inspiration of God is . . ." and its successors; cf. Geneva: "The whole Scripture is given by inspiration of God and is . . .") has at least to say for itself that it is a somewhat clumsy, perhaps, but not misleading, paraphrase of the Greek term in the theological language of the day. The Greek term has, however, nothing to say of *inspir-ing* or of *in*spiration: it speaks only of a "spiring" or "spira-tion." What it says of Scripture is, not that it is "breathed into by God" or is the product of the Divine "inbreathing" into its human authors, but that it is breathed out by God, "God-breathed," the product of the creative breath of God. In a word, what is declared by this fundamental passage is simply that the Scriptures are a Divine product, without any indica-tion of how God has operated in producing them. No term could have been chosen, however, which would have more em-phatically asserted the Divine production of Scripture than that which is here employed. The "breath of God" is in Scrip-ture just the symbol of His almighty power, the bearer of His creative word. "By the word of Jehovah," we read in the sig-nificant parallel of Ps. xxxiii. 6, "were the heavens made, and all the host of them by the breath of his mouth." And it is particularly where the operations of God are energetic that this term (whether רוּחַ, *rūªh*, or נְשָׁמָה, *nᵉshāmāh*) is employed to designate them — God's breath is the irresistible outflow of His power. When Paul declares, then, that "every scripture," or "all scripture" is the product of the Divine breath, "is God-breathed," he asserts with as much energy as he could employ that Scripture is the product of a specifically Divine operation.

(1) 2 Tim. iii. 16: In the passage in which Paul makes this energetic assertion of the Divine origin of Scripture he is en-gaged in explaining the greatness of the advantages which Tim-othy had enjoyed for learning the saving truth of God. He had had good teachers; and from his very infancy he had been, by his knowledge of the Scriptures, made wise unto salvation through faith in Jesus Christ. The expression, "sacred writ-ings," here employed (ver. 15), is a technical one, not found elsewhere in the New Testament, it is true, but occurring cur-rently in Philo and Josephus to designate that body of authori-tative books which constituted the Jewish "Law." It appears here anarthrously because it is set in contrast with the oral teaching which Timothy had enjoyed, as something still bet-

ter: he had not only had good instructors, but also always "an open Bible," as we should say, in his hand. To enhance yet further the great advantage of the possession of these Sacred Scriptures the apostle adds now a sentence throwing their nature strongly up to view. They are of Divine origin and therefore of the highest value for all holy purposes.

There is room for some difference of opinion as to the exact construction of this declaration. Shall we render "Every Scripture" or "All Scripture"? Shall we render "Every [or all] Scripture is God-breathed and [therefore] profitable," or "Every [or all] Scripture, being God-breathed, is as well profitable"? No doubt both questions are interesting, but for the main matter now engaging our attention they are both indifferent. Whether Paul, looking back at the Sacred Scriptures he had just mentioned, makes the assertion he is about to add, of them distributively, of all their parts, or collectively, of their entire mass, is of no moment: to say that every part of these Sacred Scriptures is God-breathed and to say that the whole of these Sacred Scriptures is God-breathed, is, for the main matter, all one. Nor is the difference great between saying that they are in all their parts, or in their whole extent, God-breathed and therefore profitable, and saying that they are in all their parts, or in their whole extent, because God-breathed as well as profitable. In both cases these Sacred Scriptures are declared to owe their value to their Divine origin; and in both cases this their Divine origin is energetically asserted of their entire fabric. On the whole, the preferable construction would seem to be, "Every Scripture, seeing that it is God-breathed, is as well profitable." In that case, what the apostle asserts is that the Sacred Scriptures, in their every several passage — for it is just "passage of Scripture" which "Scripture" in this distributive use of it signifies — is the product of the creative breath of God, and, because of this its Divine origination, is of supreme value for all holy purposes.

It is to be observed that the apostle does not stop here to tell us either what particular books enter into the collection which he calls Sacred Scriptures, or by what precise operations

God has produced them. Neither of these subjects entered into the matter he had at the moment in hand. It was the value of the Scriptures, and the source of that value in their Divine origin, which he required at the moment to assert; and these things he asserts, leaving to other occasions any further facts concerning them which it might be well to emphasize. It is also to be observed that the apostle does not tell us here everything for which the Scriptures are made valuable by their Divine origination. He speaks simply to the point immediately in hand, and reminds Timothy of the value which these Scriptures, by virtue of their Divine origin, have for the "man of God." Their spiritual power, as God-breathed, is all that he had occasion here to advert to. Whatever other qualities may accrue to them from their Divine origin, he leaves to other occasions to speak of.

(2) 2 Pet. i. 19–21: What Paul tells here about the Divine origin of the Scriptures is enforced and extended by a striking passage in 2 Pet. (i. 19–21). Peter is assuring his readers that what had been made known to them of "the power and coming of our Lord Jesus Christ" did not rest on "cunningly devised fables." He offers them the testimony of eyewitnesses of Christ's glory. And then he intimates that they have better testimony than even that of eyewitnesses. "We have," says he, "the prophetic word" (English versions, unhappily, "the word of prophecy"): and this, he says, is "more sure," and therefore should certainly be heeded. He refers, of course, to the Scriptures. Of what other "prophetic word" could he, over against the testimony of the eyewitnesses of Christ's "excellent glory" (Authorized Version) say that "we have" it, that is, it is in our hands? And he proceeds at once to speak of it plainly as "Scriptural prophecy." You do well, he says, to pay heed to the prophetic word, because we know this first, that "every prophecy of scripture . . ." It admits of more question, however, whether by this phrase he means the whole of Scripture, designated according to its character, as prophetic that is, of Divine origin; or only that portion of Scripture which we discriminate as particularly prophetic, the immedi-

ate revelations contained in Scripture. The former is the more likely view, inasmuch as the entirety of Scripture is elsewhere conceived and spoken of as prophetic. In that case, what Peter has to say of this "every prophecy of scripture"—the exact equivalent, it will be observed, in this case of Paul's "every scripture" (2 Tim. iii. 16)—applies to the whole of Scripture in all its parts. What he says of it is that it does not come "of private interpretation"; that is, it is not the result of human investigation into the nature of things, the product of its writers' own thinking. This is as much as to say it is of Divine gift. Accordingly, he proceeds at once to make this plain in a supporting clause which contains both the negative and the positive declaration: "For no prophecy ever came [margin "was brought"] by the will of man, but it was as borne by the Holy Spirit that men spoke from God." In this singularly precise and pregnant statement there are several things which require to be carefully observed. There is, first of all, the emphatic denial that prophecy—that is to say, on the hypothesis upon which we are working, Scripture—owes its origin to human initiative: "No prophecy ever was brought—'came' is the word used in the English version text, with 'was brought' in Revised Version margin—by the will of man." Then, there is the equally emphatic assertion that its source lies in God: it was spoken by men, indeed, but the men who spoke it "spake from God." And a remarkable clause is here inserted, and thrown forward in the sentence that stress may fall on it, which tells us how it could be that men, in speaking, should speak not from themselves, but from God: it was "as borne"—it is the same word which was rendered "was brought" above, and might possibly be rendered "brought" here—"by the Holy Spirit" that they spoke. Speaking thus under the determining influence of the Holy Spirit, the things they spoke were not from themselves, but from God.

Here is as direct an assertion of the Divine origin of Scripture as that of 2 Tim. iii. 16. But there is more here than a simple assertion of the Divine origin of Scripture. We are advanced somewhat in our understanding of how God has produced the Scriptures. It was through the instrumentality of men who "spake from him." More specifically, it was through an operation of the Holy Ghost on these men which is described as "bearing" them. The term here used is a very specific one. It is not to be confounded with guiding, or directing, or controlling, or even leading in the full sense of that word. It goes beyond all such terms, in assigning the effect produced specifically to the active agent. What is "borne" is taken up by the "bearer," and conveyed by the "bearer's" power, not its own, to the "bearer's" goal, not its own. The men who spoke from God are here declared, therefore, to have been taken up by the Holy Spirit and brought by His power to the goal of His choosing. The things which they spoke under this operation of the Spirit were therefore His things, not theirs. And that is the reason which is assigned why "the prophetic word" is so sure. Though spoken through the instrumentality of men, it is, by virtue of the fact that these men spoke "as borne by the Holy Spirit," an immediately Divine word. It will be observed that the proximate stress is laid here, not on the spiritual value of Scripture (though that, too, is seen in the background), but on the Divine trustworthiness of Scripture. Because this is the way every prophecy of Scripture "has been brought," it affords a more sure basis of confidence than even the testimony of human eyewitnesses. Of course, if we do not understand by "the prophetic word" here the entirety of Scripture described, according to its character, as revelation, but only that element in Scripture which we call specifically prophecy, then it is directly only of that element in Scripture that these great declarations are made. In any event, however, they are made of the prophetic element in Scripture as written, which was the only form in which the readers of this Epistle possessed it, and which is the thing specifically intimated in the phrase "every prophecy *of scripture*." These great declarations are made, therefore, at least of large tracts of Scripture; and if the entirety of Scripture is intended by the phrase "the prophetic word," they are made of the whole of Scripture.

(3) Jn. x. 34 f.: How far the supreme trustworthiness of Scripture, thus asserted, extends may be conveyed to us by a passage in one of Our Lord's discourses recorded by John (Jn. x. 34–35). The Jews, offended by Jesus' "making himself God," were in the act to stone Him, when He defended Himself thus: "Is it not written in your law, I said, Ye are gods? If he called them gods, unto whom the word of God came (and the scripture cannot be broken), say ye of him, whom the Father sanctified [margin "consecrated"] and sent unto the world, Thou blasphemest; because I said, I am the Son of God?" It may be thought that this defence is inadequate. It certainly is incomplete: Jesus made Himself God (Jn. x. 33) in a far higher sense than that in which "Ye are gods" was said of those "unto whom the word of God came": He had just declared in unmistakable terms, "I and the Father are one." But it was quite sufficient for the immediate end in view — to repel the technical charge of blasphemy based on His making Himself God: it is not blasphemy to call one God in any sense in which he may fitly receive that designation; and certainly if it is not blasphemy to call such men as those spoken of in the passage of Scripture adduced gods, because of their official functions, it cannot be blasphemy to call Him God whom the Father consecrated and sent into the world. The point for us to note, however, is merely that Jesus' defence takes the form of an appeal to Scripture; and it is important to observe how He makes this appeal. In the first place, He adduces the Scriptures as law: "Is it not written in your law?" He demands. The passage of Scripture which He adduces is not written in that portion of Scripture which was more specifically called "the Law," that is to say, the Pentateuch; nor in any portion of Scripture of formally legal contents. It is written in the Book of Psalms; and in a particular psalm which is as far as possible from presenting the external characteristics of legal enactment (Ps. lxxxii. 6). When Jesus adduces this passage, then, as written in the "law" of the Jews, He does it, not because it stands in this psalm, but because it is a part of Scripture at large. In other words, He here ascribes legal authority to the entirety of Scrip-

ture, in accordance with a conception common enough among the Jews (cf. Jn. xii. 34), and finding expression in the New Testament occasionally, both on the lips of Jesus Himself, and in the writings of the apostles. Thus, on a later occasion (Jn. xv. 25), Jesus declares that it is written in the "law" of the Jews, "They hated me without a cause," a clause found in Ps. xxxv. 19. And Paul assigns passages both from the Psalms and from Isaiah to "the Law" (1 Cor. xiv. 21; Rom. iii. 19), and can write such a sentence as this (Gal. iv. 21 f.): "Tell me, ye that desire to be under the law, do ye not hear the law? For it is written . . ." quoting from the narrative of Genesis. We have seen that the entirety of Scripture was conceived as "prophecy"; we now see that the entirety of Scripture was also conceived as "law": these three terms, the law, prophecy, Scripture, were indeed, materially, strict synonyms, as our present passage itself advises us, by varying the formula of adduction in contiguous verses from "law" to "scripture." And what is thus implied in the manner in which Scripture is adduced, is immediately afterward spoken out in the most explicit language, because it forms an essential element in Our Lord's defence. It might have been enough to say simply, "Is it not written in your law?" But Our Lord, determined to drive His appeal to Scripture home, sharpens the point to the utmost by adding with the highest emphasis: "and the scripture cannot be broken." This is the reason why it is worth while to appeal to what is "written in the law," because "the scripture cannot be broken." The word "broken" here is the common one for breaking the law, or the Sabbath, or the like (Jn. v. 18; vii. 23; Mt. v. 19), and the meaning of the declaration is that it is impossible for the Scripture to be annulled, its authority to be withstood, or denied. The movement of thought is to the effect that, because it is impossible for the Scripture — the term is perfectly general and witnesses to the unitary character of Scripture (it is all, for the purpose in hand, of a piece) — to be withstood, therefore this particular Scripture which is cited must be taken as of irrefragable authority. What we have here is, therefore, the strongest possible assertion of the indefectible authority of Scripture; precisely what is true of Scripture is that it "cannot be broken." Now, what is the particular thing in Scripture, for the confirmation of which the indefectible authority of Scripture is thus invoked? It is one of its most casual clauses — more than that, the very form of its expression in one of its most casual clauses. This means, of course, that in the Saviour's view the indefectible authority of Scripture attaches to the very form of expression of its most casual clauses. It belongs to Scripture through and through, down to its most minute particulars, that it is of indefectible authority.

It is sometimes suggested, it is true, that Our Lord's argument here is an *argumentum ad hominem*, and that his words, therefore, express not His own view of the authority of Scripture, but that of His Jewish opponents. It will scarcely be denied that there is a vein of satire running through Our Lord's defence: that the Jews so readily allowed that corrupt judges might properly be called "gods," but could not endure that He whom the Father had consecrated and sent into the world should call Himself Son of God, was a somewhat pungent fact to throw up into such a high light. But the argument from Scripture is not *ad hominem* but *e concessu;* Scripture was common ground with Jesus and His opponents. If proof were needed for so obvious a fact, it would be supplied by the circumstance that this is not an isolated but a representative passage. The conception of Scripture thrown up into such clear view here supplies the ground of all Jesus' appeals to Scripture, and of all the appeals of the New Testament writers as well. Everywhere, to Him and to them alike, an appeal to Scripture is an appeal to an indefectible authority whose determination is final; both He and they make their appeal indifferently to every part of Scripture, to every element in Scripture, to its most incidental clauses as well as to its most fundamental principles, and to the very form of its expression. This attitude toward Scripture as an authoritative document is, indeed, already intimated by their constant designation of it by the name of Scripture, the Scriptures, that is "the Document," by way of eminence; and by their customary citation of it with the simple formula, "It is written." What is written in this document admits so little of questioning that its authoritativeness required no asserting, but might safely be taken for granted. Both modes of expression belong to the constantly illustrated habitudes of Our Lord's speech. The first words He is recorded as uttering after His manifestation to Israel were an appeal to the unquestionable authority of Scripture; to Satan's temptations He opposed no other weapon than the final "It is written"! (Mt. iv. 4.7.10; Lk. iv. 4.8). And among the last words which He spoke to His disciples before He was received up was a rebuke to them for not understanding that all things "which are written in the law of Moses, and the prophets, and psalms" concerning Him — that is (ver. 45) in the entire "Scriptures" — "must needs be" (very emphatic) "fulfilled" (Lk. xxiv. 44). "Thus it is written," says He (ver. 46), as rendering all doubt absurd. For, as He had explained earlier upon the same day (Lk. xxiv. 25 ff.), it argues only that one is "foolish and slow at heart" if he does not "believe in" (if his faith does not rest securely on, as on a firm foundation) "all" (without limit of subject-matter here) "that the prophets" (explained in ver. 27 as equivalent to "all the scriptures") "have spoken."

The necessity of the fulfilment of all that is written in Scripture, which is so strongly asserted in these last instructions to His disciples, is frequently adverted to by Our Lord. He repeatedly explains of occurrences occasionally happening that they have come to pass "that the scripture might be fulfilled" (Mk. xiv. 49; Jn. xiii. 18; xvii. 12; cf. xii. 14; Mk. ix. 12.13). On the basis of Scriptural declarations, therefore, He announces with confidence that given events will certainly occur: "All ye shall be offended [literally "scandalized"] in me this night: *for* it is written . . ." (Mt. xxvi. 31; Mk. xiv. 27; cf. Lk. xx. 17). Although holding at His command ample means of escape, He bows before on-coming calamities, for, He asks, how otherwise "should the scriptures be fulfilled, that thus it must be?" (Mt. xxvi. 54). It is not merely the two disciples with whom He talked on the way to Emmaus (Lk. xxiv. 25) whom He rebukes for not trusting themselves more perfectly to the teaching of Scripture. "Ye search the scriptures," He says to the Jews, in the classical passage (Jn. v. 39), "because ye think that in them ye have eternal life; and these are they which bear witness of me; and ye will not come to me, that ye may have life!" These words surely were spoken more in sorrow than in scorn: there is no blame implied either for searching the Scriptures or for thinking that eternal life is to be found in Scripture; approval rather. What the Jews are blamed for is that they read with a veil lying upon their hearts which He would fain take away (2 Cor. iii. 15 f.). "Ye search the scriptures" — that is right: and "even you" (emphatic) "think to have eternal life in them" — that is right, too. But "it is these very Scriptures" (very emphatic) "which are bearing witness" (continuous process) "of me; and" (here is the marvel!) "ye will not come to me and have life!" — that you may, that is, reach the very end you have so properly in view in searching the Scriptures. Their failure is due, not to the Scriptures but to themselves, who read the Scriptures to such little purpose.

Quite similarly Our Lord often finds occasion to express wonder at the little effect to which Scripture had been read, not because it had been looked into too curiously, but because it had not been looked into earnestly enough, with sufficiently simple and robust trust in its every declaration. "Have ye not read even this scripture?" He demands, as He adduces Ps. cxviii. to show that the rejection of the Messiah was already intimated in Scripture (Mk. xii. 10; Mt. xxi. 42 varies the expression to the equivalent: "Did ye never read in the scriptures?"). And when the indignant Jews came to Him complaining of the Hosannas with which the children in the Temple were acclaiming Him, and demanding, "Hearest thou what these are saying?" He met them (Mt. xxi. 16) merely with, "Yea: did ye never read, Out of the mouths of babes and sucklings thou hast perfected praise?" The underlying thought of these passages is spoken out when He intimates that the source of all error in Divine things is just ignorance of the Scriptures: "Ye do err," He declares to His questioners, on an important occasion, "not knowing the scriptures" (Mt. xxii. 29); or, as it is put, perhaps more forcibly, in interrogative form, in its parallel in another Gospel: "Is it not for this cause that ye err, that ye know not the scriptures?" (Mk. xii. 24). Clearly, he who rightly knows the Scriptures does not err. The confidence with which Jesus rested on Scripture, in its every declaration, is further illustrated in a passage like Mt. xix. 4. Certain Pharisees had come to Him with a question on divorce and He met them thus: "Have ye not read, that he who made them from the beginning made them male and female, and said, For this cause shall a man leave his father and mother, and shall cleave to his wife; and the two shall become one flesh? . . . What therefore God hath joined together, let not man put asunder." The point to be noted is the explicit reference of Gen. ii. 24 to God as its author: "*He who made them . . . said*"; "what therefore *God* hath joined together." Yet this passage does not give us a saying of God's recorded in Scripture, but just the word of Scripture itself, and can be treated as a declaration of God's only on the hypothesis that all Scripture is a declaration of God's. The parallel in Mk. (x. 5 ff.) just as truly, though not as explicitly, assigns the passage to God as its author, citing it as authoritative law and speaking of its enactment as an act of God's. And it is interesting to observe in passing that Paul, having occasion to quote the same passage (1 Cor. vi. 16), also explicitly quotes it as a Divine word: "For, The twain, saith he, shall become one flesh" — the "he" here, in accordance with a usage to be noted later, meaning just "God."

Thus clear is it that Jesus' occasional adduction of Scripture as an authoritative document rests on an ascription of it to God as its author. His testimony is that whatever stands written in Scripture is a word of God. Nor can we evacuate this testimony of its force on the plea that it represents Jesus only in the days of His flesh, when He may be supposed to have reflected merely the opinions of His day and generation. The view of Scripture He announces was, no doubt, the view of His day and generation as well as His own view. But there is no reason to doubt that it was held by Him, not because it was the current view, but because, in His Divine-human knowledge, He knew it to be true; for, even in His humiliation, He is the faithful and true witness. And in any event we should bear in mind that this was the view of the resurrected as well as of the humiliated Christ. It was after He had suffered and had risen again in the power of His Divine life that He pronounced those foolish and slow of heart who do not believe all that stands written in all the Scriptures (Lk. xxiv. 25); and that He laid down the simple "Thus it is written" as the sufficient ground of confident belief (Lk. xxiv. 46). Nor can we explain away Jesus' testimony to the Divine trustworthiness of Scripture by interpreting it as not His own, but that of His followers, placed on His lips in their reports of His words. Not only is it too constant, minute, intimate and in part incidental, and therefore, as it were, hidden, to admit of this interpretation; but it so pervades all our channels of information concerning Jesus' teaching as to make it certain that it comes actually from Him. It belongs not only to the Jesus of our evangelical records but as well to the Jesus of the earlier sources which underlie our evangelical records, as anyone may assure himself by observing the instances in which Jesus adduces the Scriptures as Divinely authoritative that are recorded in more than one of the Gospels (e.g. "It is written," Mt. iv. 4.7.10 [Lk. iv. 4.8.10]; Mt. xi. 10; [Lk. vii. 27]; Mt. xxi. 13 [Lk. xix. 46; Mk. xi. 17]; Mt. xxvi. 31 [Mk. xiv. 21]; "the scripture" or "the scriptures," Mt. xix. 4 [Mk. x. 9]; Mt. xxi. 42 [Mk. xii. 10; Lk. xx. 17]; Mt. xxii. 29 [Mk. xii. 24; Lk. xx. 37]; Mt. xxvi. 56 [Mk. xiv. 49; Lk. xxiv. 44]). These passages alone would suffice to make clear to us the testimony of Jesus to Scripture as in all its parts and declarations Divinely authoritative.

The attempt to attribute the testimony of Jesus to His followers has in its favor only the undeniable fact that the testimony of the writers of the New Testament is to precisely the same effect as His. They, too, cursorily speak of Scripture by

that pregnant name and adduce it with the simple "It is written," with the implication that whatever stands written in it is
Divinely authoritative. As Jesus' official life begins with this
"It is written" (Mt. iv. 4), so the evangelical proclamation
begins with an "Even as it is written" (Mk. i. 2); and as Jesus
sought the justification of His work in a solemn "Thus it is
written, that the Christ should suffer, and rise again from the
dead the third day" (Lk. xxiv. 46 ff.), so the apostles solemnly
justified the Gospel which they preached, detail after detail, by
appeal to the Scriptures, "That Christ died for our sins according to the scriptures" and "That he hath been raised on
the third day according to the scriptures" (1 Cor. xv. 3.4; cf.
Acts viii. 35; xvii. 3; xxvi. 22, and also Rom. i. 17; iii. 4.10;
iv. 17; xi. 26; xiv. 11; 1 Cor. i. 19; ii. 9; iii. 19; xv. 45; Gal. iii.
10.13; iv. 22.27). Wherever they carried the gospel it was as a
gospel resting on Scripture that they proclaimed it (Acts xvii.
2; xviii. 24.28); and they encouraged themselves to test its
truth by the Scriptures (Acts xvii. 11). The holiness of life
they inculcated, they based on Scriptural requirement (1 Pet.
i. 16), and they commended the royal law of love which they
taught by Scriptural sanction (Jas. ii. 8). Every detail of duty
was supported by them by an appeal to Scripture (Acts xxiii.
5; Rom. xii. 19). The circumstances of their lives and the
events occasionally occurring about them are referred to Scripture for their significance (Rom. ii. 26; viii. 36; ix. 33; xi. 8;
xv. 9.21; 2 Cor. iv. 13). As Our Lord declared that whatever
was written in Scripture must needs be fulfilled (Mt. xxvi. 54;
Lk. xxii. 37; xxiv. 44), so His followers explained one of the
most startling facts which had occurred in their experience by
pointing out that "it was needful that the scripture should be
fulfilled, which the Holy Spirit spake before by the mouth of
David" (Acts i. 16). Here the ground of this constant appeal
to Scripture, so that it is enough that a thing "is contained in
scripture" (1 Pet. ii. 6) for it to be of indefectible authority,
is plainly enough declared: Scripture must needs be fulfilled,
for what is contained in it is the declaration of the Holy Ghost
through the human author. What Scripture says, God says;

and accordingly we read such remarkable declarations as these: "For the scripture saith unto Pharaoh, For this very purpose did I raise thee up" (Rom. ix. 17); "And the scripture, foreseeing that God would justify the Gentiles by faith, preached the gospel beforehand unto Abraham, . . . In thee shall all the nations be blessed" (Gal. iii. 8). These are not instances of simple personification of Scripture, which is itself a sufficiently remarkable usage (Mk. xv. 28; Jn. vii. 38.42; xix. 37; Rom. iv. 3; x. 11; xi. 2; Gal. iv. 30; 1 Tim. v. 18; Jas. ii. 23; iv. 5 f.), vocal with the conviction expressed by James (iv. 5) that Scripture cannot speak in vain. They indicate a certain confusion in current speech between "Scripture" and "God," the outgrowth of a deep-seated conviction that the word of Scripture is the word of God. It was not "Scripture" that spoke to Pharaoh, or gave his great promise to Abraham, but God. But "Scripture" and "God" lay so close together in the minds of the writers of the New Testament that they could naturally speak of "Scripture" doing what Scripture records God as doing. It was, however, even more natural to them to speak casually of God saying what the Scriptures say; and accordingly we meet with forms of speech such as these: "Wherefore, even as the Holy Spirit saith, To-day if ye shall hear His voice," etc. (Heb. iii. 7, quoting Ps. xcv. 7); "Thou art God . . . who by the mouth of thy servant David hast said, Why did the heathen rage," etc. (Acts iv. 25 Authorized Version, quoting Ps. ii. 1); "He that raised him from the dead . . . hath spoken on this wise, I will give you . . . because he saith also in another [place] . . ." (Acts xiii. 34, quoting Isa. lv. 3 and Ps. xvi. 10), and the like. The words put into God's mouth in each case are not words of God recorded in the Scriptures, but just Scripture words in themselves. When we take the two classes of passages together, in the one of which the Scriptures are spoken of as God, while in the other God is spoken of as if He were the Scriptures, we may perceive how close the identification of the two was in the minds of the writers of the New Testament.

This identification is strikingly observable in certain ca-

tenae of quotations, in which there are brought together a
number of passages of Scripture closely connected with one another. The first chapter of the Epistle to the Hebrews supplies
an example. We may begin with ver. 5: "For unto which of
the angels said he"—the subject being necessarily "God"
—"at any time, Thou art my Son, this day have I begotten
thee?"—the citation being from Ps. ii. 7 and very appropriate in the mouth of God— "and again, I will be to him a
Father, and he shall be to me a Son?"—from 2 S. vii. 14,
again a declaration of God's own— "And when he again bringeth in the firstborn into the world he saith, And let all the angels of God worship him"—from Deut. xxxii. 43, Septuagint,
or Ps. xcvii. 7, in neither of which is God the speaker— "And
of the angels he saith, Who maketh his angels winds, and his
ministers a flame of fire"—from Ps. civ. 4, where again God
is not the speaker but is spoken of in the third person— "but
of the Son he saith, Thy throne, O God, etc."—from Ps. xlv.
6.7 where again God is not the speaker, but is addressed—
"And, Thou, Lord, in the beginning," etc.—from Ps. cii. 25–
27, where again God is not the speaker but is addressed—
"But of which of the angels hath he said at any time, Sit thou
on my right hand?" etc.—from Ps. cx. 1, in which God is the
speaker. Here we have passages in which God is the speaker
and passages in which God is not the speaker, but is addressed
or spoken of, indiscriminately assigned to God, because they
all have it in common that they are words of Scripture, and as
words of Scripture are words of God. Similarly in Rom. xv.
9 ff. we have a series of citations the first of which is introduced
by "as it is written," and the next two by "again he saith,"
and "again," and the last by "and again, Isaiah saith," the
first being from Ps. xviii. 49; the second from Deut. xxxii. 43;
the third from Ps. cxvii. 1; and the last from Isa. xi. 10. Only
the last (the only one here assigned to the human author) is a
word of God in the text of the Old Testament.

This view of the Scriptures as a compact mass of words of
God occasioned the formation of a designation for them by
which this their character was explicitly expressed. This des-

ignation is "the sacred oracles," "the oracles of God." It occurs with extraordinary frequency in Philo, who very commonly refers to Scripture as "the sacred oracles" and cites its several passages as each an "oracle." Sharing, as they do, Philo's conception of the Scriptures as, in all their parts, a word of God, the New Testament writers naturally also speak of them under this designation. The classical passage is Rom. iii. 2 (cf. Heb. v. 12; Acts vii. 38). Here Paul begins an enumeration of the advantages which belonged to the chosen people above other nations; and, after declaring these advantages to have been great and numerous, he places first among them all their possession of the Scriptures: "What advantage then hath the Jew? or what is the profit of circumcision? Much every way: first of all, that they were intrusted with the oracles of God." That by "the oracles of God" here are meant just the Holy Scriptures in their entirety, conceived as a direct Divine revelation, and not any portions of them, or elements in them more especially thought of as revelatory, is perfectly clear from the wide contemporary use of this designation in this sense by Philo, and is put beyond question by the presence in the New Testament of habitudes of speech which rest on and grow out of the conception of Scripture embodied in this term. From the point of view of this designation, Scripture is thought of as the living voice of God speaking in all its parts directly to the reader; and, accordingly, it is cited by some such formula as "it is said," and this mode of citing Scripture duly occurs as an alternative to "it is written" (Lk. iv. 12, replacing "it is written" in Mt.; Heb. iii. 15; cf. Rom. iv. 18). It is due also to this point of view that Scripture is cited, not as what God or the Holy Spirit "said," but what He "says," the present tense emphasizing the living voice of God speaking in Scriptures to the individual soul (Heb. iii. 7; Acts xiii. 35; Heb. i. 7.8.10; Rom. xv. 10). And especially there is due to it the peculiar usage by which Scripture is cited by the simple "saith," without expressed subject, the subject being too well understood, when Scripture is adduced, to require stating; for who could be the speaker of the words of Scripture but God only (Rom.

xv. 10; 1 Cor. vi. 16; 2 Cor. vi. 2; Gal. iii. 16; Eph. iv. 8; v. 14)? The analogies of this pregnant subjectless "saith" are very widespread. It was with it that the ancient Pythagoreans and Platonists and the mediaeval Aristotelians adduced each their master's teaching; it was with it that, in certain circles, the judgments of Hadrian's great jurist Salvius Julianus were cited; African stylists were even accustomed to refer by it to Sallust, their great model. There is a tendency, cropping out occasionally, in the old Testament, to omit the name of God as superfluous, when He, as the great logical subject always in mind, would be easily understood (cf. Job xx. 23; xxi. 17; Ps. cxiv. 2; Lam. iv. 22). So, too, when the New Testament writers quoted Scripture there was no need to say whose word it was: that lay beyond question in every mind. This usage, accordingly, is a specially striking intimation of the vivid sense which the New Testament writers had of the Divine origin of the Scriptures, and means that in citing them they were acutely conscious that they were citing immediate words of God. How completely the Scriptures were to them just the word of God may be illustrated by a passage like Gal. iii. 16: "He saith not, And to seeds, as of many; but as of one, And to thy seed, which is Christ." We have seen Our Lord hanging an argument on the very words of Scripture (Jn. x. 34); elsewhere His reasoning depends on the particular tense (Mt. xxii. 32) or word (Mt. xxii. 43) used in Scripture. Here Paul's argument rests similarly on a grammatical form. No doubt it is the grammatical form of the word which God is recorded as having spoken to Abraham that is in question. But Paul knows what grammatical form God employed in speaking to Abraham only as the Scriptures have transmitted it to him; and, as we have seen, in citing the words of God and the words of Scripture he was not accustomed to make any distinction between them. It is probably the Scriptural word as a Scriptural word, therefore, which he has here in mind: though, of course, it is possible that what he here witnesses to is rather the detailed trustworthiness of the Scriptural record than its direct divinity — if we can separate two things which apparently were not separated in Paul's mind. This much we can at least say without straining, that the designation of Scripture as "scripture" and its citation by the formula, "It is written," attest primarily its indefectible authority; the designation of it as "oracles" and the adduction of it by the formula, "It says," attest primarily its immediate divinity. Its authority rests on its divinity and its divinity expresses itself in its trustworthiness; and the New Testament writers in all their use of it treat it as what they declare it to be — a God-breathed document, which, because God-breathed, as through and through trustworthy in all its assertions, authoritative in all its declarations, and down to its last particular, the very word of God, His "oracles."

That the Scriptures are throughout a Divine book, created by the Divine energy and speaking in their every part with Divine authority directly to the heart of the readers, is the fundamental fact concerning them which is witnessed by Christ and the sacred writers to whom we owe the New Testament. But the strength and constancy with which they bear witness to this primary fact do not prevent their recognizing by the side of it that the Scriptures have come into being by the agency of men. It would be inexact to say that they recognize a human element in Scripture: they do not parcel Scripture out, assigning portions of it, or elements in it, respectively to God and man. In their view the whole of Scripture in all its parts and in all its elements, down to the least minutiae, in form of expression as well as in substance of teaching, is from God; but the whole of it has been given by God through the instrumentality of men. There is, therefore, in their view, not, indeed, a human element or ingredient in Scripture, and much less human divisions or sections of Scripture, but a human side or aspect to Scripture; and they do not fail to give full recognition to this human side or aspect. In one of the primary passages which has already been before us, their conception is given, if somewhat broad and very succinct, yet clear expression. No 'prophecy,' Peter tells us (2 Pet. i. 21), 'ever came by the will of man; *but as borne by the Holy Ghost,* men spake from God.'

Here the whole initiative is assigned to God, and such complete control of the human agents that the product is truly God's work. The men who speak in this "prophecy of scripture" speak not of themselves or out of themselves, but from "God": they speak only as they are "borne by the Holy Ghost." But it is they, after all, who speak. Scripture is the product of man, but only of man speaking from God and under such a control of the Holy Spirit as that in their speaking they are "borne" by Him. The conception obviously is that the Scriptures have been given by the instrumentality of men; and this conception finds repeated incidental expression throughout the New Testament.

It is this conception, for example, which is expressed when Our Lord, quoting Ps. cx., declares of its words that "David himself said in the Holy Spirit" (Mk. xii. 36). There is a certain emphasis here on the words being David's own words, which is due to the requirements of the argument Our Lord was conducting, but which none the less sincerely represents Our Lord's conception of their origin. They are David's own words which we find in Ps. cx., therefore; but they are David's own words, spoken not of his own motion merely, but "in the Holy Spirit," that is to say — we could not better paraphrase it — "as borne by the Holy Spirit." In other words, they are "God-breathed" words and therefore authoritative in a sense above what any words of David, not spoken in the Holy Spirit, could possibly be. Generalizing the matter, we may say that the words of Scripture are conceived by Our Lord and the New Testament writers as the words of their human authors when speaking "in the Holy Spirit," that is to say, by His initiative and under His controlling direction. The conception finds even more precise expression, perhaps, in such a statement as we find — it is Peter who is speaking and it is again a psalm which is cited — in Acts i. 16, "The Holy Spirit spake by the mouth of David." Here the Holy Spirit is adduced, of course, as the real author of what is said (and hence Peter's certainty that what is said will be fulfilled); but David's mouth is expressly designated as the instrument (it is the instrumental preposition that is used) by means of which the Holy Spirit speaks the Scripture in question. He does not speak save through David's mouth. Accordingly, in Acts iv. 25, 'the Lord that made the heaven and earth,' acting by His Holy Spirit, is declared to have spoken another psalm ' through the mouth of . . . David,' His "servant"; and in Mt. xiii. 35 still another psalm is adduced as "spoken through the prophet" (cf. Mt. ii. 5). In the very act of energetically asserting the Divine origin of Scripture the human instrumentality through which it is given is constantly recognized. The New Testament writers have, therefore, no difficulty in assigning Scripture to its human authors, or in discovering in Scripture traits due to its human authorship. They freely quote it by such simple formulae as these: "Moses saith" (Rom. x. 19); "Moses said" (Mt. xxii. 24; Mk. vii. 10; Acts iii. 22); "Moses writeth" (Rom. x. 5); "Moses wrote" (Mk. xii. 19; Lk. xx. 28); "Isaiah . . . saith" (Rom. x. 20); "Isaiah said" (Jn. xii. 39); "Isaiah crieth" (Rom. ix. 27); "Isaiah hath said before" (Rom. ix. 29); "said Isaiah the prophet" (Jn. i. 23); "did Isaiah prophesy" (Mk. vii. 6; Mt. xv. 7); "David saith" (Lk. xx. 42; Acts ii. 25; Rom. xi. 9); "David said" (Mk. xii. 36). It is to be noted that when thus Scripture is adduced by the names of its human authors, it is a matter of complete indifference whether the words adduced are comments of these authors or direct words of God recorded by them. As the plainest words of the human authors are assigned to God as their real author, so the most express words of God, repeated by the Scriptural writers, are cited by the names of these human writers (Mt. xv. 7; Mk. vii. 6; Rom. x. 5.19.20; cf. Mk. vii. 10 from the Decalogue). To say that "Moses" or "David says," is evidently thus only a way of saying that "Scripture says," which is the same as to say that "God says." Such modes of citing Scripture, accordingly, carry us little beyond merely connecting the name, or perhaps we may say the individuality, of the several writers with the portions of Scripture given through each. How it was given through them is left meanwhile, if not without suggestion, yet without specific explanation. We seem safe only in inferring this much: that the gift of Scripture through its human authors took place by a process much more intimate than can be expressed by the term "dictation," and that it took place in a process in which the control of the Holy Spirit was too complete and pervasive to permit the human qualities of the secondary authors in any way to condition the purity of the product as the word of God. The Scriptures, in other words, are conceived by the writers of the New Testament as through and through God's book, in every part expressive of His mind, given through men after a fashion which does no violence to their nature as men, and constitutes the book also men's book as well as God's, in every part expressive of the mind of its human authors.

If we attempt to get behind this broad statement and to obtain a more detailed conception of the activities by which God has given the Scriptures, we are thrown back upon somewhat general representations, supported by the analogy of the modes of God's working in other spheres of His operation. It is very desirable that we should free ourselves at the outset from influences arising from the current employment of the term "inspiration" to designate this process. This term is not a Biblical term and its etymological implications are not perfectly accordant with the Biblical conception of the modes of the Divine operation in giving the Scriptures. The Biblical writers do not conceive of the Scriptures as a human product breathed into by the Divine Spirit, and thus heightened in its qualities or endowed with new qualities; but as a Divine product produced through the instrumentality of men. They do not conceive of these men, by whose instrumentality Scripture is produced, as working upon their own initiative, though energized by God to greater effort and higher achievement, but as moved by the Divine initiative and borne by the irresistible power of the Spirit of God along ways of His choosing to ends of His appointment. The difference between the two conceptions may not appear great when the mind is fixed exclusively upon the nature of the resulting product. But they are differing conceptions, and look at the production of Scripture from distinct points of view — the human and the Divine; and the involved mental attitudes toward the origin of Scripture are very diverse. The term "inspiration" is too firmly fixed, in both theological and popular usage, as the technical designation of the action of God in giving the Scriptures, to be replaced; and we may be thankful that its native implications lie as close as they do to the Biblical conceptions. Meanwhile, however, it may be justly insisted that it shall receive its definition from the representations of Scripture, and not be permitted to impose upon our thought ideas of the origin of Scripture derived from an analysis of its own implications, etymological or historical. The Scriptural conception of the relation of the Divine Spirit to the human authors in the production of Scripture is better expressed by the figure of "bearing" than by the figure of "inbreathing"; and when our Biblical writers speak of the action of the Spirit of God in this relation as a breathing, they represent it as a "breathing out" of the Scriptures by the Spirit, and not a "breathing into" the Scriptures by Him.

So soon, however, as we seriously endeavor to form for ourselves a clear conception of the precise nature of the Divine action in this "breathing out" of the Scriptures — this "bearing" of the writers of the Scriptures to their appointed goal of the production of a book of Divine trustworthiness and indefectible authority — we become acutely aware of a more deeply lying and much wider problem, apart from which this one of inspiration, technically so called, cannot be profitably considered. This is the general problem of the origin of the Scriptures and the part of God in all that complex of processes by the interaction of which these books, which we call the sacred Scriptures, with all their peculiarities, and all their qualities of whatever sort, have been brought into being. For, of course, these books were not produced suddenly, by some miraculous act — handed down complete out of heaven, as the phrase goes; but, like all other products of time, are the ultimate effect of many processes coöperating through long periods. There is to be considered, for instance, the preparation of the material which forms the subject-matter of these books: in a sacred history, say, for example, to be narrated; or in a religious experience which may serve as a norm for record; or in a logical elaboration of the contents of revelation which may be placed at the service of God's people; or in the progressive revelation of Divine truth itself, supplying their culminating contents. And there is the preparation of the men to write these books to be considered, a preparation physical, intellectual, spiritual, which must have attended them throughout their whole lives, and, indeed, must have had its beginning in their remote ancestors, and the effect of which was to bring the right men to the right places at the right times, with the right endowments, impulses, acquirements, to write just the books which were designed for them. When "inspiration," technically so called, is superinduced on lines of preparation like these, it takes on quite a different aspect from that which it bears when it is thought of as an isolated action of the Divine Spirit operating out of all relation to historical processes. Representations are sometimes made as if, when God wished to produce sacred books which would incorporate His will — a series of letters like those of Paul, for example — He was reduced to the necessity of going down to earth and painfully scrutinizing the men He found there, seeking anxiously for the one who, on the whole, promised best for His purpose; and then violently forcing the material He wished expressed through him, against his natural bent, and with as little loss from his recalcitrant characteristics as possible. Of course, nothing of the sort took place. If God wished to give His people a series of letters like Paul's, He prepared a Paul to write them, and the Paul He brought to the task was a Paul who spontaneously would write just such letters.

If we bear this in mind, we shall know what estimate to place upon the common representation to the effect that the human characteristics of the writers must, and in point of fact do, condition and qualify the writings produced by them, the implication being that, therefore, we cannot get from man a pure word of God. As light that passes through the colored glass of a cathedral window, we are told, is light from heaven, but is stained by the tints of the glass through which it passes; so any word of God which is passed through the mind and soul of a man must come out discolored by the personality through which it is given, and just to that degree ceases to be the pure word of God. But what if this personality has itself been formed by God into precisely the personality it is, for the express purpose of communicating to the word given through it just the coloring which it gives it? What if the colors of the stained-glass window have been designed by the architect for the express purpose of giving to the light that floods the cathedral precisely the tone and quality it receives from them? What if the word of God that comes to His people is framed by God into the word of God it is, precisely by means of the qualities of the men formed by Him for the purpose, through which it is given? When we think of God the Lord giving by His Spirit a body of authoritative Scriptures to His people, we must remember that He is the God of providence and of grace as well as of revelation and inspiration, and that He holds all the lines of preparation as fully under His direction as He does the specific operation which we call technically, in the narrow sense, by the name of "inspiration." The production of the Scriptures is, in point of fact, a long process, in the course of which numerous and very varied Divine activities are involved, providential, gracious, miraculous, all of which must be taken into account in any attempt to explain the relation of God to the production of Scripture. When they are all taken into account we can no longer wonder that the resultant Scriptures are constantly spoken of as the pure word of God. We wonder, rather, that an additional operation of God — what we call specifically "inspiration," in its technical sense — was thought necessary. Consider, for example, how a piece of sacred history — say the Book of Chronicles, or the great historical work, Gospel and Acts, of Luke — is brought to the writing. There is first of all the preparation of the history to be written: God the Lord leads the sequence of occurrences through the development He has designed for them that they may convey their lessons to His people: a "teleological" or "aetiological" character is inherent in the very course of events. Then He prepares a man, by birth, training, experience, gifts of grace, and, if need be, of revelation, capable of appreciating this historical development and eager to search it out, thrilling in all his being with its lessons and bent upon making them clear and effective to others. When, then, by His providence, God sets this man to work on the writing of this history, will there not be spontaneously written by him the history which it was Divinely intended should be written? Or consider how a psalmist would be prepared to put into moving verse a piece of normative religious experience: how he would be born with just the right quality of religious sensibility, of parents through whom he should receive just the right hereditary bent, and from whom he should get precisely the right religious example and training, in circumstances of life in which his religious tendencies should be developed precisely on right lines; how he would be brought through just the right experiences to quicken in him the precise emotions he would be called upon to express, and finally would be placed in precisely the exigencies which would call out their expression. Or consider the providential preparation of a writer of a didactic epistle — by means of which he should be given the intellectual breadth and acuteness, and be trained in habitudes of reasoning, and placed in the situations which would call out precisely the argumentative presentation of Christian truth which was required of him. When we give due place in our thoughts to the universality of the providential government of God, to the minuteness and completeness of its sway, and to its invariable efficacy, we may be inclined to ask what is needed beyond this mere providential government to secure the production of sacred books which should be in every detail absolutely accordant with the Divine will.

The answer is, Nothing is needed beyond mere providence to secure such books—provided only that it does not lie in the Divine purpose that these books should possess qualities which rise above the powers of men to produce, even under the most complete Divine guidance. For providence is guidance; and guidance can bring one only so far as his own power can carry him. If heights are to be scaled above man's native power to achieve, then something more than guidance, however effective, is necessary. This is the reason for the superinduction, at the end of the long process of the production of Scripture, of the additional Divine operation which we call technically "inspiration." By it, the Spirit of God, flowing confluently in with the providentially and graciously determined work of men, spontaneously producing under the Divine directions the writings appointed to them, gives the product a Divine quality unattainable by human powers alone. Thus these books become not merely the word of godly men, but the immediate word of God Himself, speaking directly as such to the minds and hearts of every reader. The value of "inspiration" emerges, thus, as twofold. It gives to the books written under its "bearing" a quality which is truly superhuman; a trustworthiness, an authority, a searchingness, a profundity, a profitableness which is altogether Divine. And it speaks this Divine word immediately to each reader's heart and conscience; so that he does not require to make his way to God, painfully, perhaps even uncertainly, through the words of His servants, the human instruments in writing the Scriptures, but can listen directly to the Divine voice itself speaking immediately in the Scriptural word to him.

That the writers of the New Testament themselves conceive the Scriptures to have been produced thus by Divine operations extending through the increasing ages and involving a multitude of varied activities, can be made clear by simply attending to the occasional references they make to this or that step in the process. It lies, for example, on the face of their expositions, that they looked upon the Biblical history as teleological. Not only do they tell us that "whatsoever things were written aforetime were written for our learning, that through patience and through comfort of the scriptures we might have hope" (Rom. xv. 4; cf. Rom. iv. 23.24); they speak also of the course of the historical events themselves as guided for our benefit: "Now these things happened unto them by way of example " — in a typical fashion, in such a way that, as they occurred, a typical character, or predictive reference impressed itself upon them; that is to say, briefly, the history occurred as it did in order to bear a message to us — "and they were written for our admonition, upon whom the ends of the ages are come" (1 Cor. x. 11; cf. ver. 6). Accordingly, it has become a commonplace of Biblical exposition that "the history of redemption itself is a typically progressive one" (Küper), and is "in a manner impregnated with the prophetic element," so as to form a "part of a great plan which stretches from the fall of man to the first consummation of all things in glory; and, in so far as it reveals the mind of God toward man, carries a respect to the future not less than to the present" (P. Fairbairn). It lies equally on the face of the New Testament allusions to the subject that its writers understood that the preparation of men to become vehicles of God's message to man was not of yesterday, but had its beginnings in the very origin of their being. The call by which Paul, for example, was made an apostle of Jesus Christ was sudden and apparently without antecedents; but it is precisely this Paul who reckons this call as only one step in a long process, the beginnings of which antedated his own existence: "But when it was the good pleasure of God, who separated me, even from my mother's womb, and called me through his grace, to reveal his Son in me" (Gal. i. 15.16; cf. Jer. i. 5; Isa. xlix. 1.5). The recognition by the writers of the New Testament of the experiences of God's grace, which had been vouchsafed to them as an integral element in their fitting to be the bearers of His gospel to others, finds such pervasive expression that the only difficulty is to select from the mass the most illustrative passages. Such a statement as Paul gives in the opening verses of 2 Cor. is thoroughly typical. There he represents that he has been afflicted and comforted to the end that he might "be able to comfort them that are in any affliction, through the comfort wherewith " he had himself been "comforted of God." For, he explains, "Whether we are afflicted, it is for your comfort and salvation; or whether we are comforted, it is for your comfort, which worketh in the patient enduring of the same sufferings which we also suffer" (2 Cor. i. 4–6). It is beyond question, therefore, that the New Testament writers, when they declare the Scriptures to be the product of the Divine breath, and explain this as meaning that the writers of these Scriptures wrote them only as borne by the Holy Spirit in such a fashion that they spoke, not out of themselves, but "from God," are thinking of this operation of the Spirit only as the final act of God in the production of the Scriptures, superinduced upon a long series of processes, providential, gracious, miraculous, by which the matter of Scripture had been prepared for writing, and the men for writing it, and the writing of it had been actually brought to pass. It is this final act in the production of Scripture which is technically called "inspiration"; and inspiration is thus brought before us as, in the minds of the writers of the New Testament, that particular operation of God in the production of Scripture which takes effect at the very point of the writing of Scripture — understanding the term "writing" here as inclusive of all the processes of the actual composition of Scripture, the investigation of documents, the collection of facts, the excogitation of conclusions, the adaptation of exhortations as means to ends and the like — with the effect of giving to the resultant Scripture a specifically supernatural character, and constituting it a Divine, as well as human, book. Obviously the mode of operation of this Divine activity moving to this result is conceived, in full accord with the analogy of the Divine operations in other spheres of its activity, in providence and in grace alike, as confluent with the human activities operative in the case; as, in a word, of the nature of what has come to be known as "immanent action."

It will not escape observation that thus "inspiration" is made a mode of "revelation." We are often exhorted, to be sure, to distinguish sharply between "inspiration" and "revelation"; and the exhortation is just when "revelation" is taken in one of its narrower senses, of, say, an external manifestation of God, or of an immediate communication from God in words. But "inspiration" does not differ from "revelation" in these narrowed senses as genus from genus, but as a species of one genus differs from another. That operation of God which we call "inspiration," that is to say, that operation of the Spirit of God by which He "bears" men in the process of composing Scripture, so that they write, not of themselves, but "from God," is one of the modes in which God makes known to men His being, His will, His operations, His purposes. It is as distinctly a mode of revelation as any mode of revelation can be, and therefore it performs the same office which all revelation performs, that is to say, in the express words of Paul, it makes men wise, and makes them wise unto salvation. All "special" or "supernatural" revelation (which is redemptive in its very idea, and occupies a place as a substantial element in God's redemptive processes) has precisely this for its end; and Scripture, as a mode of the redemptive revelation of God, finds its fundamental purpose just in this: if the "inspiration" by which Scripture is produced renders it trustworthy and authoritative, it renders it trustworthy and authoritative only that it may the better serve to make men wise unto salvation. Scripture is conceived, from the point of view of the writers of the New Testament, not merely as the record of revelations, but as itself a part of the redemptive revelation of God; not merely as the record of the redemptive acts by which God is saving the world, but as itself one of these redemptive acts, having its own part to play in the great work of establishing and building up the kingdom of God. What gives it a place among the redemptive acts of God is its Divine origination, taken in its widest sense, as inclusive of all the Divine operations, providential, gracious and expressly supernatural, by which it has been made just what it is — a body of writings able to make wise unto salvation, and profitable for making the man of God perfect. What gives it its place among the modes of revelation is, however, specifically the culminating one of these Divine operations, which we call "Inspiration"; that is to say, the action of the Spirit of God in so "bearing" its human authors in their work of producing Scripture, as that in these Scriptures they speak, not out of themselves, but "from God." It is this act by virtue of which the Scriptures may properly be called "God-breathed."

It has been customary among a certain school of writers to speak of the Scriptures, because thus "inspired," as a Divine-human book, and to appeal to the analogy of Our Lord's Divine-human personality to explain their peculiar qualities as such. The expression calls attention to an important fact, and the analogy holds good a certain distance. There are human and Divine sides to Scripture, and, as we cursorily examine it, we may perceive in it, alternately, traits which suggest now the one, now the other factor in its origin. But the analogy with Our Lord's Divine-human personality may easily be pressed beyond reason. There is no hypostatic union between the Divine and the human in Scripture; we cannot parallel the "inscripturation" of the Holy Spirit and the incarnation of the Son of God. The Scriptures are merely the product of Divine and human forces working together to produce a product in the production of which the human forces work under the initiation and prevalent direction of the Divine: the person of Our Lord unites in itself Divine and human natures, each of which retains its distinctness while operating only in relation to the other. Between such diverse things there can exist only a remote analogy; and, in point of fact, the analogy in the present instance amounts to no more than that in both cases Divine and human factors are involved, though very differently. In the one they unite to constitute a Divine-human person, in the other they coöperate to perform a Divine-human work. Even so distant an analogy may enable us, however, to recognize that as, in the case of Our Lord's person, the human nature remains truly human while yet it can never fall into sin or error because it can never act out of relation with the Divine nature into conjunction with which it has been brought; so in the case of the production of Scripture by the conjoint action of human and Divine factors, the human factors have acted as human factors, and have left their mark on the product as such, and yet cannot have fallen into that error which we say it is human to fall into, because they have not acted apart from the Divine factors, by themselves, but only under their unerring guidance.

The New Testament testimony is to the Divine origin and qualities of "Scripture"; and "Scripture" to the writers of the New Testament was fundamentally, of course, the Old Testament. In the primary passage, in which we are told that "every" or "all Scripture" is "God-breathed," the direct reference is to the "sacred writings" which Timothy had had in knowledge since his infancy, and these were, of course, just the sacred books of the Jews (2 Tim. iii. 16). What is explicit here is implicit in all the allusions to inspired Scriptures in the New Testament. Accordingly, it is frequently said that our entire testimony to the inspiration of Scripture concerns the Old Testament alone. In many ways, however, this is overstated. Our present concern is not with the extent of " Scripture " but with the nature of "Scripture"; and we cannot present here the considerations which justify extending to the New Testament the inspiration which the New Testament writers attribute to the Old Testament. It will not be out of place, however, to point out simply that the New Testament writers obviously themselves made this extension. They do not for an instant imagine themselves, as ministers of a new covenant, less in possession of the Spirit of God than the ministers of the old covenant: they freely recognize, indeed, that they have no sufficiency of themselves, but they know that God has made them sufficient (2 Cor. iii. 5.6). They prosecute their work of proclaiming the gospel, therefore, in full confidence that they speak "by the Holy Spirit" (1 Pet. i. 12), to whom they attribute both the matter and form of their teaching (1 Cor. ii. 13). They, therefore, speak with the utmost assurance of their teaching (Gal. i. 7.8); and they issue commands with the completest authority (1 Thess. iv. 2.14; 2 Thess. iii. 6.12), making it, indeed, the test of whether one has the Spirit that he should recognize what they demand as commandments of God (1 Cor. xiv. 37). It would be strange, indeed, if these high claims were made for their oral teaching and commandments exclusively.

In point of fact, they are made explicitly also for their written injunctions. It was "the things" which Paul was "writing," the recognition of which as commands of the Lord, he makes the test of a Spirit-led man (1 Cor. xiv. 37). It is his "word by this epistle," obedience to which he makes the condition of Christian communion (2 Thess. iii. 14). There seems involved in such an attitude toward their own teaching, oral and written, a claim on the part of the New Testament writers to something very much like the "inspiration" which they attribute to the writers of the Old Testament.

And all doubt is dispelled when we observe the New Testament writers placing the writings of one another in the same category of "Scripture" with the books of the Old Testament. The same Paul who, in 2 Tim. iii. 16, declared that 'every' or 'all scripture is God-breathed' had already written in 1 Tim. v. 18: "For the scripture saith, Thou shall not muzzle the ox when he treadeth out the corn. And, The laborer is worthy of his hire." The first clause here is derived from Deuteronomy and the second from the Gospel of Luke, though both are cited as together constituting, or better, forming part of the "Scripture" which Paul adduces as so authoritative as by its mere citation to end all strife. Who shall say that, in the declaration of the later epistle that "all" or "every" Scripture is God-breathed, Paul did not have Luke, and, along with Luke, whatever other new books he classed with the old under the name of Scripture, in the back of his mind, along with those old books which Timothy had had in his hands from infancy? And the same Peter who declared that every "prophecy of scripture" was the product of men who spoke "from God," being 'borne' by the Holy Ghost (2 Pet. i. 21), in this same epistle (iii. 16), places Paul's Epistles in the category of Scripture along with whatever other books deserve that name. For Paul, says he, wrote these epistles, not out of his own wisdom, but "according to the wisdom given to him," and though there are some things in them hard to be understood, yet it is only "the ignorant and unstedfast" who wrest these difficult passages — as what else could be expected of men who wrest "also the other

Scriptures" (obviously the Old Testament is meant) — "unto their own destruction"? Is it possible to say that Peter could not have had these epistles of Paul also lurking somewhere in the back of his mind, along with "the other scriptures," when he told his readers that every "prophecy of scripture" owes its origin to the prevailing operation of the Holy Ghost? What must be understood in estimating the testimony of the New Testament writers to the inspiration of Scripture is that "Scripture" stood in their minds as the title of a unitary body of books, throughout the gift of God through His Spirit to His people; but that this body of writings was at the same time understood to be a growing aggregate, so that what is said of it applies to the new books which were being added to it as the Spirit gave them, as fully as to the old books which had come down to them from their hoary past. It is a mere matter of detail to determine precisely what new books were thus included by them in the category "Scripture." They tell us some of them themselves. Those who received them from their hands tell us of others. And when we put the two bodies of testimony together we find that they constitute just our New Testament. It is no pressure of the witness of the writers of the New Testament to the inspiration of the Scripture, therefore, to look upon it as covering the entire body of "Scriptures," the new books which they were themselves adding to this aggregate, as well as the old books which they had received as Scripture from the fathers. Whatever can lay claim by just right to the appellation of "Scripture," as employed in its eminent sense by those writers, can by the same just right lay claim to the "inspiration" which they ascribe to this "Scripture."

LITERATURE. — J. Gerhard, "Loci Theolog.," Locus I; F. Turretin, "Instit. Theol.," Locus II; B. de Moor, "Comm. in J. Marckii Comp.," cap. ii; C. Hodge, "Syst. Theol.," New York, 1871, I, 151–86; Henry B. Smith, "The Inspiration of the Holy Scriptures," New York, 1855, new ed., Cincinnati, 1891; A. Kuyper, "Encyclopedie der heilige Godgeleerdheid," 1888–89, II, 347 ff., ET; "Enc of Sacred Theol.," New York, 1898, 341–563; also "De Schrift het woord Gods," Tiel, 1870; H. Bavinck, "Gereformeerde Dogmatiek²," Kampen, 1906, I,

406–527; R. Haldane, "The Verbal Inspiration of the Scriptures Established," Edinburgh, 1830; J. T. Beck, "Einleitung in das System der christlichen Lehre," Stuttgart, 1838, 2d ed., 1870; A. G. Rudelbach, "Die Lehre von der Inspiration der heil. Schrift," *Zeitschrift für die gesammte Lutherische Theologie und Kirche*, 1840, 1, 1841, 1, 1842, 1; S. R. L. Gaussen, "Théopneustie ou inspiration plénière des saintes écritures[2]," Paris, 1842, ET by E. N. Kirk, New York, 1842; also "Theopneustia; the Plenary Inspiration of the Holy Scriptures," David Scott's tr., reëdited and revised by B. W. Carr, with a preface by C. H. Spurgeon, London, 1888; William Lee, "The Inspiration of the Holy Scriptures," Donellan Lecture, 1852, New York, 1857; James Bannerman, "Inspiration: the Infallible Truth and Divine Authority of the Holy Scriptures," Edinburgh, 1865; F. L. Patton, "The Inspiration of the Scriptures," Philadelphia, 1869 (reviewing Lee and Bannerman); Charles Elliott, "A Treatise on the Inspiration of the Holy Scriptures," Edinburgh, 1877; A. A. Hodge and B. B. Warfield, "Inspiration," *Presbyterian Review*, April, 1881, also tract, Philadelphia, 1881; R. Watts, "The Rule of Faith and the Doctrine of Inspiration," Edinburgh, 1885; A. Cave, "The Inspiration of the OT Inductively Considered," London, 1888; B. Manly, "The Bible Doctrine of Inspiration," New York, 1888; W. Rohnert, "Die Inspiration der heiligen Schrift und ihre Bestreiter," Leipzig, 1889; A. W. Dieckhoff, "Die Inspiration und Irrthumlosigkeit der heiligen Schrift," Leipzig, 1891; J. Wichelhaus, "Die Lehre der heiligen Schrift," Stuttgart, 1892; J. Macgregor, "The Revelation and the Record," Edinburgh, 1893; J. Urquhart, "The Inspiration and Accuracy of the Holy Scriptures," London, 1895; C. Pesch, "De Inspiratione Sacrae Scripturae," Freiburg, 1906; James Orr, "Revelation and Inspiration," London, **1910.**

# IV
# THE REAL PROBLEM OF INSPIRATION

# THE REAL PROBLEM OF INSPIRATION[1]

A GREAT deal is being said of late of "the present problem of inspiration," with a general implication that the Christian doctrine of the plenary inspiration of the Scriptures has been brought into straits by modern investigation, and needs now to adapt itself to certain assured but damaging results of the scientific study of the Bible. Thus, because of an assumed "present distress," Canon Cheyne, in a paper read at the English Church Congress of 1888, commended a most revolutionary book of Mr. R. F. Horton's, called "Inspiration and the Bible,"[2] which explains away inspiration properly so called altogether, as the best book he could think of on the subject. And Mr. Charles Gore defends the concessive method of treating the subject of inspiration adopted in "Lux Mundi," by the plea that the purpose of the writers of that volume "was 'to succour a distressed faith,' by endeavoring to bring the Christian creed into its right relation to the modern growth of knowledge, scientific, historical, critical."[3] On our side of the water, Dr. Washington Gladden has published a volume which begins by presenting certain "new" views of the structure of the books of the Bible as established facts, and proceeds to the conclusion that: "Evidently neither the theory of verbal inspiration nor the theory of plenary inspiration can be made to fit the facts which a careful study of the writings themselves brings before us. These writings are not inspired in the sense which we have commonly given to that word." Accordingly he recommends that under the pressure of these new views we admit not only that the Bible is not "infallible," but that its laws

[1] From *The Presbyterian and Reformed Review*, vol. iv, 1893. pp. 177–221.

[2] "Inspiration and the Bible." An Inquiry. By Robert F. Horton, M.A., Late Fellow of New College, Oxford. Fourth Edition. London: T. Fisher Unwin, 1889.

[3] "Lux Mundi." Tenth Edition. London: John Murray, 1890. P. xi.

are "inadequate" and "morally defective," and its untrustworthiness as a religious teacher is so great that it gives us in places "blurred and distorted ideas about God and His truth."[4] And Prof. Joseph H. Thayer has published a lecture which represents as necessitated by the facts as now known, such a change of attitude towards the Bible as will reject the whole Reformed doctrine of the Scriptures in favor of a more "Catholic" view which will look upon some of the history recorded in the Bible as only "fairly trustworthy," and will expect no intelligent reader to consider the exegesis of the New Testament writers satisfactory.[5] A radical change in our conception of the Scriptures as the inspired Word of God is thus pressed upon us as now necessary by a considerable number of writers, representing quite a variety of schools of Christian thought.

Nevertheless the situation is not one which can be fairly described as putting the old doctrine of inspiration in jeopardy. The exact state of the case is rather this: that a special school of Old Testament criticism, which has, for some years, been gaining somewhat widespread acceptance of its results, has begun to proclaim that these results having been accepted, a "changed view of the Bible" follows which implies a reconstructed doctrine of inspiration, and, indeed, also a whole new theology. That this changed view of the Bible involves losses is frankly admitted. The nature of these losses is stated by Dr. Sanday in a very interesting little book [6] with an evident effort to avoid as far as possible "making sad the heart of the righteous whom the Lord hath not made sad," as consisting chiefly in making "the intellectual side of the connection between Christian belief and Christian practice a matter of greater difficulty than it has hitherto seemed to be," in rendering it "less

<hr>

[4] "Who Wrote the Bible?" A Book for the People. By Washington Gladden. Boston: Houghton, Mifflin & Co., 1891. See pp. 61 (cf. pp. 57, 92 seq.), 21, 25, 154 (cf. pp. 105, 166, 37, etc.).

[5] "The Change of Attitude Towards the Bible." A lecture, etc. By Joseph Henry Thayer, Professor in Harvard University. Boston: Houghton, Mifflin & Co., 1891. See pp. 9, 10, 22, 52, 65.

[6] "The Oracles of God" (Longmans, 1891), pp. 5, 45, 76.

easy to find proof texts for this or that," and in making the use of the Bible so much less simple and less definite in its details that "less educated Christians will perhaps pay more deference to the opinion of the more educated, and to the advancing consciousness of the Church at large." If this means all that it seems to mean, its proclamation of an indefinite Gospel eked out by an appeal to the Church and a scholastic hierarchy, involves a much greater loss than Dr. Sanday appears to think — a loss not merely of the Protestant doctrine of the perspicuity of the Scriptures, but with it of all that that doctrine is meant to express and safeguard — the loss of the Bible itself to the plain Christian man for all practical uses, and the delivery of his conscience over to the tender mercies of his human instructors, whether ecclesiastical or scholastic. Dr. Briggs is more blunt and more explicit in his description of the changes which he thinks have been wrought. "I will tell you what criticism has destroyed," he says in an article published a couple of years ago. "It has destroyed many false theories about the Bible; it has destroyed the doctrine of verbal inspiration; it has destroyed the theory of inerrancy; it has destroyed the false doctrine that makes the inspiration depend upon its attachment to a holy man."[7] And he goes on to remark further "that Biblical criticism is at the bottom" of the "reconstruction that is going on throughout the Church" — "the demand for revision of creeds and change in methods of worship and Christian work." It is clear enough, then, that a problem has been raised with reference to inspiration by this type of criticism. But this is not equivalent to saying that the established doctrine of inspiration has been put in jeopardy. For there is criticism and criticism. And though it may not be unnatural for these scholars themselves to confound the claims of criticism with the validity of their own critical methods and the soundness of their own critical conclusions, the Christian world can scarcely be expected to acquiesce in the identification. It has all along been pointing out that they were traveling on the

[7] The article appeared in *The Christian Union*, but we quote it from *Public Opinion*, vol. x. No. 24 (March 25, 1891), p. 576.

wrong road; and now when their conclusions clash with well-established facts, we simply note that the wrong road has not unnaturally led them to the wrong goal. In a word, it is not the established doctrine of inspiration that is brought into distress by the conflict, but the school of Old Testament criticism which is at present fashionable. It is now admitted that the inevitable issue of this type of criticism comes into collision with the established fact of the plenary inspiration of the Bible and the well-grounded Reformed doctrine of Holy Scripture based on this fact.[8] The cry is therefore, and somewhat impatiently, raised that this fact and this doctrine must " get out of the way," and permit criticism to rush on to its bitter goal. But facts are somewhat stubborn things, and are sometimes found to prove rather the test of theories which seek to make them their sport.

Nevertheless, though the strain of the present problem should thus be thrown upon the shoulders to which it belongs, it is important to keep ourselves reminded that the doctrine of inspiration which has become established in the Church, is open to all legitimate criticism, and is to continue to be held only as, and so far as, it is ever anew critically tested and approved. And in view of the large bodies of real knowledge concerning the Bible which the labors of a generation of diligent critical study have accumulated, and of the difficulty which is always experienced in the assimilation of new knowledge and

[8] This remark, of course, does not imply that there are none who assert that the results of this type of criticism leave " inspiration " untouched. Dr. Driver does not stand alone when he says, in the Preface to his " Introduction to the Literature of the Old Testament ": " Criticism in the hands of Christian scholars does not banish or destroy the inspiration of the Old Testament; it *presupposes* it " (p. xix). But Prof. Driver would be the last to maintain that the " inspiration " which criticism leaves to the Old Testament is what the Church has understood by the plenary inspiration of the Bible. Accordingly, Prof. Robertson speaks directly to the point when he remarks in the Preface to his " Early Religion of Israel " (p. xi), that " such scholars would do an invaluable service to the Church, at the present time, if they would explain what they mean by inspiration in this connection." The efforts to do this, on our side of the water, are not reassuring. On the relation of the new views to inspiration see the lucid statement by Dr. E. C. Bissell in *The Hartford Seminary Record*, ii. 1.

its correlation with previously ascertained truth, it is becoming to take this occasion to remind ourselves of the foundations on which this doctrine rests, with a view to inquiring whether it is really endangered by any assured results of recent Biblical study. For such an investigation we must start, of course, from a clear conception of what the Church doctrine of inspiration is, and of the basis on which it is held to be the truth of God. Only thus can we be in a position to judge how it can be affected on critical grounds, and whether modern Biblical criticism has reached any assured results which must or may "destroy" it.

The Church, then, has held from the beginning that the Bible is the Word of God in such a sense that its words, though written by men and bearing indelibly impressed upon them the marks of their human origin, were written, nevertheless, under such an influence of the Holy Ghost as to be also the words of God, the adequate expression of His mind and will. It has always recognized that this conception of co-authorship implies that the Spirit's superintendence extends to the choice of the words by the human authors (verbal inspiration[9]), and preserves its product from everything inconsistent with a divine authorship — thus securing, among other things, that entire truthfulness which is everywhere presupposed in and asserted for Scripture by the Biblical writers (inerrancy). Whatever minor variations may now and again have entered into the mode of statement, this has always been the core of the Church doctrine of inspiration. And along with many other modes of commending and defending it, the primary ground on which it has been held by the Church as the true doctrine is that it is the doctrine of the Biblical writers themselves, and has therefore the whole mass of evidence for it which goes to show that the Biblical writers are trustworthy as doctrinal guides. It is the testimony of the Bible itself to its own origin and character as the Oracles of the Most High, that has led the

[9] It ought to be unnecessary to protest again against the habit of representing the advocates of "verbal inspiration" as teaching that the mode of inspiration was by dictation. The matter is fully explained in the paper: "Inspiration." By Profs. A. A. Hodge and B. B. Warfield. Philadelphia: Presbyterian Board of Publication, 1881, pp. 19 *seq.*

Church to her acceptance of it as such, and to her dependence on it not only for her doctrine of Scripture, but for the whole body of her doctrinal teaching, which is looked upon by her as divine because drawn from this divinely given fountain of truth.

Now if this doctrine is to be assailed on critical grounds, it is very clear that, first of all, criticism must be required to proceed against the evidence on which it is based. This evidence, it is obvious, is twofold. First, there is the exegetical evidence that the doctrine held and taught by the Church is the doctrine held and taught by the Biblical writers themselves. And secondly, there is the whole mass of evidence — internal and external, objective and subjective, historical and philosophical, human and divine — which goes to show that the Biblical writers are trustworthy as doctrinal guides. If they are trustworthy teachers of doctrine and if they held and taught this doctrine, then this doctrine is true, and is to be accepted and acted upon as true by us all. In that case, any objections brought against the doctrine from other spheres of inquiry are inoperative; it being a settled logical principle that so long as the proper evidence by which a proposition is established remains unrefuted, all so-called objections brought against it pass out of the category of objections to its truth into the category of difficulties to be adjusted to it. If criticism is to assail this doctrine, therefore, it must proceed against and fairly overcome one or the other element of its proper proof. It must either show that this doctrine is not the doctrine of the Biblical writers, or else it must show that the Biblical writers are not trustworthy as doctrinal guides. If a fair criticism evinces that this is not the doctrine of the Biblical writers, then of course it has "destroyed" the doctrine which is confessedly based on that supposition. Failing in this, however, it can "destroy" the doctrine, strictly speaking, only by undermining its foundation in our confidence in the trustworthiness of Scripture as a witness to doctrine. The possibility of this latter alternative must, no doubt, be firmly faced in our investigation of the phenomena of the Bible; but the weight of the evidence, be it small or great, for the general trustworthiness of the Bible as a source of doctrine, throws itself, in the form of a presumption, against the reality of any phenomena alleged to be discovered which make against its testimony. No doubt this presumption may be overcome by clear demonstration. But clear demonstration is requisite. For, certainly, if it is critically established that what is sometimes called, not without a touch of scorn, "the traditional doctrine," is just the Bible's own doctrine of inspiration, the real conflict is no longer with "the traditional theory of inspiration," but with the credibility of the Bible. The really decisive question among Christian scholars (among whom alone, it would seem, could a question of inspiration be profitably discussed), is thus seen to be, "What does an exact and scientific exegesis determine to be the Biblical doctrine of inspiration?"

## The Biblical Doctrine of Inspiration Clear

The reply to this question is, however, scarcely open to doubt. The stricter and the more scientific the examination is made, the more certain does it become that the authors of the New Testament held a doctrine of inspiration quite as high as the Church doctrine. This may be said, indeed, to be generally admitted by untrammeled critics, whether of positive or of negative tendencies. Thus, for instance — to confine our examples to a few of those who are not able personally to accept the doctrine of the New Testament writers — Archdeacon Farrar is able to admit that Paul "shared, doubtless, in the views of the later Jewish schools — the Tanaim and Amoraim — on the nature of inspiration. These views . . . made the words of Scripture coextensive and identical with the words of God." [10] So also Otto Pfleiderer allows that Paul "fully shared the assumption of his opponents, the irrefragable authority of the letter as the immediately revealed Word of God." [11] Similarly, Tholuck recognizes that the application of the Old Testament made by the author of the Epistle to the Hebrews,

[10] "Life of Paul," i. 49.  [11] "Paulinism," i. 88.

"rests on the strictest view of inspiration, since passages where God is not the speaker are cited as words of God or of the Holy Ghost (i. 6, 7, 8, iv. 4, 7, vii. 21, iii. 7, x. 15)."[12] This fact is worked out also with convincing clearness by the writer of an odd and sufficiently free Scotch book published a few years ago,[13] who formulates his conclusion in the words: "There is no doubt that the author of Hebrews, in common with the other New Testament writers, regards the whole Old Testament as having been dictated by the Holy Ghost, or, as we should say, plenarily, and, as it were, mechanically inspired." And more recently still Prof. Stapfer, of Paris,[14] though himself denying the reality not only of an infallibility for the Bible, but also of any inspiration for it at all, declaring that "the doctrine of an Inspiration distinct from Revelation and legitimating it, is an error"—yet cannot deny that Paul held a different doctrine—a doctrine which made the Old Testament to him the divine Word and the term, "It is written," equivalent to "God says."[15]

A detailed statement of the evidence is scarcely needed to support a position allowed by such general consent. But it will not be improper to adjoin a brief outline of the grounds on which the general consent rests. In the circumstances, however, we may venture to dispense with an argument drawn up from our own point of view,[16] and content ourselves with an extract from the brief statement of the grounds of his decision

[12] "Old Testament in the New," *Bibliotheca Sacra*, xi. 612.

[13] "Principles of Christianity," by James Stuart (1888), p. 346.

[14] "Séance de Rentrée des Cours de la Faculté de Théologie Protestante de Paris, le Mardi 3 Novembre," 1891. *Leçon d'Ouverture de M. le Prof. Edm. Stapfer.* Paris: Fischbacher, 1891. Pp. 26, 42.

[15] Compare also Kuenen, "Prophets," p. 449; Reuss, "History of Christian Theology in the Apostolic Age," i. p. 352 *seq.*; Riehm, "Der Lehrbegr. des Hebräerbriefes," i. pp. 173, 177, etc.

[16] Those who wish to see a very conclusive and thorough statement of Paul's doctrine of inspiration should consult Dr. Purves's paper on "St. Paul and Inspiration," published in *The Presbyterian and Reformed Rev.*, January, 1893. For our Lord's doctrine, see Dr. Caven's paper on "Our Lord's Testimony to the Old Testament," in the number of the *Review* for July, 1892.

given by another of those critical scholars who do not believe the doctrine of plenary inspiration, but yet find themselves constrained to allow that it is the doctrine of the New Testament writers. Richard Rothe [17] seeks, wrongly, to separate Christ's doctrine of the Old Testament from that of the apostles; our Lord obviously spoke of the Scriptures of His people out of the same fundamental conception of their nature and divinity as His apostles. But he more satisfactorily outlines the doctrine of the apostles as follows:

"We find in the New Testament authors the same theoretical view of the Old Testament and the same practice as to its use, as among the Jews of the time in general, although at the same time in the handling of the same conceptions and principles on both sides, the whole difference between the new Christian spirit and that of contemporary Judaism appears in sharp distinctness. Our authors look upon the words of the Old Testament as *immediate* words of God, and adduce them expressly as such, even those of them which are not at all related as direct sayings of God. They see nothing at all in the sacred volume which is simply the word of its human author and not at the same time the very Word of God Himself. In all that stands ' written ' God Himself speaks to them, and so entirely are they habituated to think only of this that they receive the sacred Word written itself, as such, as God's Word, and hear God speaking in it *immediately*, without any thought of the human persons who appear in it as speaking and acting. The *historical* conception of their Bible is altogether foreign to them. Therefore they cite the abstract ἡ γραφή or αἱ γραφαί or γραφαὶ ἅγιαι (Rom. i. 2), or again τὰ ἱερὰ γράμματα (2 Tim. iii. 15), without naming any special author, as self-evidently God's Word, e.g., John vii. 38, x. 35, xix. 36, 37, xx. 9; Acts i. 16; James ii. 8; Rom. ix. 17; Gal. iii. 8, 22, iv. 30; 1 Pet. ii. 6; 2 Pet. i. 20, etc.; and introduce Old Testament citations with the formulas, now that God (Matt. i. 22, ii. 15; Acts iv. 25, xiii. 34; Rom. i. 2), now that the Holy Spirit (Acts i. 16, xxviii. 25; Heb. iii. 7, ix. 8, x. 15; cf. also Acts iv. 25; 1 Pet. i. 11; 2 Pet. i. 20) so speaks or has spoken. The Epistle to the Hebrews unhesitatingly adduces with a ὁ θεὸς λέγει and the like, even passages in which God is spoken of expressly in the third person (i. 6, 7, 8 *seq.*, iv. 4, 7, vii. 21, x. 30), and even (i. 10) cites a passage in which in the Old Testament text God

[17] " Zur Dogmatik," p. 177 *seq.*

Himself (according to the view of the author it is, however, the Son of God) is addressed, as a word spoken by God. In 2 Tim. iii. 16 the ἱερὰ γράμματα (verse 15) are expressly called θεόπνευστα, however the sentence may be construed or expounded; and however little a special theory of the inspiration of the Bible can be drawn from an expression of such breadth of meaning, nevertheless this *datum* avails to prove that the author shared in general the view of his Jewish contemporaries as to the peculiar character of the Old Testament books, and it is of especial importance inasmuch as it attributes the inspiration, without the least ambiguity, directly to the writings themselves, and not merely to their authors, the prophets. No doubt, in the teaching of the apostles the conception of prophetic inspiration to which it causally attributes the Old Testament, has not yet the sharp exactness of our ecclesiastical dogmatic conception; but it stands, nevertheless, in a very express analogy with it. . . . Moreover, it must be allowed that the apostolical writers, although they nowhere say it expressly, refer the prophetic inspiration also to the *actus scribendi* of the Biblical authors. The whole style and method of their treatment of the Old Testament text manifestly presupposes in them this view of this matter, which was at the time the usual one in the Jewish schools. With Paul particularly this is wholly incontrovertibly the case. For only on that view could he, in such passages as Rom. iv. 23, 24, xv. 4; 1 Cor. ix. 10, x. 11 — in which he distinguishes between the occurrence of the Old Testament facts and the recording of them — maintain of the latter that it was done with express teleological reference to the needs of the New Testament believers, at least so far as the selection of the matter to be described is concerned; and only on that view could he argue on the details of the letter of the Old Testament Scriptures, as he does in Gal. iii. 15, 16. We can, moreover, trace the continuance of this view in the oldest post-apostolical Church. . . . So far as the Old Testament is concerned, our ecclesiastical-dogmatic doctrine of inspiration can, therefore, in very fact, appeal to the authority, not indeed of the Redeemer Himself — for He stands in an entirely neutral attitude towards it — but no doubt of the apostles."

A keen controversialist like Rothe does not fail, of course —
as the reader has no doubt observed — to accompany his exposition of the apostolic doctrine with many turns of expression
designed to lessen its authority in the eyes of the reader, and to
prepare the way for his own refusal to be bound by it; but
neither does he fail to make it clear that this doctrine, although
it is unacceptable to him, is the apostles' doctrine. The apostles' *doctrine,* let it be observed that we say. For even so bald
a statement as Rothe's will suffice to uncover the fallacy of the
assertion, which is so often made, that the doctrine of verbal
inspiration is based on a few isolated statements of Scripture
to the neglect, if not to the outrage, of its phenomena — a form
of remark into which even so sober a writer as Dr. W. G. Blaikie
has lately permitted himself to fall.[18] Nothing, obviously, could
be more opposite to the fact. The doctrine of verbal inspiration
is based on the broad foundation of the carefully ascertained
*doctrine* of the Scripture writers on the subject. It is a product
of Biblical Theology. And if men will really ask, not, "What do
the creeds teach? What do the theologians say? What is the
authority of the Church? but, What does the Bible itself teach
us?" and "fencing off from the Scriptures all the speculations,
all the dogmatic elaborations, all the doctrinal adaptations that
have been made in the history of doctrine in the Church,"
"limit themselves strictly to the theology of the Bible itself"
— according to the excellent programme outlined by Dr.
Briggs[19] — it is to the doctrine of verbal inspiration, as we
have seen, that they must come. It is not Biblical criticism that
has "destroyed" verbal inspiration, but Dr. Briggs' scholastic
theories that have drawn him away in this matter from the
pure deliverances of Biblical Theology.[20]

Much more, of course, does such a statement as even

[18] " Letter to the Rev. Andrew A. Bonar, D.D.," etc. Edinburgh, 1890.

[19] " The Edward Robinson Chair of Biblical Theology in the Union
Theological Seminary," New York (1891), pp. 5, 6.

[20] The substance of some of the preceding paragraphs was printed in
*The Homiletical Review* for May, 1891, under the title of " The Present
Problem of Inspiration."

Rothe's uncover the even deeper error of the assertion latterly becoming much too common, that, the doctrine of verbal inspiration, as a recent writer puts it,[21] "is based wholly upon an *a priori* assumption of what inspiration *must be,* and not upon the Bible as it actually exists." It is based wholly upon an exegetical fact. It is based on the exegetical fact that our Lord and His apostles held this doctrine of Scripture, and everywhere deal with the Scriptures of the Old Testament in accordance with it, as the very Word of God, even in their narrative parts. This is a commonplace of exegetical science, the common possession of the critical schools of the left and of the right, a prominent and unmistakable deliverance of Biblical Theology. And on the establishment of it as such, the real issue is brought out plainly and stringently. If criticism has made such discoveries as to necessitate the abandonment of the doctrine of plenary inspiration, it is not enough to say that we are compelled to abandon only a "particular theory of inspiration," though that is true enough. We must go on to say that that "particular theory of inspiration" is the theory of the apostles and of the Lord, and that in abandoning *it* we are abandoning *them* as our doctrinal teachers and guides, as our "exegetes," in the deep and rich sense of that word which Dr. Vincent vindicates for it.[22] This real issue is to be kept clearly before us, and faced courageously. Nothing is gained by closing our eyes to the seriousness of the problem which we are confronting. Stated plainly it is just this: Are the New Testament writers trustworthy guides in doctrine? Or are we at liberty to reject their authority, and frame contrary doctrines for ourselves? If the latter pathway be taken, certainly the doctrine of plenary inspiration is not the only doctrine that is "destroyed," and the labor of revising our creeds may as well be saved and the shorter process adopted of simply throwing them

[21] "Exegesis." An address delivered at the Opening of the Autumn Term of Union Theological Seminary, September 24, 1891. By Marvin R. Vincent, D.D. New York: C. Scribner's Sons, 1891. P. 40.

[22] *Op. cit.,* p. 5 *seq.*

away. No wonder we are told that the same advance in knowledge which requires a changed view of the Bible necessitates also a whole new theology. If the New Testament writers are not trustworthy as teachers of doctrine and we have to go elsewhere for the source and norm of truth as to God and duty and immortality, it will not be strange if a very different system of doctrine from that delivered by the Scriptures and docilely received from them by the Church, results.

And now, having uncovered the precise issue which is involved in the real problem of inspiration, let us look at it at various angles and thus emphasize in turn two or three of the more important results that spring from it.

## I

### MODIFICATIONS OF THE BIBLICAL DOCTRINE UNDERMINE THE AUTHORITY OF THE SCRIPTURES

First, we emphasize the fact that, this being the real state of the case, we cannot modify the doctrine of plenary inspiration in any of its essential elements without undermining our confidence in the authority of the apostles as teachers of doctrine.

Logically, this is an immediate corollary of the proposition already made good. Historically, it is attested by the driftage of every school of thought which has sought to find a ground of faith in any lower than the Church's doctrine of a plenarily inspired Bible. The authority which cannot assure of a hard fact is soon not trusted for a hard doctrine. Sooner or later, in greater or less degree, the authority of the Bible in doctrine and life is replaced by or subordinated to that of reason, or of the feelings, or of the "Christian consciousness"—the "conscious experience by the individual of the Christian faith"— or of that corporate Christian consciousness which so easily hardens into simple ecclesiastical domination. What we are to accept as the truth of God is a comparatively easy question, if we can open our Bibles with the confident belief that what we read there is commended to us by a fully credible "Thus saith the Lord." But in proportion as we allow this or that element in it not to be safeguarded to us by this divine guarantee, do we begin to doubt the trustworthiness of more and more of the message delivered, and to seek other grounds of confidence than the simple "It is written" which sufficed for the needs of our Lord and His apostles. We have seen Dr. Sanday pointing to "the advancing consciousness of the Church at large," along with the consensus of scholars, as the ground of acceptance of doctrines as true, which will be more and more turned to when men can no longer approach the Bible so simply as heretofore. This is the natural direction in which to look, for men trained to lay that great stress on institutional Christianity which leads Mr. Gore to describe the present situation as one in which "it is becoming more and more difficult to believe in the Bible without believing in the Church." [23] Accordingly Dr. Sterrett also harmonizes his Hegelianism and Churchliness in finding the ground of Christian certitude in the "communal Christian consciousness," which is defined as the Church, as "objective, authoritative reason for every Christian," to which he must subordinate his individual reason.[24] Men of more individualistic training fall back rather on personal reason or the individual "Christian consciousness"; but all alike retire the Bible as a source of doctrine behind some other safeguard of truth.

It may not be without interest or value to subject the various pathways which men tread in seeking to justify a lower view of Scripture than that held and taught by the New Testament writers, to a somewhat close scrutiny, with a view to observing how necessarily they logically involve a gradual undermining of the trustworthiness of those writers as teachers

[23] " Lux Mundi." American Ed. New York: John W. Lovell Co. P. 283.

[24] " Reason and Authority in Religion." By J. MacBride Sterrett, D.D., Professor in Seabury Divinity School. New York: T. Whittaker, 1891. P. 176.

of doctrine. From the purely formal point of view proper to our present purpose, four types of procedure may be recognized.

### CHRIST VERSUS THE APOSTLES

1. There is first, that, of which Richard Rothe is an example, which proceeds by attempting to establish a distinction between the teaching of Christ and the teaching of His apostles, and refusing the latter in favor of the former.

As we have already remarked, this distinction cannot be made good. Rothe's attempt to establish it proceeds on the twofold ground, on the one hand, of an asserted absence from our Lord's dealings with the Scriptures of those extreme facts of usage of it as the Word of God, and of those extreme statements concerning its divine character, on the ground of which in the apostles' dealing with it we must recognize their high doctrine of Scripture; and on the other hand, of an asserted presence in Christ's remarks concerning Scripture of hints that He did not share the conception of Scripture belonging to contemporary Judaism, which conception we know to have been the same high doctrine that was held by the apostles. He infers, therefore, that the apostles, in this matter, represent only the current Jewish thought in which they were bred, while Christ's divine originality breaks away from this and commends to us a new and more liberal way.

But in order to make out the first member of the twofold ground on which he bases this conclusion, Rothe has to proceed by explaining away, by means of artificial exegetical expedients, a number of facts of usage and deliverances as to Scripture, in which our Lord's dealings with Scripture culminate, and which are altogether similar in character and force to those on the basis of which he infers the apostles' high doctrine. These are such passages as the quotation in Matt. xix. 4, 5, of Adam's words as God's Word, which Lechler appeals to as decisive just as Rothe appeals to similar passages in the epistles —but which Rothe sets aside in a footnote simply with the remark that it is not decisive here; the assertion in John x. 35, that the "Scripture cannot be broken," which he sets aside as probably not a statement of Christ's own opinion but an *argumentum ad hominem,* and as in any case not available here, since it does not explicitly assert that the authority it ascribes to Scripture is due "to its origination by inspiration"—but which, as Dr. Robert Watts has shown anew,[25] is conclusive for our Saviour's view of the entire infallibility of the whole Old Testament; the assertion in Matt. v. 18 (and in Luke xiv. 17) that not "one jot or one tittle ( ἰῶτα ἒν ἢ μία κεραία ) shall pass away from the law till all be fulfilled," which he sets aside with the remark that it is not the law-codex, but the law itself, that is here spoken of, forgetful of the fact that it is the law itself *as written* that the Lord has in mind, in which form alone, moreover, do "yodhs and horns" belong to it; the assertion in Matt. xxii. 43, that it was "in the Spirit" that David called the Messiah, " Lord," in the one hundred and tenth Psalm which he sets aside with the remark that this does prove that Jesus looked upon David as a prophet, but not necessarily that he considered the one hundred and tenth Psalm inspired, as indeed he does not say γράφει but καλεῖ — forgetful again that it is to the written David alone that Christ makes His appeal and on the very language written in the Psalm that He founds His argument.

No less, in order to make out the second member of the ground on which he bases his conclusion, does Rothe need to press passages which have as their whole intent and effect to

[25] " Faith and Inspiration." The Carey Lectures for 1884. By Robert Watts, D.D. London: Hodder & Stoughton, 1885. P. 139. " The sole question is: What, according to the language employed by Him, was His estimate of the Old Testament Scripture? It will be observed that He does not single out the passage on which He bases His argument, and testify of it that it is unbreakable, making its infallibility depend on His authority. Stated formally, His argument is as follows: Major — The Scripture cannot be broken. Minor — ' I said ye are God's,' is written in your law, which is Scripture. Conclusion — ' I said ye are God's ' cannot be broken. . . . He argues the infallibility of the clause on which He founds His argument from the infallibility of the record in which it occurs. According to His infallible estimate, it was sufficient proof of the infallibility of any sentence or phrase of a clause, to show that it constituted a portion of what the Jews called ' the Scripture ' ( ἡ γραφή )."

rebuke the scribes for failure to understand and properly to use Scripture, into indications of rejection on Christ's part of the authority of the Scriptures to which both He and the scribes appealed. Lest it should be thought incredible that such a conclusion should be drawn from such premises, we transcribe Rothe's whole statement.

" On the other hand, we conclude with great probability that the Redeemer did *not* share the conception of His Israelitish contemporaries as to the inspiration of their Bible, as stated above, from the fact that He repeatedly expresses his dissatisfaction with the manner usual among them of looking upon and using the sacred books. He tells the scribes to their face that they do not understand the Scriptures (Matt. xxii. 29; Mark xii. 24), and that it is delusion for them to think to possess eternal life in *them,* therefore in a *book* (John v. 39), even as He also (in the same place) seems to speak disapprovingly of their searching of the Scriptures, because it proceeds from such a perverted point of view." [26]

Thus Jesus' *appeal* to the Scriptures as testifying to Him, and His rebuke to the Jews for not following them while professing to honor them, are made to do duty as a proof that He did not ascribe plenary authority to them.[27]

Furthermore, Rothe's whole treatment of the matter omits altogether to make account of the great decisive consideration of the general tone and manner of Christ's allusions and appeal to the Scriptures, which only culminate in such passages as he has attempted to explain away, and which not only are inconsistent with any other than the same high view of their authority, trustworthiness and inspiration, as that which Rothe infers from similar phenomena to have been the conception of the apostles, but also are necessarily founded on it as its natural expression. The distinction attempted to be drawn between

[26] " Zur Dogmatik," p. 177.

[27] Compare Meyer, *in loc.* (E. T., i. p. 262, note) : " Even Rothe . . . takes δοκεῖτε in the sense of a *delusion*, namely, that they possessed eternal *life* in a *book*. Such explanations are opposed to the high veneration manifested by Jesus towards the Holy Scriptures, especially apparent in John. . . ."

Christ's doctrine of Holy Scripture and that of His apostles is certainly inconsistent with the facts.

But we are more concerned at present to point out that the attempt to draw this distinction must result in undermining utterly all confidence in the New Testament writers as teachers of doctrine. So far as the apostles are concerned, indeed, it would be more correct to say that it is the outgrowth and manifestation of an already present distrust of them as teachers of doctrine. Its very principle is appeal from apostolic teaching to that of Christ, on the ground that the former is not authoritative. How far this rejection of apostolic authority goes is evidenced by the mode of treatment vouchsafed to it. Immediately on drawing out the apostles' doctrine of inspiration, Rothe asks, "But now what dogmatic value has this fact?" And on the ground that "by their fruits ye shall know them," he proceeds to declare that the apostles' doctrine of Scripture led them into such a general use and mode of interpretation of Scripture as Rothe deems wholly unendurable.[28] It is not, then, merely the teaching of the apostles as to what the Scriptures are, but their teaching as to what those Scriptures teach, in which Rothe finds them untrustworthy. It would be impossible but that the canker should eat still more deeply.

Nor is it possible to prevent it from spreading to the undermining of the trustworthiness of even the Lord's teaching itself, for the magnifying of which the distinction purports to be drawn. The artificial manner in which the testimony of the Lord to the authority of the Scriptures is explained away in the attempt to establish the distinction, might be pleaded indeed as an indication that trust in it was not very deeply rooted. And there are other indications that had the Lord been explained to be of the apostles' mind as to Scripture, a way would have been found to free us from the duty of following His teaching.[29] For even *His* exegesis is declared not to be authoritative, seeing that "exegesis is essentially a scientific function, and conditioned on the existence of scientific means, which in relation to the Old Testament were completely at the com-

[28] *Op. cit.*, pp. 181, 182.          [29] *Op. cit.*, pp. 174, 175.

mand of Jesus as little as of His contemporaries"; and the principle of partial limitation at least to the outlook of His day which is involved in such a statement is fully accepted by Rothe.[30] All this may, however, be thought more or less personal to Rothe's own mental attitude, whereas the ultimate undermining of our Lord's authority as teacher of doctrine, as well as that of His apostles, is logically essential to the position assumed.

This may be made plain at once by the very obvious remark that we have no Christ except the one whom the apostles have given to us. Jesus Himself left no treatises on doctrine. He left no written dialogues. We are dependent on the apostles for our whole knowledge of Him, and of what He taught. The portraiture of Jesus which has glorified the world's literature as well as blessed all ages and races with the revelation of a God-man come down from heaven to save the world, is limned by his followers' pencils alone. The record of that teaching which fell from His lips as living water, which if a man drink of he shall never thirst again, is a record by his followers' pens alone. They have painted for us, of course, the Jesus that they knew, and as they knew Him. They have recorded for us the teachings that they heard, and as they heard them. Whatever untrustworthiness attaches to them as deliverers of doctrine, must in some measure shake also our confidence in their report of what their Master was and taught.

But the logic cuts even deeper. For not only have we no

---

[30] Even on an extreme Kenotic view, it is, however, not so certain that *error* should be attributed to the God-man. Prof. Gretillat, of Neuchatel, a Kenotist of the type of Gess and his own colleague Godet, is able to teach that " by reason of the relation which unites the intelligence with the will," our Lord must needs be free not only from sin, but also from all error (*Exposé de Theol. Syst.*, iv. 288). Tholuck occupied a position similar to Rothe's; yet he reminds us that: " Proofs might be brought to show that, even in questions pertaining to learned exegesis " — which are such as our Lord needed to *learn* as a man — " such as those concerning the historical connection of a passage, the author and age of a book, an original spiritual discernment without the culture of the schools may often divine the truth " (" Citations of the Old Testament in the New," tr. in *Bibliotheca Sacra*, xi. p. 615).

Christ but Him whom we receive at the apostles' hands, but this Christ is committed to the trustworthiness of the apostles as teachers. His credit is involved in their credit. He represents His words on earth as but the foundation of one great temple of doctrine, the edifice of which was to be built up by Him through their mouths, as they spoke moved by His Spirit; and thus He makes Himself an accomplice before the fact in all they taught. In proportion as they are discredited as doctrinal guides, in that proportion He is discredited with them. By the promise of the Spirit, He has forever bound His trustworthiness with indissoluble bands to the trustworthiness of His accredited agents in founding His Church, and especially by that great promise recorded for us in John xvi. 12–15: "I have yet many things to say unto you, but ye cannot bear them now. Howbeit when he, the Spirit of truth, is come, he will guide you into all truth; for he shall not speak of himself; but whatsoever he shall hear, that shall he speak: and he will show you things to come. He shall glorify me: for he shall receive of mine, and shall show it unto you. All things that the Father hath are mine: therefore said I, that he shall take of mine and shall show it unto you." Says Dr. C. W. Hodge:[31]

" It is impossible to conceive how the authority of the Master could be conveyed to the teaching of the disciples more emphatically than is here done by Christ. He identifies His teaching and the teaching of the Spirit as parts of one whole; His teaching is carrying out My teaching, it is calling to remembrance what I have told you; it is completing what I have begun. And to make the unity emphatic, He explains why He had reserved so much of His own teaching, and committed the work of revelation to the Spirit. He, in His incarnation and life, comprised all saving truth. He was the revealer of God and the truth and the life. But while some things He had taught while yet with them, He had many things to say which must be postponed because they could not yet bear them. . . . If Christ has re-

---

[31] Sermon on " The Promise of the Spirit," in the volume: " Princeton Sermons." By the Faculty of the Seminary. New York: Fleming H. Revell Co., 1893. P. 33. The whole of this noble sermon should be read.

ferred us to the apostles as teachers of the truths which He would have us know, certainly this primary truth of the authority of the Scriptures themselves can be no exception. All questions as to the extent of this inspiration, as to its exclusive authority, as to whether it extends to words as well as doctrines, as to whether it is infallible or inerrant, or not, are simply questions to be referred to the Word itself."

In such circumstances the attempt to discriminate against the teaching of the apostles in favor of that of Christ, is to contradict the express teaching of Christ Himself, and thus to undermine our confidence in it. We cannot both believe Him and not believe Him. The cry, "Back to Christ!" away from all the imaginations of men's hearts and the cobweb theories which they have spun, must be ever the cry of every Christian heart. But the cry, "Back to Christ!" away from the teachings of His apostles, whose teachings He Himself represents as His own, only delivered by His Spirit through their mouths, is an invitation to desert Christ Himself. It is an invitation to draw back from the Christ of the Bible to some Christ of our own fancy, from the only real to some imaginary Christ. It is to undermine the credit of the whole historical revelation in and through the Christ of God, and to cast us for the ascertainment and authentication of truth on the native powers of our own minds.

### Accommodation or Ignorance?

2. Another method is that of those who seek to preserve themselves from the necessity of accepting the doctrine of inspiration held by the writers of the New Testament, by representing it as merely a matter of accommodation to the prejudices of the Jews, naturally if not necessarily adopted by the first preachers of the Gospel in their efforts to commend to their contemporaries their new teaching as to the way of life.

This position is quite baldly stated by a recent Scotch writer, to whose book, written with a frank boldness, a force and a logical acumen which are far above the common, too little heed has been paid as an indication of the drift of the times.[32] Says Mr. James Stuart:

" The apostles had not merely to reveal the Gospel scheme of salvation to their own and all subsequent ages, but they had to present it in such a form, and support it by such arguments, as should commend it to their more immediate hearers and readers. Notwithstanding its essentially universal character, the Gospel, as it appears in the New Testament, is couched in a particular form, suited to the special circumstances of a particular age and nation. Before the Gospel could reach the hearts of those to whom it was first addressed, prejudices had to be overcome, prepossessions had to be counted on and dealt with. The apostles, in fact, had just to take the men of their time as they found them, adapting their teaching accordingly. Not only so, but there is evidence that the apostles were themselves, to a very great extent, men of their own time, sharing many of the common opinions and even the common prejudices, so that, in arguing *ex concessis*, they were arguing upon grounds that would appear to themselves just and tenable. Now one of the things universally conceded in apostolic times was the inspiration and authority of the Old Testament; another was the legitimacy of certain modes of interpreting and applying the Old Testament. The later Jews, as is well known, cherished a superstitious reverence and attached an overwhelming importance to the letter of the Old Testament, which they regarded as the ' Word of God ' in the fullest and most absolute sense that can possibly be put upon such an expression. The doctors taught and the people believed that the sacred writings were not only inspired, but inspired to the utmost possible or conceivable extent. In the composition of Scripture, the human author was nowhere, and the inspiring Spirit everywhere; not the thoughts alone, but the very words of Scripture were the Word of God, which He communicated by the mouth of the human author, who merely discharged the duty of spokesman and amanuensis, so that what the Scripture contains is the Word of God in as complete and full a sense as if it had been dictated by the lips of God to the human authors, and recorded with something approaching to perfect accuracy. . . . Such being the prevalent view of the inspiration and authority of the Old Testa-

[32] " The Principles of Christianity." Being an Essay towards a More Correct Apprehension of Christian Doctrine, Mainly Soteriological. By James Stuart, M.A. London: Williams & Norgate, 1888. P. 67 *seq.*

ment writings, what could be more natural than that the apostles should make use of these writings to enforce and commend their own ideas? And if the Old Testament were to be used for such a purpose at all, evidently it must be used according to the accepted methods; for to have followed any other — assuming the possibility of such a thing — would have defeated the object aimed at, which was to accommodate the Gospel to established prejudices."

Now, here too, the first remark which needs to be made is that the assertion of "accommodation" on the part of the New Testament writers cannot be made good. To prove "accommodation," two things need to be shown: first, that the apostles did not share these views, and, secondly, that· they nevertheless accommodated their teaching to them. "Accommodation" properly so called cannot take place when the views in question are the proper views of the persons themselves. But even in the above extract Mr. Stuart is led to allow that the apostles shared the current Jewish view of the Scriptures, and at a later point [33] he demonstrates this in an argument of singular lucidity, although in its course he exaggerates the character of their views in his effort to fix a stigma of mechanicalness on them. With what propriety, then, can he speak of "accommodation" in the case? The fact is that the theory of "accommodation" is presented by Mr. Stuart only to enable him the more easily to refuse to be bound by the apostolic teaching in this matter, and as such it has served him as a stepping stone by which he has attained to an even more drastic principle, on which he practically acts: that whenever the apostles can be shown to agree with their contemporaries, their teaching may be neglected. In such cases, he conceives of the New Testament writers "being inspired and guided by current opinion," [34] and reasons thus: [35]

" Now it is unquestionable that the New Testament writers in so regarding the Old Testament were not enunciating a new theory of inspiration or interpretation, they were simply adopting and follow-

[33] P. 345 *seq.*
[34] P. 213.
[35] Pp. 348, 349.

**ing out** the current theory. . . . In matters of this kind . . . the
New Testament writers were completely dominated by the spirit of
the age, so that their testimony on the question of Scripture inspiration possesses no independent value." " If these popular notions were
infallibly correct before they were taken up and embodied in the
New Testament writings, they are infallibly correct still; if they
were incorrect before they were taken up and embodied in the New
Testament writings, they are incorrect still." [36]

   This is certainly most remarkable argumentation, and the
principle asserted is probably one of the most singular to which
thinking men ever committed themselves, viz., that a body of
religious teachers, claiming authority for themselves as such,
are trustworthy *only* when they teach *novelties*. It is the
apotheosis of the old Athenian and new modern spirit, which
has leisure and heart " for nothing else but either to tell or
hear some new thing." Nevertheless, it is a principle far from
uncommon among those who are seeking justification for themselves in refusing the leadership of the New Testament writers
in the matter of the authority and inspiration of the Scriptures. And, of late, it is, of course, taking upon itself in certain
quarters a new form, the form imposed by the new view of the
origin of Christian thought in Hellenic sources, which has
been given such vogue by Dr. Harnack and rendered popular
in English-speaking lands by the writings of the late Dr. Hatch.
For example, we find it expressed in this form in the recent
valuable studies on the First Epistle of Clement of Rome, by
Lic. Wrede.[37] Clement's views of the Old Testament Scriptures
are recognized as of the highest order; he looks upon them as
a marvelous and infallible book whose very letters are sacred,
as a veritable oracle, the most precious possession of the
Church. These high views were shared by the whole Church of
his day, and, indeed, of the previous age: "The view which

   [36] P. 70. The immediate reference of these last words is to matters of
criticism and exegesis; but according to the contextual connection they
would also be used of matters of inspiration.

   [37] " Untersuchungen zum ersten Klemensbriefe." Von Lic. Theol. W.
Wrede, Privatdocent der Theologie in Göttingen. Göttingen: Vanderhoeck
& Ruprecht's Verlag, 1891. Pp. 60, 75 *seq.*

Clement has of the Old Testament, and the use which he makes of it, show in themselves no essential peculiarities in comparison with the most nearly related Christian writings, especially the Pauline epistles, the Epistle to the Hebrews and the Epistle of Barnabas." And yet, according to Wrede, this view rests on "the Hellenistic conception of inspiration, according to which the individual writers were passive instruments of God."[38] Whether, however, the contemporary influence is thought to be Jewish or Greek, it is obvious that the appeal to it in such matters has, as its only intention, to free us from the duty of following the apostles and can have as its only effect to undermine their authority. We may no doubt suppose at the beginning that we seek only to separate the kernel from the husk; but a principle which makes husk of all that can be shown to have anything in common with what was believed by any body of contemporaries, Hebrew or Greek, is so very drastic that it will leave nothing which we can surely trust. On this principle the Golden Rule itself is not authoritative, because something like it may be found in Jewish tradition and among the heathen sages. It certainly will not serve to make novelty the test of authority.

From the ethical point of view, however, this theory is preferable to that of "accommodation," and it is probable that part, at least, of the impulse which led Mr. Stuart to substitute it for the theory of "accommodation," with which he began, arose from a more or less clear perception of the moral implications of the theory of "accommodation." Under the impulse of that theory he had been led to speak of the procedure of the apostles in such language as this: "The sole principle that regulates all their appeals to the Old Testament, is that of obtaining, at whatever cost, support for their own favorite ideas."[39] Is it any wonder that the reaction took place and an attempt was made to shift the burden from the *veracity* to the *knowledge* of the New Testament writers?[40] In Mr. Stuart's

---

[38] Compare the review of Wrede by Prof. H. M. Scott, in *The Presbyterian and Reformed Review*, January, 1893, p. 163.

[39] P. 66.         [40] P. 353.

case we see very clearly, then, the effect of a doctrine of "accommodation" on the credit of the New Testament writers. His whole book is written in order to assign reason why he will not yield authority to these writers in their doctrine of a sacrificial atonement. This was due to their Jewish type of thought. But when the doctrine of accommodation is tried as a ground for the rejection of their authority, it is found to cut too deeply even for Mr. Stuart. He wishes to be rid of the authority of the New Testament writers, not to impeach their veracity; and so he discards it in favor of the less plausible, indeed, but also less deeply cutting canon, that the apostles are not to be followed when they agree with contemporary thought, because in these elements they are obviously speaking out of their own consciousness, as the products of their day, and not as proclaimers of the *new* revelation in Christ. Their inspiration, in a word, "was not *plenary* or *universal* — extending, that is, to all matters whatever which they speak about — but *partial* or *special,* being limited to securing the accurate communication of that plan of salvation which they had so profoundly experienced, and which they were commissioned to proclaim." [41] In all else "the New Testament writers are simply on a level with their contemporaries." It may not be uninstructive to note that under such a formula Mr. Stuart not only rejects the teachings of these writers as to the nature and extent of inspiration, but also their teaching as to the sacrificial nature of the very plan of salvation which they were especially commissioned to proclaim. But what it is our business at present to point out is that the doctrine of accommodation is so obviously a blow at not only the trustworthiness, but the very veracity of the New Testament authors, that Mr. Stuart, even after asserting it, is led to permit it to fall into neglect.

And must it not be so? It may be easy indeed to confuse it with that progressive method of teaching which every wise teacher uses, and which our Lord also employed (John xvi. 12 *seq.*); it may be easy to represent it as nothing more than that harmless wisdom which the apostle proclaimed as the

[41] P. 258.

principle of his life, as he went about the world becoming all things to all men. But how different it is from either! It is one thing to adapt the teaching of truth to the stage of receptivity of the learner; it is another thing to adopt the errors of the time as the very matter to be taught. It is one thing to refrain from unnecessarily arousing the prejudices of the learner, that more ready entrance may be found for the truth; it is another thing to adopt those prejudices as our own, and to inculcate them as the very truths of God. It was one thing for Paul to become "all things to all men" that he might gain them to the truth; it was another for Peter to dissemble at Antioch, and so confirm men in their error. The accommodation attributed to the New Testament writers is a method by which they did and do not undeceive but deceive; not a method by which they teach the truth more winningly and to more; but a method by which they may be held to have taught along with the truth also error. The very object of attributing it to them is to enable us to separate their teaching into two parts — the true and the false; and to justify us in refusing a part while accepting a part at their hands. At the best it must so undermine the trustworthiness of the apostles as deliverers of doctrine as to subject their whole teaching to our judgment for the separation of the true from the false; at the worst, it must destroy their trustworthiness by destroying our confidence in their veracity. Mr. Stuart chose the better path; but he did so, as all who follow him must, by deserting the principle of accommodation, which leads itself along the worse road. With it as a starting point we must impeach the New Testament writers as lacking either knowledge or veracity.

### TEACHING VERSUS OPINION

3. A third type of procedure, in defense of refusal to be bound by the doctrine of the New Testament writers as to inspiration, proceeds by drawing a distinction between the belief and the teaching of these writers; and affirming that, although it is true that they did believe and hold a high doctrine of in-

spiration, yet they do not explicitly teach it, and that we are bound, not by their opinions, but only by their explicit teaching.

This appears to be the conception which underlies the treatment of the matter by Archdeacon (then Canon) Farrar, in his " Life and Work of St. Paul." Speaking of Paul's attitude towards Scripture, Dr. Farrar says: [42]

" He shared, doubtless, in the views of the later Jewish schools — the Tanaim and Amoraim — on the nature of inspiration. These views, which we find also in Philo, made the words of Scripture co-extensive and identical with the words of God, and in the clumsy and feeble hands of the more fanatical Talmudists often attached to the dead letter an importance which stifled or destroyed the living sense. But as this extreme and mechanical literalism — this claim to absolute infallibility even in accidental details and passing allusions — this superstitious adoration of the letters and vocables of Scripture, as though they were the articulate vocables and immediate autograph of God — finds no encouragement in any part of Scripture, and very distinct discouragement in more than one of the utterances of Christ, so there is not a single passage in which any approach to it is dogmatically stated in the writings of St. Paul."

This passage lacks somewhat more in point of clearness than it does in point of rhetorical fire. But three things seem to be sufficiently plain: (1) That Dr. Farrar thinks that Paul shared the views of the Tanaim, the Amoraim and Philo as to the nature of inspiration. (2) That he admits that these views claimed for Scripture " absolute infallibility even in accidental details and passing allusions." (3) That nevertheless he does not feel bound to accept this doctrine at Paul's hands, because, though Paul held it, he is thought not to have " dogmatically stated " it.

Now, the distinction which is here drawn seems, in general, a reasonable one. No one is likely to assert infallibility for the apostles in aught else than in their official teaching. And whatever they may be shown to have held apart from their official teaching, may readily be looked upon with only that respect

[42] *Op. cit.*, Vol. i. p. 49

which we certainly must accord to the opinions of men of such exceptional intellectual and spiritual insight. But it is more difficult to follow Dr. Farrar when it is asked whether this distinction can be established in the present matter. It does not seem to be true that there are no didactic statements as to inspiration in Paul's letters, or in the rest of the New Testament, such as implicate and carry into the sphere of matters taught, the whole doctrine that underlies their treatment of Scripture. The assertion in the term "theopneustic" in such a passage as II Tim. iii. 16, for example, cannot be avoided by any construction of the passage; and the doctrine taught in the assertion must be understood to be the doctrine which that term connoted to Paul who uses it, not some other doctrine read into it by us.

It is further necessary to inquire what sources we have in a case like that of Paul, to inform us as to what his opinions were, apart from and outside of his teachings. It might conceivably have happened that some of his contemporaries should have recorded for us some account of opinions held by him to which he has given no expression in his epistles; or some account of actions performed by him involving the manifestation of judgment — somewhat similar, say, to Paul's own account of Peter's conduct in Antioch (Gal. ii. 11 *seq.*). A presumption may be held to lie also that he shared the ordinary opinions of his day in certain matters lying outside the scope of his teachings, as, for example, with reference to the form of the earth, or its relation to the sun; and it is not inconceivable that the form of his language, when incidentally adverting to such matters, might occasionally play into the hands of such a presumption. But it is neither on the ground of such a presumption, nor on the ground of such external testimony, that Dr. Farrar ascribes to him views as to inspiration similar to those of his Jewish contemporaries. It is distinctly on the ground of what he finds on a study of the body of official teaching which Paul has left to us. Dr. Farrar discovers that these views as to the nature of Scripture so underlie, are so assumed in, are so implied by, are so interwoven with Paul's official teaching that he is unwillingly driven to perceive that they were Paul's opinions. With what color of reason then can they be separated from his teaching?

There is raised here, moreover, a very important and far-reaching question, which few will be able to decide in Dr. Farrar's sense. What is taught in the New Testament? And what is the mode of its teaching? If we are to fall in with Dr. Farrar and say that nothing is taught except what is "dogmatically stated" in formal didactic form, the occasional character of the New Testament epistles would become a source of grave loss to us, instead of, as it otherwise is, a source of immense gain; the parabolic clothing of much of Christ's teaching would become a device to withhold from us all instruction on the matters of which the parables treat; and all that is most fundamental in religious truth, which, as a rule, is rather assumed everywhere in Scripture as a basis for particular applications than formally stated, would be removed out of the sphere of Biblical doctrine. Such a rule, in a word, would operate to turn the whole of Biblical teaching on its head, and to reduce it from a body of principles inculcated by means of examples into a mere congeries of instances hung in the air. The whole advance in the attitude of Dogmatics towards the Scriptures which has been made by modern scholarship is, moreover, endangered by this position. It was the fault of the older dogmatists to depend too much on isolated proof-texts for the framing and defense of doctrine. Dr. Farrar would have us return to this method. The alternative, commended justly to us by the whole body of modern scholarship, is, as Schleiermacher puts it, to seek "a form of Scripture proof on a larger scale than can be got from single texts," to build our systematic theology, in a word, on the basis, not of the occasional dogmatic statements of Scripture alone, taken separately and, as it were, in shreds, but on the basis of the theologies of the Scripture — to reproduce first the theological thought of each writer or group of writers and then to combine these several theologies (each according to its due historical place) into the one consistent system, consentaneous parts of which they are found to be.[43] In rejecting this method, Dr. Farrar discredits the whole science of Biblical Theology. From its standpoint it is incredible that one should attribute less importance and authoritativeness to the fundamental conceptions that underlie, color and give form to all of Paul's teaching than to the chance didactic statements he may have been led to make by this or that circumstance at the call of which his letters happened to be written. This certainly would be tithing mint and anise and cummin and omitting the weightier matters of the law.

That this mode of presenting the matter must lead, no less than the others which have already come under review, to undermining the authority of the New Testament writers as deliverers of doctrine, must already be obvious. It begins by discrediting them as leaders in doctrinal thought and substituting for this a sporadic authority in explicit dogmatic statements. In Dr. Farrar's own hands it proceeds by quite undermining our confidence in the apostles as teachers, through an accusation lodged against them, not only of holding wrong views in doctrine, but even of cherishing as fundamental conceptions theological fancies which are in their very essence superstitious and idolatrous, and in their inevitable outcome ruinous to faith and honor. For Dr. Farrar does not mince matters when he expresses his opinion of that doctrine of inspiration — in its nature and its proper effects — which Philo held and the Jewish Rabbis and in which Paul, according to his expressed conviction, shared. "To say that every word and sentence and letter of Scripture is divine and supernatural, is a mechanical and useless shibboleth, nay, more, a human idol, and (constructively, at least) a dreadful blasphemy." It is a superstitious — he tells us that he had almost said fetish-worshiping — dogma, and "not only unintelligible, but profoundly dangerous." It

---

[43] The present writer has tried to state the true relations of Systematic and Biblical theology in a discussion of " The Idea of Systematic Theology Considered as a Science " (Inaugural Address), pp. 22-28. A. D. F. Randolph & Co., 1888. He ventures to refer the reader to it.

"has in many ages filled the world with misery and ruin," and "has done more than any other dogma to corrupt the whole of exegesis with dishonest casuistry, and to shake to its centre the religious faith of thousands, alike of the most ignorant and of the most cultivated, in many centuries, and most of all in our own."[44] Yet these are the views which Dr. Farrar is forced to allow that Paul shared! For Philo "held the most rigid views of inspiration"; than him indeed "Aqiba himself used no stronger language on the subject"[45]—Aqiba, "the greatest of the Tanaites";[46] and it was the views of the Tanaim, Amoraim and Philo, which Dr. Farrar tells us the apostle shared. How after this Dr. Farrar continues to look upon even the "dogmatic statements" of Paul as authoritative, it is hard to see. By construction he was a fetish worshiper and placed Scripture upon an idol's pedestal. The doctrines which he held and which underlie his teaching were unintelligible, useless, idolatrous, blasphemous and profoundly dangerous, and actually have shaken to its centre the religious faith of thousands. On such a tree what other than evil fruits could grow?

No doubt something of this may be attributed to the exaggeration characteristic of Dr. Farrar's language and thought. Obviously Paul's view of inspiration was not altogether identical with that of contemporary Judaism; it differed from it somewhat in the same way that his use of Scripture differed from that of the Rabbis of his day. But it is one with Philo's and Aqiba's on the point which with Dr. Farrar is decisive: alike with them he looked upon Scripture as "absolutely infallible, even in accidental details and passing allusions," as the very Word of God, His "Oracles," to use his own high phrase, and therefore Dr. Farrar treats the two views as essentially one. But the situation is only modified, not relieved, by the recognition of this fact.

In any event the pathway on which we enter when we begin

[44] "Inspiration.' 'A Clerical Symposium. By the Rev. Archdeacon Farrar and others. London: James Nisbet and Co., 1888. 2d ed. Pp. 219, 241.

[45] "History of Interpretation." Bampton Lectures. By F. W. Farrar, D.D. London: Macmillan, 1880. P. 147.          [46] P. 71.

to distinguish between the didactic statements and the fundamental conceptions of a body of incidental teaching, with a view to accepting the former and rejecting the latter, cannot but lead to a general undermining of the authority of the whole. Only if we could believe in a quite mechanical and magical process of inspiration (from believing in which Dr. Farrar is no doubt very far) by which the subject's " dogmatical statements " were kept entirely separate from and unaffected by his fundamental conceptions, could such an attitude be logically possible. In that case we should have to view these " dogmatical statements " as not Paul's at all, standing, as they do *ex hypothesi,* wholly disconnected with his own fundamental thought, but as spoken through him by an overmastering spiritual influence; as a phenomenon, in a word, similar to the oracles of heathen shrines, and without analogy in Scripture except perhaps in such cases as that of Balaam. In proportion as we draw back from so magical a conception of the mode of inspiration, in that proportion our refusal of authority to the fundamental conceptions of the New Testament writers must invade also their " dogmatical statements." We must logically, in a word, ascribe like authority to the whole body of their teaching, in its foundation and superstructure alike, or we must withhold it in equal measure from all; or, if we withhold it from one and not the other, the discrimination would most naturally be made against the superstructure rather than against the foundation.

## Facts versus Doctrine

4. Finally, an effort may be made to justify our holding a lower doctrine of inspiration than that held by the writers of the New Testament, by appealing to the so-called phenomena of the Scriptures and opposing these to the doctrine of the Scriptures, with the expectation, apparently, of justifying a modification of the doctrine taught by the Scriptures by the facts embedded in the Scriptures.

The essential principle of this method of procedure is shared

by very many who could scarcely be said to belong to the class
who are here more specifically in mind, inasmuch as they do
not begin by explicitly recognizing the doctrine of inspiration
held by the New Testament writers to be that high doctrine
which the Church and the best scientific exegesis agree in understanding them to teach.[47] Every attempt to determine or

[47] On the contrary these writers usually minimize the Biblical definition of inspiration. Thus Dr. Marvin R. Vincent, who is immediately to be
quoted (*op. c.* p. 15), tells us " Scripture does not define the nature and
extent of its own inspiration. The oft-quoted passage of II Tim. iii. 16
really gives us no light on that point. . . . The passage does indeed point
out certain *effects* which attend the use of inspired writings. . . . But after
all, we are no nearer than ever to an answer to the question, What *is*
inspiration? . . . So that we must fall back on the facts, on the phenomena
of the Bible as we have it." But the deck is not cleared by such remarks;
after all, Paul does assert *something* by calling the Scriptures Theopneustic, and what the thing is that he asserts in the use of this predicate,
is not discoverable from an examination into what the Scriptures *are*, but
only by an examination into what Paul *means;* but what Paul *understands*
by theopneustic, Dr. Vincent makes no effort to investigate. This whole
procedure is typical. Thus, for example, the Rev. J. Paterson Smyth, in
his recent book, " How God Inspired the Bible " (p. 64), proceeds in an
exactly similar manner. " Our theory of inspiration must be learned from
the facts presented in the Bible ,and in order to be correct it must be consistent with all these facts. . . . I want to find out what I can about inspiration. God has nowhere revealed to me exactly what it is. He has told me
it is a divine influence, an in-breathing of the Holy Ghost on the spirit of
the ancient writers. But I cannot tell how much that means or what effects
I should expect from it. I have, therefore, no way of finding out except by
examining the phenomena presented by the Bible itself." This method
amounts simply to discarding the guidance of the doctrine of Scripture in
favor of our own doctrine founded on our examination of the nature of
Scripture. Mr. Smyth cannot close his eyes to certain outstanding facts on
the surface of Scripture, indicatory of the doctrine as to Scripture held by
the Biblical writers (pp. 36 and 106), though he makes no effort to collect
and estimate all such phenomena. And when he realizes that some may be
affected even by his meagre statement of them so far as to say that " the
strong expressions just here quoted from some of the Bible writers, and
even from our Lord Himself, convince me that the theory of verbal inspiration is most probably true," he has only such an answer as the following: " Well, reader, you will find a good many thoughtful people disagree-
ing with you. Why? Because, while fully receiving these arguments as a
proof of God's inspiration of the Bible, they have looked a little further
than the surface to judge how much God's inspiration implies, and they
cannot believe from their examination of Scripture that it implies what is
known as verbal inspiration " (p. 109). Mr. Smyth means by " verbal

modify the Biblical doctrine of inspiration by an appeal to the actual characteristics of the Bible must indeed proceed on an identical principle. It finds, perhaps, as plausible a form of assertion possible to it in the declaration of Dr. Marvin R. Vincent[48] that "our only safe principle is that *inspiration is consistent with the phenomena of Scripture*"—to which one of skeptical turn might respond that whether *the inspiration claimed by Scripture* is consistent with the phenomena of Scripture after all requires some proof, while one of a more believing frame might respond that it is a safer principle that the phenomena of Scripture are consistent with its inspiration. Its crudest expression may be seen in such a book as Mr. Horton's "Inspiration and the Bible," which we have already had occasion to mention. Mr. Horton chooses to retain the term, "inspiration," as representing "the *common sense* of Christians of all ages and in all places" as to the nature of their Scriptures,[49] but asserts that this term is to be understood to mean just what the Bible *is*—that is to say, whatever any given writer chooses to think the Bible to be. When Paul affirms in II Tim. iii. 16 that every Scripture is "inspired by God," therefore, we are not to enter into a philological and exegetical investigation to discover what Paul meant to affirm by the use of this word, but simply to say that Paul must have meant to affirm the Bible to be what we find it to be. Surely no way could be invented which would more easily enable us to substitute our thought for the apostles' thought, and to pro-

inspiration" the theory of mechanical dictation. But putting that aside as a man of straw, what it is difficult for us to understand is how "thoughtful people" can frame a theory of inspiration after only such shallow investigation of the Scriptural doctrine of inspiration, and how "thoughtful people" can assign their inability to believe a doctrine, an inability based on their own conception of what Scripture is, as any proof that that doctrine is not taught by the "strong expressions" of the Bible writers and the Lord Himself. Is it any more rationalistic to correct the Scriptural doctrine of the origin of the universe from our investigations of the nature of things, than it is to correct the Scriptural doctrine of inspiration from our investigations of the nature of Scripture?

[48] *Mag. of Christian Lit.*, April 1892.

[49] *Op. cit.*, p. 5.

claim our crudities under the sanction of their great names. Operating by it, Mr. Horton is enabled to assert that the Bible is "inspired," and yet to teach that God's hand has entered it only in a providential way, by His dealings through long ages with a people who gradually wrought out a history, conceived hopes, and brought all through natural means to an expression in a faulty and often self-contradictory record, which we call inspired only "because by reading it and studying it we can find our way to God, we can find what is His will for us and how we can carry out that will." [50] The most naïve expression of the principle in question may be found in such a statement as the following, from the pen of Dr. W. G. Blaikie: "In our mode of dealing with this question the main difference between us is, that you lay your stress on certain general considerations, and on certain specific statements of Scripture. We, on the other hand, while accepting the specific statements, lay great stress also on the *structure* of Scripture as we find it, on certain phenomena which lie on the surface, and on the inextricable difficulties which are involved in carrying out your view in detail." [51] This statement justly called out the rebuke of Dr. Robert Watts,[52] that "while the principle of your theory is a mere inference from apparent discrepancies not as yet explained, the principle of the theory you oppose is the formally expressed utterances of prophets and apostles, and of Christ Himself."

Under whatever safeguards, indeed, it may be attempted, and with whatever caution it may be prosecuted, the effort to modify the teaching of Scripture as to its own inspiration by an appeal to the observed characteristics of Scripture, is an attempt not to obtain a clearer knowledge of what the Scriptures teach, but to *correct* that teaching. And to *correct* the teaching of Scripture is to proclaim Scripture untrustworthy as a witness to doctrine. The procedure in question is precisely similar

[50] *Op. cit.*, p. 240.

[51] " Letter to the Rev. Andrew A. Bonar, D.D." By William G. Blaikie, D.D., LL.D. 2d ed. Edinburgh: Macniven & Wallace, 1890. P. 5.

[52] " A Letter to the Rev. Prof. William G. Blaikie, D.D., LL.D." By Robert Watts, D.D., LL.D. Edinburgh: R. W. Hunter, 1890. P. 30.

to saying that the Bible's doctrine of creation is to be derived not alone from the teachings of the Bible as to creation, but from the facts obtained through a scientific study of creation; that the Bible's doctrine as to man is to be found not in the Bible's deliverances on the subject, but "while accepting these, we lay great stress also on the *structure* of man as we find him, and on the inextricable difficulties which are involved in carrying out the Bible's teaching in detail"; that the Bible's doctrine of justification is to be obtained by retaining the term as commended by the common sense of the Christian world and understanding by it just what we find justification to be in actual life. It is precisely similar to saying that Mr. Darwin's doctrine of natural selection is to be determined not solely by what Mr. Darwin says concerning it, but equally by what we, in our own independent study of nature, find to be true as to natural selection. A historian of thought who proceeded on such a principle would scarcely receive the commendation of students of history, however much his writings might serve certain party ends. Who does not see that underlying this whole method of procedure — in its best and in its worst estate alike — there is apparent an unwillingness to commit ourselves without reserve to the *teaching* of the Bible, either because that teaching is distrusted or already disbelieved; and that it is a grave logical error to suppose that the teaching of the Bible as to inspiration can be corrected in this way any otherwise than by showing it not to be in accordance with the facts? The proposed method, therefore, does not conduct us to a somewhat modified doctrine of inspiration, but to a disproof of inspiration; by correcting the doctrine delivered by the Biblical writers, it discredits those writers as teachers of doctrine.

Let it not be said that in speaking thus we are refusing the inductive method of establishing doctrine. We follow the inductive method. When we approach the Scriptures to ascertain their doctrine of inspiration, we proceed by collecting the whole body of relevant facts. Every claim they make to inspiration is a relevant fact; every statement they make concerning inspiration is a relevant fact; every allusion they make to the subject is a relevant fact; every fact indicative of the attitude they hold towards Scripture is a relevant fact. But the characteristics of their own writings are not facts relevant to the determination of *their doctrine*. Nor let it be said that we are desirous of determining the true, as distinguished from the Scriptural, doctrine of inspiration otherwise than inductively. We are averse, however, to supposing that in such an inquiry the relevant "phenomena" of Scripture are not first of all and before all the claims of Scripture and second only to them its use of previous Scripture. And we are averse to excluding these primary "phenomena" and building our doctrine solely or mainly upon the characteristics and structure of Scripture, especially as determined by some special school of modern research by critical methods certainly not infallible and to the best of our own judgment not even reasonable. And we are certainly averse to supposing that this induction, if it reaches results not absolutely consentaneous with the teachings of Scripture itself, has done anything other than discredit those teachings, or that in discrediting them, it has escaped discrediting the doctrinal authority of Scripture.

Nor again is it to be thought that we refuse to use the actual characteristics of Scripture as an aid in, and a check upon, our exegesis of Scripture, as we seek to discover its doctrine of inspiration. We do not simply admit, on the contrary, we affirm that in every sphere the observed fact may throw a broad and most helpful light upon the written text. It is so in the narrative of creation in the first chapter of Genesis; which is only beginning to be adequately understood as science is making her first steps in reading the records of God's creative hand in the structure of the world itself. It is preëminently so in the written prophecies, the dark sayings of which are not seldom first illuminated by the light cast back upon them by their fulfillment. As Scripture interprets Scripture, and fulfillment interprets prediction, so may fact interpret assertion. And this is as true as regards the Scriptural assertion of the fact of inspiration as elsewhere. No careful student of the Bible doctrine of inspiration will neglect anxiously to try his conclusions as to the teachings of Scripture by the observed characteristics and "structure" of Scripture, and in trying he may and no doubt will find occasion to modify his conclusions as at first apprehended. But it is one thing to correct our exegetical processes and so modify our exegetical conclusions in the new light obtained by a study of the facts, and quite another to modify, by the facts of the structure of Scripture, the Scriptural teaching itself, as exegetically ascertained; and it is to this latter that we should be led by making the facts of structure and the facts embedded in Scripture co-factors of the same rank in the so-called inductive ascertainment of the doctrine of inspiration. Direct exegesis after all has its rights: we may seek aid from every quarter in our efforts to perform its processes with precision and obtain its results with purity; but we cannot allow it results to be "modified" by extraneous considerations. Let us by all means be careful in determining the doctrine of Scripture, but let us also be fully honest in determining it; and if we count it a crime to permit our ascertainment of the facts recorded in Scripture to be unduly swayed by our conception of the doctrine taught in Scripture, let us count it equally a crime to permit our ascertainment of its doctrine to be unduly swayed or colored by our conception of the nature of the facts of its structure or of the facts embedded in its record. We cannot, therefore, appeal from the doctrine of Scripture as exegetically established to the facts of the structure of Scripture or the facts embedded in Scripture, in the hope of modifying the doctrine. If the teaching and the facts of Scripture are in harmony the appeal is useless. If they are in disharmony, we cannot follow both — we must choose one and reject the other. And the attempt to make the facts of Scripture co-factors of equal rank with the teaching of Scripture is ascertaining the true doctrine of inspiration, is really an attempt to modify the doctrine taught by Scripture by an appeal to the facts, while concealing from ourselves the fact that we have modified it, and in modifying corrected it, and, of course, in correcting it, discredited Scripture as a teacher of doctrine.

Probably these four types of procedure will include most of

the methods by which men are to-day seeking to free themselves from the necessity of following the Scriptural doctrine of inspiration, while yet looking to Scripture as the source of doctrine. Is it not plain that on every one of them the outcome must be to discredit Scripture as a doctrinal guide? The human mind is very subtle, but with all its subtlety it will hardly be able to find a way to refuse to follow Scripture in one of the doctrines it teaches without undermining its authority as a teacher of doctrine.

## II

### IMMENSE WEIGHT OF EVIDENCE FOR THE BIBLICAL DOCTRINE

It is only to turn another face of the proposition with which we are dealing towards us, to emphasize next the important fact, that, the state of the case being such as we have found it, the evidence for the truth of the doctrine of the plenary inspiration of Scripture is just the whole body of evidence which goes to show that the apostles are trustworthy teachers of doctrine.

Language is sometimes made use of which would seem to imply that the amount or weight of the evidence offered for the truth of the doctrine that the Scriptures are the Word of God in such a sense that their words deliver the truth of God without error, is small. It is on the contrary just the whole body of evidence which goes to prove the writers of the New Testament to be trustworthy as deliverers of doctrine. It is just the same evidence in amount and weight which is adduced in favor of any other Biblical doctrine. It is the same weight and amount of evidence precisely which is adducible for the truth of the doctrines of the Incarnation, of the Trinity, of the Divinity of Christ, of Justification by Faith, of Regeneration by the Holy Spirit, of the Resurrection of the Body, of Life Everlasting. It is, of course, not absurdly intended that every Biblical doctrine is taught in the Scriptures with equal clearness, with equal explicitness, with equal frequency. Some doctrines are stated with an explicit precision that leaves little to systematic theology in its efforts to define the truth on all sides, except to repeat the words which the Biblical writers have used to teach it — as for example the doctrine of Justification by Faith. Others are not formulated in Scripture at all, but are taught only in their elements, which the systematician must collect and combine and so arrive finally at the doctrine — as for example the doctrine of the Trinity. Some are adverted to so frequently as to form the whole warp and woof of Scripture — as for example the doctrine of redemption in the blood of Christ. Others are barely alluded to here and there, in connections where the stress is really on other matters — as for example the doctrine of the fall of the angels. But however explicitly or incidentally, however frequently or rarely, however emphatically or allusively, they may be taught, when exegesis has once done its work and shown that they are taught by the Biblical writers, all these doctrines stand as supported by the same weight and amount of evidence — the evidence of the trustworthiness of the Biblical writers as teachers of doctrine. We cannot say that we will believe these writers when they assert a doctrine a hundred times and we will not believe them if they assert it only ten times or only once; that we will believe them in the doctrines they make the main subjects of discourse, but not in those which they advert to incidentally; that we will believe them in those that they teach as conclusions of formal arguments, but not in those which they use as premises wherewith to reach those conclusions; that we will believe them in those they explicitly formulate and dogmatically teach, but not in those which they teach only in their separate parts and elements. The question is not *how* they teach a doctrine, but *do* they teach it; and when that question is once settled affirmatively, the weight of evidence that commends this doctrine to us as true is the same in every case; and that is the whole body of evidence which goes to show that the Biblical writers are trustworthy as teachers of doctrine. The Biblical doctrine of inspiration, therefore, has in its favor just this whole weight and amount of evidence. It follows on the one hand that it cannot rationally be rejected save on the ground of evidence which will outweigh the whole body of evidence which goes to authenticate the Biblical writers as trustworthy witnesses to and teachers of doctrine. And it follows, on the other hand, that if the Biblical doctrine of inspiration is rejected, our freedom from its trammels is bought logically at the somewhat serious cost of discrediting the evidence which goes to show that the Biblical writers are trustworthy as teachers of doctrine. In this sense, the fortunes of distinctive Christianity are bound up with those of the Biblical doctrine of inspiration.

Let it not be said that thus we found the whole Christian system upon the doctrine of plenary inspiration. We found the whole Christian system on the doctrine of plenary inspiration as little as we found  it upon the doctrine of angelic existences. Were there no such thing as inspiration, Christianity would be true, and all its essential doctrines would be credibly witnessed to us in the generally trustworthy reports of the teaching of our Lord and of His authoritative agents in founding the Church, preserved in the writings of the apostles and their first followers, and in the historical witness of the living Church. Inspiration is not the most fundamental of Christian doctrines, nor even the first thing we prove about the Scriptures. It is the last and crowning fact as to the Scriptures. These we first prove authentic, historically credible, generally trustworthy, before we prove them inspired. And the proof of their authenticity, credibility, general trustworthiness would give us a firm basis for Christianity prior to any knowledge on our part of their inspiration, and apart indeed from the existence of inspiration. The present writer, in order to prevent all misunderstanding, desires to repeat here what he has said on every proper occasion — that he is far from contending that without inspiration there could be no Christianity. "Without any inspiration," he added, when making this affirmation on his induction into the work of teaching the

Bible [53] — "without any inspiration we could have had Christianity; yea, and men could still have heard the truth and through it been awakened, and justified, and sanctified, and glorified. The verities of our faith would remain historically proven to us — so bountiful has God been in His fostering care — even had we no Bible; and through those verities, salvation." We are in entire harmony in this matter with what we conceive to be the very true statement recently made by Dr. George P. Fisher, that "if the authors of the Bible were credible reporters of revelations of God, whether in the form of historical transactions of which they were witnesses, or of divine mysteries that were unveiled to their minds, their testimony would be entitled to belief, even if they were shut up to their unaided faculties in communicating what they had thus received." [54] We are in entire sympathy in this matter, therefore, with the protest which Dr. Marcus Dods raised in his famous address at the meeting of the Alliance of the Reformed Churches at London, against representing that "the infallibility of the Bible is the ground of the whole Christian faith." [55] We judge with him that it is very important indeed that such a misapprehension, if it is anywhere current, should be corrected. What we are at present arguing is something entirely different from such an overstrained view of the importance of inspiration to the very existence of Christian faith, and something which has no connection with it. We do not think that the

[53] " Discourses Occasioned by the Inauguration of Benj. B. Warfield, D.D., to the Chair of New Testament Exegesis and Literature in the Western Theological Seminary, April 25, 1880." Pittsburgh, 1880. P. 46. Cf. " Inspiration." By Prof. A. A. Hodge and Prof. B. B. Warfield. Philadelphia: Presbyterian Board of Publication, 1881. Pp. 7, 8 (also in *The Presbyterian Review* for April, 1881). Also, " The Inspiration of the Scriptures." By Francis L. Patton, D.D. Philadelphia: Presbyterian Board of Publication, 1869. Pp. 22, 23, 54.

[54] *The Congregationalist*, Nov. 3, 1892; *The Magazine of Christian Literature*, Dec., 1892, p. 236, first column. This whole column should be read; its statement and illustration are alike admirable.

[55] This address may be most conveniently consulted in *The Expositor* for October, 1888, pp. 301, 302. In expressing our concurrence with portions of this address and of Dr. Fisher's papers just quoted, we are not to be understood, of course, as concurring with their whole contents.

doctrine of plenary inspiration is the ground of Christian faith, but if it was held and taught by the New Testament writers, we think it an element in the Christian faith; a very important and valuable element; [56] an element that appeals to our acceptance on precisely the same ground as every other element of the faith, viz., on the ground of our recognition of the writers of the New Testament as trustworthy witnesses to doctrine; an element of the Christian faith, therefore, which cannot be rejected without logically undermining our trust in all the other elements of distinctive Christianity by undermining the evidence on which this trust rests. We must indeed prove the authenticity, credibility and general trustworthiness of the New Testament writings before we prove their inspiration; and even were they not inspired this proof would remain valid and we should give them accordant trust. But just because this proof is valid, we must trust these writings in their witness to their inspiration, if they give such witness; and if we refuse to trust them here, we have in principle refused them trust everywhere. In such circumstances their inspiration is bound up inseparably with their trustworthiness, and therefore with all else that we receive on trust from them.

On the other hand, we need to remind ourselves that to

[56] How important and valuable this element of the Christian faith is, it is not the purpose of this paper to point out. Let it suffice here to say briefly that it is (1) the element which gives detailed certitude to the delivery of doctrine in the New Testament, and (2) the element by which the individual Christian is brought into immediate relation to God in the revelation of truth through the prophets and apostles. The importance of these factors in the Christian life could not be overstated. The importance of the recognition of plenary inspiration to the preservation of sound doctrine is negatively illustrated by the progress of Rationalism, as thus outlined briefly by Dr. Charles Hodge ("Syst. Theol.," iii. p. 195): "Those who admitted the divine origin of the Scriptures got rid of its distinctive doctrines by the adoption of a low theory of inspiration and by the application of arbitrary principles of interpretation. Inspiration was in the first instance confined to the religious teachings of the Bible, then to the ideas or truths, but not to the form in which they were presented, nor to the arguments by which they were supported. . . . In this way a wet sponge was passed over all the doctrines of redemption and their outlines obliterated." It looks as if the Church were extremely slow in reading the most obvious lessons of history.

say that the amount and weight of the evidence of the truth
of the Biblical doctrine of inspiration is measured by the
amount and weight of the evidence for the general credibility and trustworthiness of the New Testament writers
as witnesses to doctrine, is an understatement rather than
an overstatement of the matter. For if we trust them at all
we will trust them in the account they give of the person and
in the report they give of the teaching of Christ; whereupon,
as they report Him as teaching the same doctrine of Scripture that they teach, we are brought face to face with divine
testimony to this doctrine of inspiration. The argument,
then, takes the form given it by Bishop Wordsworth: "The
New Testament canonizes the Old; the INCARNATE WORD
sets His seal on the WRITTEN WORD. The Incarnate Word
is God; therefore, the inspiration of the Old Testament is
authenticated by God Himself." [57] And, again, the general
trustworthiness of the writers of the New Testament gives
us the right and imposes on us the duty of accepting their
witness to the relation the Holy Ghost bears to their teaching, as, for example, when Paul tells us that the things which
they uttered they uttered "not in words taught by human
wisdom, but in those taught by the Spirit; joining Spirit-
given things with Spirit-given things" (1 Cor. ii. 13), and
Peter asserts that the Gospel was preached by them "in
the Holy Spirit" (I Peter i. 12); and this relation asserted
to exist between the Holy Ghost and their teaching, whether
oral or written (I Cor. xiv. 37; II Thess. ii. 15, iii. 6–14), gives
the sanction of the Holy Ghost to their doctrine of Holy
Scripture, whatever that is found to be. So that, even
though we begin on the lowest ground, we may find ourselves
compelled to say, as Bishop Wilberforce found himself compelled to say: "In brief, my belief is this: The whole Bible
comes to us as 'the Word of God' under the sanction of God,
the Holy Ghost." [58] The weight of the testimony to the
Biblical doctrine of inspiration, in a word, is no less than

[57] Wordsworth, " On the Canon," p. 51, Am. Ed.
[58] " Life of the Rt. Rev. S. Wilberforce, D.D.," Vol. III. p. 149.

the weight to be attached to the testimony of God — God the Son and God the Spirit.

But our present purpose is not to draw out the full value of the testimony, but simply to emphasize the fact that on the emergence of the exegetical fact that the Scriptures of the New Testament teach this doctrine, the amount and weight of evidence for its truth must be allowed to be the whole amount and weight of the evidence that the writers of the New Testament are trustworthy as teachers of doctrine. It is not on some shadowy and doubtful evidence that the doctrine is based — not on an *a priori* conception of what inspiration ought to be, not on a "tradition" of doctrine in the Church, though all the *a priori* considerations and the whole tradition of doctrine in the Church are also thrown in the scale for and not in that against this doctrine; but first on the confidence which we have in the writers of the New Testament as doctrinal guides, and ultimately on whatever evidence of whatever kind and force exists to justify that confidence. In this sense, we repeat, the cause of distinctive Christianity is bound up with the cause of the Biblical doctrine of inspiration. We accept Christianity in all its distinctive doctrines on no other ground than the credibility and trustworthiness of the Bible as a guide to truth; and on this same ground we must equally accept its doctrine of inspiration. "If we may not accept its account of itself," asks Dr. Purves, pointedly, "why should we care to ascertain its account of other things?" [59]

## III

IMMENSE PRESUMPTION AGAINST ALLEGED FACTS
CONTRADICTORY OF THE BIBLICAL DOCTRINE

We are again making no new affirmation but only looking from a slightly different angle upon the same proposition

---

[59] "St. Paul and Inspiration." Inaugural Address, etc. A. D. F. Randolph & Co., 1892. P. 52. *Presbyterian and Reformed Review*, January, 1893, p. 21.

with which we have been dealing from the first, when we emphasize next the fact, that the state of the case being as we have found it, we approach the study of the so-called " phenomena " of the Scriptures with a very strong presumption that these Scriptures contain no errors, and that any "phenomena" apparently inconsistent with their inerrancy are so in appearance only: a presumption the measure of which is just the whole amount and weight of evidence that the New Testament writers are trustworthy as teachers of doctrine.

It seems to be often tacitly assumed that the Biblical doctrine of inspiration cannot be confidently ascertained until all the facts concerning the contents and structure and characteristics of Scripture are fully determined and allowed for. This is obviously fallacious. What Paul, for example, believed as to the nature of Scripture is obviously an easily separable question from what the nature of Scripture really is. On the other hand, the assumption that we cannot confidently accept the Biblical doctrine of inspiration as true until criticism and exegesis have said their last word upon the structure, the text, and the characteristics of Scripture, even to the most minute fact, is more plausible. But it is far from obviously true. Something depends upon our estimate of the force of the mass of evidence which goes to show the trustworthiness of the apostles as teachers of truth, and of the clearness with which they announce their teaching as to inspiration. It is conceivable, for example, that the force of the evidence of their trustworthiness may be so great that we should be fully justified in yielding implicit confidence to their teaching, even though many and serious difficulties should stand in the way of accepting it. This, indeed, is exactly what we do in our ordinary use of Scripture as a source of doctrine. Who doubts that the doctrines of the Trinity and of the Incarnation present difficulties to rational construction? Who doubts that the doctrines of native demerit and total depravity, inability and eternal punishment raise objections in the natural heart? We accept these doctrines and others which ought to be much harder to credit, such as the Biblical teaching that God so loved sinful man as to give His only-begotten Son to die for him, not because their acceptance is not attended with difficulties, but because our confidence in the New Testament as a doctrinal guide is so grounded in unassailable and compelling evidence, that we believe its teachings despite the difficulties which they raise. We do not and we cannot wait until all these difficulties are fully explained before we yield to the teaching of the New Testament the fullest confidence of our minds and hearts. How then can it be true that we are to wait until all difficulties are removed before we can accept with confidence the Biblical doctrine of inspiration? In relation to this doctrine alone, are we to assume the position that we will not yield faith in response to due and compelling evidence of the trustworthiness of the teacher, until all difficulties are explained to our satisfaction — that we must fully understand and comprehend before we will believe? Or is the point this — that we can suppose ourselves possibly mistaken in everything else except our determination of the characteristics and structure of Scripture and the facts stated therein? Surely if we do not need to wait until we understand how God can be both one and three, how Christ can be both human and divine, how man can be both unable and responsible, how an act can be both free and certain, how man can be both a sinner and righteous in God's sight, before we accept, on the authority of the teaching of Scripture, the doctrines of the Trinity, of the Incarnation, of man's state as a sinner, of God's eternal predestination of the acts of free agents, and of acceptance on the ground of Christ's righteousness, because of the weight of the evidence which goes to prove that Scripture trustworthy as a teacher of divine truth; we may on the same compelling evidence accept, in full confidence, the teaching of the same Scripture as to the nature of its own inspiration, prior to a full understanding of how all the phenomena of Scripture are to be adjusted to it.

No doubt it is perfectly true and is to be kept in mind that the claim of a writing to be infallible may be mistaken or false. Such a claim has been put forth in behalf of and by other writings besides the Bible, and has been found utterly inconsistent with the observed characteristics of those writings. An *a priori* possibility may be asserted to exist in the case of the Bible, that a comparison of its phenomena with its doctrine may bring out a glaring inconsistency. The test of the truth of the claims of the Bible to be inspired of God through comparison with its contents, characteristics and phenomena, the Bible cannot expect to escape; and the lovers of the Bible will be the last to deny the validity of it. By all means let the doctrine of the Bible be tested by the facts and let the test be made all the more, not the less, stringent and penetrating because of the great issues that hang upon it. If the facts are inconsistent with the doctrine, let us all know it, and know it so clearly that the matter is put beyond doubt. But let us not conceal from ourselves the greatness of the issues involved in the test, lest we approach the test in too light a spirit, and make shipwreck of faith in the trustworthiness of the apostles as teachers of doctrine, with the easy indifference of a man who corrects the incidental errors of a piece of gossip. Nor is this appeal to the seriousness of the issues involved in any sense an appeal to deal deceitfully with the facts concerning or stated in the Bible, through fear of disturbing our confidence in a comfortable doctrine of its infallibility. It is simply an appeal to common sense. If you are told that a malicious lie has been uttered by some unknown person you may easily yield the report a languid provisional assent; such things are not impossible, unfortunately in this sinful world not unexampled. But if it is told you of your loved and trusted friend, you will probably demand the most stringent proof at the point of your walking stick. So far as this, Robert Browning has missed neither nature nor right reason, when he makes his Ferishtah point out how much more evidence we require in proof of a fact which brings us loss than what is sufficient to command.

> " The easy acquiescence of mankind
> In matters nowise worth dispute."

If it is right to test most carefully the claim of every settled and accepted faith by every fact asserted in rebuttal of it, it must be equally right, nay incumbent, to scrutinize most closely the evidence for an asserted fact, which, if genuine, wounds in its vitals some important interest. If it would be a crime to refuse to consider most carefully and candidly any phenomena of Scripture asserted to be inconsistent with its inerrancy, it would be equally a crime to accept the asserted reality of phenomena of Scripture, which, if real, strike at the trustworthiness of the apostolic witness to doctrine, on any evidence of less than demonstrative weight.

But we approach the consideration of these phenomena alleged to be inconsistent with the Biblical doctrine of inspiration not only thus with what may be called, though in a high sense, a sentimental presumption against their reality. The presumption is an eminently rational one, and is capable of somewhat exact estimation. We do not adopt the doctrine of the plenary inspiration of Scripture on sentimental grounds, nor even, as we have already had occasion to remark on a *priori* or general grounds of whatever kind. We adopt it specifically because it is taught us as truth by Christ and His apostles, in the Scriptural record of their teaching, and the evidence for its truth is, therefore, as we have also already pointed out, precisely that evidence, in weight and amount, which vindicates for us the trustworthiness of Christ and His apostles as teachers of doctrine. Of course, this evidence is not in the strict logical sense "demonstrative"; it is "probable" evidence. It therefore leaves open the metaphysical possibility of its being mistaken. But it may be contended that it is about as great in amount and weight as "probable" evidence can be made, and that the strength of conviction which it is adapted to produce may be and should be practically equal to that produced by demonstration itself. But whatever weight it has, and whatever strength of conviction it is adapted to produce, it is with this weight of evidence behind us and with this strength of conviction as to the unreality of any alleged phenomena contradictory of the Biblical doctrine of inspiration, that we approach the study of the characteristics, the structure, and the detailed statements of the Bible. Their study is not to be neglected; we have not attained through "probable" evidence apodeictic certainty of the Bible's infallibility. But neither is the reality of the alleged phenomena inconsistent with the Bible's doctrine, to be allowed without sufficient evidence. Their reality cannot be logically or rationally recognized unless the evidence for it be greater in amount and weight than the whole mass of evidence for the trustworthiness of the Biblical writers as teachers of doctrine.

It is not to be thought that this amounts to a recommendation of strained exegesis in order to rid the Bible of phenomena adverse to the truth of the Biblical doctrine of inspiration. It amounts to a recommendation of great care in the exegetical determination of these alleged phenomena; it amounts to a recommendation to allow that our exegesis determining these phenomena is not infallible. But it is far from recommending either strained or artificial exegesis of any kind. We are not bound to harmonize the alleged phenomena with the Bible doctrine; and if we cannot harmonize them save by strained or artificial exegesis they would be better left unharmonized. We are not bound, however, on the other hand, to believe that they are unharmonizable, because we cannot harmonize them save by strained exegesis. Our individual fertility in exegetical expedients, our individual insight into exegetical truth, our individual capacity of understanding are not the measure of truth. If we cannot harmonize without straining, let us leave unharmonized. It is not necessary for us to see the harmony that it should exist or even be recognized by us as existing. But it is necessary for us to believe the harmony to be possible and real, provided that we are not prepared to say that we clearly see that on any conceivable hypothesis (conceivable to us or conceivable to any other intelligent beings) the harmony is impossible — if the trustworthiness of the Biblical writers who teach us the doctrine of plenary inspiration is really safeguarded to us on evidence which we cannot disbelieve. In that case every unharmonized passage remains a case of difficult harmony and does not pass into the category of objections to plenary inspiration. It can pass into the category of objections only if we are prepared to affirm that we clearly see that it is, on any conceivable hypothesis of its meaning, clearly inconsistent with the Biblical doctrine of inspiration. In that case we would no doubt need to give up the Biblical doctrine of inspiration; but with it we must also give up our confidence in the Biblical writers as teachers of doctrine. And if we cannot reasonably give up this latter, neither can we reasonably allow that the phenomena apparently inconsistent with the former are real, or really inconsistent with it. And this is but to say that we approach the study of these phenomena with a presumption against their being such as will disprove the Biblical doctrine of inspiration — or, we may add (for this is but the same thing in different words), correct or modify the Biblical doctrine of inspiration — which is measured precisely by the amount and weight of the evidence which goes to show that the Bible is a trustworthy guide to doctrine.

The importance of emphasizing these, as it would seem, very obvious principles, does not arise out of need for a very great presumption in order to overcome the difficulties arising from the "phenomena" of Scripture, as over against its doctrine of inspiration. Such difficulties are not specially numerous or intractable. Dr. Charles Hodge justly characterizes those that have been adduced by disbelievers in the plenary inspiration of the Scriptures, as "for the most part trivial," "only apparent," and marvelously few "of any real importance." They bear, he adds, about the same relation to the whole that a speck of sandstone detected here and there in the marble of the Parthenon would bear to that building.[60] They do not for the most part require explaining away, but only to be fairly understood in order to void them. They constitute no real strain upon faith, but when approached in a candid spirit one is left continually marveling at the excessive fewness of those which do not, like ghosts, melt away from vision as soon as faced. Moreover, as every student of the history of exegesis and criticism knows, they are a progressively vanishing quantity. Those which seemed most obvious and intractable a generation or two ago, remain today as only too readily forgotten warnings against the ineradicable and inordinate dogmatism of the opponents of the inerrancy of the Bible, who over-ride continually every canon of historical and critical caution in their eager violence against the doctrine that they assail. What scorn they expressed of "apologists" who doubted whether Luke was certainly in error in assigning a "proconsul" to Cyprus, whether he was in error in making Lysanias a contemporary tetrarch with the Herodian rulers, and the like. How easily that scorn is forgotten as the progress of discovery has one by one vindicated the assertions of the Biblical historians. The matter has come to such a pass, indeed, in the progress of discovery, that there is a sense in which it may be said that the doctrine of the inerrancy of the Bible can now be based, with considerable confidence, on its observed "phenomena." What marvelous accuracy is characteristic of its historians! Dr. Fisher, in a paper already referred to, invites

[60] "Systematic Theology," i. pp. 169, 170: We have purposely adduced this passage here to enable us to protest against the misuse of it, which, in the exigencies of the present controversy, has been made, as if Dr. Hodge was in this passage admitting the reality of the alleged errors. The passage occurs in the reply to objections to the doctrine, not in the development of the doctrine itself, and is of the nature of an *argumentum ad hominem*. How far Dr. Hodge was from admitting the reality of error in the original Biblical text may be estimated from the frequency with which he asserts its freedom from error in the immediately preceding context — pp. 152, 155, 163 (no less than three times on this page), 165, 166, 169 (no less than five times).

his readers to read Archibald Forbes' article in the *Nineteenth Century* for March, 1892, on "Napoleon the Third at Sedan," that they may gain some idea of how the truth of history as to the salient facts may be preserved amid "hopeless and bewildering discrepancies in regard to details," in the reports of the most trustworthy eye-witnesses. The article is instructive in this regard. And it is instructive in another regard also. What a contrast exists between this mass of "hopeless and bewildering discrepancies in regard to details," among the accounts of a single important transaction, written by careful and watchful eye-witnesses, who were on the ground for the precise purpose of gathering the facts for report, and who were seeking to give an exact and honest account of the events which they witnessed, and the marvelous accuracy of the Biblical writers! If these "hopeless and bewildering discrepancies" are consistent with the honesty and truthfulness and general trustworthiness of the uninspired writers, may it not be argued that the so much greater accuracy attained by the Biblical writers when describing not one event but the history of ages — and a history filled with pitfalls for the unwary — has something more than honesty and truthfulness behind it, and warrants the attribution to them of something more than general trustworthiness? And, if in the midst of this marvel of general accuracy there remain here and there a few difficulties as yet not fully explained in harmony with it, or if in the course of the historical vindication of it in general a rare difficulty (as in the case of some of the statements of Daniel) seems to increase in sharpness, are we to throw ourselves with desperate persistency into these "last ditches" and strive by our increased insistence upon the impregnability of *them* to conceal from men that the main army has been beaten from the field? Is it not more reasonable to suppose that these difficulties, too, will receive their explanation with advancing knowledge? And is it not the height of the unreasonable to treat them like the Sibylline books as of everincreasing importance in proportion to their decreasing number? The importance of keeping in mind that there is a presumption against the reality of these "inconsistent phenomena," and that the presumption is of a weight measurable only by the weight of evidence which vindicates the general trustworthiness of the Bible as a teacher of doctrine, does not arise from the need of so great a presumption in order to overcome the weight of the alleged opposing facts. Those facts are not specially numerous, important or intractable, and they are, in the progress of research, a vanishing quantity.

The importance of keeping in mind the principle in question arises rather from the importance of preserving a correct logical method. There are two ways of approaching the study of the inspiration of the Bible. One proceeds by obtaining first the doctrine of inspiration taught by the Bible as applicable to itself, and then testing this doctrine by the facts as to the Bible as ascertained by Biblical criticism and exegesis. This is good logical procedure; and in the presence of a vast mass of evidence for the general trustworthiness of the Biblical writings as witnesses of doctrine, and for the appointment of their writers as teachers of divine truth to men, and for the presence of the Holy Spirit with and in them aiding them in their teaching (in whatever degree and with whatever effect) — it would seem to be the only logical and proper mode of approaching the question. The other method proceeds by seeking the doctrine of inspiration in the first instance through a comprehensive induction from the facts as to the structure and contents of the Bible, as ascertained by critical and exegetical processes, treating all these facts as co-factors of the same rank for the induction. If in this process the facts of structure and the facts embedded in the record of Scripture — which are called, one-sidedly indeed but commonly, by the class of writers who adopt this procedure, "the phenomena" of Scripture — alone are considered, it would be difficult to arrive at a precise doctrine of inspiration, at the best: though, as we have already pointed out, a degree and kind of accuracy might be vindicated for the Scriptures which might lead us to suspect and to formulate as the best account of it, some divine assistance to the writers' memory, mental processes and expression. If the Biblical facts and teaching are taken as co-factors in the induction, the procedure (as we have already pointed out) is liable to the danger of modifying the teaching by the facts without clear recognition of what is being done; the result of which would be the loss from observation of one main fact of errancy, viz., the inaccuracy of the teaching of the Scriptures as to their own inspiration. This would vitiate the whole result: and this vitiation of the result can be avoided only by ascertaining separately the teaching of Scripture as to its own inspiration, and by accounting the results of this ascertainment one of the facts of the induction. Then we are in a position to judge by the comparison of this fact with the other facts, whether this fact of teaching is in accord or in disaccord with those facts of performance. If it is in disaccord, then of course this disaccord is the main factor in the case: the writers are convicted of false teaching. If it is in accord, then, if the teaching is not proved by the accord, it is at least left credible, and may be believed with whatever confidence may be justified by the evidence which goes to show that these writers are trustworthy as deliverers of doctrine. And if nice and difficult questions arise in the comparison of the fact of teaching with the facts of performance, it is inevitable that the relative weight of the evidence for the trustworthiness of the two sets of facts should be the deciding factor in determining the truth. This is as much as to say that the asserted facts as to performance must give way before the fact as to teaching, unless the evidence on which they are based as facts outweighs the evidence on which the teaching may be accredited as true. But this correction of the second method of procedure, by which alone it can be made logical in form or valid in result, amounts to nothing less than setting it aside altogether and reverting to the first method, according to which the teaching of Scripture is first to be determined, and then this teaching to be tested by the facts of performance.

The importance of proceeding **according to the true**

logical method may be illustrated by the observation that the conclusions actually arrived at by students of the subject seem practically to depend on the logical method adopted. In fact, the difference here seems mainly a difference in point of view. If we start from the Scripture doctrine of inspiration, we approach the phenomena with the question whether they will negative this doctrine, and we find none able to stand against it, commended to us as true, as it is, by the vast mass of evidence available to prove the trustworthiness of the Scriptural writers as teachers of doctrine. But if we start simply with a collection of the phenomena, classifying and reasoning from them, whether alone or in conjunction with the Scriptural statements, it may easily happen with us, as it happened with certain of old, that meeting with some things hard to be understood, we may be ignorant and unstable enough to wrest them to our own intellectual destruction, and so approach the Biblical doctrine of inspiration set upon explaining it away. The value of having the Scripture doctrine as a clue in our hands, is thus fairly illustrated by the ineradicable inability of the whole negative school to distinguish between *difficulties* and *proved errors*. If then we ask what we are to do with the numerous phenomena of Scripture inconsistent with verbal inspiration, which, so it is alleged, "criticism" has brought to light, we must reply: Challenge them in the name of the New Testament doctrine, and ask for their credentials. They have no credentials that can stand before that challenge. No single error has as yet been demonstrated to occur in the Scriptures as given by God to His Church. And every critical student knows, as already pointed out, that the progress of investigation has been a continuous process of removing difficulties, until scarcely a shred of the old list of "Biblical Errors" remains to hide the nakedness of this moribund contention. To say that we do not wish to make claims "for which we have only this to urge, that they cannot be absolutely disproved," is not to the point; what is to the point is to say, that we cannot set aside the presumption arising from the general trustworthiness of Scripture, that its doctrine of inspiration is true, by any array of contradictory facts, each one of which is fairly disputable. We must have indisputable errors — which are not forthcoming.

The real problem brought before the Churches by the present debate ought now to be sufficiently plain. In its deepest essence it is whether we can still trust the Bible as a guide in doctrine, as a teacher of truth. It is not simply whether we can explain away the Biblical doctrine of inspiration so as to allow us to take a different view from what has been common of the structure and characteristics of the Bible. Nor, on the other hand, is it simply whether we may easily explain the facts, established as facts, embedded in Scripture, consistently with the teaching of Scripture as to the nature, extent and effects of inspiration. It is specifically whether the results proclaimed by a special school of Biblical criticism — which are of such a character, as is now admitted by all, as to necessitate, if adopted, a new view of the Bible and of its inspiration — rest on a basis of evidence strong enough to meet and overcome the weight of evidence, whatever that may be in kind and amount, which goes to show that the Biblical writers are trustworthy as teachers of doctrine. If we answer this question in the affirmative, then no doubt we shall have not only a new view of the Bible and of its inspiration but also a whole new theology, because we must seek a new basis for doctrine. But if we answer it in the negative, we may possess our souls in patience and be assured that the Scriptures are as trustworthy witnesses to truth when they declare a doctrine of Inspiration as when they declare a doctrine of Incarnation or of Redemption, even though in the one case as in the other difficulties may remain, the full explanation of which is not yet clear to us. The real question, in a word, is not a new question but the perennial old question, whether the basis of our doctrine is to be what the Bible teaches, or what men teach. And this is a question which is to be settled on the old method, viz., on our estimate of the weight and value of the evidence which places the Bible in our hands as a teacher of doctrine.

# V
# THE TERMS "SCRIPTURE" AND "SCRIPTURES" AS EMPLOYED IN THE NEW TESTAMENT

# THE TERMS "SCRIPTURE" AND "SCRIPTURES" AS EMPLOYED IN THE NEW TESTAMENT[1]

THE scope of this article does not permit the discussion in it of the employment of Scripture, or of the estimate put upon Scripture, by either our Lord or the Evangelists. It is strictly limited to the use of the term 'Scripture' in the NT, particularly in the Gospels: and to the immediate implications of that use.

1. The use of this term in the NT was an inheritance, not an invention. The idea of a 'canon' of 'Sacred Scriptures' (and with the idea the thing) was handed down to Christianity from Judaism. The Jews possessed a body of writings, consisting of 'Law, Prophets, and (other) Scriptures (*Kethubhim*),' though they were often called, for brevity's sake, merely 'the Law and the Prophets' or simply 'the Law.' These 'Sacred Scriptures,' or this 'Scripture' (*hakkethibh*) as it was frequently called, or these 'Books,' or simply this 'Book' (*hassepher*), they looked upon as originating in Divine inspiration, and as therefore possessed everywhere of Divine authority. Whatever stood written in these Scriptures was a word of God, and was therefore referred to indifferently as something which 'Scripture says' ('*amar qara*', or '*amar hakkethibh*, or *kethibh qera*'), or 'the All-Merciful says' ('*amar rachmana*'), or even simply 'He says' (*wekhen hu'* '*amar* or merely (*we'amar*); that God is the Speaker in the Scriptural word being too fully understood to

[1] Reprinted from Hastings' " Dictionary of Christ and the Gospels " (Vol. II, pp. 583–588) by permission of Charles Scribner's Sons. This article is a condensation by Dr. Warfield himself of the much longer article published in " Revelation and Inspiration " (pp. 115–165) and in *The Princeton Theological Review* (1910, pp. 561–612). In this article Greek and Hebrew words have been transliterated as it proved impossible by photoengraving to reproduce it in a manner suitable for this volume by reason of the narrow columns and small type in which it was printed. It is believed that the shorter article will meet the needs of most readers.

require explicit expression. Every precept or dogma was supposed to be grounded in Scriptural teaching, and possessed authority only as buttressed by a Scripture passage, introduced commonly by one or the other of the formulas 'for it is said' (*shenne'emar*) or 'as it is written' (*dakhethibh* or *kedhakhethibh*), though, of course, a great variety of more or less frequently occurring formulas of adduction are found. Greek-speaking Jews naturally tended merely to reproduce in their new language the designations and forms of adduction of their sacred books current among their people. This process was no doubt facilitated by the existence among the Greeks of a pregnant legislative use of *grapho, graphe, gramma,* by which these terms were freighted with an implication of authority. But it is very easy to make too much of this. In Josephus, and even more plainly in the LXX, the influence of the Greek usage may be traced; but in a writer like Philo, Jewish habits of thought appear to be absolutely determinative. The fact of importance is that there was nothing left for Christianity to invent here. It merely took over in their entirety the established usages of the Synagogue, and the NT evinces itself in this matter at least a thoroughly Jewish book. The several terms it employs are made use of, to be sure, with some sensitiveness to their inherent implications as Greek words, and the Greek legislative use of some of them gave them, no doubt, peculiar fitness for the service asked of them. But the application made of them by the NT writers had its roots set in Jewish thought, and from it they derive a fuller and deeper meaning than the most pregnant classical usage could impart to them.

2. To the NT writers, as to other Jews, the sacred books of what was now called by them 'the old covenant' (2 Cor. iii. 14), described according to their contents as 'the Law, the Prophets, and the Psalms' (Lk. xxiv. 44), or more briefly as 'the Law and the Prophets' (Matt. vii. 12, Lk. xvi. 16; cf. Acts xxviii. 23, Lk. xvi. 29, 31), or merely as 'the Law' (Jno. x. 34, 1 Cor. xiv. 21), or even perhaps 'the Prophets' (Matt. ii. 23, xi. 13, xxvi. 56, Lk. i. 70, xviii. 31, xxiv. 25, 27, Acts iii. 24,

xiii. 27, Rom. i. 2, xvi. 26), were, when thought of according to
their nature, a body of 'sacred scriptures' (Rom. i. 2, 2 Tim.
iii. 16), or, with the omission of the unnecessary, because well-
understood adjective, simply by way of eminence, 'the Scriptures,' 'Scripture.' For employment in this designation either
of the substantives *graphe* or *gramma* offered itself, although,
of course, each brought with it its own suggestions arising from
the implication of the form and the general usage of the word.
The more usual of the two in this application, in Philo and
Josephus, is *gramma,* or more exactly *grammata;* for, although
it is sometimes so employed in the singular (but apparently
only late, e.g. Callimachus, *Epigr.* xxiv. 4, and the Church
Fathers, *passim*), it is in the plural that this form more properly denotes that congeries of alphabetical signs which constitutes a book. In the NT, on the other hand, this form is
rare. The complete phrase *hiera grammata,* found also both in
Josephus and in Philo, occurs in 2 Tim. iii. 15 as the current
title of the sacred books, freighted with all its implications as
such. Elsewhere in the NT, however, *grammata* is scarcely
used as a designation of Scripture (cf. Jno. v. 47, vii. 15). Practically, therefore, *graphe,* in its varied uses, remains the sole
form employed in the NT in the sense of 'Scripture,' 'Scriptures.'

3. This term occurs in the NT about fifty times (Gospels
23, Acts 7, Catholic Epistles 6, Paul 14); and in every case it
bears that technical sense in which it designates the Scriptures by way of eminence, the Scriptures of the OT. It is true
there are a few instances in which passages adduced as *graphe*
are not easily identified in the OT text; but there is no reason
to doubt that OT passages were intended (cf. Hühn, *Die alttest.
Citate,* 270; and Mayor on Jas. iv. 5, Lightfoot on 1 Cor. ii. 9,
Westcott on Jno. vii. 38, and Godet on Lk. xi. 49). We need to
note in modification of the broad statement, therefore, only
that it is apparent from 2 Pet. iii. 16 (cf. 1 Tim. v. 18) that
the NT writers were well aware that the category 'Scripture,'
in the high sense, included also the writings they were producing, as along with the books of the OT constituting the com-

plete 'Scripture' or authoritative Word of God. In 20 out of the 50 instances in which *graphe* occurs in the NT, it is the plural form which is used, and in all but two of these cases the article is present—*hai graphai*, the well- known Scriptures of the Jewish people; and the two exceptions are exceptions only in appearance, since adjectival definitions are present (*graphai hagiai*, Rom. i. 2, here first in extant literature; *graphai prophetikai*, Rom. xvi. 26). The singular form occurs some 30 times, all but four of which have the article; and here again the exceptions are only apparent, the term being definite in every case (Jno. xix. 37 'another Scripture'; 1 Pet. ii. 6, 2 Pet. i. 20, 2 Tim. iii. 16, used as a proper name). The distribution of the singular and plural forms is perhaps worth noting. In Acts the singular (3 times) and plural (4) occur almost equally frequently: the plural prevails in the Synoptics (Matt. plural only; Mk. two to one; Lk. three to one), and the singular in the rest of the NT (John 11 to 1, James 3 to 0, Peter 2 to 1, Paul 2 to 5). In the Gospels the plural form occurs exclusively in Matt., prevailingly in Mk. and Lk., and rarely in Jno., of which the singular is characteristic. No distinction seems to be traceable between the usage of the Evangelists in their own persons and that of our Lord as reported by them. Matt. and Mk. do not on their own account use the term at all; in Lk. and Jno., on the other hand, it occurs not only in reports of our Lord's sayings and of the sayings of others, but also in the narrative itself. To our Lord is ascribed the use indifferently of the plural (Matt. xxi. 42, xxii. 49, xxvi. 54, 56, Mk. xii. 24, xiv, 9, Jno. v. 39) and the singular (Mk. xii. 10, Lk. iv. 21, Jno. vii. 38, 42, x. 35, xiii. 18, xvii. 12).

The history of *graphe, graphai*, as applied to literary documents, does not seem to have been exactly the same as that of its congener *gramma, grammata*. The latter appears to have been current first as the appropriate appellation of an alphabetical character, and to have grown gradually upward from that lowly employment to designate documents of less or greater extent, as ultimately made up of alphabetical characters. Although, therefore, the singular *to gramma* is used of any written thing, it is apparently, when applied to 'writings,' most naturally employed of brief pieces like short inscriptions or proverbs, or of the shorter portions of documents such as clauses—though it is also used of those larger sections of works which are more commonly designated as 'books.' It is rather the plural, *ta grammata,* which seems to have suggested itself not only for extended treatises, but indeed for documents of all kinds. When so employed, the plural form is not to be pressed. Such a phrase as 'Moses' *grammata*' (Jno. v. 47), for example, probably ascribes to Moses only a single book— what we call the Pentateuch; and such a phrase as *hiera grammata* (2 Tim. iii. 15) does not suggest to us a 'Divine library,' but brings the OT before us as a unitary whole. On the other hand, *graphe,* in its application to literary ·products, seems to have sprung lightly across the intermediate steps to designate which *gramma* is most appropriately used, and to have been carried over at once from the 'writing' in the sense of the script to the 'writing' in the sense of the Scripture. Kindred with *gramma* as it is, its true synonymy in its literary application is rather with such words as *biblos* (*biblion*) and *logos,* in common with which it most naturally designates a complete literary piece, whether 'treatise' or 'book.' Where thought of from the material point of view as so much paper, so to speak, a literary work was apt to be called a *biblos* (*biblion*); when thought of as a rational product, thought presented in words, it was apt to be spoken of as a *logos:* intermediate between the two stood *graphe* (*gramma*), which was apt to come to the lips when the 'web of words' itself was in mind. In a word, *biblos* (*biblion*) was the most exact word for the 'book,' *graphe* (*gramma*) for the 'document' inscribed in the 'book,' *logos* for the 'treatise' which the 'document' records; while as between *graphe* and *gramma, gramma,* pre-serving the stronger material flavour, gravitates somewhat towards *biblos* (*biblion*), and *graphe* looks upward somewhat toward *logos.* When, in the development of the publisher's trade, the system of making books in great rolls gave way to the 'small-roll system,' and long works came to be broken up into 'books,' each of which was inscribed in a 'volume,' these separate 'books' attached to themselves this whole series of designations, each with its appropriate implication. Smaller sections were properly called *periochai, topoi, choria, grammata* (the last of which is the proper term for 'clauses'), but very seldom, if ever, in classical Greek, *graphai*.

5. The current senses of these several terms are, of course, more or less reflected in their NT use. But we are struck at once with the fact that *graphe* occurs in the NT solely in its pregnant technical usage as a designation of the Sacred Scriptures. There seems no intrinsic reason why it should not, like *grammata,* be freely used for non-sacred 'writings.' In point of fact, however, throughout the NT *graphe* is ever something 'which the Holy Ghost has spoken through the mouth' of its human authors (Acts 1.16), and which is therefore of indefectible, because Divine, authority. It is perhaps even more remarkable that even on this high plane of technical reference it never occurs, in accordance with its most natural, and in the classics its most frequent, sense of 'treatise,' as a term to describe the several books of which the OT is composed. It is tempting, no doubt, to seek to give it such a sense in some of the passages where, occurring in the singular, it yet does not seem to designate the Scriptures in their entirety, and Dr. Hort appears for a moment almost inclined to yield to the temptation (on 1 Pet. ii. 6, note the 'probable'). It is more tempting still to assume that behind the common use of the plural *hai graphai* to designate the Scriptures as a whole, there lies a previous current usage by which each book which enters into the composition of these 'Scriptures' was designated by the singular *he graphe*. But in no single passage where *he graphe* occurs does it seem possible to give it a reference to the 'treatise' to which the appeal is made; and the common employment in profane Greek of *graphai* (in the plural) for a single document, discourages the assumption that (like *ta biblia*) when applied to the Scriptures it has reference to their composite character. The truth seems to be that whether the plural *hai graphai* or the singular *he graphe* is employed,

the application of the term to the OT writings by the writers
of the NT is based upon the conception of these OT writings
as a unitary whole, and designates this body of writings in their
entirety as the one well-known authoritative documentation
of the Divine word. This is the fundamental fact with respect
to the use of these terms in the NT from which all the other
facts of their usage flow.

6. It is true that in one unique passage, 2 Pet. iii. 16 (on
the meaning of which see Bigg, *in loc.*), *hai graphai* does occur
with a plural signification. But the units of which this plural
is made up, as the grammatical construction suggests, appear
to be not 'treatises' (Huther, Kühl), but 'passages' (de
Wette). Peter seems to say that the unlearned and unstable
of course wrested the hard sayings of Paul's letters as they
were accustomed to wrest *tas loipas graphas*, i.e. the other
Scripture statements (cf. Eurip. *Hipp.* 1311; Philo, *de Praem.
et Poen.* §11 near end)—the implication being that no part
of Scripture was safe in their hands. This is a sufficiently remarkable use of the plural, no other example of which occurs
in the NT; but it is an entirely legitimate one for the NT, and
in its context a perfectly natural one. In the Church Fathers
the plural *hai graphai* is formed freely upon *he graphe* both in
the sense of 'book' of Scripture and in the sense of 'passage'
of Scripture. But in the NT, apart from the present passage,
there is in no instance of the use of *hai graphai* the slightest
hint of a series whether of 'treatises' or of 'passages' underlying it. Even a passage like Lk. xxiv. 27 forms no exception;
for if *graphai* is employed in a singular sense of a single document, then *pasai hai graphai* remains just the whole of that
document, and is the exact equivalent of *pasa he graphe*, or
(if *graphe* has acquired standing as a quasi-proper name) as
*pasa graphe* (2 Tim. iii. 16). Similarly *hai graphai ton
propheton* (Matt. xxvi. 56), *graphai prophetikai* (Rom. xvi.
26) appear to refer not to particular passages deemed prophetic, or to the special section of the OT called 'the Prophets,'
but to the entire OT conceived as prophetic in character (cf.
2 Pet. i. 20, Acts ii. 30, 2 Pet. iii. 16).

7. In 2 Pet. iii. 16, however, we have already been brought face to face with what is probably the most remarkable fact about the usage of *graphe* in the NT. This is its occasional employment to refer not merely, as from its form and previous history was to be expected, to the Scripture as a whole, or even, as also would have been only a continuation of its profane usage, to the several treatises which make up that whole, but to the individual passages of Scripture. This employment finds little support from the classics, in which *gramma* rather than *graphe* is the current form for the adduction of 'clauses' or fragmentary portions of documents (cf. *e.g.* Plato, *Parmen.* 128 A-D, *Ep.* 3[317 B]; Thucyd. v. 29; Philo, *de Congr. Erud. Grat.* 12, *Quod Deus immut* 2). It has been customary, accordingly, to represent it as a peculiarity of NT and Patristic Greek. It seems to be found, however, though rarely, in Philo (*Quis rerum div. haer.* 53, *de Proem, et Poen.* 11; cf. Euripides, *Hipp.* 1311), and is probably an extreme outgrowth of the habit of looking upon the Scriptures as a unitary book of Divine oracles, every portion and passage of which is clothed with the Divine authority which belongs to the whole and is therefore manifested in all its parts. When the entirety of Scripture is 'Scripture' to us, each passage may readily be adduced as 'Scripture,' because 'Scripture' is conceived as speaking through and in each passage. The transition is easy from saying, 'The Scripture says, namely, in this or that passage,' to saying, of this and that passage, severally, 'This Scripture says,' and 'Another Scripture says'; and a step so inviting was sure sooner or later to be taken. The employment of *he graphe* in the NT to denote a particular passage of Scripture does not appear then to be a continuation of a classical usage, but a new development on Jewish or Judaeo-Christian ground from the pregnant use of *graphe* for the Sacred Scriptures, every clause of which is conceived as clothed with the authority of the whole. So far from throwing in doubt the usage of *graphe* pregnantly of Scripture as a whole, therefore, it rather presupposes this usage and is a result of it. So it will

not surprise us to find the two usages standing side by side in the NT.

8. It has indeed been called in question whether both these usages do stand side by side in the NT. Possibly a desire to find some well-marked distinction between the usage of the plural and singular forms has not been without influence here. At all events, it has every now and then been suggested that the singular *he graphe* bears in the NT the uniform sense of 'passage of Scripture,' while it is the plural *hai graphai* alone which in the NT designates Scripture as a whole. The younger Schulthess, for example (*Lucubr. pro divin. discip. ac pers. Jesu*, 1828, p. 36 n.) having occasion to comment briefly on the words *pasa graphe theopneustos* of 2 Tim. iii. 16, among other assertions of equal dubiety makes this one: '*graphe* in the singular never means *biblos* in the NT, much less the entirety of *ton hieron grammaton*, but some particular passage.' Hitherto it has been thought enough to meet such assertions with a mere expression of dissent: Christiaan Sepp, for example (*De Leer des NT over de HS des OV*, 1849, p. 69), meets this one with equal brevity and point by the simple statement: 'Passages like Jno. x. 35 prove the contrary.' Of late, however, under the influence of a comment of Bishop Lightfoot's on Gal. iii. 22 which has become famous, Schulthess' doctrine has become almost traditional in a justly influential school of British exegesis (cf. Westcott on Jno. ii. 22, x. 35; Hort on 1 Pet. ii. 6; Swete on Mk. xii. 10; Page on Acts i. 10; Knowling on Acts viii. 32; Plummer on Lk. iv. 21). The attempt to carry this doctrine through, however, appears to involve a violence of exegesis which breaks down of itself. Of the 30 instances in which the singular *graphe* occurs, about a score seem intractable to the proposed interpretation (Jno. ii. 22, vii. 38, 42, x. 35, xvii. 12, xix. 28, xx. 9, Acts viii. 32, Rom. iv. 3, ix. 17, x. 11, xi. 2, Gal. iii. 8, 22, iv. 30, 1 Tim. v. 18, Jas. iv. 5, 1 Pet. ii. 6, 2 Pet. i. 20 [cf. Cremer, *sub voc.*, who omits Jno. xvii. 12, xx. 9; E. Hühn, *Die alttest. Citate*, etc., 1900, p. 276, who adds Jno. xiii. 18, xix. 24, 36, Jas. ii. 8; and Vaughan on Rom. iv. 3,

Meyer on Jno. x. 35, Weiss on Jno. x. 35, Kübel on 2 Pet. i. 20, Abbott on Eph. iv. 8, Beet on Rom. ix. 17, Mayor on 2 Pet. iii. 16; *EBi* 4329; Franke, *Das AT bei Johannes*, 48; E. Haupt, *Die alttest. Citate in den vier Evang.* 201]). In some of these passages it would seem quite impossible to refer *graphe* to a particular passage of Scripture. No particular passage is suggested, for example, in Jno. ii. 22 or in Gal. iii. 22, and it is sought and conjecturally supplied by the commentators only under the pressure of the theory. The reference of Jno. xx. 9 is quite as broad as that of Lk. xxiv. 45. In Jno. x. 35 the argument depends on the wide reference to Scripture as a whole, which forms its major premise. The personification of Scripture in such passages as Jas. iv. 5 and Gal. iii. 8 carries with it the same implication. And the anarthrous use of *graphe* in 1 Pet. ii. 6, 2 Pet. i. 20, 2 Tim. iii. 16, is explicable only on the presupposition that *graphe* had acquired the value of a proper name. Perhaps the two passages, 1 Pet. ii. 6 and 2 Pet. i. 20, are fairly adapted to stand as the tests of the possibility of carrying through the reference of *graphe* in the singular to particular passages: and the artificial explanations which are given of these passages by the advocates of that theory (cf. Zahn, *Einleitung*, etc., ii. 108; Hort on 1 Pet. ii. 6) may stand for its sufficient refutation. There seems no reason why we should fail to recognize that the employment of *graphe* in the NT so far follows its profane usage, in which it is prevailingly applied to entire documents and carries with it a general implication of completeness, that in its more common reference it designates the OT to which it is applied in its completeness as a unitary whole (cf. Franke, *op. cit.* p. 48). It remains only to add that the same implication is present in the designation of the OT as *hai graphai*, which, as has already been pointed out, does not suggest that the OT is a collection of 'treatises,' but is merely a variant of *he graphe* in accordance with good Greek usage, employed interchangeably with it at the dictation of nothing more recondite than literary habit. Whether *hai graphai* is used, then, or *he graphe*, or the anarthrous *graphe*, in each case alike the OT is thought of as a single document set over against all other documents by reason of its unique Divinity and indefectible authority, by which it is constituted in every passage and declaration the final arbiter of belief and practice.

9. It is an outgrowth of this conception of the OT that it is habitually adduced for the ordinary purposes of instruction or debate by such simple formulas as 'it is said,' 'it is written,' with the implication that what is thus said or written is of Divine and final authority. Both of these usages are illustrated in a variety of forms, and with all possible high implications, not only in the NT at large, but also in the Gospels,—and not only in the comments of the Evangelists, but also in the reported sayings of our Lord. We are concerned here only with the formula, 'It is written,' in which the consciousness of the written form—the documentary character—of the authority appealed to finds expression. In its most common form, this formula is the simple *gegraptai*, used either absolutely, or, with none of its authoritative implication thereby evacuated, with more or less clear intimation of the place where the cited words are to be found written. By its side occurs also the resolved formula *gegrammenon estin* (peculiar to Jno.; cf. Plummer on Lk. iv. 17), or some similar formula, with the same implications. These modes of expression have analogies in profane Greek, especially in legislative usages; but their use with reference to the Divine Scriptures, as it involves the adduction of an authority which rises immeasurably above all legislative authority, is also freighted with a significance to which the profane usage affords no key. In the Gospels, *gegraptai* occurs exclusively in Matt. and Mk., and predominately in Lk., but only once in Jno.; most commonly in reports of our Lord's sayings. In the latter part of Lk., on the other hand, the authoritative citation of the OT is accomplished by the use of the participle *gegrammenon*, while in Jno. the place of *gegraptai* (viii. 17 only) is definitely taken by the resolved formula *gegrammenon estin*. The significance of these formulas is perhaps most manifest where they stand alone as the bare adduction of authority without indication of

any kind whence the citation is derived (so *gegraptai*, Matt. iv. 4, 6, 7, 10, [xi. 10,] xxi. 13, [xxvi. 24,] xxvi. 31, Mk. vii. 6, ix. 12, 13, xi. 17, xiv. 21, 27, Lk. iv. 4, 8, 10, vii. 27, xix. 46, xx. 17, xxii. 37; *gegrammenon estin*, Jno. ii. 17, vi. 31, xii. 14, [16]). The adjunction of an indication of the place where the citation may be found does not, however, really affect the authoritativeness of its adduction. This adjunction is rare in Matt. and Mk. (Matt. ii. 5, Mk. i. 2 only), more frequent in Lk. (ii. 23, iii. 4, x. 26, xviii. 31, xxiv. 44, 46) and Jno. (vi. 45, viii. 17, x. 34, xv. 25); and by its infrequency it emphasizes the absence of all necessity for such identification. When a NT writer says, 'It is written,' there can arise no doubt where what he thus adduces as possessing absolute authority over the thought and consciences of men is to be found written. The simple adduction in this solemn and decisive manner of a written authority, carries with it the implication that the appeal is made to the indefectible authority of the Scriptures of God, which in all their parts and in every one of their declarations are clothed with the authority of God Himself.

Literature.—Lightfoot, *Hor. Heb. et Talm.* (ed. Pitman) xi, xii; Schöttgen, *Hor. Heb. et Talm.* 1732; Surenhusius, *Sepher hammishna sive biblos katallages*, 1713 (pp. 1-36); Döpke, *Hermeneutik d. NT Schriften*, 1829 (i. pp. 60-69); Edersheim, *LT* i. 187, n. 2; Weber, Jüd. Theol.[2] (1897) § 20; H. J. Holtzmann, *NT Theol.*, Index; Weiss, *Theol. of NT*, § 74a, n. 3, § 136b. n. 5, § 152b, n. 4; Sepp, *De Leer des NT over de HS des OV*, 1849, Tholuck, *Ueber die Citate der AT im NT*[6]; Turpie, *The NT View of the Old*, 1872; Böhl, *Die alttest. Citate in NT*, 1878; Toy, *Quotations in NT*, 1884; Dittmar, *VT in Novo*, i. 1899; Hühn, *Die alttest. Citate im NT*, 1900; Anger, *Ratio qua loci VT in Evang. Mat. laudantur*, 1801; E. Haupt, *Die alttest. Citate in d. 4 Evangg.* 1871; Clemen, *Der Gebrauch d. AT im NT und speciell in den Reden Jesu*, 1891-1893, *Der Gebrauch der AT in den NT Schriften*, 1895 (full literature, p. 19); Massebieau, *Examen des Citations de l'Ancien Test. dans l'Evang. selon S. Matthieu*, 1885; Swete, *Gospel acc. to Mark*, pp. lxx-lxxiv; Franke, *Das AT bei*

*Johannes,* 1885 (pp. 46-88, 225-281); Lechler, '*Das AT in den Reden Jesu*' (TSK, 1854, 4); Grau, *Das Selbstbewusstsein Jesu,* iv. 1887; Barth, *Die Hauptprobleme des Lebens Jesu,* ii. 1899 [2nd ed. 1903]; Kautzsch, *de VT locis in Paulo,* 1809; Monnet, *Les citations de S. Paul,* 1874; Vollmer, *Die alttest. Citate Paulus,* 1895.

# VI
## "GOD-INSPIRED SCRIPTURE"

# "GOD-INSPIRED SCRIPTURE"

THE phrase, "Given by inspiration of God," or "Inspired of God," occurs, as is well-known, but once in the New Testament — in the classical passage, to wit, II Tim. iii. 16, which is rendered in the Authorized Version, "All Scripture *is* given by inspiration of God," and by the Revised Version, "Every Scripture inspired of God *is*, etc." The Greek word represented by it, and standing in this passage as an epithet or predicate of "Scripture" — θεόπνευστος — though occurring here only in the New Testament and found nowhere earlier in all Greek literature, has nevertheless not hitherto seemed of doubtful interpretation. Its form, its subsequent usage, the implications of parallel terms and of the analogy of faith, have combined with the suggestions of the context to assign to it a meaning which has been constantly attributed to it from the first records of Christian interpretation until yesterday.

This unvarying understanding of the word is thus reported by the leading lexicographers: Schleusner "New Test. Lexicon." Glasgow reprint of fourth Leipzig edition, 1824:

"Θεόπνευστος, ου, ὁ, ἡ, *afflatu divino actus, divino quodam spiritu afflatus*, et partim de *hominibus* usurpatur, *quorum sensus et sermones ad vim divinam referendi sunt*, v. c. *poëtis, faticidis, prophetis, auguribus*, qui etiam θεοδίδακτοι vocantur, partim de *ipsis rebus, notionibus, sermonibus, et scriptis, a Deo suggestis, et divino instructu natis*, ex θεός et πνέω *spiro*, quod, ut Latinum *afflo*, de diis speciatim usurpatur, quorum vi homines interdum ita agi existimabantur, ut notiones rerum, antea ignotarum, insolito quodam modo conciperent atque mente vehementius concitata in sermones sublimiores et elegantiores erumperent. Conf. *Cic.* pro Archia c. 14; *Virgil*. Aen. iii, 358, vi, 50. In N. T. semel legitur II Tim. iii. 16, πᾶσα γραφὴ θεόπνευστος omnis

---

[1] From *The Presbyterian and Reformed Review*, v. XI, pp. 89–130.

Scriptura divinitus inspirata, seu, quæ est originis divinæ. coll. II Pet i. 21. Syrus. . . . scriptura, quæ per spiritum scripta est. Conjunxit nempe actionem scribendi cum actione inspirandi. Apud *Plutarchum* T. ix. p. 583. ed. *Reiske.* θεόπνευστοι ὄνειροι sunt *somnia a diis immissa.*"

Robinson "Greek and English Lexicon of the New Testament," new ed., New York, 1872:

"θεόπνευστος, ου, ὁ, ἡ, adj. (θεός, πνέω), *God-inspired, inbreathed of God*, II Tim. iii. 16 πᾶσα γραφὴ θεόπνευστος. — Plut. de Placit. Philosoph. 5. 2, τοὺς ὀνείρους τοὺς θεοπνεύστους. Phocylid. 121 τῆς δὲ θεοπνεύστου σοφίης λόγος ἐστὶν ἄριστος. Comp. Jos. c. Ap. 1. 7 [αἱ γραφαὶ] τῶν προφητῶν κατὰ τὴν ἐπίπνοιαν τὴν ἀπὸ τοῦ θεοῦ μαθόντων. Cic. pro Arch. 8, 'poetam . . . quasi divino quodam spiritu inflari.' "

Thayer-Grimm "Greek-English Lexicon of the New Testament," New York, 1887:

"θεόπνευστος, —ον, (θεός and πνέω), *inspired by God*: γραφή, i. e. the contents of Scripture, II Tim. iii. 16 [see πᾶς I. 1 c.]; σοφίη, [pseudo-] Phocyl. 121; ὄνειροι, Plut. de plac. phil. 5, 2, 3 p. 904f.; [Orac. Sibyll. 5, 406 (cf. 308); Nonn. paraphr. ev. Ioan. 1, 99]. (ἔμπνευστος also is used passively, but ἄπνευστος, εὔπνευστος, πυρίπνευστος, [δυσδιάπνευστος], actively [and δυσανάπνευστος appar. either act. or pass.; cf. W. 96 (92) note].) "

Cremer "Biblico-Theological Lexicon of New Testament Greek" ed. 2, E. T., Edinburgh, 1878:

"θεόπνευστος, *prompted by God, divinely inspired*. II Tim. iii. 16, πᾶσα γραφὴ θ. In profane Greek it occurs only in Plut. *de placit. philos.* v. 2, ὄνειροι θεόπνευστοι (κατ' ἀνάγκην γίνονται), opposed to φυσικοί. The formation of the word cannot be traced to the use of πνέω, but only of ἐμπνέω. Cf. Xen. *Hell.* vii. 4, 32, τὴν ἀρετὴν θεὸς μὲν ἐμπνεύσας; Plat. *Conv.* 179 B, μένος ἐμπνεῦσαι ἐνίοις τῶν ἡρώων τὸν θεόν; Hom. *Il.* xx. 110; *Od.* xix. 138. The simple verb is never used of divine action. How much the word corresponds with the Scriptural view is evident from II Pet. i. 21."

And the commentators generally will be found to speak no otherwise.

The completeness of this lexical consent has recently, however, been broken, and that by no less an authority than Prof.

Hermann Cremer himself, the second edition of whose great "Biblico-theological Lexicon" we have just adduced as in entire agreement with the current view. The date of issue of this edition, in its original German form, was 1872. The third edition was delayed until 1883. In the interval Dr. Cremer was called upon to write the article on "Inspiration" in the second edition of Herzog's "Realencyklopædie" (Vol. vi, *sub voc.*, pp. 746 *seq.*), which saw the light in 1880. In preparing this article he was led to take an entirely new view [2] of the meaning of θεόπνευστος, according to which it defines Scripture, in II Tim. iii. 16, not according to its origin, but according to its effect — not as "inspired of God," but as "inspiring its readers." The statement of his new view was transferred to the third edition of his "Lexicon" (1883; E. T. as "Supplement," 1886) very much in the form in which it appears in Herzog; and it has retained its place in the "Lexicon," with practically no alteration, ever since.[3] As its expression in Herzog was the earliest, and therefore is historically the most important, and as the article in the "Lexicon" is easily accessible in both German and English, and moreover does not

[2] The novelty of the view in question must not be pressed beyond measure. It was a new view in the sense of the text, but, as we shall subsequently see, it was no invention of Prof. Cremer's, but was derived by him from Ewald.

[3] That is at least to the eighth edition (1895), which is the last we have seen. The chief differences between the Herzog and "Lexicon" articles are found at the beginning and end — the latter being fuller at the beginning and the former at the end. The "Lexicon" article opens thus: "Θεόπνευστος, -ον, *gifted with God's Spirit, breathing the Divine Spirit* (but not, as Weiss still maintains = *inspired by God*). The term belongs only to Hellenistic and Ecclesiastical Greek, and as peculiar thereto is connected with expressions belonging to the sphere of heathen prophecy and mysteries, θεοφόρος, θεοφόρητος, θεοφορούμενος, θεήλατος, θεοκίνητος, θεοδέγμων, θεοδέκτωρ, θεοπρόπος, θεόμαντις, θεόφρων, θεοφράδμων, θεοφραδής, ἔνθεος, ἐνθουσιαστής, *et al.*, to which Hellenistic Greek adds two new words, θεόπνευστος and θεοδίδακτος, without, however, denoting what the others do — an ecstatic state." The central core of the article then runs parallel in both forms. Nothing is added in the "Lexicon," except (in the later editions) immediately after the quotations from Nonnus this single sentence: "This usage in Nonnus shows just that it is not to be taken as = *inspiratus*, inspired by God but as = filled with God's Spirit and therefore radiating it." Then follows immediately the next sentence, precisely as in Herzog, with which the "Lexicon" article then runs parallel to the quotation from Origen, immediately after which it breaks off.

essentially differ from what is said in Herzog, we shall quote here Dr. Cremer's statement of the case in preference from Herzog. He says:

"In theological usage, Inspiration denotes especially the influence of the Holy Spirit in the origination of the sacred Scriptures, by means of which they become the expression to us of the will of God, or the Word of God. The term comes from the Vulgate, which renders II Tim. iii. 16 πᾶσα γραφὴ θεόπνευστος, by *omnis Scriptura divinitus inspirata*. Whether the meaning of the Greek term is conveyed by this is at least questionable. It clearly belongs only to Hellenistic and Christian Greek. The notion that it was used also in classical Greek of poets and seers (Huther in his Commentary) and to express what Cicero says in his *pro Archia*, p. 8, *nemo vir magnus sine aliquo afflatu divino unquam fuit*, is certainly wrong. For θεόπνευστος does not occur at all in classical Greek or in profane Greek as a whole. In the unique passage, Plutarch, *de placit. phil.*, 5, 2 (Mor. 904, 2): τοὺς ὀνείρους τοὺς θεοπνεύστους κατ' ἀνάγκην γίνεσθαι· τοὺς δὲ φυσικοὺς ἀνειδωλοποιουμένης ψυχῆς τὸ συμφέρον αὐτῇ κτλ., it is very probably to be ascribed to the copyist, and stands, as Wyttenbach conjectures, in the place of θεοπέμπτους. Besides this it occurs in Pseudo-Phocylides, v. 121: τῆς δὲ θεοπνεύστου σοφίης λόγος ἐστὶν ἄριστος — unless the whole line is, with Bernays, to be deleted as disturbing to the sense — as well as in the fifth book of the "Sibyllines," v. 308: Κύμη δ' ἡ μωρὰ σὺν νάμασι τοῖς θεοπνεύστοις, and v. 406, 'Αλλὰ μέγαν γενετῆρα θεὸν πάντων θεοπνεύστων 'Εν θυσίαις ἐγέραιρον καὶ ἁγίας ἑκατόμβας. The Pseudo-Phocylides was, however, a Hellenist, and the author of the fifth book of the "Sibyllines" was, most probably, an Egyptian Jew living in the time of Hadrian. On Christian ground we find it in II Tim. iii. 16, which is possibly the earliest written employment of it to which we can point. Wetstein, on this passage, adduces the sentence from the *Vita Sabae* 16 (in Cotelerii *Monum.*): ἔφθασε τῇ τοῦ Χυ χάριτι ἡ πάντων θεοπνεύστων, πάντων χριστοφόρων αὐτοῦ συνοδία μέχρι ὁ ὀνομάτων, as well as the designation of Marcus Eremita as ὁ θεόπνευστος ἀνήρ. That the term has a passive meaning = 'gifted with God's Spirit,' 'divinely spirited,' (not 'inspired' as Ewald rightly distinguishes [4]) may be taken as indubitable from 'Sibyll.', v. 406 and the two passages last adduced. Never-

---

The contrast is between "*göttlich begeistet*" and "*göttlich begeistert*." The reference to Ewald is given in the "Lexicon": *Jahrb. f. bibl. Wissenschaft*, vii. 68, seq.; ix. 91 seq.

theless γραφὴ θεόπνευστος does not seem easily capable of meaning 'inspired by God's Spirit' in the sense of the Vulgate; when connected with such conceptions as γραφή here, νᾶμα, 'fountain,' 'Sibyll.' v. 308, it would rather signify 'breathing a divine spirit,' in keeping with that ready transition of the passive into the active sense which we see in ἄπνευστος, εὔπνευστος, 'ill- or well-breathed' = 'breathing ill or well.' Compare Nonnus, paraphr. ev Jo., i, 102: οὗ ποδὸς ἄκρου ἀνδρομέην παλάμην οὐκ ἄξιος εἰμὶ πελάσσας, λῦσαι μοῦνον ἱμάντα θεοπνεύστοιο πεδίλου, with v. 129: βαπτίζειν ἀπύροισι καὶ ἀπνεύστοισι λοέτροις. In harmony with this, it might be understood also in Phocyl. 121; the explanation, 'Wisdom gifted with the Divine Spirit,' at all events has in its favor the fact that θεόπνευστος is given the same sense as when it is connected with ἀνήρ, ἄνθρωπος. Certainly a transition to the sense, 'breathed by God' = 'inspired by God' seems difficult to account for, and it would fit, without forcing, only Phocyl. 121, while in II Tim. iii. 16, on the assumption of this sense, there would be required a not altogether easy metonyme. The sense 'breathing God's Spirit' is moreover in keeping with the context, especially with the ὠφέλιμος πρὸς διδασκαλίαν κτλ. and the τὰ δυνάμενά σε σοφίσαι, v. 15, as well as with the language employed elsewhere, e. g., in the Epistle to the Hebrews, where what the Scripture says is, as is well known, spoken of as the saying, the word of the Holy Ghost. Cf. also Acts xxviii. 25. Origen also, in Hom. 21 in Jerem., seems so to understand it: sacra volumina Spiritus pleni-tudinem spirant. Let it be added that the expression 'breathed by God, inspired by God,' though an outgrowth of the Biblical idea, certainly, so far as it is referred to the prophecy which does not arise out of the human will (II Pet. i. 21), yet can scarcely be applied to the whole of the rest of the sacred Scriptures — unless we are to find in II Tim. iii. 16 the expression of a conception of sacred Scripture similar to the Philonian. There is no doubt, however, that the Peshito understood it simply = 'inspired by God' — yet not differently than as in Matt. xxii. 43 we find: Δαυὶδ ἐν πνεύματι λαλεῖ. It translates כָּל כְּתָב גֵּיר בְּרוּחָא אֶתְכְּתֵב, 'for every Scripture which is written ἐν πνεύματι' — certainly keeping prominently in the foreground the inspiration of the writer. Similarly the Æthiopic renders: 'And every Scripture is in the (by the) Spirit of the Lord and profits'; while the Arabic (deriving from the original text) reads: 'And every Scripture which is divinely of spiratio, divinam sapiens auram.' The rendering of the Peshito and the explanations of the Greek exegetes would certainly lend great weight to the divinitus inspirata, were not they explicable from the dominant idea of the time — for which, it was thought, a suitable term was found in II Tim. iii. 16, nowhere else used indeed and coined for the purpose — but which was itself more or less taken over from the Alexandrian Judaism, that is to say, from heathenism."

Here, we will perceive, is a carefully reasoned attempt to reverse the previous lexical *consensus* as to the meaning of this important word. We have not observed many traces of the influence of this new determination of its import. The present writer, after going over the ground under Prof. Cremer's guidance, too hastily adopted his conclusion in a paper on "Paul's Doctrine of the Old Testament" published in *The Presbyterian Quarterly* for July, 1899; and an adverse criticism of Dr. Cremer's reasoning, from the pen of Prof. Dr. L. Schulze, of Rostock, appeared in the *Theologisches Literaturblatt* for May 22, 1896 (xvii. 21, pp. 253, 254), in the course of a review of the eighth edition of the "Lexicon." But there has not met our eye as yet any really thorough reëxamination of the whole matter, such as a restatement of it like Dr. Cremer's might have been expected to provoke. The case surely warrants and indeed demands it. Dr. Cremer's statement is more than a statement — it is an argument; and his conclusion is revolutionary, not indeed as to doctrine — for that rests on a broader basis than a single text or an isolated word — but as to the meaning borne by an outstanding New Testament term. It would seem that there is, then, no apology needed for undertaking a somewhat minute examination of the facts in the case under the guidance of Dr. Cremer's very full and well-reasoned statement.

It may conduce, in the end, to clearness of presentation if we begin somewhat *in medias res* by raising the question of the width of the usage of the word. Is it broadly a Greek word, or distinctively a Hellenistic word, or even a purely Christian word?

So far as appears from the usage as ascertained,[5] it would

[5] Of which the facts given by Cremer may for the present be taken as a fair conspectus, only adding that the word occurs not only in the editions of Plutarch, "De plac. phil.," v. 2, 3, but also in the printed text of the

seem to be post-Christian. Whether we should also call it Christian, coined possibly by Paul and used only in Christian circles, depends, in the present state of our knowledge, on the determination of two rather nice questions. One of these concerns the genuineness of the reading θεοπνεύστους in the tract on "The Opinions of Philosophers" (v, 2, 3), which has come down to us among the works of Plutarch, as well as in its dependent document, the "History of Philosophy" (106), transmitted among the works of Galen. The other concerns the character, whether Jewish or Jewish-Christian, of certain portions of the fifth book of the "Sibylline Oracles" and of the "Poem of Admonition," once attributed to Phocylides but now long recognized to be the work of a late Alexandrian Jew,[6] —in both of which the word occurs. Dr. Cremer considers the reading to be false in the Plutarchian tract, and thinks the fifth book of the "Sybillines" and the Pseudo-Phocylidian poem Jewish in origin. He therefore pronounces the word a Hellenistic one. These decisions, however, can scarcely be looked upon as certain; and they will bear scrutiny, especially as they are accompanied with some incidental errors of statement.

It would certainly require considerable boldness to decide with confidence upon the authorship of any given portion of the fifth book of the "Sibyllines." Friedlieb (whom Dr. Cremer follows) and Badt ascribe the whole book to a Jewish, but Alexandre, Reuss and Dechent to a Christian author; while others parcel it out variously between the two classes of sources—the most assigning the sections containing the word in question, however, to a Jewish author (Bleck, Lücke, Gfrörer; Ewald, Hilgenfeld; Schürer). Schürer practically gives up in despair the problem of distributing the book to its several authors, and contents himself with saying that Jewish pieces preponderate and run in date from the first Christian century to Hadrian.[7] In these circumstances surely

dependent document printed among Galen's works under the title of "De-hist. phil.," 106.

[6] Cf. Mahaffy, "History of Greek Literature" (American ed.), i 188, note 1.

[7] "The Jewish People in the Time of Jesus Christ," E. T., II, iii. 286, whence the account given in the text is derived.

a certain amount of doubt may fairly be thought to rest on the Jewish or Christian origin of our word in the Sibylline text. On the other hand, there seems to be pretty good positive reason for supposing the Pseudo-Phocylidian poem to be in its entirety a Christian production. Its Jewish origin was still strenuously maintained by Bernays,[8] but its relation to the "Teaching of the Apostles" has caused the subject to be reopened, and we think has brought it to at least a probable settlement in favor of Scaliger's opinion that it is the work "ἀνωνύμου Christiani."[9] In the face of this probability the brilliant and attractive, but not always entirely convincing conjectures by which Bernays removed some of the Christian traits from the text may now be neglected: and among them that by which he discarded the line containing our word. So far then as its occurrence in the fifth book of the "Sibyllines" and in Pseudo-Phocylides is concerned, no compelling reason appears why the word may not be considered a distinctively Christian one: though it must at the same time be recognized that the sections in the fifth "Sibyl" in which it occurs are more probably Jewish than Christian.

With reference to the Plutarchian passage something more needs to be said. "In the unique passage, Plutarch de plac. phil. 5, 2 (904 F.): τῶν ὀνείρων τοὺς μὲν θεοπνεύστους κατ' ἀνάγκην γίνεσθαι· τοὺς δὲ φυσικοὺς ἀνειδωλοποιουμένης ψυχῆς τὸ συμφέρον αὐτῇ κτλ." says Dr. Cremer, "it is with the greatest probability to be ascribed to the transcriber, in whose mind θεόπνευστος lay in the sense of the Vulgate rendering, divinitus inspirata, and it stands, as Wyttenbach conjectures, for θεοπέμπτους." The remark concerning Wyttenbach is erroneous — only one of a series of odd misstatements which have dogged the textual notes on this passage. Wyttenbach prints θεοπνεύστους in his text and accompanies it with this textual

---

[8] See his "Gesammelte Abhandlungen," edited by Usener in 1885. Usener's Preface should be also consulted.

[9] So Harnack, "Theologische Literaturzeitung," 1885, No. 7, p. 160: also, J. R. Harris, "The Teaching of the Apostles and the Sibylline Books" (Cambridge, 1888): both give internal evidences of the Christian origin of the book. Cf. what we have said in *The Andover Review* for August, 1886, p. 219.

note: [10] "θεοπέμπτους *reposuit editor Lips. ut ex Gal. et Mosc. At in neutro haec reperio. Sane non est quare compilatori elegantias obtrudamus.*" Θεοπέμπτους is therefore not Wyttenbach's conjecture: Wyttenbach does not even accept it, and this has of late been made a reproach to him: [11] he ascribes it to "the Leipzig editor," that is to Christian Daniel Beck, whose edition of this tract was published at Leipzig, in 1787. But Wyttenbach even more gravely misquotes Beck than he has himself been misquoted by Dr. Cremer. For Beck, who prints in his text: τῶν ὀνείρων τοὺς μὲν θεοπνεύστους, annotates as follows: "Olim: τοὺς ὀνείρους τοὺς θεοπνεύστους — *Reddidi textis elegantiorem lectionem, quae in M. et G. est. θεοπνεύστους sapere Christianum librarium videtur pro θεοπέμπτους.*" [12] That is to say, Wyttenbach has transferred Beck's note on τῶν ὀνείρων τοὺς μὲν to θεοπέμπτους. It is this clause and not θεοπέμπτους that Beck professes to have got out of the Moscow MS. and Galen: θεοπέμπτους he presents merely as a pure conjecture founded on the one consideration that θεοπνεύστους has a flavor of Christian scribe about it; and he does not venture to put θεοπέμπτους into the text. The odd thing is that Hutten follows Wyttenbach in his misrepresentation of Beck, writing in his note: "Beck. dedit θεοπέμπτους ut elegantiorem lectionem e Mosq. et Gal. sumptam. In neutro se hoc reperisse W. notat, addens, non esse quare compilatori elegantias obtrudamus. Cors. e Gal. notat τῶν ὀνείρων τοὺς μὲν θεοπνεύστους." [13] Corsini does indeed so report, his note running: "Paullo aliter" (i. e., from the ordinary text which he reprints from Stephens) "Galenus, τῶν ὀνείρων τοὺς μὲν θεοπνεύστους, somniorum ea quidem quae divinitus inspirata sint, etc." [14] But this is exactly what Beck says, and nothing other,

[10] Oxford 8vo edition, 1795–1830, Vol. IV, ii. 650.

[11] As by Diels in his "Doxographi Graci," p. 15: "*fuit scilicet* θεοπέμπτους, *quod sero intellectum est a Wyttenbachio in indice Plutarcheo. si Galenum inspexissit, ipsum illud* θεοπέμπτους *inventurus erat.*" But Diels' presentation of Galen was scarcely open to Wyttenbach's inspection: and the editions then extant read θεοπνεύστους as Corsini rightly tells us.

[12] "Plutarchi de Physicis Philosophorum Decretis," ed. Chr. Dan. Beckius, Leipzig, 1787. [13] Tübingen, 1791–1804, Vol. XII (1800), p. 467.

[14] "Plutarchi de Placitis Philosophorum Libb. v." (Florentiæ, 1750).

except that he adds that this form is also found in the Moscow MS. We must conclude that Hutten in looking at Beck's note was preoccupied with Wyttenbach's misreport of it. The upshot of the whole matter is that the reading θεοπέμπτους was merely a conjecture of Beck's, founded solely on his notion that θεοπνεύστους was a purely Christian term, and possessing no diplomatic basis whatsoever. Accordingly it has not found its way into the printed text of Plutarch: all editions, with one exception, down to and including those of Dübner-Döhner (Didot's "Bibliotheca") of 1856 and Bernardakis (Teubner's series) of 1893 read θεοπνεύστους.

A new face has been put on the matter, however, by the publication of 1879 of Diels' "Doxographi Græci," in which the whole class of ancient literature to which Plutarch's "De plac. philos." belongs is subjected to a searching study, with a view to tracing the mutual relations of the several pieces and the sources from which they are constructed.[15] With this excursion into "higher criticism," into which there enters a highly speculative element, that, despite the scientific thoroughness and admirable acuteness which give the whole an unusually attractive aspect, leaves some doubts in the mind of the sober reader,[16] we have now happily little to do. Suffice it to say that Diels looks upon the Plutarchian tract as an epitome of a hypothetical Aëtios, made about 150 A.D. and already used by Athenagoras (c. 177 A.D.):[17] and on the Galenic tract as in its later portion an excerpt from the Plutarchian tract, made about A.D. 500.[18] In the course of his work, he has

[15] A very clear account of Diels' main conclusions is given by Franz Susemihl in his "Geschichte der Griechischen Literatur in der Alexandrinerzeit" (Leipzig, 1891-1892), ii. pp. 250, 251, as well as in Bursian's *Jahresbericht* for 1881 (VII, i. 289 *seq.*). A somewhat less flattering notice by Max Heinze appears in Bursian for 1880, p. 3 *seq.*

[16] Cf. the remarks of Max Heinze as above.

[17] It would be possible to hold, of course, that Athenagoras used not the [Pseudo?-] Plutarch, but the hypothetical Aëtios, of which Diels considers the former an excerpt: but Diels does not himself so judge: "anceps est quæstio utrum excerpserit Athenagoras Plutarchi Placita an maius illud opus, cuius illa est epitome. illud mihi probatur, hoc R. Volkmanno 'Leben Plut.,' i .169. . . ." (p. 51).

[18] The relation of the Pseudo-Galen to the [Pseudo?-] Plutarch Diels ex-

framed and printed a careful recension of the text of both tracts,[19] and in both of them he reads at the place of interest to us, θεοπέμπτους.[20] Here for the first (and as yet only [21]) time θεοπέμπτους makes its appearance in the text of what we may, in deference to Diels' findings and after the example of Gerke,[22] call, at least, the "[Pseudo?-] Plutarch."[23] The key to the situation, with Diels, lies in the reading of the Pseudo-Galen: for as an excerpt from the [Pseudo?-] Plutarch the Pseudo-Galen becomes a valuable witness to its text, and is treated in this case indeed as a determinative witness, inasmuch as the whole MS. transmission of [Pseudo?-] Plutarch, so far as known, reads here θεοπνεύστους. Editing θεοπέμπτους in Pseudo-Galen, Diels edits it also, on that sole documentary ground, in [Pseudo?-] Plutarch. That we may form some estimate of the likelihood of the new reading, we must, therefore, form some estimate of its likelihood in the text of the Pseudo-Galen, as well as of the principles on which the text of the [Pseudo?-] Plutarch is to be framed.

The editions of Pseudo-Galen — including that of Kühn[24] — presses thus: "Alter liber quo duce ex generali physicorum tanquam promulside ad largiorem dapam Galenus traducit est 'Plutarchus de Placidis philosophorum physicis.' Unde cum in prioribus pauca suspensa manu ut condimentum adspersa sint (c. 5, 20, 21), jam a c. 25 ad finem Plutarchus ita regnat, nihil aliud ut praeterea adscitum esse appareat . . . ergo foedioribus Byzantiorum soloecismis amputatis hanc partem ad codicum fidem descripsimus, non nullis Plutarcheae emendationis auxilium, pluribus fortasse humanae perversitatis insigne testimonium" (pp. 252, 253).      [19] Plutarch's, pp. 267 seq.; Galen's, pp. 595 seq.

[20] Plutarch's "Ep.," v. 2, 3 (p. 416); Galen's "Hist. Phil.," 106 (p. 640).

[21] For Bernardakis reads θεοπνεύστους in his text (Teubner series, Plutarch's "Moralia," v. 351), recognizing at the same time in a note that the reading of Galen is θεοπέμπτους.

[22] In Pauly's "Real-Encyclopædie," new ed., s. v.

[23] It is not meant, of course, that Diels was the first to deny the tract to Plutarch. It has always been under suspicion. Wyttenbach, for example, rejects its Plutarchian claim with decision, and speaks of the tract in a tone of studied contempt, which is, indeed, reflected in the note already quoted from him, in the remark that we would not be justified in obtruding elegancies on a mere compiler. Cf. i. p. xli: "Porro, si quid hoc est, spurius liber utriusque nomine perperam fertur idem, Plutarchi qui dicitur De Philosophorum Placitis, Galeni Historia philosophiæ."

[24] Diels does not think highly of this portion of Kühn's edition: "Kuehnius, qui prioribus sui corporis voluminibus manum subinde admovit quamvis parum

have hitherto read θεοπνεύστους at our place, and from this we may possibly infer, that this is the reading of the common run of the MSS.[25] Diels constructs his text for this portion of the treatise from two kindred MSS. only, and records the readings of no others: as no variation is given upon our word, we may infer that these two MSS. at least agree in reading θεοπέμπτους. The former of them (Codex Laurentianus lxxiv, 3), of the twelfth or early thirteenth century, is described as transcribed "with incredible corruptness"; the latter (Codex Laurentianus lviii, 2), of the fifteenth century, as written more carefully: both represent a common very corrupt archetype.[26] This archetype is reconstructed from the consent of the two, and where they differ the preference is given to the former. The text thus framed is confessedly corrupt: [27] but though it must therefore be cautiously used, Diels considers it nevertheless a treasure house of the best readings for the [Pseudo?-] Plutarch.[28] Especially in the latter part of the [Pseudo?-] Plutarch, where the help of Eusebius and the other *eclogæ* fails, he thinks the case would often be desperate if we did not have the Pseudo-Galen. Three examplse of the preservation of the right reading by it alone he gives us, one of them being our present passage, in which he follows, therefore, the reading of the Pseudo-Galen against the entire MS. transmission.

Diels considers the whole MS. transmission of the [Pseudo?-] Plutarch to take us back to an archetype of

felicem, postremo urgenti typothetæ ne inspectas quidem Charterianæ plagulas typis discribendas tradidisse fertur. neque aliter explicari potest, quod editio ambitiose suscepta tam misere absoluta est" (p. 241, 2).

[25] Though Diels informs us that the editors have made very little effort to ascertain the readings of the MSS.

[26] "Ex archetypo haud vetusto eodemque mendosissimo quattuor exempla transcripta esse, ac fidelius quidem Laur. A, peritius sed interpolate Laur. B." (p. 241).

[27] Diels' language is: "dolendum sane est libri condicionem tam esse desperatam ut etiam Plutarcheo archetypo comparato haud semel plane incertus hæreas, quid sibi velit compilator" (p. 12).

[28] "Verum quamvis sit summa opus cautione ne ventosi nebulonis commenta pro sincera memoria amplexemur, inest tamen in Galeno optimarum lectionum pæne intactus thesaurus" (p. 13).

about A.D. 1000, and selects from it three codices as nearest to the archetype,[29] viz., A = Codex Mosquensis 339 (nunc 352) of saec. xi. or xii. (the same as the Mosq. quoted by Beck), collated by Matthaei and in places reëxamined for Diels by Voelkelius; B = Codex Marcianus 521 [xcii, 7], of saec. xiv, very closely related to A, collated by Diels himself; and C = Codex Parisinus 1672 of saec. xiii. ex. vel. xiv. in which is a copy of a corpus of Plutarch put together by Planudes or a contemporary. Through these three codices he reaches the original apograph which stands at the root of all the extant MSS., and from it, by the aid of the excerpts from the tract — in our passage the Pseudo-Galen's only — he attains his text.

His note on our reading runs thus: "θεοπέμπτους G cf. Arist. de divinat. 2 p. 463b 13: θεοπνεύστους (A) B C, cf. Prol. p. 15." The parenthesis in which A is enclosed means that A is here cited from the silence of Matthaei's collation.[30] The reference to the Prolegomena is to the passage already alluded to, in which the Galenic reading θεοπέμπτους is cited as one of three chosen instances of excellent readings preserved by Galen alone. The note there runs thus: "alteri loco christiani librarii pius fraus nocuit. V. 2, 3, 'Ηρόφιλος τῶν ὀνείρων τοὺς μὲν θ ε ο π ν ε ύ σ τ ο υ ς κατ' ἀνάγκην γίνεθαι. fuit scilicet θεοπέμπτους, quod sero intellectum est a Wyttenbachio in indice Plutarcheo. si Galenum inspexisset, ipsum illud θεοπέμπτους inventurus erat. simili fraude versus 121 Phocylideis a Byzantinis insertus est, ubi vox illa sacra [II Tim. iii. 16] I. Bernaysio interpolationis originem manifesto aperuit."

---

[29] "Codices manu scripti quotquot noti sunt ex archetypo circa millesimum annum scripto deducti sunt" (p. 33). "duo autem sunt recensendi Plutarchi instrumenta . . . unum recentius ex codicis petendum, inter quos A B C archetypo proximos ex ceterorum turba segregavi . . . alterum genus est excerptorum . . ." (p. 42).

[30] The readings of A are drawn from a collation of it with the Frankfort edition of 1620 published by C. F. Matthæi in his "Lectiones Mosquenses." In a number of important readings, the MS. has been reinspected for Diels by Voelkel with the result of throwing some doubt on the completeness of Matthæi's collation. Accordingly the MS. is cited in parenthesis whenever it is cited *e silentio* (see Diels, p. 33).

That is to say, the reading of the Pseudo-Galen is preferred to that of the MSS., because the reading θεοπνεύστους explains itself as a pious fraud of a Christian scribe, giving a place in the text of Plutarch to "this sacred word" — another example of which procedure is to be found in Pseudo-Phoc. 121, extruded by Bernays from the text on this very ground. On this remark, as on a hinge, turns, it would seem, the decision of the whole question. The problem of the reading, indeed, may be set forth at this point in the form of this alternative: — Which is most likely, — that θεοπνεύστους in the [Pseudo?-] Plutarch originated in the pious fraud of a Christian scribe? — or that θεοπέμπτους in the text of Pseudo-Galen edited by Diels originated in the error of a careless scribe?

When we posit the problem in this definite form we cannot feel at all certain that Diels' solution is the right one. There is an à priori unlikelihood in its way: deliberate corruption of texts is relatively rare and not to be assumed without good reason. The parallel from the Pseudo-Phocylides fails, now that it seems probable that the whole poem is of Christian origin. There seems no motive for such a pious fraud as is charged: what gain could be had from intruding θεοπνεύστους into the Plutarchian text? and what special sanctity attached to this word? And if a sacrosanct character be attributed to the word, could it not be equally plausibly argued that it was therefore offensive to the Christian consciousness in this heathen connection, and was accordingly replaced by the less sacred θεοπέμπτους, a word of heathen associations and indeed with a secondary sense not far from "extraordinary." [31] Or if it be now said that it is not intended to charge conscious fraud, it is pertinent to ask what special associations Christians had with the word θεόπνευστος in connection with dreams which would cause it to obtrude itself

---

[31] The general use of θεόπεμπτος is illustrated in the Lexicons, by the citation of Arist., "Ethic. Nic.," i. 9, 3, where happiness is spoken of as θεόπεμπτος in contrast to the attainment of virtue in effort; Longinus, c. 34, where we read of θεόπεμπτά τινα δωρήματα in contrast with ἀνθρώπινα; Themist, "Or." 13, p. 178 D, where ὁ Θ. νεανίος is found; Dion. Hal., T. 14. Liddell and Scott quote for the secondary sense of "extraordinary," Longus, 3, 18; Artem., i. 7.

unconsciously in such a connection. One is almost equally at a loss to account for the intrusion of the word in the place of the simpler θεόπεμπτος, whether the intrusion be looked upon as deliberate or unconscious. On the other hand, the substitution of θεόπεμπτος for θεόπνευστος in the text of Pseudo-Galen seems quite readily accountable, and that whether it be attributed to the original excerpter or to some later copyist of the tract. The term was associated with dreams in the minds of all acquainted with the literature of the subject. Diels himself refers us to a passage in Aristotle where the collocation occurs,[32] and familiar passages from Philo [33] and the "Clementina"[34] will suggest themselves to others. "God-sent dreams" must have almost had the rank of a "terminus technicus."[35] Moreover the scribe had just written the word

---

[32] Arist., de divinat, 2 p. 463ᵇ 13: ὅλως δ'ἐπεὶ καὶ τῶν ἄλλων ζώων ὀνειρώττει τινά, θεόπεμπτα μὲν οὐκ ἄν εἴη τὰ ἐνύπνια, οὐδὲ γέγονε τούτου χάριν, δαιμόνια μέντοι· ἡ γὰρ φύσις δαιμονία, ἀλλ' οὐ θεία.

[33] Cf. Philo's tract περὶ τοῦ θεοπέμπτους εἶναι τοὺς ὀνείρους (Mangey., i. 620). Its opening words run (Yonge's translation, ii. 292): "The treatise before this one has contained our opinions as to those of τῶν ὀνείρων θεοπέμπτων classed in the first species ... which are defined as dreams in which the Deity sends the appearances beheld in dreams according to his own suggestion (τὸ θεῖον κατὰ τὴν ἰδίαν ὑποβολῆς τὰς ἐν τοῖς ὕπνοις ἐπιπέμπειν φαντασίας)," whereas this later treatise is to discuss the second species of dreams, in which, "our mind being moved along with that of the universe, has seemed to be hurried away from itself and to be God-borne (θεοφορεῖσθαι) so as to be capable of preapprehension and foreknowledge of the future." Cf. also § 22, τῆς θεοπέμπτου φαντασίας: § 33, θεοπέμπτους ὀνείρους: ii. § 1, τῶν θεοπέμπτων ὀνείρων. The superficial parallelism of Philo with what is cited from Herophilus is close enough fully to account for a scribe harking back to Philo's language — or even for the compiler of the Pseudo-Galen doing so.

[34] "Clementine Homilies," xvii. 15: "And Simon said: 'If you maintain that apparitions do not always reveal the truth, yet for all that visions and dreams, being God-sent (τὰ ὁράματα καὶ τὰ ἐνύπνια θεόπεμπτα ὄντα οὐ ψεύδεται) do not speak falsely in regard to those matters which they wish to tell.' And Peter said: 'You were right in saying that, being God-sent, they do not speak falsely (θεόπεμπτα ὄντα οὐ ψεύδεται. But it is uncertain if he who sees has seen a God-sent dream (εἰ ὁ ἰδὼν θεόπεμπτον ἑώρακεν ὄνειρον)." What has come to the "Clementine Homilies" is surely already a Christian commonplace.

[35] The immediately preceding paragraph in the Pseudo-Galen (§ 105), corresponding with [Pseudo?-] Plutarch, v. i. 1, 2.3 is edited by Diels thus: Πλάτων καὶ οἱ Στωικοὶ τὴν μαντικὴν εἰσάγουσι· καὶ γὰρ θεόπεμπτον εἶναι, ὅπερ ἐστὶν ἐνθεαστικὸν καὶ κατὰ τὸ θειότατον τῆς ψυχῆς, ὅπερ ἐστὶν ἐνθουσιαστικόν, καὶ τὸ ὀνειροπυλικὸν καὶ τὸ ἀστρονομικὸν καὶ τὸ ὀρνεοσκοπικόν. Ξενοφάνης καὶ Ἐπίκουρος ἀναιροῦσι τὴν μαντικήν.

in the immediate context, and that not without close con-
tiguity with the word ὀνείρους,[36] and may be readily supposed
to have had it still lingering in his memory when he came to
write the succeeding section. In fine, the intrusion into the
text of θεοπνεύστους, a rare word and one suggested to a dull
or inattentive scribe by nothing, seems far less easy to account for than the intrusion of θεοπέμπτους, a common word,
an ordinary term in this connection, and a term suggested
to the scribe by the immediate context. On transcriptional
grounds certainly the former appears far more likely to be
original — "proclivi scriptioni praestat ardua."

The decisive consideration against θεοπνεύστους in the
mind of Diels — as it had been before him in the mind of
Beck — seems to have been, indeed, nothing but the assumption that θεόπνευστος, as a distinctively Christian word, must
argue a Christian hand, wherever it is found. That, however,
in our present study is precisely the matter under investigation; and we must specially guard against permitting to
intrude decisively into our premises what we propose to
arrive at only by way of conclusion. Whether the word be
genuine in the [Pseudo?-] Plutarch or not, is just one of the
most important factors in deciding whether it be a peculiarly
Christian word or not. An instructive parallel may be found
in the treatment accorded by some great authorities to the
cognate word θεόπνοος when it turned up in an inscription
which seems obviously heathen.[37] This inscription, inscribed
(about the third century) on the face of a man-headed sphinx
at Memphis, sings the praises of the sphinx's beauty—

---

Πυθαγόρας δὲ μόνον τὸ θυτικὸν οὐκ ἐγκρίνει. Ἀριστοτέλης καὶ Δικαίαρχος τοὺς ὀνείρους
εἰσάγουσιν, ἀθάνατον μὲν τὴν ψυχὴν οὐ νομίζοντες, θείου δέ τινος μετέχειν. Surely the scribe
or compiler who could transmute the section περὶ μαντικῆς in the [Pseudo?-]
Plutarch into this, with its intruded θεόπεμπτον before him and its allusion to
Aristotle on dreams, might be credited without much rashness with the intrusion
of θεοπέμπτους into the next section.

[36] Cf. in general E. Thrämer. Hastings *ERE*, VI, p. 542.

[37] It is duly recorded in Boeckh, "Corpus Inscript. Graec," 4700 b. (Add. iii).
It is also printed by Kaibel, "Epigrammata Græca" (Berlin, 1878), p. 428, but
not as a Christian inscription, but under the head of "Epigrammata dedicatoria:
V. proscynemata."

among the items mentioned being that ἐφύπερ[θ]ε πρόσωπον ἔχει τὸ θ[ε]ό[πν]ουν, while, below, the body is that of the lion, king of beasts. Boeckh comments on this: "Vs. 4, 5, recte legit Letronnius, qui θεόπνοον monet Christianum quidam sonare." But why should Letronnius infer Christianity from the word θεόπνοον, or Boeckh think it worth while to record the fact? Fortunately the heathen use of θεόπνοος is beyond question.[38] It provides an excellent illustration, therefore, of the rashness of pronouncing words of this kind to be of Christian origin; and suggests the hesitancy with which we should extrude such a word from the text of [Pseudo?-] Plutarch on the sole ground that it "tastes of a Christian scribe." Surely if a heathen could invent and use the one word, he might equally well invent and use the other. And certainly it is a great mistake to look upon compounds with θεός of this kind as in any sense exclusively Christian. The long list of heathen terms of this character given by Dr. Cremer, indeed, is itself enough to indicate the heathen facility for their coinage. Many such words, we may well believe, were found by Christians ready made to their hand, and had only to be adapted to their richer usage. What is more distinctively Christian is the parallel list of words compounded with πνεῦμα [39] or even χριστός [40] which were placed by their side,

[38] Porphyry: "Ant. Nymph.," 116: ἡγοῦντο γὰρ προσιζάνειν τῷ ὕδατι τὰς ψυχὰς θεοπνόῳ ὄντι, ὥς φησιν ὁ Νουμήνιος· διὰ τοῦτο λέγων καὶ τὸν προφήτην εἰρηκέναι, ἐμφέρεσθαι ἐπάνω τοῦ ὕδατος θεοῦ πνεῦμα — a passage remarkable for containing an appeal to Moses (Gen. i. 5) by a heathen sage. "God-breathed water" is rendered by Holstenius: "aquae quae divino spiritu foveretur"; by Gesnerus: "aquae divinitus afflatae"; by Thomas Taylor: "water which is inspired by divinity." Pisid. "Hexaem.," 1489: ἡ θεόπνους ἀκρότης (quoted unverified from Hase-Dindorf's Stephens). The Christian usage is illustrated by the following citations, taken from Sophocles: Hermes Tris., "Poem," 17. 14: τῆς ἀληθείας; Anastasius of Sinai, Migne, 89. 1169 A: Those who do not have the love of God, "these, having a diabolical will and doing the desires of their flesh, παραιτοῦνται ὡς πονηρὸν τὸ θεόμοιον, καὶ θεόκτιστον, καὶ θεόμοιον τῆς νοερᾶς καὶ θεοχαράκτου ἡμῶν ψυχῆς ὁμολογεῖν ἐν Χριστῷ, καὶ τὴν ζωοποιὸν αὐτῆς καὶ συστατικὴν θεόπνουν ἐνέργειαν."

[39] πνευματοφόρος and πνευματοφορεῖσθαι are pre-Christian Jewish words, already used in the LXX. (Hos. ix. 7, Zeph. iii. 4, Jer. ii. 24). Compounds of θεός found in the LXX. are θεόκτιστος, II Macc. vi. 23; θεομαχεῖν, II Macc. vii. 19 [θεομάχος Sm., Job xxvi. 5, et al.]; θεοσέβεια, Gen. xx. 11 et al.; θεοσεβής Ex. xviii. 21 et al.

[40] No derivative of χριστός except χριστιανός is found in the New Testament.

such as [πνευματικός], πνευματοκίνητος, πνευματοφόρος, πνευματέμφορος; χριστόγραφος, χριστοδίδακτος, χριστοκίνητος, χριστόληπτος, χριστοφόρος.

As the reasons which have been determining with Diels in framing his text do not appear to us able to bear the weight laid on them, we naturally cannot adopt his text with any confidence. We doubt whether θεοπέμπτους was the original reading in the Pseudo-Galen; we doubt whether, if that were the case, we should on that ground edit it in the [Pseudo?-] Plutarch. Our feeling is decided that the intrusion of θεοπέμπτους into a text which originally read θεοπνεύστους would be far more easily accounted for than the reverse. One should be slow, of course, in rejecting a reading commended by such a scholarly tact as Diels'. But we may take courage from the fact that Bernardakis, with Diels' text before him, continues to read θεοπνεύστους even though recognizing θεοπέμπτους as the reading of Galen. We think we must be permitted to hold the matter still at least *sub judice* and to profess our inability in the circumstances to look upon the word as a purely Christian term.[41] It would be interesting to know what phraseology was used by Herophilus himself (born c. B.C. 300) in the passage which the [Pseudo?-] Plutarch excerpts. But this excerpt seems to be the only source of information we have in the matter,[42] and it would perhaps be overbold

The compounds are purely Patristic. See Lightfoot's note on Ignatius, Eph. ix; Phil. viii and the note in Migne's "Pat. Græc.," xi. 1861, at Adamantii "Dialogus de recta fide," § 5.

[41] In the Hase-Dindorf Stephens, *sub-voc.* θεόπνευστος, the passage, from the [Pseudo?-] Plutarch is given within square brackets in this form: ["Plut. Mor. p. 904F: τοὺς ὀνείρους τοὺς θεοπλούτους]." What is to be made of this new reading, we do not know. One wonders whether it is a new conjecture or a misprint. No earlier reference is given for θεόπλουτος in the "Thesaurus" than Chrysostom: "Ita Jobum appellat Jo. Chrystom, Vol. iv, p. 297, Suicer." Sophocles cites also Anast. Sinai. for the word: *Hexæmeron* XII *ad fin.* (Migne, 1076 D., Vol. 89): ὅπως τοῦτο καταβαλὼν ἐν ταῖς ψυχαῖς τραπεζισῶν σῶν ἄρρων σε δι' αὐτῶν τὴν θεόπλουτον καταπλουτήσω.

[42] So it may be confidently inferred from the summary of what we know of Herophilus given in Susemihl's "Geschichte der Griechisch. Literatur in d. Alexandrinerzeit," Vol. i, p. 792, or from Marx's "De Herophili . . . vita scriptis atque in medicina mentis" (Göttingen, 1840), p. 38. In both cases Herophilus' doctrine

to suppose that the compiler had preserved the very words of the great physician. Were such a presumption deemed plausible we should be forced to carry back the first known use of the word θεόπνευστος to the third century before Christ, but not to a *provenance* other than that Alexandria where its earliest use is otherwise traceable. Perhaps if we cannot call it a purely Christian term nor yet, with Dr. Cremer, an exclusively Hellenistic one, we may venture to think of it, provisionally at least, as belonging to Alexandrian Greek. Whether we should also say to late Alexandrian usage will possibly depend on the degree of likelihood we ascribe to its representing in the text of the [Pseudo?-] Plutarch an actual usage of Herophilus.

Our interest in determining the reading in the [Pseudo?-] Plutarch culminates, of course, in its bearing on the meaning of θεόπνευστος. Prof. Schulze's remark [43] that no copyist would have substituted θεόπνευστος here for θεόπεμπτος if linguistic usage had attached an active sense to the former, is no doubt quite just. This is admitted, indeed, by Dr. Cremer, who considers that the scribe to whom the substitution is thought to be due "had θεόπνευστος in his mind in the sense of the Vulgate rendering, *divinitus inspirata*"; and only seeks to break the force of this admission by urging that the constant exegetical tradition which assigned this meaning to θεόπνευστος, rests on a misunderstanding of the word and reads into it a sense derived from Alexandrian-Jewish conceptions of inspiration. This appeal from a fixed later to an assumed original sense of the word possesses force, no doubt, only in case that traces of such an assumed original sense can be adduced; and meanwhile the presence of θεόπνευστος as a synonym of θεόπεμπτος, even in the vocabulary of somewhat late scribes, must rank as one item in the evidence by which its meaning is to be ascertained. The whole face of the matter is changed, however, if θεόπνευστος be allowed to be probably

---

of dreams is gathered solely from our excerpts — in the case of Susemihl from "Aëtius" and in the case of Marx primarily from Galen with the support of Plutarch.　　　　　　　　　　　　　　[43] *Loc. cit.*

or even possibly genuine in the [Pseudo?-] Plutarch. In that case it could scarcely be thought to reflect the later Christian conception of inspiration, imposed on Paul's term by thinkers affected by Philo's doctrine of Scripture, but would stand as an independent bit of evidence as to the original meaning of the term. The clerical substitution of θεόπεμπτος for it under the influence of literary associations would indeed, in this case too, only witness to a synonymy in the mind of the later scribes, who may well be supposed Christians and sharers in the common conception that Christians read into θεόπνευστος. But the implications of the passage itself would be valid testimony to the original import of the term here used. And it would seem quite clear that the implications of the passage itself assign to it a passive sense, and that a sense not very remote from θεόπεμπτος. "Herophilus says," we read, "that theopneustic dreams" ("dreams divinely inspired," Holland; "the dreams that are caused by divine instinct," Goodwin), "come by necessity; but natural ones" ("natural dreams," Holland; "dreams which have their origin from a natural cause," Goodwin), "from the soul's imagery of what is fitting to it and its consequences," etc.[44] The contrast here between dreams that are θεόπνευστοι and those that are φυσικοί, the former of which are imposed on the soul while the latter are its own production, would seem certainly to imply that θεόπνευστος here imports something nearly akin to "God-given," though naturally with implications of its own as to the mode of the giving. It might be

[44] In the common text the passage goes on to tell us of the dreams of mixed nature, i. e., presumably partly divine and partly human in origin. But the idea itself seems incongruous and the description does not very well fit the category. Diels, therefore, conjectures πνευματικούς in its place in which case there are *three* categories in the enumeration: Theopneustic, physical (i. e., the product of the ψυχή or lower nature), and pneumatic, or the product of the higher nature. The whole passage in Diels' recension runs as follows: Aët. 'Plac.,' p. 416 (Pseudo-Plut., v. 2, 3): Ἡρόφιλος τῶν ὀνείρων τοὺς μὲν θεοπέμπτους κατ' ἀνάγκην γίνεσθαι, τοὺς δὲ φυσικοὺς ἀνειδωλοποιουμένης ψυχῆς τὸ συμφέρον αὐτῇ καὶ τὸ πάντως ἐσόμενον, τοὺς δὲ συγκραματικοὺς [πνευματικοὺς? Diels, but this is scarcely the right correction, cf. Susemihl, "Gesch. d. Gr. Lit.," etc. i. 792] [ἐκ τοῦ αὐτομάτου] κατ' εἰδώλων πρόσπτωσιν, ὅταν ἃ βουλόμεθα βλέπωμεν, ὡς ἐπὶ τῶν τὰς ἐρωμένας ὁρώντων ἐν ὕπνῳ γίνεται."

possible to read it as designating dreams that are breathed into by God, filled with His inspiration and thus made the vehicles of His message, if we otherwise knew that such is the implication of the term. But nothing so subtle as this is suggested by the language as it stands, which appears to convey merely the simple notion that theopneustic dreams differ from all natural ones, whether the latter belong to the higher or lower elements of our nature, in that they come from God and are therefore not necessarily agreeable to the soul's own image-making faculties or the product of its immanent desires, but take form and bear a meaning imposed on them from without.

There are few other instances of the occurrence of the word which have much chance of lying entirely outside the sphere of influence of its use in II Tim. iii. 16. In the first rank of these will certainly be placed the two instances in the fifth book of the "Sibyllines." The former of these occurs in a description of the city of Cyme, which is called the "foolish one," and described as cast down by wicked hands, "along with her theopneustic streams (νάμασι θεοπνεύστοις)" no longer to shout her boasts into the air but henceforth to remain "dead amid the Cymean streams." [45] The description skillfully brings together all that we know of Cyme — adverts to her former greatness ("the largest and noblest of all the Æolian cities," Strabo tells us,[46] and with Lesbos, "the metropolis" of all the rest), her reputation for folly (also adverted to and quaintly explained by Strabo), her present decadence, and her situation by running waters (a trait indicated also by her coins which show that there was a stream

---

[45] V. 308 *seq.* The full text, in Rzach's edition, runs:

Κύμη δ' ἡ μωρὴ σὺν νάμασιν οἷς θεοπνεύστοις
'Εν παλάμαις ἀθέων ἀνδρῶν ἀδίκων καὶ ἀθέσμων
'Ριφθεῖσ' οὐκ ἔτι τίσσον ἐς αἰθέρα ῥῆμα προδώσει·
'Αλλὰ μενεῖ νεκρὴ ἐνὶ νάμασι κυμαίοισιν.

[46] Strabo, "Rerum Geographicarum," liber xiii, iii. 6, pp. 622, 623 (Amsterdam ed., 1707, p. 924). A good summary may be read in Smith's "Dictionary of Greek and Roman Geography," i. 724, 725.

near by called Xanthus). It has been customary to understand by "the theopneustic streams" mentioned, some streams or fountains in the neighborhood known for the presumptively oracular powers of their waters.[47] But there does not seem to have been preserved any notice of the existence of such oracular waters belonging to Cyme, and it makes against this assumption that the Cymeans, like the rest of the Ionians and Æolians, were accustomed to resort for their oracles to the somewhat distant Branchidæ, in the south.[48] It appears much more likely, then, that the streams adverted to are natural streams and stand here only as part of the rather full and very exact description of the town — the reference being primarily to the Xanthus and to it as an element merely in the excellence of the situation. In that case "theopneustic," here too, would seem to mean something akin to "God-given," or perhaps more broadly still "divine," in the sense of specially excellent and desirable.

The second Sibylline passage is a portion of a lament over the destruction of the Temple at Jerusalem, wherein (we are told) gold, "deceiver of the world and souls," was not worshiped, but men "adored in sacrifices, with pure and noble hecatombs, the great Father-God of all theopneustic things."[49] Here Alexandre translates, "Qui cælestis vitam pater omnibus afflat"; and Terry, "The God and mighty maker of all breathing things." [50] And they seem supported in their general conception by the fact that we appear to have before us here only a slightly varied form of a formula met with elsewhere in the Sibyllines. Thus, as Rzach points out, we

[47] Alexandre translates "plenis numine lymphis"; Dr. Terry, "inspired streams."

[48] So Herodotus observes (i, 157).

[49] V. 408 *seq.* In Rzach's text the lines run:

Οὐ γὰρ ἀκηδέστως αἰνεῖ θεὸν ἐξ ἀφανοῦς γῆς
οὐδὲ πέτρην ποίησε σοφὸς τέκτων παρὰ τούτοις,
οὐ χρυσὸν κόσμου ἀπάτην ψυχῶν τ' ἐσεβάσθη,
ἀλλὰ μέγαν γενετῆρα θεὸν πάντων θεοπνεύστων
ἐν θυσίαις ἐγέραιρ' ἁγίαις καλαῖς θ' ἑκατόμβαις.

[50] In this second edition, Dr. Terry has altered this to "The Mighty Father, God of all things God-inspired": but this scarcely seems an improvement.

have at iii, 278 [51] a condemnation of those who "neither fear nor desire to honor the deathless Father-God of all men," [52] and at iii, 604, essentially the same phrase is repeated. We seem, in a word, to meet here only with the Sibylline equivalent of the Homeric "πατὴρ ἀνδρῶν τε θεῶν τε." Accordingly θεοπνεύστων would seem to stand here in the stead of ἀνθρώπων in the parallel passages, and merely to designate men, doubtless with a reminiscence of Gen. ii. 7 — or perhaps, more widely, creatures, with a reminiscence of such a passage as Ps. civ. 30. In either event it is the creative power of God that is prominently in the mind of the writer as he writes down the word θεοπνεύστων, which is to him obviously the proper term for "creatures" in correlation with the γενέτης θεός.

By the side of these Sibylline passages it is perhaps natural to place the line from the Pseudo-Phocylides, which marks the culmination of his praise of "speech" as the greatest gift of God — a weapon, he says, sharper than steel and more to be desired than the swiftness of birds, or the speed of horses, or the strength of lions, or the horns of bulls or the stings of bees — "for best [of all] is the speech of theopneustic wisdom," so that the wise man is better than the strong one, and it is wisdom that rules alike in the field, the city and the sea. It is certainly simplest to understand "theopneustic wisdom" here shortly as "God-given wisdom." Undoubtedly it is itself the inspirer of the speech that manifests it, and we might manage to interpret the θεοπνεύστου as so designating it —"God-inspiring, God-breathing wisdom." But this can scarcely be considered natural; and it equally undoubtedly lies more closely at hand to interpret it as designating the source of the wisdom itself as lying in God. Wisdom is conceived as theopneustic, in a word, because wisdom itself is thought of as coming from God, as being the product of the divine activity — here

[51] οὐδὲ φοβηθεὶς ἀθάνατον γενετῆρα θεὸν πάντων ἀνθρώπων οὐκ ἔθελες τιμᾶν. Rzach compares also Xenophon. "Fragm.," i. 1, M., ε'ὶς θεὸς ἔν τε θεοῖσι καὶ ἀνθρώποισι μέγιστος·

[52] Terry, Ed. 2: "the immortal Father, God of all mankind."

designated, as so frequently in the Old Testament, as operating as a breathing.

A passage that has come to light since Dr. Cremer's investigation for this word-study was made, is of not dissimilar implication. It is found in the recently published "Testament of Abraham,"[53] a piece which in its original form, its editor, Prof. James, assigns to a second-century Egyptian Jewish-Christian, though it has suffered much mediævalization in the ninth or tenth century. It runs as follows: "And Michael the archangel came immediately with a multitude of angels, and they took his precious soul (τὴν τιμίαν αὐτοῦ ψυχήν) in their hands in a God-woven cloth (σινδόνι θεοϋφαντῷ); and they prepared (ἐκήδευσαν) the body of righteous Abraham unto the third day of his death with theopneustic ointments and herbs (μυρίσμασι θεοπνεύστοις καὶ ἀρώμασιν), and they buried him in the land of promise." Here θεόπνευστος can hardly mean "God-breathing," and "God-imbued" is not much better; and though we might be tempted to make it mean "divinely sweet" (a kind of derivative sense of "God-redolent ointment"; for πνέω means also "to smell," "to breathe of a thing"), it is doubtless better to take it simply, as the parallel with θεοϋφαντῷ suggests, as importing something not far from "God-given." The cloth in which the soul was carried up to God and the unguents with which the body was prepared for burial were alike from God — were "God-provided"; the words to designate this being chosen in each case with nice reference to their specific application, but covering to their writer little more specific meaning than the simple adjective "divine" would have done.

It is surely in this same category also that we are to place the verse of Nonnus which Dr. Cremer adduces as showing distinctly that the word θεόπνευστος "is not to be taken as equivalent to *inspiratus*, inspired by God, but as rather meaning filled with God's spirit and therefore radiating it." Nonnus is paraphrasing John i. 27 and makes the Baptist say: "And he that cometh after me stands to-day in your

[53] Recension A, chap. xx. p. 103, ed. James.

midst, the tip of whose foot I am not worthy to approach
with human hand though only to loose the thongs of the
theopneustic sandal." [54] Here surely the meaning is not directly that our Lord's sandal "radiated divinity," though
certainly that may be one of the implications of the epithet,
but more simply that it partook of the divinity of the divine
Person whose property it was and in contact with whom it
had been. All about Christ was divine. We should not go
far wrong, therefore, if we interpreted θεόπνευστος here simply
as "divine." What is "divine" is no doubt "redolent of
Divinity," but it is so called not because of what it does,
but because of what it is, and Nonnus' mind when he called
the sandal theopneustic was occupied rather with the divine
influence that made the sandal what it was, viz., something
more than a mere sandal, because it had touched those divine
feet, than with any influence which the sandal was now calculated to exert. The later line which Dr. Cremer asks us
to compare is not well calculated to modify this decision.
In it John i. 33 is being paraphrased and the Baptist is contrasting his mission with that of Christ who was to baptize
with fire and the Holy Spirit ἐν πυρὶ βαπτίζων καὶ πνεύματι).
He, John, was sent, on the contrary, he says, to baptize the
body of already regenerate men, and to do it in lavers that
are destitute of both fire and the spirit — fireless and spirit-
less (ἀπύροισι καὶ ἀπνεύστοισι λοετροῖς). [55] It may indeed be
possible to interpret, "unburning and unspiritualizing"; but
this does not seem the exact shade of thought the words are
meant to express; though in any case the bearing of the
phrase on the meaning of θεόπνευστος in the former line is of
the slightest.

Of the passages cited by Dr. Cremer there remain only
the two he derives from Wetstein, in which θεόπνευστος ap-

[54] Nonni Panopolitani "Paraphrasis in Joannem" (i. 27), in Migne, xliii. 753:

Καὶ ὀπίστερος ὅστις ἱκάνει
Σήμερον ὑμείων μέσος ἵσταται, οὗ ποδὸς ἄκρου,
'Ανδρομέην παλάμην οὐκ ἄξιός εἰμι πελάσσας,
Δῦσαι μοῦνον ἱμάντα θεοπνεύστοιο πεδίλου.

[55] Op. cit., p. 756.

pears as an epithet of certain men. To these should be added an inscription found at Bostra, in which a certain ecclesiastic is designated an ἀρχιερεὺς θεόπνευστος.[56] Dr. Cremer himself thinks it clear that in such passages we have a passive sense, but interprets it as *divinely spirited*, "endued with the divine spirit," rather than as "*divinely inspired*," — in accordance with a distinction drawn by Ewald. Certainly it is difficult to understand the word in this connection as expressing simple origination by God; it was something more than the mere fact that God made them that was intended to be affirmed by calling Marcus and Antipater theopneustic men. Nor does it seem very natural to suppose that the intention was to designate them as precisely what we ordinarily mean by God-inspired men. It lies very near to suppose, therefore, that what it was intended to say about them, is that they were God-pervaded men, men in whom God dwelt in an especial manner; and this supposition may be thought to be supported by the parallel, in the passage from the "Vita Sabæ," with χριστοφόρος. Of whom this "caravan of all theopneustics, of all his christophers," was composed, we have no means of determining, as Cotelerius' "Monumenta," from which Wetstein quoted the passage, is not accessible to us as we write. But the general sense of the word does not seem to be doubtful. Ignatius, ("ad Ephes." ix.) tells us that all Christians constitute such a caravan, of "God-bearers and shrine-bearers, Christ-bearers, holy-thing-bearers, completely clothed in the commandments of Christ"; and Zahn rightly comments that thus the Christians appear as the real "ἐνιθεοι or ἐνθουσιάζοντες, since they carry Christ and God in them-

---

[56] It is given in Kaibel's "Epigrammata Græca," p. 477. Waddington supposes the person meant to be a certain Archbishop of Bostra, of date 457–474, an opponent of Origenism, who is commemorated in the Greek Church on June 13. The inscription runs as follows:

Δόξης] ὀρθοτό[ν]ου ταμίης καὶ ὑπέρμαχος ἐσθλός,
ἀρχιερεὺς θεόπνευστος ἐδείματο κάλλος ἄμετρον
'Αντίπατρ]ο[ς] κλυτόμητις ἀεθλοφόρους μετ' ἀγῶνας,
κυ[δ]αίνων μεγάλως θεομήτορα παρθένον ἀγνήν
Μαρίαν πολύυμνον, ἀκήρατον ἀγλαόδωρον·

selves." Particularly distinguished Christians might therefore very properly be conceived in a supereminent sense as
filled with God and bearers of Christ; and this might very
appropriately be expressed by the double attribution of θεόπ
νευστος and χριστοφόρος. Only it would seem to be necessary
to understand that thus a secondary and derived sense would
be attributed to θεόπνευστος, about which there should still
cling a flavor of the idea of origination. The θεόπνευστος ἀνήρ
is God-filled by the act of God Himself, that is to say, he is
a God-endowed man, one made what he is by God's own
efficiency. No doubt in usage the sense might suffer still
more attrition and come to suggest little more than "divine"
— which is the epithet given to Marcus of Scetis [57] by Nicephorus Callistus, ("H. E.,"xi, 35) — ὁ θεῖος Μάρκος — that is
to say "Saint Mark," of which ὁ θεόπνευστος Μάρκος is doubtless a very good synonym. The conception conveyed by θεό
πνευστος in this usage is thus something very distinct from
that expressed by the Vulgate rendering, *a Deo inspiratus*,
when taken strictly; that would seem to require, as Ewald
suggests, some such form as θεέμπνευστος; the theopneustic
man is not the man "breathed into by God." But it is equally
distinct from that expressed by the phrase, "pervaded by
God," used as an expression of the character of the man so
described, without implication of the origin of this characteristic. What it would seem specifically to indicate is that
he has been framed by God into something other than what
he would have been without the divine action. The Christian
as such is as much God-made as the man as such; and the
distinguished Christian as such as much as the Christian at
large; and the use of θεόπνευστος to describe the one or the
other would appear to rest ultimately on this conception. He

[57] Wetstein cites the expression as applied (where, he does not say) to
"Marcus Ægyptus," by which he means, we suppose, Marcus of Scetis, mentioned
by Sozomen, H. E., vi. 29, and Nicephorus Callistus, H. E., xi. 35. Dr. Cremer
transmutes the designation into Marcus Eremita, who is mentioned by Nicephorus Callistus, H. E., xiv. 30, 54, and whose writings are collected in Migne,
lxv. 905 *seq.* The two are often identified, but are separately entered in Smith and
Wace.

is, in what he has become, the product of the divine energy —
of the divine breath.

We cannot think it speaking too strongly, therefore, to
say that there is discoverable in none of these passages the
slightest trace of an active sense of θεόπνευστος, by which it
should express the idea, for example, of "breathing the
divine spirit," or even such a quasi-active idea as that of
"redolent of God." Everywhere the word appears as purely
passive and expresses production by God. And if we proceed
from these passages to those much more numerous ones, in
which it is, as in II Tim. iii. 16, an epithet or predicate of
Scripture, and where therefore its signification may have
been affected by the way in which Christian antiquity understood that passage, the impression of the passive sense of the
word grows, of course, ever stronger. Though these passages
may not be placed in the first rank of material for the determination of the meaning of II Tim. iii. 16, by which they
may have themselves been affected; it is manifestly improper
to exclude them from consideration altogether. Even as part
bearers of the exegetical tradition they are worthy of adduction: and it is scarcely conceivable that the term should have
been entirely voided of its current sense, had it a different
current sense, by the influence of a single employment of it
by Paul — especially if we are to believe that its natural
meaning as used by him differed from that assigned it by
subsequent writers. The patristic use of the term in connection with Scripture has therefore its own weight, as evidence
to the natural employment of the term by Greek-speaking
Christian writers.

This use of it does not seem to occur in the very earliest
patristic literature: but from the time of Clement of Alexandria the term θεόπνευστος appears as one of the most common technical designations of Scripture. The following scattered instances, gathered at random, will serve to illustrate
this use of it sufficiently for our purpose. Clement of Alexandria: "Strom.," vii. 16, § 101 (Klotz, iii. 286; Potter,
894), "Accordingly those fall from their eminence who follow

not God whither He leads; and He leads us in the inspired Scriptures (κατὰ τὰς θεοπνεύστους γραφάς)"; "Strom.," vii. 16, § 103 (Klotz, iii. 287; Potter, 896), "But they crave glory, as many as willfully sophisticate the things wedded to inspired words (τοῖς θεοπνεύστοις λόγοις) handed down by the blessed apostles and teachers, by diverse arguments, opposing human teaching to the divine tradition for the sake of establishing the heresy"; "Protrept." 9, § 87 (Klotz., i. 73, 74; Potter 71), "This teaching the apostle knows as truly divine (θείαν): 'Thou, O Timothy,' he says, 'from a child hast known the holy letters which are able to make thee wise unto salvation, through faith that is in Jesus Christ'; for truly holy are those letters that sanctify and deify; and the writings or volumes that consist of these holy letters or syllables, the same apostle consequently calls 'inspired by God, seeing that they are profitable for doctrine,' etc." Origen: "De Principiis," iv, 8 (cf. also title to Book iv), "Having thus spoken briefly on the subject of the Divine inspiration of the Holy Scriptures (περὶ τοῦ θεοπνεύστου τῆς θείας γραφῆς)"; Migne, (11, 1276), "The Jews and Christians agree as to the inspiration of the Holy Scripture (θείῳ γεγράφθαι πνεύματι), but differ as to its interpretation"; (12, 1084), "Therefore the inspired books (θεόπνευστα βιβλία) are twenty-two"; (14, 1309), "The inspired Scripture"; (13, 664–5), "For we must seek the nourishment of the whole inspired Scripture (πάσης τῆς θεοπνεύστου γραφῆς); "Hom. xx. in Joshuam," 2 (Robinson's "Origen's Philocalia," p. 63), "Let us not then be stupefied by listening to Scriptures which we do not understand, but let it be to us according to our faith by which we believe that 'every Scripture, seeing that it is inspired (θεόπνευστος), is profitable': for you must needs admit one of two things regarding these Scriptures, either that they are not inspired (θεόπνευστοι) because they are not profitable, as the unbeliever takes it, or, as a believer, you must admit that since they are inspired (θεόπνευστοι) they are profitable"; "Selecta in Psalmos," Ps. i, 3 (Migne XII, ii. 1080; De la Rue, 527), "Being about to begin the interpretation of the Psalms, we prefix a very excellent tradition handed down by the Hebrew [58] to us generally concerning the whole divine Scripture (καθολικῶς περὶ πάσης θείας γραφῆς); for he affirmed that the whole inspired Scripture (τὴν ὅλην θεόπνευστον γραφήν). . . . But if 'the words of the Lord are pure words, fined silver, tried as the earth, purified seven times' (Ps. ii. 7) and the Holy Spirit has with all care dictated them accurately through the ministers of the word (μετὰ πάσης ἀκριβείας ἐξητασμένως τὸ ἅγιον πνεῦμα ὑποβέβληκεν αυτὰ διὰ τῶν ὑπηρετῶν τοῦ λόγου), let the proportion never escape us, according to which the wisdom of God is first with respect to the whole theopneustic Scripture unto the last letter (καθ' ἣν ἐπὶ πᾶσαν ἔφθασε γραφὴν ἡ σοφία τοῦ θεοῦ θεόπνεύστον μέχρι τοῦ τυχόντος γράμματος); and haply it was on this account that the Saviour said, 'One iota or one letter shall not pass from the law till all be fulfilled': and it is just so that the divine art in the creation of the world, not only appeared in the heaven and sun and moon and stars, interpenetrating their whole bodies, but also on earth did the same in paltry matter, so that not even the bodies of the least animals are disdained by the artificer. . . . So we understand concerning all the things written by the inspiration (ἐξ ἐπιπνοίας) of the Holy Spirit . . . ." Athanasius (Migne, 27, 214): πᾶσα γραφὴ ἡμῶν τῶν χριστιανῶν θεόπνευστός ἐστιν; (Migne, 25, 152): θεόπνευστος κάλεῖται; (Bened. Par., 1777, i. 767): "Saying also myself, 'Since many have taken in hand to set forth to themselves the so-called apocrypha and to sing them with τῇ θεοπνεύστῳ γραφῇ . . . .'" Cyrillus Hier., "Catechet.,"iv. 33: "This is taught us by αἱ θεόπνευστοι γραφαί of both the Old and New Covenant." Basil, "On the Spirit," xxi (ad fin.): "How can he who calls Scripture 'God-inspired' because it was written through the inspiration of the Spirit (ὁ θεόπνευστον τὴν γραφὴν ὀνομάζων, διὰ τῆς ἐπιπνοίας τοῦ ἁγίου πνεύματος συγγραφεῖσαν), use the language of one who insults and belittles Him?" "Letters," xvii. 3: "All bread is nutri-

[58] That is doubtless the Jewish teacher to whom he elsewhere refers, as, e. g., "De Principiis," iv. 20 (Ante-Nicene Library, N. Y. ed., iv. 375), where the same general subject is discussed.

tious, but it may be injurious to the sick; just so, all Scripture
is God-inspired (πᾶσα γραφὴ θεόπνευστος) and profitable";
(Migne, xxx. 81): "The words of God-inspired Scripture (οἱ
τῆς θεοπνεύστου γραφῆς λόγοι) shall stand on the tribune of
Christ"; (Migne, 31, 744): "For every word or deed must
be believed by the witness of the θεοπνεύστου γραφῆς, for the
assurance of the good and the shame of the wicked"; (Migne,
31, 1080): "Apart from the witness of the θεοπνεύστων γραφῶν
it is not possible, etc."; (Migne, 31, 1500): "From what sort
of Scripture are we to dispute at this time? Πάντα ὁμότιμα,
καὶ πάντα πνευματικά· πάντα θεόπνευστα, καὶ πάντα ὠφέλιμα";
(Migne, 31, 1536): "On the interpretation and remarking of
the names and terms τῆς θεοπνεύστου γραφῆς"; (Migne, 32,
228): μεγίστη δὲ ὁδὸς πρὸς τὴν τοῦ καθήκοντος εὕρεσιν καὶ ἡ μελέτη
τῶν θεοπνεύστων γραφῶν. Gregory Naz. (Migne, 35, 504): περὶ
τοῦ θεοπνεύστου τῶν ἁγίων γραφῶν; (Migne, 36, 472, cf. 37, 589),
περὶ τῶν γηησίων βιβλίων τῆς θεοπνεύστου γραφῆς; (Migne, 36,
1589), τοῖς θεοπνεύστοις γραφαῖς. Gregory Nyssen, "Against
Eunom.," vii. 1: "What we understand of the matter is as
follows: Ἡ θεόπνευστος γραφή, as the divine apostle calls it,
is the Scripture of the Holy Spirit and its intention is the
profit of men"; (Migne, 44, 68), μόνης τῆς θεοπνεύστου διαθήκης.
Cyrillus Alex. (Migne, 68, 225), πολυμερῶς καὶ πολυτρόπως ἡ
θεόπνευστος γραφὴ τῆς διὰ χριστοῦ σωτηρίας προαναφωνεῖ τοὺς
τύπους. Neilos Abbas (Migne, 79, 141, cf. 529): γραφὴ ἡ θεόπνευστος οὐδὲν λέγει ἀκαίρως κτλ. Theodoret of Cyrrhus (" H.
E.", i. 6; Migne, iii. 920). John of ·Damascus (Migne, 85,
1041), etc.

If, then, we are to make an induction from the use of the
word, we shall find it bearing a uniformly passive significance,
rooted in the idea of the creative breath of God. All that is,
is God-breathed ("Sibyll." v. 406); and accordingly the rivers
that water the Cymean plain are God-breathed (" Sibyll." v.
308), the spices God provides for the dead body of His friend
("Testament of Abraham," A. xx), and above all the wisdom
He implants in the heart of man (Ps.-Phocyl. 121), the dreams
He sends with a message from Him (Ps.-Plut., v. 2, 3) and

the Scriptures He gives His people (II Tim. iii. 16). By an extension of meaning by no means extreme, those whom He has greatly honored as His followers, whom He has created into His saints, are called God-breathed men ("Vita Sabæ" 16. Inscription in Kaibel); and even the sandals that have touched the feet of the Son of God are called God-breathed sandals (Nonnus), i. e., sandals that have been made by this divine contact something other than what they were: in both these cases, the word approaching more or less the broader meaning of "divine." Nowhere is there a trace of such an active significance as "God-breathing"; and though in the application of the word to individual men and to our Lord's sandals there may be an approach to the sense of "God-imbued," this sense is attained by a pathway of development from the simple idea of God-given, God-determined, and the like.

It is carefully to be observed, of course, that, although Dr. Cremer wishes to reach an active signification for the word in II Tim. iii. 16, he does not venture to assign an active sense to it immediately and directly, but approaches this goal through the medium of another signification. It is fully recognized by him that the word is originally passive in its meaning; it is merely contended that this original passive sense is not "God-inspired," but rather "God-filled" — a sense which, it is pleaded, will readily pass into the active sense of "God-breathing," after the analogy of such words as ἄπνευστος, εὔπνευστος, which from "ill- or well-breathed" came to mean "breathing ill or well." What is filled with God will certainly be redolent of God, and what is redolent of God will certainly breathe out God. His reasons for preferring the sense of "gifted or filled with God's Spirit, divinely spirited," to "God-inspired" for the original passive connotation of the word are drawn especially from what he thinks the unsuitableness of the latter idea to some of the connections in which the word is found. It is thought that, as an epithet of an individual man, as an epithet of Scripture or a fountain, and (in the later editions of the "Lexicon" at least) especially, as an epithet of a sandal, "God-inspired" is incongruous, and something like "filled with God's Spirit and therefore radiating it" is suggested. There is obviously some confusion here arising from the very natural contemplation of the Vulgate translation "*a Deo inspiratus*" as the alternative rendering to what is proposed. There is, we may well admit, nothing in the word θεόπνευστος to warrant the *in-* of the Vulgate rendering: this word speaks not of an "*in*spiration" by God, but of a "spiration" by God. The alternatives brought before us by Dr. Cremer's presentation are not to be confined, therefore, to the two, "Divinely spirited" and "Divinely *in*spired," but must be made to include the three, "Divinely spirited," "Divinely *in*spired," and "Divinely spired." The failure of Dr. Cremer to note this introduces, as we say, some confusion into his statement. We need only thus incidentally refer to it at this point, however. It is of more immediate importance to observe that what we are naturally led to by Dr. Cremer's remarks, is to an investigation of the natural meaning of the word θεόπνευστος under the laws of word-formation. In these remarks he is leaning rather heavily on the discussion of Ewald to which he refers us, and it will conduce to a better understanding of the matter if we will follow his directions and turn to our Ewald.

Ewald, like Dr. Cremer, is dissatisfied with the current explanation of θεόπνευστος and seeks to obtain for it an active sense, but is as little inclined as Dr. Cremer to assign an active sense directly to it. He rather criticises Winer,[59] for using language when speaking of θεόπνευστος which would seem to imply that such compounds could really be active — as if "it were to be taken as a passive, although such words as εὔπνευστος, ἄπνευστος are used actively." He cannot admit that any compound of a word like -πνευστος can be really active in primary meaning, and explains that εὔπνευστος means not so much "breathing good," i. e., propelling something good by the breath, as "endowed with good breath," and expresses, therefore, just like ἄπνευστος, "breathless,"

[59] "Jahrb. f. bibl. Wissenschaft," vii. 114.

i. e., "*dead*," a subjective condition, and is therefore to be compared with a half-passive verb, as indeed the word-form suggests. Just so, θεόπνευστος, he says, is not so much our "God-breathing" as our "full of God's Spirit," "permeated and animated by God's Spirit." Thus, he supposes θεόπνευστος to mean "blown through by God" (*Gottdurchwehet*, "God-pervaded"), rather than "blown into by God" (*Gotteingewehet*, "God-inspired") as the Vulgate (*inspiratus*) and Luther (*eingegeben*) render it — an idea which, as he rightly says, would have required something like θεέμπνευστος [60] (or we may say θεείσπνευστος) [61] to express it.

At first he seems to have thought that by this explanation he had removed all implication as to the origination of Scrip-

---

[60] In a note on p. 89, Ewald adds as to θεέμπνευστος that it is certainly true that such compounds are not common, and that this particular one does not occur: but that they are possible is shown by the occurrence of such examples as θεοσύνακτος, θεοκατασκεύαστος, in which the preposition occurs: and *dem Laute nach*, the formation is like θεήλατος. There seems to be no reason, we may add, why, if it were needed, we should not have had a θεέμπνευστος by the side of θεόπνευστος, just as by the side of πνευματοφόρος we have πνευματέμφορος ("Etymologicum Magnum," 677, 28; John of Damascus, in Migne, 96, 837c.: Ἧσε προφητῶν πνευματέμφορον στόμα).

[61] For not even θεεμπνέω would properly signify "breathe into" but rather "breathe *in*," "inhale." It is by a somewhat illogical extension of meaning that the verb and its derivatives (ἔμπνευσις, ἔμπνοια) are used in the theological sense of "inspiration," in which sense they do not occur, however, either in the LXX. or the New Testament. In the LXX. ἔμπνευσις means a "blast," a "blowing" (Ps. xvii. (xviii.) 15; cf. the participle ἐμπνέων, Acts ix. 1); ἔμπνους, "living," "breathing" (II Macc. vii. 5, xiv. 45); and the participle πᾶν ἐμπνέον, "every living, breathing thing" (Deut. xx. 16; Josh. x. 28, 30, 35, 37, 39, 40; xi. 14; Wisd. xv. 11). Εἰσπνέω is properly used by the classics in the sense of "breathing into," "inspiring": it is not found in itself or derivatives in LXX. or the New Testament — though it occurs in Aq. at Ex. i. 5. How easily and in what a full sense, however, ἐμπνέω is used by ecclesiastical writers for "inspire" may be noted from such examples as Ign. " ad Mag.," 8: "For the divine (θειότατοι) prophets lived after Christ; for this cause also they were persecuted, being inspired by His grace (ἐμπνεόμενοι ὑπὸ τῆς χάριτος αὐτοῦ) for the full persuasion of those that are disobedient." Theoph. of Antioch, " ad. Autol.," ii. 9: "Butt he men of God, πνευματοφόροι of the Holy Ghost, and becoming prophets ὑπ' αὐτοῦ τοῦ θεοῦ ἐμπνευσθέντες καὶ σοφισθέντες, became θεοδίδακτοι and holy and righteous." The most natural term for "inspired" in classic Greek one would be apt to think, would be ἔνθεος (ἔνθους), with τὸ ἔνθεον for "inspiration"; and after it, participial or other derivatives of ἐνθουσιάζω: but both εἰσπνέω and ἐμπνέω were used for the "inspiration" that consisted of "breathing *into*" even in profane Greek.

ture from the epithet: it expresses, he said,[62] what Scripture is — viz., pervaded by God, full of His Spirit — without the least hint as to how it got to be so. He afterwards came to see this was going too far, and contented himself with saying that though certainly implicating a doctrine of the origin of the Scriptures, the term throws the *emphasis* on its quality.[63] He now, therefore, expressed himself thus: "It is certainly undeniable that the new expression θεόπνευστος, II Tim. iii. 16, is intended to say very much what Philo meant, but did not yet know how to express sharply by means of such a compressed and strong term. For θεόπνευστος (like εὔπνευστος, accurately, 'well-breathed') must mean 'God-breathed' or 'God-animated' (*Gottbeathmet,* or *Gottbegeistert*), and, in accordance with the genius of the compressed, clear Greek compounds, this includes in itself the implication that the words are *spoken by the Spirit of God,* or by those who are inspired by God," — a thing which, he adds, is repeatedly asserted in Scripture to have been the case, as, for example, in II Pet. i. 21. On another occasion,[64] he substantially repeats this, objecting to the translations *inspiratus, eingegeben,* as introducing an idea not lying in the word and liable to mislead, affirming a general but not perfect accord of the idea involved in it with Philo's conception of Scripture, and insisting on the incomplete parallelism between the term and our dogmatic idea of "inspiration." "This term," he says, "no doubt expresses only what is everywhere presupposed by Philo as to Scripture and repeatedly said by him in other words; still his usage is not yet so far developed; and it is accordant with this that in the New Testament, also, it is only in one of the latest books that the word is thus used. This author was possibly the first who so applied it." Again, θεόπνευστος "means, purely passively, God-spirited (*Gottbegeistet*), or full of God's Spirit, not at all, when taken strictly what we call discriminatingly God-inspired (*Gottbegeistert*) or filled with God's inspiration (*Begeisterung*), but in itself only,

---

[62] P. 88.          [63] "Geschichte des Volkes Israel," vi. 245, note.
[64] "Jahrb. f. bibl. Wissenschaft," ix. 91.

in a quite general sense, God-breathed, God-inspired (*Gott-beathmet, Gottbegeistert*), or filled with the divine spirit. In itself, therefore, it permits the most divers applications and we must appeal purely to the context in each instance in order to obtain its exact meaning."

Here we have in full what Dr. Cremer says so much more briefly in his articles. In order to orient ourselves with reference to it, we shall need to consider in turn the two points that are emphasized. These are, first, the passive form and sense of the word; and, secondly, the particular passive sense attributed to it, to wit: *Gottbegeistet* rather than *Gottbegeistert*, "endowed with God's Spirit," rather than "inspired by God."

On the former point there would seem to be little room for difference of opinion. We still read in Schmiedel's Winer: "Verbals in -τος correspond sometimes to Latin participles in -*tus*, sometimes to adjectives in -*bilis*"; and then in a note (despite Ewald's long-ago protest), after the adduction of authorities, "θεόπνευστος, *inspiratus* (II Tim. iii. 16; passive like ἔμπνευστος, while εὔπνευστος, ἄπνευστος are active)."[65] To these Thayer-Grimm adds also πυρίπνευστος and δυσδιάπνευστος as used actively and δυσανάπνευστος as used apparently either actively or passively. Ewald, however, has already taught us to look beneath the "active" usage of εὔπνευστος and ἄπνευστος for the "half-passive" background, and it may equally be found in the other cases; in each instance it is a state or condition at least, that is described by the word, and it is often only a matter of point of view whether we catch the passive conception or not. For example, we shall look upon δυσδιάπνευστος as active or passive according as we think of the object it describes as a "slowly evaporating" or a "slowly evaporated" object — that is, as an object that only slowly evaporates, or as an object that can be only with difficulty evaporated. We may prefer the former expression; the Greeks preferred the latter: that is all. We fully accord

---

[65] Sec. 16, 2, p. 135. Cf. Thayer's Winer, p. 96; Moulton's, p. 120. Also Thayer's Buttmann, p. 190. The best literature of the subject will be found adduced by Winer.

with Prof. Schulze, therefore, when he says that all words compounded with -πνευστος have the passive sense as their original implication, and the active sense, when it occurs, is always a derived one. On this showing it cannot be contended, of course, that θεόπνευστος may not have, like some of its relatives, developed an active or quasi-active meaning, but a passive sense is certainly implied as its original one, and a certain presumption is thus raised for the originality of the passive sense which is found to attach to it in its most ordinary usage.[66]

This conclusion finds confirmation in a consideration which has its bearing on the second point also — the consideration that compounds of verbals in -τος with θεός normally express an effect produced by God's activity. This is briefly adverted to by Prof. Schulze, who urges that "the closely related θεοδίδακτος, and many, or rather most, of the compounds of θεο- in the Fathers, bear the passive sense," adducing in illustration: θεόβλαστος, θεοβούλητος, θεογέννητος, θεόγραπτος, θεόδμητος, θεόδοτος, θεοδώρητος, θεόθρεπτος, θεοκίνητος, θεόκλητος, θεοποίητος, θεοφόρητος, θεόχρηστος, θεόχριστος. The statement may be much broadened and made to cover the whole body of such compounds occurring in Greek literature. Let any one run his eye down the list of compounds of θεός with verbals in -τος as they occur on the pages of any Greek *Lexicon*, and he will be quickly convinced that the notion normally expressed is that of a result produced by God. The sixth edition of Liddell and Scott happens to be the one lying at hand as we write; and in it we find entered (if we have

---

[66] Compounds of -πνευστος do not appear to be very common. Liddell and Scott (ed. 6) do not record either ἀνά- or διά- or ἐπί- or even εὐ-; though the cognates are recorded, and further compounds presupposing them. The rare word εὔπνευστος might equally well express "breathing-well" quasi-actively, or "well-aired" passively; just as ἄπνευστος is actually used in the two senses of "breathless" and "unventilated": and a similar double sense belongs to δυσανάπνευστος. Ἔμπνευστος does not seem to occur in a higher sense; its only recorded usage is illustrated by Athenaeus, iv. 174, where it is connected with ὄργανα in the sense of wind-instruments: its cognates are used of "inspiration." Only πυρίπνευστος = πυρίπνοος = "fire-breathing" is distinctively active in usage: cf. ἀνάπνευστυς, poetic for ἄπνευστος = "breathless."

counted aright), some eighty-six compounds of this type, of which, at least, seventy-five bear quite simply the sense of a result produced by God. We adjoin the list: θεήλατος, θεοβάστακτος, θεόβλυστος, θεοβούλητος, θεοβράβευτος, θεογένητος, θεόγνωστος, θεόγραπτος, θεοδέκτος, θεοδίδακτος, θεόδμητος, θεοδόμητος, θεόδοτος, θεοδώρητος, θεόθετος, θεοκατάρατος, θεοκατασκεύαστος, θεοκέλευστος, θεοκίνητος, θεόκλητος, θεόκμητος, θεόκραντος, θεόκριτος, θεόκτητος, θεόκτιστος, θεόκτιτος, θεοκυβέρνητος, θεοκύρωτος, θεόλεκτος, θεόληπτος, θεομακάριστος, θεομίσητος, θεόμυστος, θεόπαιστος, θεοπαράδοτος, θεοπάρακτος, θεόπεμπτος, θεοπέρατος, θεόπληκτος, θεόπλουτος, θεοποίητος, θεοπόνητος, θεοπρόσδεκτος, θεόπτυστος, θεόργητος, θεόρρητος, θέορτος, θεόσδοτος, θεόστρεπτος, θεοστήρικτος, θεοστύγητος, θεοσύλλεκτος, θεοσύμφυτος, θεοσύνακτος, θεόσυτος, θεοσφράγιστος, θεόσωστος, θεοτέρατος, θεότευκτος, θεοτίμητος, θεότρεπτος, θεοτύπωτος, θεοϋπόστατος, θεοΰφαντος, θεόφαντος, θεόφθεγκτος, θεοφίλητος, θεόφοιτος, θεοφόρητος, θεοφρούρητος, θεοφύλακτος, θεοχόλωτος, θεόχρηστος, θεόχριστος. The eleven instances that remain, as in some sort exceptions to the general rule, include cases of different kinds. In some of them the verbal is derived from a deponent verb and is therefore passive only in form, but naturally bears an active sense: such are θεοδήλητος (God-injuring), θεομίμητος (God-imitating), θεόσεπτος (feared as God). Others may possibly be really passives, although we prefer an active form in English to express the idea involved: such are, perhaps, θεόκλυτος ("God-heard," where we should rather say, "calling on the gods"), θεοκόλλητος ("God-joined," where we should rather say, "united with God"), θεόπρεπτος ("God-distinguished," where we should rather say, "meet for a god"). There remain only these five: θεαίτητος ("obtained from God"), θεόθυτος ("offered to the gods"), θεορράστος and the more usual θεόρροτος ("flowing from the gods"), and θεοχώρητος ("containing God"). In these the relation of θεός to the verbal idea is clearly not that of producing cause to the expressed result, but some other: perhaps what we need to recognize is that the verbal here involves a relation which we ordinarily express by a preposition, and that the sense would be suggested by some such phrases as "God-asked-of," "God-offered-to-," "God-flowed-from," "God-made-room-for." In any event, these few exceptional cases cannot avail to set aside the normal sense of this compound, as exhibited in the immense majority of the cases of its occurrence. If analogy is to count for anything, its whole weight is thrown thus in favor of the interpretation which sees in θεόπνευστος, quite simply, the sense of "God-breathed," i. e., produced by God's creative breath.

If we ask, then, what account is to be given of Ewald's and, after him, Prof. Cremer's wish, to take it in the specific sense of "God-spirited," that is, "imbued with the Spirit of God," we may easily feel ourselves somewhat puzzled to return a satisfactory answer. We should doubtless not go far wrong in saying, as already suggested, that their action is proximately due to their not having brought all the alternatives fairly before them. They seem to have worked, as we have said, on the hypothesis that the only choice lay between the Vulgate rendering, "God-inspired," and their own "God-imbued." Ewald, as we have seen, argues (and as we think rightly) that "God-*inspired*" is scarcely consonant with the word-form, but would have required something like θεέμ-πνευστος. Similarly we may observe Dr. Cremer in the second edition of his " Lexicon " (when he was arguing for the current conception) saying that "the formation of the word cannot be traced to the use of πνέω, but only of ἐμπνέω," and supporting this by the remark that "the simple verb is never used of divine action"; and throughout his later article, operating on the presumption that the rendering "*inspired*" solely will come into comparison with his own newly proposed one. All this seems to be due, not merely to the traditional rendering of the word itself, but also to the conception of the nature of the divine action commonly expressed by the term, "inspiration," and indeed to the doctrine of Holy Scripture, dominant in the minds of these scholars.[67] If we will shake ourselves loose from these obscur-

[67] Two fundamental ideas, lying at the root of all their thinking of Scripture, seem to have colored somewhat their dealing with this term:

ing prepossessions and consider the term without preoccupation of mind, it would seem that the simple rendering "God-breathed" would commend itself powerfully to us: certainly not, with the Vulgate and Luther, "God-*in*breathed," since the preposition "in" is wholly lacking in the term and is not demanded for the sense in any of its applications; but equally certainly not "God-imbued" or "God-infused" in the sense of imbued or infused *with* (rather than *by*) God, since, according to all analogy, as well as according to the simplest construction of the compound, the relation of "God" to the act expressed is that of "agent." On any other supposition than that this third and assuredly the most natural alternative, "God-breathed," was not before their minds, the whole treatment of Ewald and Dr. Cremer will remain somewhat inexplicable.

Why otherwise, for example, should the latter have remarked, that the "word must be traced to the use of ἐμπνέω and not to the simple verb πνέω?" Dr. Cremer, it is true, adds, as we have said, that the simple verb is never used of divine action. In any case, however, this statement is overdrawn. Not only is πνέω applied in a physical sense to God in such passages of the LXX. as Ps. cxlvii. 7 (18) (πνεύσει τὸ πνεῦμα αὐτοῦ) and Isa. xl. 24, and of Symmachus and Theodotion as Isa. xl. 7; and not only in the earliest Fathers is it used of the greatest gifts of Christ the Divine Lord, in such passages as Ign., "Eph." 17: — "For this cause the Lord received ointment on His head, that He might breathe incorruption upon His Church (ἵνα πνέῃ τῇ ἐκκλησίᾳ ἀφθαρσίαν)"; but in what may be rightly called the normative passage,

the old Lutheran doctrine of the Word of God, and the modern rationalizing doctrine of the nature of the Divine influence exerted in the production of Scripture. On account of the latter point of view they seem determined not to find in Scripture itself any declaration that will shut them up to "a Philonian conception of Scripture" as the Oracles of God — the very utterances of the Most High. By the former they seem predisposed to discover in it declarations of the wonder-working power of the Word. The reader cannot avoid becoming aware of the influence of both these dogmatic conceptions in both Ewald's and Cremer's dealing with θεόπνευστος. But it is not necessary to lay stress on this.

Gen. ii. 7, it is practically justified, in its application to God, by the LXX. use of πνοή in the objective clause, and actually employed for the verb itself by both Symmachus and Theodotion. And if we will penetrate beneath the mere matter of the usage of a word to the conception itself, nothing could be more misleading than such a remark as Dr. Cremer's. For surely there was no conception more deeply rooted in the Hebrew mind, at least, than that of the creative "breath of God"; and this conception was assuredly not wholly unknown even in ethnic circles. To a Hebrew, at all events, the "breath of God" would seem self-evidently creative; and no locution would more readily suggest itself to him as expressive of the Divine act of "making" than just that by which it would be affirmed that He breathed things into existence. The "breath of the Almighty" — πνοὴ παντοκράτορος — was traditionally in his mouth as the fit designation of the creative act (Job xxxii. 8, xxxiii. 4); and not only was he accustomed to think of man owing his existence to the breathing of the breath of God into his nostrils (Gen. ii. 7, especially Symm. Theod.) and of his life as therefore the "breath of God" (πνεῦμα θεῖον, LXX., Job xxvii. 8), which God needs but to draw back to Himself that all flesh should perish (Job xxxiv. 14): but he conceived also that it was by the breath of God's mouth (πνεύματι τοῦ στώματος, Ps. xxxiii. 6), that all the hosts of the heavens were made, and by the sending forth of His breath, (πνεῦμα, Ps. civ. 30) that the multiplicity of animal life was created. By His breath even (πνοή, Job xxxvii. 10), he had been told, the ice is formed; and by His breath (πνεῦμα, Isa. xi. 5, cf. Job iv. 9) all the wicked are consumed. It is indeed the whole conception of the Spirit of God as the executive of the Godhead that is involved here: the conception that it is the Spirit of God that is the active agent in the production of all that is. To the Hebrew consciousness, creation itself would thus naturally appear as, not indeed an "*inspiration*," and much less an "infusion of the Divine essence," but certainly a "spiration"; and all that exists would appeal to it as, therefore, in the proper sense theopneustic, i. e., simply, "breathed by God," produced by the creative breath of the Almighty, the πνοὴ παντοκράτορος.

This would not, it needs to be remembered, necessarily imply an "immediate creation," as we call it. When Elihu declares that it is the breath of the Almighty that has given him life or understanding (Job xxxii. 8, xxxiii. 4), he need not be read as excluding the second causes by which he was brought into existence; nor need the Psalmist (civ. 30) be understood to teach an "immediate creation" of the whole existing animal mass. But each certainly means to say that it is God who has made all these things, and that by His breath: He breathed them into being — they are all θεόπ-νευστοι. So far from the word presenting a difficulty there-fore from the point of view of its conception, it is just, after the nature of Greek compounds, the appropriate crystalli-zation into one concise term of a conception that was a ruling idea in every Jewish mind. Particularly, then, if we are to suppose (with both Ewald and Cremer) that the word is a coinage of Paul's, or even of Hellenistic origin, nothing could be more natural than that it should have enshrined in it the Hebraic conviction that God produces all that He would bring into being by a mere breath. From this point of view, therefore, there seems no occasion to seek beyond the bare form of the word itself for a sense to attribute to it. If we cannot naturally give it the meaning of "God-*in*spired," we certainly do not need to go so far afield as to attribute to it the sense of "filled with God": the natural sense which be-longs to it by virtue of its formation, and which is com-mended to us by the analogy of like compounds, is also most consonant with the thought-forms of the circles in which it perhaps arose and certainly was almost exclusively used. What the word naturally means from this point of view also, is "God-spirited," "God-breathed," "produced by the cre-ative breath of the Almighty."

Thus it appears that such a conception as "God-breathed" lies well within the general circle of ideas of the Hellenistic writers, who certainly most prevailingly use the word. An application of this conception to Scripture, such as is made in II Tim. iii. 16, was no less consonant with the ideas concerning the origin and nature of Scripture which prevailed in the circles out of which that epistle proceeded. This may indeed be fairly held to be generally conceded.

The main object of Ewald's earlier treatment of this passage, to be sure, was to void the word θεόπνευστος of all implication as to the origination of Scripture. By assigning to it the sense of "God-pervaded," "full of God's Spirit," he supposed he had made it a description of what Scripture is, without the least suggestion of how it came to be such; and he did not hesitate accordingly, to affirm that it had nothing whatever to say as to the origin of Scripture.[68] But he afterwards, as we have already pointed out, saw the error of this position, and so far corrected it as to explain that, of course, the term θεόπνευστος includes in itself the implication that the words so designated are spoken by the Spirit of God or by men inspired by God — in accordance with what is repeatedly said elsewhere in Scripture, as, for example, in II Pet. i. 21 — yet still to insist that it throws its *chief emphasis* rather on the nature than the origin of these words.[69] And he never thought of denying that in the circles in which the word was used in application to Scripture, the idea of the origination of Scripture by the act of God was current and indeed dominant. Philo's complete identification of Scripture with the spoken word of God was indeed the subject under treatment by him, when he penned the note from which we have last quoted; and he did not fail explicitly to allow that the conceptions of the writer of the passage in II Timothy were very closely related to those of Philo. "It is certainly undeniable," he writes, "that the new term θεόπνευστος, II Tim. iii. 16, is intended to express very much what Philo meant, and did not yet know how to say sharply by means of so compressed and direct a term"; and again, in another place, "this term, no doubt, embodies only what is everywhere presupposed by

---

[68] "Jahrb. f. bibl. Wissenschaft," vii. 88, 114.
[69] "Geschichte des Volkes Israel," i. 245, note.

Philo as to the Scriptures, and is repeatedly expressed by him in other words; yet his usage is not yet so far developed; and it is in accordance with this that in the New Testament, too, it is only one of the latest writings which uses the term in this way."[70]

It would seem, to be sure, that it is precisely this affinity with Philo's conception of Scripture which Dr. Cremer wishes to exclude in his treatment of the term. "Let it be added," he writes, near the close of the extract from his *Herzog* article which we have given above, "that the expression 'breathed by God, inspired by God,' though an outgrowth of the Biblical idea, certainly, so far as it is referred to the prophecy which does not arise out of the human will II Pet. i. 20), yet can scarcely be applied to the whole of the rest of Scripture — unless we are to find in II Tim. iii. 16 the expression of a conception of sacred Scripture similar to the Philonian." And a little later he urges against the testimony of the exegetical tradition to the meaning of the word, that it was affected by the conceptions of Alexandrian Judaism — that is, he suggests, practically of heathenism. There obviously lies beneath this mode of representation an attempt to represent the idea of the nature and origin of Scripture exhibited in the New Testament, as standing in some fundamental disaccord with that of the Philonian tracts; and the assimilation of the conception expressed in II Tim. iii. 16 to the latter as therefore its separation from the former. Something like this is affirmed also by Holtzmann when he writes:[71] "It is accordingly clear that the author shares the Jewish conception of the purely supernatural origin of the Scriptures in is straitest acceptation, according to which, therefore, the theopneusty is ascribed immediately to the Scriptures themselves, and not merely, as in II Pet. i. 21, to their writers; and so far as the thing itself is concerned there is nothing incorrect implied in the translation, *tota Scriptura.*" The notion that the Biblical and the Philonian ideas of Scripture somewhat markedly

[70] "Jahrb.," etc., ix. 92.
[71] "Die Pastoralbriefe" u. s. w., p. 163.

differ is apparently common to the two writers: only Holtz-mann identifies the idea expressed in II Tim. iii. 16 with the Philonian, and therefore pronounces it to be a mark of late origin for that epistle; while Cremer wishes to detach it from the Philonian, that he may not be forced to recognize the Philonian conception as possessing New Testament authorization.

No such fundamental difference between the Philonian and New Testament conceptions as is here erected, however, can possibly be made out; though whatever minor differences may be traceable between the general New Testament conception and treatment of Scripture and that of Philo, it remains a plain matter of fact that no other general view of Scripture than the so-called Philonian is discernible in the New Testament, all of whose writers — as is true of Jesus Himself also, according to His reported words, — consistently look upon the written words of Scripture as the express utterances of God, owing their origin to His direct spiration and their character to this their divine origin. It is peculiarly absurd to contrast II Pet. i. 21 with II Tim. iii. 16 (as Holtz-mann does explicitly and the others implicitly), on the ground of a difference of conception as to "inspiration," shown in the ascription of inspiration in the former passage to the writers, in the latter immediately to the words of Scripture. It is, on the face of it, the "word of prophecy" to which Peter as-cribes divine surety; it is written prophecy which he declares to be of no "private interpretation"; and if he proceeds to exhibit how God produced this sure written word of prophecy — viz., through men of God carried onward, apart from their own will, by the determining power of the Holy Ghost [72] — surely this exposition of the mode of the divine action in producing the Scriptures can only by the utmost confusion of ideas be pleaded as a denial of the fact that the Scriptures were produced by the Divine action. To Peter as truly as to Paul, and to the Paul of the earlier epistles as truly as to the

[72] For the implications of the term φερόμενοι here (as distinguished from ἀγόμενοι) consult the fruitful discussion of the words in Schmidt's "Synonymik."

Paul of II Timothy, or as to Philo himself, the Scriptures are the product of the Divine Spirit, and would be most appropriately described by the epithet of "God-breathed," i. e., produced by the breath, the inspiration, of God.

The entire distinction which it is sought to erect between the New Testament and the Philonic conceptions of Scripture, as if to the New Testament writers the Scriptures were less the oracles of God than to Philo, and owed their origin less directly to God's action, and might therefore be treated as less divine in character or operation, hangs in the mere air. There may be fairly recognized certain differences between the New Testament and the Philonic conceptions of Scripture; but they certainly do not move in this fundamental region. The epithet "God-breathed," "produced by the creative breath of the Almighty," commends itself, therefore, as one which would lie near at hand and would readily express the fundamental view as to the origination of Scripture current among the whole body of New Testament writers, as well as among the whole mass of their Jewish contemporaries, amid whom they were bred. The distinction between the inspiration of the writers and that of the record, is a subtlety of later times of which they were guiltless: as is also the distinction between the origination of Scripture by the action of the Holy Ghost and the infusing of the Holy Spirit into Scriptures originating by human activity. To the writers of this age of simpler faith, the Scriptures are penetrated by God because they were given by God: and the question of their effects, or even of their nature, was not consciously separated from the question of their origin. The one sufficient and decisive fact concerning them to these writers, inclusive of all else and determinative of all else that was true of them as the Word of God, was that they were "God-given," or, more precisely, the product of God's creative "breath."

In these circumstances it can hardly be needful to pause to point out in detail how completely this conception accords with the whole New Testament doctrine of Scripture, and with the entire body of phraseology currently used in it to express its divine origination. We need only recall the declarations that the Holy Spirit is the author of Scripture (Heb. iii. 7, x. 15), "in whom" it is, therefore, that its human authors speak (Matt. xxii. 43; Mark xii. 36), because it is He that speaks what they speak "through them" (Acts i. 16, iv. 25), they being but the media of the prophetic word (Matt. i. 22, ii. 15, iii. 3, iv. 14, viii. 17, xii. 17, xiii. 35, xxi. 4, xxiv. 15, xxvii. 9, Luke xviii. 31, Acts ii. 16, xxvii. 25, Rom. i. 2, Luke i. 76, Acts i. 16, iii. 18, 21). The whole underlying conception of such modes of expression is in principle set forth in the command of Jesus to His disciples, that, in their times of need, they should depend wholly on the Divine Spirit speaking in them (Matt. x. 20; Mark xiii. 11; cf. Luke i. 41, 67, xii. 12; Acts iv. 8): and perhaps even more decidedly still in Peter's description of the prophets of Scripture as "borne by the Holy Ghost," as πνευματόφοροι, whose words are, therefore, of no "private interpretation," and of the highest surety (II Pet. i. 21). In all such expressions the main affirmation is that Scripture, as the product of the activity of the Spirit, is just the "breath of God"; and the highest possible emphasis is laid on their origination by the divine agency of the Spirit. The primary characteristic of Scripture in the minds of the New Testament writers is thus revealed as, in a word, its Divine origin.

That this was the sole dominating conception attached from the beginning to the term θεόπνευστος as an epithet of Scripture, is further witnessed by the unbroken exegetical tradition of its meaning in the sole passage of the New Testament in which it occurs. Dr. Cremer admits that such is the exegetical tradition, though he seeks to break the weight of this fact by pleading that the unanimity of the patristic interpretation of the passage is due rather to preconceived opinions on the part of the Fathers as to the nature of Scripture, derived from Alexandrian Judaism, than to the natural effect on their minds of the passage itself. Here we are pointed to the universal consent of Jewish and Christian students of the Word as to the divine origin of the Scriptures they held

in common — a fact impressive enough of itself — as a reason
for discrediting the testimony of the latter as to the meaning
of a fundamental passage bearing on the doctrine of Holy
Scripture. One is tempted to ask whether it can be really
proved that the theology of Alexandrian Judaism exercised
so universal and absolute a dominion over the thinking of the
Church, that it is likely to be due to its influence alone that
the Christian doctrine of inspiration took shape, in despite
(as we are told) of the natural implications of the Christian
documents themselves. And one is very likely to insist that,
whatever may be its origin, this conception of the divine
origination of Scripture was certainly shared by the New
Testament writers themselves, and may very well therefore
have found expression in II Tim. iii. 16 — which would therefore need no adjustment to current ideas to make it teach
it. At all events, it is admitted that this view of the teaching
of II Tim. iii. 16 is supported by the unbroken exegetical
tradition; and this fact certainly requires to be taken into
consideration in determining the meaning of the word.

It is quite true that Dr. Cremer in one sentence does not
seem to keep in mind the unbrokenness of the exegetical tradition. We read: "Origen also, in 'Hom. 21 in Jerem.', seems
so [i. e., as Dr. Cremer does] to understand it [that is,
θεόπνευστος ]:—*sacra volumina spiritus plenitudinem spirant.*"
The unwary reader may infer from this that these words of
Origen are explanatory of II Tim. iii. 16, and that they therefore break the exegetical tradition and show that Origen assigned to that passage the meaning that "the Holy Scriptures
breathe out the plenitude of the Spirit." Such is, however,
not the case. Origen is not here commenting on II Tim. iii. 16,
but only freely expressing his own notion as to the nature of
Scripture. His words here do not, therefore, break the constancy of the exegetical tradition, but at the worst only the
universality of that Philonian conception of Scripture, to the
universality of which among the Fathers, Dr. Cremer attributes the unbrokenness of the exegetical tradition. What results from their adduction is, then, not a weakening of the
patristic testimony to the meaning of θεόπνευστος in II Tim.

iii. 16, but (at the worst) a possible hint that Dr. Cremer's explanation of the unanimity of that testimony may not, after all, be applicable. When commenting on II Tim. iii. 16, Origen uniformly takes the word θεόπνευστος as indicatory of the origin of Scripture; though when himself speaking of what Scripture is, he may sometimes speak as Dr. Cremer would have him speak. It looks as if his interpretation of II Tim. iii. 16 were expository of its meaning to him rather than impository of his views on it. Let us, by way of illustration, place a fuller citation of Origen's words, in the passage adduced by Dr. Cremer, side by side with a passage directly dealing with II Tim. iii. 16, and note the result.

Secundum istiusmodi expositiones decet sacras litteras credere nec unum quidem apicem habere vacuum sapientia Dei. Qui enim mihi homini præcipit dicens: *Non apparebis ante conspectum meum vacuus,* multo plus hoc ipse agit, ne aliquid vacuum loquatur. Ex plenitudine ejus accipientes prophetæ, ea, quæ erant de plenitudine sumpta, cecinerunt: et idcirco sacra volumina spiritus plenitudinem spirant, nihilque est sive in prophetia, sive in lege, sive in evangelio, sive in apostolo, quod non a plenitudine divinæ majestatis descendat. Quamobrem spirant in scripturis sanctis hodieque plenitudinis verba. Spirant autem his, qui habent et oculos ad videnda cœlestia et aures ad audienda divina, et nares ad ea, quæ sunt plenitudinis, sentienda (Origen, "in Jeremiam Homilia," xxi, 2. Wirceburg ed., 1785, ix, 733).

Here Origen is writing quite freely: and his theme is the divine fullness of Scripture. There is nothing in Scripture which is vain or empty and all its fullness is derived from Him from whom it is dipped by the prophets. Contrast his manner, now, when he is expounding II Tim. iii. 16.

" Let us not be stupefied by hearing Scriptures which we do not understand; but let it be to us according to our faith, by which also we believe that every Scripture because it is theopneustic (πᾶσα γραφὴ θεόπνευστος οὖσα) is profitable. For you must needs admit one of two things regarding these Scriptures: either that they are not theopneustic since they are not profitable, as the unbeliever takes it; or, as a believer, you must admit that since they are theopneustic, they are profitable. It is to be admitted, of course, that the profit is often received by us unconsciously, just as often we are assigned certain food for the benefit of the eyes, and only after two or three days does the digestion of the food that was to benefit the eyes give us assurance by trial that the eyes are benefited. . . . So, then, believe also concerning the divine Scriptures, that thy soul is profited, even if thy understanding does not perceive the fruit of the profit that comes from the letters, from the mere bare reading" [Origen, "Hom. XX in Josuam" 2, in J. A. Robinson's Origen's "Philocalia," p. 63).

It is obvious that here Origen does not understand II Tim. iii. 16, to teach that Scripture is inspired only because it is profitable, and that we are to determine its profitableness first and its inspiration therefrom; what he draws from the passage is that Scripture is profitable because it is inspired, and that though we may not see in any particular case how, or even that, it is profitable, we must still believe it to be profitable because it is inspired, i. e., obviously because it is given of God for that end.

It seemed to be necessary to adduce at some length these passages from Origen, inasmuch as the partial adduction of one of them, alone, by Dr. Cremer might prove misleading to the unwary reader. But there appears to be no need of multiplying passages from the other early expositors of II Tim. iii. 16, seeing that it is freely confessed that the exegetical tradition runs all in one groove. We may differ as to the weight we allow to this fact; but surely as a piece of testimony corroborative of the meaning of the word derived from other considerations, it is worth noting that it has from the beginning been understood only in one way — even by those, such as Origen and we may add Clement, who may not themselves be absolutely consistent in preserving the point of view taught them in this passage.[73]

[73] Cf. Prof. Schulze, *loc. cit.*: "Further, it should not be lost sight of (and Dr. Cremer does not do so) how the Church in its defenders has understood this word. There can be no doubt that in the conflict with Montanism, the traditional doctrine of theopneusty was grounded in the conception of θεπνευστος, but *never* that of the Scriptures breathing out the Spirit of God. The passage which Cremer adduces from Origen gives no interpretation of this word, but only points to a quality of Scripture consequent on their divine origination by the Holy Spirit: and elsewhere when he adduces the rule of faith, the words run, *quod per spiritum dei*

The final test of the sense assigned to any word is, of course, derived from its fitness to the context in which it is found. And Dr. Cremer does not fail to urge with reference to θεόπνευστος in II Tim. iii. 16, that the meaning he assigns to it corresponds well with the context, especially with the succeeding clauses; as well as, he adds, with the language elsewhere in the New Testament, as, for example, in the Epistle to the Hebrews, where what Scripture says is spoken of as the utterance, the saying of the Holy Ghost, with which he would further compare even Acts xxviii. 25.

That the words of Scripture are conceived, not only in Hebrews but throughout the New Testament, as the utterances of the Holy Ghost is obvious enough and not to be denied. But it is equally obvious that the ground of this conception is everywhere the ascription of these words to the Holy Ghost as their responsible author: *littera scripta manet* and remains what it was when written, viz., the words of the writer. The fact that all Scripture is conceived as a body of Oracles and approached with awe as the utterances of God certainly does not in the least suggest that these utterances may not be described as God-given words or throw a preference for an interpretation of θεόπνευστος which would transmute it into an assertion that they are rather God-giving words.

And the same may be said of the contextual argument. Naturally, if θεόπνευστος means "God-giving," it would as an epithet or predicate of Scripture serve very well to lay a foundation for declaring this "God-giving Scripture" also profitable, etc. But an equal foundation for this declaration is laid by the description of it as "God-given." The passage just quoted from Origen will alone teach us this. All that can be said on this score for the new interpretation, therefore,

*sacræ scripturæ conscriptæ sint,* or *a verbo dei et spirita dei dictæ sunt:* just as Clem. Alex. also, when, in *Coh.* 71, he is commenting on the Pauline passage, takes the word in the usual way, and yet, like Origen, makes an inference from the God-likeness (as θεοποιεῖν ) in Plato's manner, from the whole passage—though not deriving it from the word itself. For the use of the word in Origen, we need to note: *Sel. in Ps.,* ii. 527; *Hom. in Joh.,* vi. 134, Ed. de la R."

is that it also could be made accordant with the context; and as much, and much more, can be said for the old. We leave the matter in this form, since obviously a detailed interpretation of the whole passage cannot be entered into here, but must be reserved for a later occasion. It may well suffice to say now that obviously no advantage can be claimed for the new interpretation from this point of view. The question is, after all, not what can the word be made to mean, but what does it mean; and the witness of its usage elsewhere, its form and mode of composition, and the sense given it by its readers from the first, supply here the primary evidence. Only if the sense thus commended to us were unsuitable to the context would we be justified in seeking further for a new interpretation — thus demanded by the context. This can by no means be claimed in the present instance, and nothing can be demanded of us beyond showing that the more natural current sense of the word is accordant with the context.

The result of our investigation would seem thus, certainly, to discredit the new interpretation of θεόπνευστος offered by Ewald and Cremer. From all points of approach alike we appear to be conducted to the conclusion that it is primarily expressive of the origination of Scripture, not of its nature and much less of its effects. What is θεόπνευστος is "God-breathed," produced by the creative breath of the Almighty. And Scripture is called θεόπνευστος in order to designate it as "God-breathed," the product of Divine spiration, the creation of that Spirit who is in all spheres of the Divine activity the executive of the Godhead. The traditional translation of the word by the Latin *inspiratus a Deo* is no doubt also discredited, if we are to take it at the foot of the letter. It does not express a breathing *into* the Scriptures by God. But the ordinary conception attached to it, whether among the Fathers or the Dogmaticians, is in general vindicated. What it affirms is that the Scriptures owe their origin to an activity of God the Holy Ghost and are in the highest and truest sense His creation. It is on this foundation of Divine origin that all the high attributes of Scripture are built.

# VII
## "IT SAYS:" "SCRIPTURE SAYS:" "GOD SAYS"

# "IT SAYS:" "SCRIPTURE SAYS:" "GOD SAYS"[1]

IT would be difficult to invent methods of showing profound reverence for the text of Scripture as the very Word of God, which will not be found to be characteristic of the writers of the New Testament in dealing with the Old. Among the rich variety of the indications of their estimate of the written words of the Old Testament as direct utterances of Jehovah, there are in particular two classes of passages, each of which, when taken separately, throws into the clearest light their habitual appeal to the Old Testament text as to God Himself speaking, while, together, they make an irresistible impression of the absolute identification by their writers of the Scriptures in their hands with the living voice of God. In one of these classes of passages the Scriptures are spoken of as if they were God; in the other, God is spoken of as if He were the Scriptures: in the two together, God and the Scriptures are brought into such conjunction as to show that in point of directness of authority no distinction was made between them.

Examples of the first class of passages are such as these: Gal. iii. 8, "The Scripture, foreseeing that God would justify the heathen through faith, preached before the gospel unto Abraham, saying, In thee shall all the nations be blessed" (Gen. xii. 1–3); Rom. ix. 17, "The Scripture saith unto Pharaoh, Even for this same purpose have I raised thee up" (Ex. ix. 16). It was not, however, the Scripture (which did not exist at the time) that, foreseeing God's purposes of grace in the future, spoke these precious words to Abraham, but God Himself in His own person: it was not the not yet existent Scripture that made this announcement to Pharaoh, but God Himself through the mouth of His prophet Moses. These acts could be attributed to "Scripture" only as the

[1] From *The Presbyterian and Reformed Review*, Vol. x, 1899, pp. 472–510.

result of such a habitual identification, in the mind of the writer, of the text of Scripture with God as speaking, that it became natural to use the term "Scripture says," when what was really intended was "God, as recorded in Scripture, said."

Examples of the other class of passages are such as these: Matt. xix. 4, 5, "And he answered and said, Have ye not read that he which made them from the beginning made them male and female, and said, For this cause shall a man leave his father and mother, and shall cleave to his wife, and the twain shall become one flesh?" (Gen. ii. 24); Heb. iii. 7, "Wherefore, even as the Holy Ghost saith, Today if ye shall hear his voice," etc. (Ps. xcv. 7); Acts iv. 24, 25, "Thou art God, who by the mouth of thy servant David hast said, Why do the heathen rage and the people imagine vain things" (Ps. ii. 1); Acts xiii. 34, 35, "He that raised him up from the dead, now no more to return to corruption, . . . hath spoken in this wise, I will give you the holy and sure blessings of David" (Isa. lv. 3); "because he saith also in another [Psalm], Thou wilt not give thy holy one to see corruption" (Ps. xvi. 10); Heb. i. 6, "And when he again bringeth in the first born into the world, he saith, And let all the angels of God worship him" (Deut. xxxii. 43); "and of the angels he saith, Who maketh his angels wings, and his ministers a flame of fire" (Ps. civ. 4); "but of the Son, *He saith,* Thy throne, O God, is for ever and ever," etc., (Ps. xlv. 7) and, "Thou, Lord, in the beginning," etc. (Ps. cii. 26). It is not God, however, in whose mouth these sayings are placed in the text of the Old Testament: they are the words of others, recorded in the text of Scripture as spoken to or of God. They could be attributed to God only through such habitual identification, in the minds of the writers, of the text of Scripture with the utterances of God that it had become natural to use the term "God says" when what was really intended was "Scripture, the Word of God, says."

The two sets of passages, together, thus show an absolute identification, in the minds of these writers, of "Scripture" with the speaking God.

In the same line with these passages are commonly ranged certain others, in which Scripture seems to be adduced with a subjectless λέγει or φησί, the authoritative subject — whether the divinely given Word or God Himself — being taken for granted. Among these have been counted such passages, for example, as the following: Rom. ix. 15, "For he saith to Moses, I will have mercy on whom I have mercy, and I will have compassion on whom I have compassion" (Ex. xxxiii. 19); Rom. xv. 10, "And again he saith, Rejoice, ye Gentiles, with his people" (Deut. xxxii. 43); and again, "Praise the Lord, all ye Gentiles; and let all the people praise him" (Ps. cvii. 1); Gal. iii. 16, "He saith not, And to seeds, as of many; but as of one, And to thy seed (Gen. xiii. 15), which is Christ"; Eph. iv. 8, "Wherefore he saith, When he ascended on high, he led captivity captive, and gave gifts unto men" (Ps. lxviii. 18); Eph. v. 14, "Wherefore he saith, Awake thou that sleepest and arise from the dead and Christ shall shine upon thee" (Isa. lx. 1); I Cor. vi. 16, "For the twain, saith he, shall become one flesh" (Gen. ii. 24); I Cor. xv. 27, "But when he saith, All things are put in subjection" (Ps. viii. 7); II Cor. vi. 2, "For he saith, At an acceptable time, I heark-ened unto thee, and in a day of salvation did I succor thee" (Isa. xlix. 8); Heb. viii. 5, "For see, saith he, that thou make all things according to the pattern that was showed thee in the mount" (Ex. xxv. 40); James iv. 6, "Wherefore he saith, God resisteth the proud but giveth grace to the humble" (Prov. iii. 34).

There is room for difference of opinion, of course, whether all these passages are cases in point. And there has certainly always existed some difference of opinion among commenta-tors as to the proper *subauditum* in such instances as are allowed. The state of the case would seem to be fairly indi-cated by Alexander Buttmann, when he says:

"The predicates λέγει or φησίν are often found in the New Testa-ment in quotations, ὁ θεός or even merely ἡ γραφή being always to be supplied as subject; as I Cor. vi. 16, II Cor. vi. 2, Gal. iii. 16, Eph. iv. 8, v. 14, Heb. viii. 5, iv. 3 (εἴρηκεν). These subjects are also expressed, as in Gal. iv. 30, I Tim. v. 18, or to be supplied from the preceding context, as in Heb. i. 5 *seq.*" [2]

Of the alternatives thus offered, Jelf apparently prefers the one:

"In the New Testament we must supply προφήτης, ἡ γραφή, πνεῦμα, etc., before φησί, λέγει, μαρτυρεῖ." [3]

Winer and Blass take the other:

"The formulas of citation — λέγει, II Cor. vi. 2, Gal. iii. 16, Eph. iv. 8 al., φησί, I Cor. vi. 16, Heb. viii. 5; εἴρηκε, Heb. iv. 4 (cf. the Rabbinical אומר); μαρτυρεῖ, Heb. vii. 17 (εἶπε, I Cor. xv. 27) — are probably in no instance impersonal in the minds of the New Testament writers. The subject (ὁ θεός) is usually contained in the context, either directly or indirectly; in I Cor. vi. 16 and Matt. xix. 5, φησί, there is an apostolic ellipsis (of ὁ θεός); in Heb. vii. 17, the best authorities have μαρτυρεῖται." [4]

"In the formulas of citation such as λέγει, II Cor. vi. 2, Gal. iii. 16, etc.; φησίν, I Cor. vi. 16, Heb. viii. 5; εἴρηκε, Heb. iv. 4 — ὁ θεός is to be understood ('*He* says'); in II Cor. x. 10, φησίν (א DE, etc. [?], 'one says'), appears to be a wrong reading for φασίν (B), unless perhaps a τις has dropped out (but cp. Clem. Hom., xi. 9 *ad init.*)." [5]

The commentators commonly range themselves with Winer and Blass. Thus, on Rom. ix. 15, Sanday and Headlam comment: "λέγει without a nominative for θεὸς λέγει is a common idiom in quotations," referring to Rom. xv. 10 as a parallel case. On Gal. iii. 16, Meyer says: "sc. Θεός, which is derived from the historical reference of the previous ἐρρέθησαν, so well known to the reader"; and Alford: "viz., He who gave the promises — God"; and Sieffert: "οὐ λέγει sc. θεός which flows out of the historical relation (known to the reader) of the preceding ἐρρέθησαν (cf. Eph. iv. 8, v. 14)."

[2] "A Grammar of the New Testament Greek," Thayer's translation p. 134.
[3] Sec. 373, 3.
[4] Winer, Sec. 58, 9, γ; p. 656 of Moulton's translation.
[5] Blass' "Grammar of N. T. Greek"; English translation by H. St. J. Thackeray, M.A., p. 75.

On Eph. iv. 8, Meyer's comment runs: "*Who* says it (comp. v. 14) is obvious of itself, namely, *God*, whose word the Scripture is. See on I Cor. vi. 16; Gal. iii. 16; the supplying ἡ γραφή or τὸ πνεῦμα must have been suggested by the context (Rom. xv. 10). The manner of citation with the simple λέγει, obviously meant of God, has as its necessary presupposition, in the mind of the writer and readers, the Theopneustia of the Old Testament." Haupt, similarly: "The introduction of a citation with the simple λέγει, with which, of course, 'God' is to be supplied as subject, not 'the Scripture,' is found in Paul again v. 14, II Cor. vi. 2, Rom. xv. 10; similarly φησί, I Cor. vi. 16 (εἶπεν with the addition ὁ θεός, II Cor. vi. 16)." A similar comment is given by Ellicott, who adds at Eph. v. 14: "scil. ὁ θεός, according to the usual form of St. Paul's quotations; see notes on chap. iv. 8 and on Gal. iii. 16": though on I Cor. vi. 16 he speaks with less decision: "It may be doubted what nominative is to be supplied to this practically impersonal verb, whether ἡ γραφή (comp. John vii. 38, Rom. iv. 3, ix. 17, *al.*) or ὁ θεός (comp. Matt. xix. 5, II Cor. vi. 2, where this nominative is distinctly suggested by the context): the latter is perhaps the more natural: comp. Winer, *Gr.*, § 58, 9, and notes on Eph. iv. 8." On I Cor. vi. 16, Edwards comments: "*sc.* ὁ θεός, as in Rom. ix. 15. Cf. Matt. xix. 4, 5, where ὁ ποιήσας supplies a nom. to εἶπεν. Similarly in Philo and Barnabas φησί introduces citations from Scripture." On II Cor. vi. 2, Waite says: "A statement of God Himself is adduced"; and De Wette: "*sc.* θεός, who Himself speaks." On Heb. viii. 5, Bleek comments: "That there is to be understood as the subject of φησί, not, as Böhme thinks, ἡ γραφή, but ὁ θεός, can least of all be doubtful here, where actual words of God are adduced"; and Weiss: "This statement is now established (γάρ) by appeal to Ex. xxv. 40, which passage is characterized only by the interpolated φησίν (cf. Acts xxv. 22) as a divine oracle. . . . The subject of φησίν is, of course, God, neither ὁ χρηματισμός (Lün.) nor ἡ γραφή (Bhm.)." On James iv. 6, Mayor comments: "The subject understood is probably God, as above, i. 12, ἐπηγγείλατο, and Eph. iv. 8, v. 14, where the same phrase occurs; others take it as ἡ γραφή. Cf. above, v. 5." [6]

Most of these passages have, on the other hand, been explained by some commentators on the supposition that it is ἡ γραφή that is to be supplied, as has sufficiently appeared indeed from the controversial remarks in the notes quoted above. This circumstance may be taken as precluding the necessity of adducing examples here.[7] Suffice it to say that those so filling in the *subauditum* are entirely at one with the commentators already quoted in looking upon the citations as treated by the New Testament writers as of divine authority, it being, in their apprehension, all one in this regard whether the *subauditum* is conceived as ἡ γραφή or as ὁ θεός.

In the meantime, however, there has occasionally showed itself a tendency to treat these subjectless verbs more or less as true impersonals. Thus we read in Delitzsch's note on Heb. viii. 5: "For 'see,' *saith He,* i. e., ὁ θεός, or taking φησί impersonally (that is, without a definite subject), '*it is said*' (i. e., in Scripture), (Bernhardy, 'Synt.,' 419)." So Kern on James iv. 6 comments: "λέγει here *impersonaliter,* instead of the foregoing λέγει ἡ γραφή"; and accordingly Beyschlag, in his recent commentary says: "to λέγει, ἡ γραφή is to be supplied, or it is to be taken with Kern impersonally." Similarly Godet on I Cor. vi. 16 says: "The subject of the verb φησίν, *says he,* may be either Adam or Moses, or Scripture, or God Himself, or finally, as is shown by Heinrici, the verb may be a simple formula of quotation like our '*It is said.*' This form is frequently found in Philo." [8] Some such usage as is here

---

[6] So also Wandel: "James then cites the passage Prov. iii. 24, in which we must simply supply 'God' to λέγει."

[7] As a single example, take, e. g., Oltramare, on Eph. iv. 8: "Διὸ λέγει, scil. ἡ γραφή: In accord with the extreme frequency with which the New Testament is cited, Paul often cites by saying simply λέγει (v. 14, Rom. xv. 10, II Cor. vi. 2, Gal. iii. 16; cf. Rom. iv. 3, x. 17, I Tim. v. 18), or φησί (I Cor. vi. 16; cf. Heb. viii. 15), or εἶπε (I Cor. xv. 27). He understands the subject, which is understood of itself, γραφή or θεός (see Winer, *Gr.,* p. 486)."

[8] Earlier still De Wette explained the phrase in a somewhat similar way. His note on Eph. v. 8 runs: "Old Testament support. διὸ λέγει] *therefore* (because

supposed may seem actually to occur in the common text of Wisdom xv. 12 [9] and II Cor. x. 10.[10] But in both passages the true reading is probably φασίν; in neither instance is it clear that, if φησίν be read, it has no subject implied in the context; if φησίν be read and taken as equivalent to φασίν it still is not purely indefinite; and in any case the instances are not parallel, inasmuch as in neither of these passages is it Scripture, or indeed any document, that is adduced.

The fact that a few very able commentators have taken this unlikely line of exposition would call for nothing more than this incidental remark, were not our attention attracted somewhat violently to it by the dogmatic tone and extremity of contention of a recent commentator who has adopted this opinion. We refer to Dr. T. K. Abbott's comment on Eph. iv. 8, in his contribution to "The International Critical Commentary." It runs to a considerable length, but as on this very account it opens out somewhat more fully than usual this

Christ gives the gifts and according to the presupposition that all that concerns Christ is predicted in the Old Testament *it is said*, [heisst es] (cf. Gal. iii. 16, I Cor. vi. 16 — a formula of citation (also v. 14) like Jas. iv. 6, Acts xiii. 35, Heb. x. 5, not elsewhere found in the apostle (cf., however, II Cor. vi. 17) . . ." And again on Eph. v. 14 we read: "διὸ λέγει] *therefore it is said* [heisst es] (in the Scriptures). Cf. iv. 8." He supposes that, in the latter passage, Paul confuses a customary application of Scripture with the very words of Scripture.

[9] Grimm's note on the passage runs: "Instead of the rec. reading, φησίν, Alex. Ephr., 157, 248, 296, Compl. have φασίν. Nevertheless the author may here return to the singular, referring to the potter before depicted (see the following verses). Or φησί may stand impersonally, in the sense of 'heisst es,' 'sagt man,' Win., p. 462, 6th ed.; Müller, 'Philo's Buch von d. Weltschöpfung,' p. 44." Cf. further, below, p. 316.

[10] φησίν is placed by Tischendorf, Tregelles and Westcott and Hort in their texts: while φασίν is read by Lachmann and placed in their margins by Tregelles and Westcott and Hort. The former is read by אDEFGKLP, etc., by the cursives, and by the Vulgate and Coptic versions, while the latter is the reading of B, Old Latin and Syriac. Heinrici pertinently remarks (in his own "Commentary," 1887): "The reading φασίν, which Lachmann accepts, is just as strongly witnessed by B, the Itala and Peschitto as φησίν (אDFG Vulg. Copt.) and it almost looks as if φησίν were a correction occasioned by the succeeding ὁ τοιοῦτος (against Meyer)." Alford, who continues to read φησίν equally pertinently on that hypothesis, remarks: "φησίν, taken by Winer (Ed. 6, § 58, 96), De Wette and Meyer as impersonal, 'heisst es,' 'men say'; but why should not the τις of ver. 7, and ὁ τοιοῦτος of ver. 11, be the subject?" See further below, p. 316.

rather unwonted view of the construction, we shall venture to quote it *in extenso*. Dr. Abbott says:

"Διὸ λέγει. 'Wherefore it saith' = 'it is said.' If any substantive is to be supplied, it is ἡ γραφή; but the verb may well be taken impersonally, just as in colloquial English one may often hear: 'it says' or the like. Many expositors supply, however, ὁ Θεός. Meyer even says, 'Who says it is obvious of itself, namely, God, whose word the Scripture is.[11] Similarly Alford [12] and Ellicott.[13] If it were St. Paul's habit to introduce quotations from the Old Testament, by whomsoever spoken in the original text, with the formula ὁ Θεὸς λέγει, then this supplement here might be defended. But it is not. In quoting he sometimes says λέγει, frequently ἡ γραφὴ λέγει, at other times Δαβὶδ λέγει, Ἡσαΐας λέγει. There is not a single instance in which ὁ Θεός is either expressed or implied as the subject, except where in the original context God is the speaker, as in Rom. ix. 15. Even when that is the case

[11] [See above, p. 287.]

[12] ["*He* (viz., God, whose word the Scriptures are. See reff. [i. e., Rom. xii. 3, II Cor. x. 13, iv. 13, 16 = Paul only], and notes: not merely 'it,' *es heisst*, as, De Wette, *al.*: nor ἡ γραφή: had it been the subject it must have been expressed, as in Rom. iv. 3, ix. 17, *al.*) *says* (viz., Ps. lxviii. 18, see below: not in some Christian hymn, as Flatt and Storr — which would not agree with λέγει, nor with the treatment of the citation, which is plainly regarded as carrying the weight of Scripture.")]

[13] ["'*He saith,*' *sc.* ὁ Θεός,, not ἡ γραφή. This latter nominative is several times inserted by St. Paul (Rom. iv. 3, ix. 17, x. 11, Gal. iv. 30, I Tim. v. 18), but is not therefore to be regularly supplied whenever there is an ellipsis (Bos, *Ellips.*, p. 54) without reference to the nature of the passages. The surest and in fact only guide is the context; when that affords no certain hint, we fall back upon the natural subject, ὁ Θεός, whose words the Scriptures are; see notes on Gal. iii. 16." See further above, p. 287. At Gal. iii. 16, Ellicott had said: "'*He saith not*'; not ἡ γραφή (Bos, *Ellips.*, p. 54), as in Rom. xv. 10 — where the subst. is supplied from γέγραπται, ver. 9 — or τὸ πνεῦμα (Rück., Winer, *Gr.*, §39, 1), which appears arbitrary, but the natural subject ὁ Θεός, as in Eph. iv. 8, v. 14, and (φησὶ) I Cor. vi. 16, Heb. viii. 5. So apparently Syr., which here inserts *illi* after λέγει." The passage referred to in Bos (London ed. of 1825, pp. 57, 58) is as follows: "In the New Testament, where the Scripture of the Old Testament is cited, φησὶ or λέγει often occurs with ἡ γραφή understood — a word which actually stands in other passages: I Cor. vi. 16, Eph. v. 14, Gal. iii. 16. The same thing occurs in the Greek fathers. Marcus Eremita, in his earlier aphorisms, No. 106, οὐδεὶς, φησί, στρατευόμενος ἐμπλέκεται ταῖς τοῦ βίου πραγματείαις, 'No one, says (the Scripture, II Tim. ii. 4) going a-soldiering is entangled in the affairs of this life.' So, No. 134: φησὶ γὰρ, ὁ ὑψῶν ἑαυτὸν ταπεινωθήσεται, 'For, says (Scripture), he that exalteth himself shall be brought low.' There may be also understood *pro re nata εὐαγγελιστής, προφήτης, ἀπόστολος*: but the other is more general and suits excellently. Schoettg."]

he does not hesitate to use a different subject, as in Rom. x. 19, 20: 'Moses saith,' 'Isaiah is very bold, and saith'; Rom. ix. 17, 'The Scripture saith to Pharaoh.'

"This being the case, we are certainly not justified in forcing upon the apostle here and in chap. v. 14 a form of expression consistent only with the extreme view of verbal inspiration. When Meyer (followed by Alford and Ellicott) says that ἡ γραφή must not be supplied unless it is given by the context, the reply is obvious, namely, that, as above stated, ἡ γραφή λέγει does, in fact, often occur, and therefore the apostle might have used it here, whereas ὁ Θεὸς λέγει does not occur (except in cases unlike this), and we have reason to believe could not be used by St. Paul here. It is some additional confirmation of this that both here and in chap. v. 14 (if that is a Biblical quotation) he does not hesitate to make important alterations. This is the view taken by Braune, Macpherson, Moule; the latter, however, adding that for St. Paul 'the word of the Scripture and the word of its Author are convertible terms.'

"It is objected that although φησί is used impersonally, λέγει is not. The present passage and chap. v. 14 [14] are enough to prove the usage for St. Paul, and there are other passages in his Epistles where this sense is at least applicable; cf. Rom. xv. 10, where λέγει is parallel to γέγραπται in ver. 9; Gal. iii. 16, where it corresponds to ἐρρήθησαν. But, in fact, the impersonal use of φησί in Greek authors is quite different, namely = φασί, 'they say' (so II Cor. x. 10). Classical authors had no opportunity of using λέγει as it is used here, as they did not possess any collection of writings which could be referred to as ἡ γραφή, or by any like word. They could say: ὁ νόμος λέγει and τὸ λεγόμενον."

It is not, it will be observed, the fact that Dr. Abbott decides against the *subauditum*, ὁ θεός, in these passages, which calls for remark. As he himself points out, many others have been before him in this. It is the extremity of his opinion that first of all attracts attention. For it is to be noticed that, though he sometimes speaks as if he understood an implied ἡ γραφή, or some like term, as the subject of λέγει, that is not his real contention. What he proposes is to take the verb wholly indefinitely — as equivalent to "it is said," as if the

[14] [The text actually has "ver. 14," but we venture to correct the obvious slip.]

source of the quotation were unimportant and its authority
insignificant. This interpretation of his proposal is placed beyond doubt by his remarks on chap. v. 14. There we read:

"Διὸ λέγει. 'Wherefore it is said.' It is generally held that this
formula introduces a quotation from canonical Scripture. . . . The
difficulties disappear when we recognize that λέγει need not be taken
to mean ὁ Θεὸς λέγει — an assertion which has been shown in iv. 8 to
be untenable. It means, 'it says,' or 'it is said,' and the quotation may
probably be from some liturgical formula or hymn — a supposition
with which its rhythmical character agrees very well. . . . Theodoret
mentions this opinion. . . . Stier adopts a similar view, but endeavors
to save the supposed limitation of the use of λέγει by saying that in
the Church the Spirit speaks. As there are in the Church prophets and
prophetic speakers and poets, so there are liturgical expressions and
hymns which are holy words. Comparing *vv.* 18, 19, Col. iii. 16, it
may be said that the apostle is here giving us an example of this self-
admonition by new spiritual songs."

So extreme an opinion, as we have already hinted, naturally finds, however, little support in the commentators, even
in those quoted to buttress it, — of course, in its fundamental point. Braune says: "We must naturally supply ἡ
γραφή, the Scripture, with λέγει, 'saith,' (James iv. 6, Rom.
xv. 10, Gal. iii. 16, I Cor. vi. 16: φησίν), and not ὁ θεὸς (Meyer,
Schenkel [15]), or ὁ λέγων (Bleek: the writer)": to which Dr.
M. T. Riddle, his translator, however, adds: "The fact that
Paul frequently supplies ἡ γραφή (Rom. iv. 3, ix. 17, x. 11,
Gal. iv. 30, I Tim. v. 18) is against Braune's view; for in some
of these passages there is a reason for its insertion (see
"Romans," p. 314), and as the Scriptures are God's Word
(Meyer), the natural aim and obvious subject is ὁ θεὸς. So
Alford, Ellicott and most." Moule's comment runs: "*Where-
fore he saith*] Or *it*, i. e., the Scripture, *saith*. St. Paul's usage

[15] ["With λέγει God is to be supplied as subject. From this way of adducing
it, it is already clear that the cited words cannot be taken from a Christian hymn
in use in the Church at Ephesus (Storr, Flatt), but must belong to the sacred,
God-given Scripture." Accordingly at v. 14 he says: "In accordance with the
formula (λέγει, chap. iv. 8) usual in adducing Scripture, it can scarcely be doubtful
that the apostle intended to cite an Old Testament passage."]

in quotation leaves the subject of the verb undetermined here and in similar cases (see, e. g., chap. v. 14[16]). For him the word of the Scripture and the word of its author are convertible terms." Macpherson alone, of those appealed to by Dr. Abbott, supports, in a somewhat carelessly written note, the indefinite interpretation put forward by Dr. Abbott, — being misled apparently by remarks of Lightfoot's and Westcott's. His comment runs:

"A very simple quotation formula is here employed, the single word λέγει. It is also similarly used (chap. v. 14; II Cor. vi. 2; Gal. iii. 16; Rom. xv. 10).[17] This word is frequently employed in the fuller formula, *The Scripture saith*, λέγει ἡ γραφή (Rom. iv. 3, x. 11, xi. 2; Jas. ii. 23, etc.); or the name of the writer of the particular scripture, Esaias, David, the Holy Spirit, the law (Rom. xv. 12; Acts xiii. 35; Heb. iii. 7; I Cor. xiii. 34, etc.).[18] Of λέγει, φησί, εἴρηκε, and similar words thus used, Winer ("Grammar," p. 656, 1882) says that probably in no instance are they impersonal in the minds of the New Testament writers, but that the subject, ὁ θεός, is somewhere in the context, and is to be supplied.[19] On the contrary, Lightfoot, in his note on Gal. iii. 16, remarks that λέγει, like the Attic φησί, seems to be used impersonally, the nominative being lost sight of. In our passage we have no nominative in the context which we can supply, and it seems better to render the phrase impersonally, *It is said*. The same word is used very frequently in the Epistle to the Hebrews, but always with God or Christ understood from the immediate context. Westcott very correctly remarks (p. 457) that the use of the formula in Eph. iv. 8, v. 14, seems to be of a different kind."[20]

[16] The comment there is simply: "he *saith*] or possibly *it* (the Scripture) *saith*."        [17] [The parenthetical marks should doubtless be removed.]

[18] [This sentence seems formally incomplete; probably "is frequently employed" is to be supplied from the preceding clause.]

[19] [This scarcely gives a complete view of Winer's remark: he says that "the subject ὁ θεός) is *usually* contained in the context, either directly *or indirectly*," and proceeds to adduce cases of ellipsis.]

[20] [What Westcott apparently says is not that "the two passages in the Epistle to the Ephesians (iv. 8, v. 14, διὸ λέγει) appear to be different in kind" from the usage of Hebrews, but from the cases in the rest of the New Testament, where God is the subject of λέγει indeed, but "the reference is to words directly spoken by God." He possibly means, "different in kind" from the usage both of Hebrews and of the rest of the New Testament: but he does not seem to say this directly. See post, p. 305.]

Outside of these commentators quoted by himself, however, Prof. Abbott's extreme view has (as has, indeed, already incidentally appeared) the powerful support of Lightfoot and Heinrici. The former expresses his opinion not only in his note on Gal. iii. 16, to which Macpherson refers, but more fully and argumentatively in his note on I Cor. vi. 16 printed in his posthumous "Notes on the Epistles of St. Paul." In the former of these places he says:

"οὐ λέγει seems to be used impersonally, like the Attic φησί in quoting legal documents, the nominative being lost sight of. If so, we need not inquire whether ὁ θεός or ἡ γραφή is to be understood. Comp. λέγει, Rom. xv. 10, Eph. iv. 8, v. 14; and φησίν, I Cor. vi. 16, II Cor. x. 10 (v. l)."

In the latter, speaking more at large "as to the authority assigned to the passage" quoted by St. Paul, he says:

"What are we to understand by φησίν? Is ὁ θεός to be supplied or ἡ γραφή? To this question it is safest to reply that we cannot decide. The fact is that, like λέγει, φησίν when introducing a quotation seems to be used impersonally. This usage is common in Biblical Greek (λέγει, Rom. xv. 10, Gal. iii. 16, Eph. iv. 8, v. 14; φησίν, Heb. viii. 5, II Cor. x. 10 (v. l.), more common in classical Greek. Alford, after Meyer, objects to rendering φησίν impersonally here, as contrary to St. Paul's usage. But the only other occurrence of the phrase in St. Paul is II Cor. x. 10, where he is not introducing Scripture, but the objections of human critics and of more than one critic. If then φησίν be read there at all, it must be impersonal. The apostle's analogous use of λέγει points to the same conclusion. In Eph. v. 14 it introduces a quotation which is certainly not in Scripture, and apparently belonged to an early Christian hymn. We gather therefore that St. Paul's usage does not suggest any restriction here to ὁ θεός or ἡ γραφή. But we cannot doubt from the context that the quotation is meant to be authoritative."

In his own commentary on I Corinthians (1880), Heinrici writes as follows:

"To φησί, just as to λέγει (II Cor. vi. 2, Gal. iii. 16) nothing at all is to be supplied, but like *inquit* it stands, sometimes as the introduction to an objection (II Cor. x. 10, where Holsten refers to Bentley on Horat., *Serm.*, i, 4, 78), sometimes as a general formula of citation. It is especially often used in the latter sense by Philo, in the quotation of Scripture passages, and by Arrian-Epictetus, who supplies many most interesting parallels to the Pauline forms of speech. Schweighäuser, in his Index, under φησί, remarks of it: nec enim semper in proferenda objectione locum habet illa formula, verum etiam in citando exemplo ad id quod agitur pertinente. J. G. Müller (*Philo the Jew's Book on the Creation*, Berlin, 1841, p. 44) says that φησί, after the example of Plato (?), became gradually among the Hellenistic Jews the standing formula of citation."

In his edition of Meyer's " Commentary on I Corinthians " (eighth edition, 1896), this note reappears in this form:

"φησίν). Who? According to the usual view, God, whose words the sayings of the Scripture are, even when they, like Gen. ii. 24 through Adam, are spoken through another. Winer, 7 § 58, 9, 486: Buttmann, 117. But the impersonal sense 'es heisst,' 'inquit,' lies nearer the Pauline usage; he coincides in this with Arrian-Epictetus and Philo, with whom φησί sometimes introduces an objection, sometimes is the customary formula of citation. Cf. II Cor. x. 10, vi. 2, I Cor. xv. 27, Eph. iv. 8; Winer, as above; Müller, in Philo, *De op. mund.*, 44; Heinrici, i. 181. In accordance with this, are the other supplements of subject — ἡ γραφή or τὸ πνεῦμα (Rückert) — to be estimated."

Even in the extremity of his contention, therefore, Dr. Abbott, it seems, is not without support — on the philological side, at least — in previous commentators of the highest rank.

He himself does not seem, however, quite clear in his own mind: and his confusion of both considerations and commentators which make for the fundamentally diverse positions that there is to be supplied with λέγει some such subject as ἡ γραφή, and that there is nothing at all to be supplied but the word is to be taken with entire indefiniteness, is indicatory of the main thing that calls for remark in Dr. Abbott's note. For, why should this confusion take place? It is quite evident that in interpreting the phrase the fundamental distinction lies between the view which supposes that a subject to λέγει is so implied as to be suggested either by the context or by the mind of the reader from the nature of the case, and that which takes λέγει as a case of true impersonal usage, of entirely indefinite subject. It is a minor difference among the advocates of the first of these views, which separates them into two parties—those which would supply as subject ὁ θεός, and those which would supply ἡ γραφή. That one of these subdivisions of the first class of views should be violently torn from its true comradeship and confused with the second view, betrays a preoccupation on Dr. Abbott's part, when dealing with this passage, with considerations not of purely exegetical origin. He is for the moment less concerned with ascertaining the meaning of the apostle than with refuting a special interpretation of his words: and therefore everything which stands opposed in any measure to the obnoxious interpretation appears to him to be "on his side." Put somewhat brusquely, this is as much as to say that Dr. Abbott is in this note dominated by dogmatic prejudice.

There do not lack other indications of this fact. The most obtrusive of them is naturally the language—scarcely to be called perfectly calm—with which the second paragraph of the note opens: "We are certainly not justified in forcing upon the apostle here and in chap. v. 14 a form of expression consistent only with the extreme view of verbal inspiration." Certainly not. But because we chance not to like "the extreme view of verbal inspiration," are we justified in forbidding the apostle to use a form of expression consistent only with it, and forcing upon him some other form of expression which we may consider consistent with a view of inspiration which we like better? Would it not be better to permit the apostle to choose his own form of expression and confine ourselves, as expositors, to ascertaining from his form of expression what view of inspiration lay in his mind, rather than seek to force his hand into consistency with our preconceived ideas? The whole structure of the note evinces, however, that it was not written in this purely expository spirit. Thus only can be explained a certain exaggerated

dogmatism in its language, as if doubt were to be silenced by
decision of manner if not by decisiveness of evidence. So also
probably is to be explained a certain narrowness in the appeal
to usage — that rock on which much factitious exegesis splits.
Only, it is intimated, in case "it were St. Paul's habit to
introduce quotations from the Old Testament, by whomsoever spoken in the original text, with the formula ὁ θεὸς
λέγει," "could this supplement here be defended." One asks
in astonishment whether St. Paul really could make known
his estimate of Scripture as the very voice of God which
might naturally be quoted with the formula "God says,"
and so render the occurrence of that formula occasionally in
his writings no matter of surprise, only by a habitual use of
this exact formula in quoting Scripture. And one notes without surprise that the narrowness of Dr. Abbott's rule for the
adduction of usage supplies no bar to his practice when he is
arguing "on the other side." At the opening of the very next
paragraph we read, "It is objected that although φησί is used
impersonally, λέγει is not": and to this the answer is returned,
"The present passage and chap. v. 14 are sufficient to prove
the usage for St. Paul"; with the supplement, "And there
are other passages in his epistles where this sense is at least
applicable"; and further, "But in fact, the impersonal use
of φησί in Greek authors is quite different." One fancies Dr.
Abbott must have had a grim controversial smile upon his
features when he wrote that last clause, which pleads that
the meaning assigned to λέγει here is absolutely unexampled
in Greek literature, not only for λέγει but even for φησί, as a
reason for accepting it for λέγει here! But apart from this
remarkable instance of skill in marshaling adverse facts —
a skill not unexampled elsewhere in the course of this note,
as any one who will take the trouble to examine the proof-
texts adduced in it will quickly learn — might not the advocates of the supplement, ὁ θεός, say equally that "the present
passage and chap. v. 14 are sufficient to prove the usage for
St. Paul, and there are other passages in his epistles where
this sense is at least applicable." And might they not support

this statement with better proof-texts than those adduced by Dr. Abbott, or indeed with the same with better right; as well as with a more applicable supplementary remark than the one with which he really subverts his whole reasoning — such as this, for example, that elsewhere, in the New Testament, as for instance in the Epistle to the Hebrews, the usage contended for undoubtedly occurs, and a satisfactory basis is laid for it in the whole attitude of the entire body of New Testament writers, inclusive of Paul, toward the Old Testament? Certainly, reasoning so one-sided and dominated by preconceived opinions so blinding is thoroughly inconclusive. The note is, indeed, an eminent example of that form of argumentation which, to invert a phrase of Omar Khayyam's, "goes out at the same door at which it came in": and even though its contention should prove sound, can itself add nothing to the grounds on which we embrace it. At best it may serve as the starting-point of a fresh investigation into the proper interpretation of the phrase with which it deals.

For such a fresh investigation we should need to give our attention particularly to two questions. The first would inquire into the light thrown by Paul's method of introducing quotations from the Old Testament, upon his estimate of the text of the Old Testament, — with a view to determining whether it need cause surprise to find him adducing it with such a formula as "God says." Subsidiary to this it might be inquired whether it is accurate to say that "there is not a single instance in which ὁ θεός is either expressed or implied as the subject, except where in the original context God is the speaker," and further, if Paul's usage elsewhere can be accurately so described, whether that fact will warrant us in denying such an instance to exist in Eph. iv. 8. The second question would inquire into the general usage of the subjectless λέγει or φησί in and out of the New Testament, with a view to discovering what light may be thrown by it upon the interpretation of the passages in question. It might be incidentally asked in this connection whether it is a complete account to give of φησί in profane Greek to say that the "impersonal use of φησί in Greek authors is quite different from that of the New Testament, inasmuch as with them φησί = φασί, 'they say.'"

It is really somewhat discouraging at this late date to find it treated as still an open question, how Paul esteemed the written words of the Old Testament. And it brings us, as the French say, something akin to stupefaction, when Dr. Abbott goes further and uses language concerning Paul's attitude toward the Old Testament text which implies that Paul habitually distinguished, in point of authority, between those passages "where in the original context God is the speaker" and the rest of the volume, so that "we have reason to believe" that the formula ὁ θεὸς λέγει "could not be used by Paul" in introducing Scriptural language not recorded as spoken by God in the original context. He even suggests, indeed, that Paul shows an underlying doubt as to the Divine source of even the words attributed to God in the Old Testament text — "not hesitating to use a different subject" when quoting them, "as in Rom. x. 19, 20, 'Moses saith,' 'Isaiah is very bold and saith'; Rom. ix. 17, 'The Scripture saith to Pharaoh'" — and deals with the text of other portions with a freedom which exhibits his little respect for them — "not hesitating to make important alterations" in them. It would seem to require a dogmatic prejudice of the very first order to blind one to a fact so obvious as that with Paul "Scripture," as such, is conceived everywhere as the authoritative declaration of the truth and will of God — of which fact, indeed, no better evidence can be needed than the very texts quoted by Dr. Abbott in a contrary sense.

For, when Paul, in Rom. ix. 15, supports his abhorrent rejection of the supposition that there may be unrighteousness with God, with the divine declaration taken from Ex. xxxiii. 19, introduced with the formula, "For he" — that is, as Dr. Abbott recognizes, God — "saith to Moses," and then immediately, in Rom. ix. 17, supports the teaching of this declaration with the further word of God taken from Ex. ix. 16, introduced with the formula, "For the Scripture saith unto Pharaoh"—the one thing which is thrown into a relief above all others is that, with Paul, "God saith" and "Scripture saith" are synonymous terms, so synonymous in his habitual thought that he could not only range the two together in consecutive clauses, but use the second in a manner in which, taken literally, it is meaningless and can convey an appropriate sense only when translated back into its equivalent of "God saith." The present tense in both formulas, moreover, advises us that, despite the fact that in both instances they are words spoken by God which are cited, it is rather as part of that Scripture which to Paul's thinking is the ever-present and ever-speaking word of God that they are adduced. It is not as words which God once spoke (εἶπεν, LXX.) to Moses that the former passage is here adduced, but as living words still speaking to us—it is not as words Moses was once commanded to speak to Pharaoh that the second is here adduced, but as words recorded in the ever-living Scripture for our admonition upon whom the ends of the world have come. They are thus not assigned to Scripture in order to lower their authority: but rather as a mark of their abiding authority. And similarly when in that catena of quotations in Rom. x. 16–21, we read at ver. 19, "first Moses saith," and then at ver. 20, "and Isaiah is very bold and saith," both adducing words of God—the implication is not that Paul looks upon them as something less than the words of God and so cites them by the names of these human authors; but that it is all one to him to say, "God says," and "Moses says," or "Isaiah says"; and therefore in this catena of quotations—in which are included four, not two, quotations—all the citations are treated as alike authoritative, though some are in the original context words of God and others (ver. 16) words of the prophet—and though some are adduced by the name of the prophet and some without assignment to any definitely named human source. The same implication, again, underlies the fact that in the catena of quotations on Rom. xv. 9 *seq.*, the first is introduced by καθὼς γέγραπται, the next two by καὶ πάλιν λέγει and καὶ πάλιν, and the last by καὶ πάλιν 'Ησαΐας λέγει — the first being from Ps. lxxviii. 50, the second from Deut. xxxii. 43, the third from Ps. cxvii. 1, and only the last from Isaiah — Isa. xi. 10: clearly it is all one to the mind of Paul how Scripture is adduced — it is the fact that it is *Scripture* that is important. So also it is no more true that in Gal. iii. 16, the λέγει "corresponds to ἐρρήθησαν" of the immediately preceding context, than that it stands in line with the "and the Scripture foreseeing that God would justify the Gentiles by faith, preached the Gospel beforehand unto Abraham" of iii. 8 — a thing which the Scripture as such certainly did not do; and with the "for it is written" of iii. 10 and iii. 13, and the unheralded quotations of the Scriptures as unquestioned authority of iii. 11 and iii. 12; and with the general appeal in iii. 22 to the teaching of Scripture as a whole as the sole testimony needed: the effect of the whole being to evince in the clearest manner that to Paul the whole text of Scripture, inclusive of Gen. xii. 3, Deut. xxvii. 26, Hab. ii. 4, Lev. xviii. 5, and Gen. xxii. 18, was as such the living word of the living God profitable to all ages alike for divine instruction.

We need not go, indeed, beyond the first sentence of this Epistle to the Romans from which all but one of Dr. Abbott's citations are drawn, to learn Paul's conception of Scripture as the crystallized voice of God. There he declares himself to have been "separated unto the gospel of God which he promised afore by his prophets in the Holy Scriptures" (Rom. i. 2). Dr. George T. Purves, in a singularly well-considered and impressive paper on "St. Paul and Inspiration," printed in *The Presbyterian and Reformed Review* for January, 1893,[21] justly draws out the meaning of this compressed statement thus:

"Not only did Moses and the prophets speak from God, but the sacred Scriptures themselves were in some way composed under divine

[21] Vol. iv, p. 13.

control. He not only affirms with Peter that 'moved by the Holy Ghost, *men* spake from God,' but that ' *the Scriptures themselves* are inspired by God.' Paul plainly recognizes the human authorship of the books, and quotes Moses and David and Isaiah as speaking therein. But not only *through them*, but *in these books* of theirs did God also speak. Many readers notice the first part of Paul's statement, but not the second. God spake 'through the prophets *in the Holy Scriptures.*' "

This emphasis on the *written* Scriptures as themselves the product of a divine activity, making them as such the divine voice to us, is characteristic of the whole treatment of Scripture by Paul (I Cor. x. 11, Rom. xv. 4, iv. 23, I Cor. ix. 10, iv. 6): and it is thoroughly accordant with the point of view so exhibited, that he explicitly declares, not of the writers of Scripture, but of the sacred writings themselves, that they are theopneustic—breathed out, or breathed into by God (II Tim. iii. 16). For he applies this epithet not to "every prophet," but to "every *Scripture*"—that is, says Dr. Purves, to "the whole collection to which he had just referred as the 'sacred writings,' and all their parts": these *writings* are theopneustic. "By their inspiration, he evidently meant," continues Dr. Purves justly, "that, as writings, they were so composed under God's particular direction that both in substance and in form they were the special utterances of His mind and will."

It could be nothing more thas an accident if Paul, under the dominance of such a conception of Scripture, has nowhere happened to adduce from it a passage, taken out of a context in which God is not expressly made in the Old Testament narrative itself the speaker, with the formula, ὁ θεὸς λέγει, expressed or implied. If no instance of such an adduction occurs, it is worth while to note that fact, to be sure, as one of the curious accidents of literary usage; but as there is no reason to doubt that such a formula would be entirely natural on the lips of Paul, so there is no propriety in calling it impossible in Paul, or even in erecting a distinction between him and other New Testament writers on the ground that they do and he does not quote Scripture by such a formula. As a matter of fact, the distinction suggested between passages in Scripture "where in the original context God is the speaker" and passages where He is not the speaker —as if the one could be cited with a "God says," and the other not,—is foreign to Paul's conception and usage, as has abundantly appeared already: so that whatever passages of the former kind occur—"as in Rom. ix. 15," says Dr. Abbott—are really passages in which Scripture is quoted with a "God says." It cannot be held to be certain, moreover, that passages do not occur in which the "God says" introduces words not ascribed to God in the original context—so long, at least, as it is not obvious that "God" is not the *subauditum* in passages like Acts xiii. 35, Rom. xv. 10, Gal. iii. 16. It is no doubt, however, also worth observing that it is equally matter of fact, that it is rather to the Epistle to the Hebrews than to those that bear the name of Paul that we shall need to go to find a body of explicit instances of the usage in question. This is, as we have said, an interesting fact of literary usage, but it is not to be pressed into an indication of a divergent point of view toward "Scripture" between the Epistle to the Hebrews and the epistles that bear Paul's name.

Even Dr. Westcott seems, to be sure, so to press it. In the interesting dissertation "On the Use of the Old Testament in the Epistle," which he has appended to his "Commentary on the Epistle to the Hebrews," he sets out in some detail the facts that bear on the mode in which that epistle cites the Old Testament:

"The quotations," he tells us, "are without exception made anonymously. There is no mention anywhere of the name of the writer (iv. 7 is no exception to the rule). God is presented as the speaker through the person of the prophet, except in the one place where He is directly addressed (ii. 6). . . . In two places the words are attributed to Christ. . . . In two other places the Holy Spirit specially is named as the speaker. . . . But it is worthy of notice that in each of these two cases the words are also quoted as the words of God (iv. 7, viii. 8). This assignment of the written word to God, as the

Inspirer of the message, is most remarkable when the words spoken by the prophet in his own person are treated as divine words — as words spoken by Moses: i. 6 (Deut. xxxii. 43); iv. 4, comp. vv. 5, 7, 8 (Gen. ii. 2); x. 30 (Deut. xxxii. 36); and by Isaiah: ii. 13 (Isa. viii. 17 f), comp. also xiii. 5 (Deut. xxxi. 6). Generally it must be observed that no difference is made between the word spoken and the word written. For us and for all ages the record is the voice of God. The record is the voice of God, and as a necessary consequence the record is itself living. . . . The constant use of the present tense in quotations emphasizes this truth: ii. 11, iii. 7, xii. 5. Comp. xii. 26." [22]

Every careful student will recognize this at once as a very clear and very true statement of the attitude of the author of the Epistle to the Hebrews toward the Old Testament. But we cannot help thinking that Dr. Westcott overshoots the mark when he throws it into strong contrast with the attitude of the rest of the New Testament writers to the Old Testament. When he says, for example: "There is nothing really parallel to this general mode of quotation in the other books of the New Testament"—meaning apparently to suggest, as the subsequent context indicates, that the author of this Epistle exhibits an identification in his mind of the written text of the Scriptures with the voice of God which is foreign to the other writers of the New Testament—he would seem to have attached far too great significance to what is, after all, so far as it is real, nothing more than one of those surface differences of individual usage which are always observable among writers who share the same fundamental viewpoint, or even in different treatises from the same hand. Entirely at one in looking upon the Scriptures as nothing less than τὰ λόγια τοῦ θεοῦ (Rom. iii. 2, Heb. v. 12 [23])—in all their parts and phrases the utterance of God—the epistles that bear the name of Paul and this epistle yet chance to differ in the prevalent mode in which these "oracles" are adduced: the one in its formulas of citation emphasizing the sole fact that they are "oracles" it is quoting, the others,

[22] *Op. cit.*, pp. 285, 286, 287.

[23] Westcott, *in loc.*, "it seems more natural to refer it to the collected writings of the Old Testament."

that these "oracles" lie before them in *written* form. Let the fact of this difference, of course, be noted: but let it not be overstrained and, as if it were the sole relevant fact in the field of view, made to bear the whole weight of a theory of the relations of the two in their attitude toward Scripture.

Impossible as such a procedure should be in any case, it becomes doubly so when we note the extremely narrow and insecure basis for the conclusion drawn, which is offered by the differences in usage adduced between Hebrews and the rest of the New Testament — which means for us primarily the epistles that bear the name of Paul. Says Dr. Westcott in immediate sequence to what we have quoted from him:

"There is nothing really parallel to this general mode of quotation in the other books of the New Testament. Where the word λέγει occurs elsewhere, it is for the most part combined either with the name of the prophet or with 'Scripture': e.g., Rom. x. 16, Ἠσαΐας λέγει; x. 19, Μωυσῆς λέγει; xi. 9, Δαυείδ λέγει; iv. 3, ἡ γραφὴ λέγει; ix. 17, λέγει ἡ γραφή, etc. Where God is the subject, as is rarely the case, the reference is to words directly spoken by God: II Cor. vi. 2, λέγει γὰρ (ὁ θεός); Rom. ix. 15, τῷ Μωυσεῖ λέγει; ix. 25, ἐν τῷ Ὡσηὲ λέγει. Comp. Rom. xv. 9–12 (γέγραπται . . . λέγει . . . . Ἠσαΐας λέγει). The two passages in the Epistle to the Ephesians (iv. 8, v. 14, διὸ λέγει) appear to be different in kind."

The last remark is apparently intended to exclude Eph. iv. 8 and v. 14 from consideration.[24] The immediately preceding one seems intended to suggest that the subject to be supplied to λέγει in Rom. xv. 10, which carries with it also Rom. xv. 11, is ἡ γραφή; if we rather supply with Sanday-Headlam θεός, this citation would afford an instance to the contrary. Other cases similar to this, e. g., Acts xiii. 35 [25] and (with the

[24] What is meant may possibly be that these two passages in Ephesians are analogous neither to the usage of Hebrews nor to that of the rest of the New Testament, but stand out by themselves. In that case Dr. Westcott probably means to take them as instances of the indefinite use of λέγει. Cf. above, p. 293.

[25] Cf. Meyer's note: "λέγει], the subject is necessarily that of εἴρηκεν, ver. 34, and so, neither David (Bengel, Heinrichs and others), nor the Scriptures (Herrmann), but *God*, although Ps. xvi. 10 contains David's words addressed to God. But David is considered as the interpreter of God, who has put the prayer into his mouth. Comp. on Matt. xix. 5."

parallel $\phi\eta\sigma\iota$) I Cor. vi. 16,[26] are simply passed by in silence. If such cases were considered, perhaps the induction would be different.

It is possible, on the other hand, that the usage of the Epistle to the Hebrews also is conceived by Dr. Westcott a shade too narrowly. It scarcely seems sufficient to say of ii. 6, for example, that this passage is not an exception to the more general usage of the Epistle inasmuch as it is "the one place where God is directly addressed"—and is therefore not ascribed to Him, but to "some one somewhere." According to Dr. Westcott's own exposition,[27] we have in i. 10 also words addressed *to* God and yet cited as spoken *by* God, and in a number of passages words spoken *of* God nevertheless cited as spoken *by* Him; and, in a word, the fundamental principle of the mode of quotation used by this Epistle is that the words of Scripture as such are the living words of God and are cited as such indifferently—whether in the original context spoken by Him or by another of Him, to Him, or apart from Him. In any event, therefore, the citation in the present passage by the formula "someone hath somewhere borne witness" is an exception to the general usage of the Epistle, and evidences that the author of it, though conceiving Scripture as such as a body of divine oracles, did not really lose sight of the fact that these oracles were delivered through men, and might therefore be cited on occasion as the deliverances of these men. In other words, here is a mode of citation of the order affirmed to be charac-

[26] Cf. Meyer's note: "$\phi\eta\sigma\iota\nu$], who it is that says it, is self-evident, namely, *God*, the utterances of Scripture being His words, even when they may be spoken through another, as Gen. ii. 24 was through Adam. Comp. on Matt. xix. 5. Similarly Gal. iii. 16, Eph. iv. 8, Heb. viii. 5, I Cor. xv. 27. Ἡ γραφή, which is usually supplied here, would need to be suggested by the context, as in Rom. xv. 10. Rückert arbitrarily prefers τὸ πνεῦμα." "To take it *impersonally*, '*it is said*' as in II Cor. x. 10, according to the well-known usage in the classics, would be without warrant from any other instance of Paul's quotations from Scripture. Comp. Winer, *Gr.*, p. 486 [English translation, 656]; Buttmann, *Neut. Gr.*, p. 117 [English translation, 134]."

[27] For he supposes the words quoted in i. 10 to be addressed not to Christ, but to God: "God through His Spirit so speaks in the Psalmist that words not directly addressed to Christ find their fulfillment in Him."

teristic of the letters bearing the name of Paul. It is at least not beyond the limits of possibility that another such instance occurs in iv. 7: "saying in David." No doubt, "in David," may be taken here, as Dr. Westcott takes it, as meaning "in the person of David," i. e., through his prophetic utterances; but it seems, on the whole, much more natural to take it as parallel to ἐν τῇ βίβλῳ Μωυσέως (Mark xii. 26), ἐν τῷ Ὡσηέ (Rom. ix. 25), and as meaning "in the book of David "[28] — exhibiting the consciousness of the author that he is quoting not merely "God," but God in the *written Scripture* — written by the hand of men. This is the more worth insisting on that it is really not absolutely certain that the subject of the λέγων here is immediately "God" at all. There is no subject expressed either for it or the ὁρίζει on which it depends; and when we go back in the context for an express subject it eludes us, and we shall not find it until we arrive at the "even as the Holy Ghost saith" of iii. 7. From that point on, we have a series of quotations, introduced, quite in the manner of Philo, with formulæ which puzzle us as to their reference — whether to God, who is the general subject of the whole context, or to Scripture, conceived as the voice of God (e. g., iii. 15, ἐν τῷ λέγεσθαι — by whom? God? or "the Scripture" already quoted? iv. 4, εἴρηκεν — who? God? or Scripture? iv. 5, καὶ ἐν τούτῳ πάλιν). Something of the same kind meets us in the eighth chapter, where quite in the manner of Philo, we begin at ver. 5: "Even as Moses was oracularly warned when about to make the tabernacle, for 'see,' φησίν, etc." and proceed at ver. 8, with a subjectless λέγει, to close with ver. 13 with an equally subjectless ἐν τῷ λέγειν. It certainly is not obvious that the subject to be supplied to these three verbs is "God" rather than "oracular Scripture."

One can but feel that with a due regard to these two classes of neglected facts, a somewhat broader comparison of the usage of the Epistle to the Hebrews and that of those

---

[28] So (according to Lünemann), Dindorf, Schulz, Böhme, Bleek, Ebrard Alford, Woerner: add Lowrie, Riggenbach.

letters that bear the name of Paul would not leave an impression of such sharp and indubitable divergence in point of view as Dr. Westcott's statement is apt to suggest. In the Epistle to the Hebrews, the verb λέγω is used to introduce citations, (1) with *expressed* subject: ii. 6, "But someone somewhere hath borne witness, saying . . . ."; iii. 7, "Even as the Holy Ghost saith . . . ."; vi. 14, "God . . . . sware by himself, saying . . . .": (2) with subject to be *supplied from the preceding context*: i. 6, "And when he (God) again bringeth in the firstborn into the world, he saith . . . ."; i. 7, "And of the angels he (God) saith . . . ."; ii. 12, "He (Christ) is not ashamed to call them brethren, saying . . . ."; v. 6, "As he (God) saith also in another place . . . .": (3) with subject to be *supplied from the general knowledge of the reader*: x. 5, "Wherefore when he (Christ) cometh into the world, he saith . . . ."; x. 8, "Saying (Christ) above . . . ."; xii. 26, "But now hath he (God) promised, saying . . . .": (4) *without obvious subject:* iii. 15, "While it is said, To day, etc." (by whom? God? or the Scripture quoted, iii. 7 *seq.?*); iv. 7, "He [or it?] again defineth a certain time, saying in David . . . ."; viii. 8, "For finding fault with them, he [or it?] saith . . . ." (cf. viii. 13, "in that he [or it?] saith . . . ."). On the other hand, in the epistles that bear the name of Paul we may distinguish some four cases of the adduction of Scripture by the formula λέγει. (1) Sometimes, quoting Scripture *as a divine whole*, the formula runs ἡ γραφὴ λέγει or λέγει ἡ γραφή: Rom. iv. 3, ix. 17 (λέγει ἡ γραφὴ τῷ Φαραώ), xi. 2 (ἡ γραφὴ ἐν Ἡλείᾳ), Gal. iv. 30, I Tim. v. 18. (2) Sometimes it is adduced *by the name of the author:* Δαυεὶδ λέγει, Rom. iv. 6, xi. 9; Ἡσαίας λέγει, Rom. x. 16, 20, xv. 12. (3) Sometimes it is quoted *by its contents:* ὁ νόμος λέγει, Rom. iii. 19, vii. 7, I Cor. ix. 8, 10, xiv. 34; the righteousness that is of faith λέγει, Rom. x. 6 (cf. ver. 10); ὁ χρηματισμός λέγει, Rom. xi. 4. (4) Sometimes it is adduced by the verb λέγει *without expressed subject.* (A) In some of these cases *the subject is plainly indicated* in the preceding context: Rom. ix. 25 = "God," from ver. 22; x. 10 = "the righteousness of faith," (?) from ver. 6; x. 21 =

"Isaiah," from ver. 20. (B) In others it is less clearly indicated and is *not altogether obvious:* [Acts xiii. 34 = "God,"
from εἴρηκεν?]; Rom. ix. 15 = "God," from ver. 14?; Rom.
xv. 10 = "Scripture," from γέγραπται?; II Cor. vi. 2 =
"God," from preceding context; Gal. iii. 16 = "God,"
from the promises?; Eph. iv. 8 and v. 12. It should be added
that parallel to the use of the subjectless φησί in Heb. viii. 5
we have the similar use of it in I Cor. vi. 16.

When we glance over these two lists of phenomena we
shall certainly recognize a difference between them: but the
difference is not suggestive of such an extreme distinction as
Dr. Westcott appears to indicate. The fact is that for its
proper estimation we must rise to a higher viewpoint and
look upon the two lists in the light of a much larger fact.
For we cannot safely study this difference of usage as an
isolated phenomenon: and we shall get the key to its interpretation into our hands only when we correlate it with a
more general view of the estimate of Scripture and mode of
adducing Scripture prevalent at the time and in the circles
which are represented by these epistles. Dr. Westcott already
points the way to this wider outlook, when at the end of his
discussion he adds these words:

" The method of citation on which we have dwelt is peculiar to
the Epistle [to the Hebrews] among the writings of the New Testament; but it is interesting to notice that there is in the Epistle of
Clement a partial correspondence with it. Clement generally quotes
the LXX. anonymously. He attributes the prophetic words to God
(15, 21, 46), to Christ (16, 22), to the Holy Word (13, 56), to the
Holy Spirit (13, 16). But he also, though rarely, refers to the writers
(26, Job; 52, David), and to Books (57, Proverbs, ' the all virtuous
Wisdom '), and not unfrequently uses the familiar form γέγραπται
(14, 39, etc.). The quotations in the Epistle of Barnabas are also
commonly anonymous, but Barnabas mentions several names of the
sacred writers, and gives passages from the Law, the Prophets and
the Psalms with the formula, ' the Prophet saith ' (vi. 8; 2; 4, 6)."

And, he should have added, Barnabas also repeatedly adduces what he held to be the Word of God with the formulas

γέγραπται (iv. 3, 14, v. 2, xi. 1, xiv. 6, xv. 1, xvi. 6) and λέγει ἡ γραφή (iv. 7, 11, v. 4, vi. 12, xiii. 2, xv. 5) : and indeed passes from the one mode of citation to the other without the least jar, as, for example, in chap. v.: "For *it is written* concerning him, some things indeed with respect to Israel, and some with respect to us. For *it saith* this (Isa. liii. 5, 7). . . . . And the *Scripture saith* (Prov. i. 17). . . . And *still also this* (Jer. i. 25). . . . . For *God saith* (Zech. xiii. 6). . . . . For the *prophesier saith* (Ps. xxii. 21, etc.). . . . . And again *it saith* (Isa. l. 6)." Though adverting thus to these facts, however, Dr. Westcott quite misses their significance. What they mean is shortly this: that the two modes of citing Scripture thought to distinguish Hebrews and the letters that bear the name of Paul, do not imply well-marked distinctive modes of conceiving Scripture; but coëxist readily within the limits of one brief letter, like the letter of Clement or that of Barnabas. No wonder, when laid side by side, we found the usages of the two to present no sharply marked division line, but to crumble into one another along the edges. And when we look beyond Clement and Barnabas and take a general glance over the literature of the time, it is easily seen that we are looking in the two cases only at two fragments of one fact, and are seeing in each only one of the everywhere current methods of citing Scripture as the very Word of God. It seems inconceivable that one could rise from reading, say, twenty pages of Philo, for example, without being fully convinced of this.

Philo's fundamental conception of Scripture is that it is a book of oracles; each passage of it is a χρησμός or λόγιον, and the whole is therefore οἱ χρησμοί or τὰ λόγια: he currently quotes it, accordingly, as "the living voice" of God, and whole treatises of his may be read without meeting with a single citation introduced by γέγραπται or with the Scriptures once called ἡ γραφή. Nevertheless, when occasion serves, he adduces Scripture readily enough as ἡ γραφή, and cites it with γέγραπται, and calls it τὰ γράμματα. We have no more reason for assuming that such modes of citing Scripture would have been foreign to the author of the Epistle to the Hebrews (whose mode of citing Scripture is markedly Philonic) than we have for assuming that the author of the tract *de Mutatione Nominum*, in which they do not occur, but where Scripture is almost exclusively οἱ χρησμοί, or the author of the tracts *de Somniis*, where again they do not occur, but where Scripture is almost exclusively ὁ ἱερὸς (or ὁ θεῖος) λόγος (i. 14, 22, 33, 35, 37, 39, 42, ii. 4, 9, 37, etc.; i. 33, ii. 37) — which designations are rare again in *de Mutatione Nominum* (ὁ θ. λ., 20; ὁ ἱ. λ., 38) — held a different conception of Scripture from the author of the tract *de Legatione ad Caium* (§ 29) or the tract *de Abrahamo* (§ 1), in which the Scriptures are spoken of as τὰ γράμματα or αἱ γραφαί. There is no reason, in a word, why, if the Epistle to the Hebrews had contained even a single other verse, it might not have presented the "exotic," ἡ γραφή or γέγραπται. Because Philo or the author of this Epistle was especially accustomed to look on Scripture as a body of *oracles* and to cite it accordingly, is no reason why he should forget that it is a body of *written* oracles and be incapable on occasion of citing it from that point of view. Similarly because Paul ordinarily cites Scripture as *written* is no reason why he should not be firmly convinced that what is written in it is *oracles*, or should not occasionally cite it from that point of view. In a word, the two modes of citing Scripture brought into contrast by Bishop Westcott are not two mutually exclusive ways of citing Scripture, but two mutually complementary methods. The use of the one by any writer does not argue that the other is foreign to him; if we have enough written material from his hand, we are sure rather to find in him traces of the other usage also. This is the meaning of the presence in the Epistle to the Hebrews of suggestive instances of an approach to the citation of Scripture as a document: and of the presence in the epistles bearing the name of Paul of instances of modes of citation which hint of his conception of Scripture as an oracular book. Where and when the sense of the oracular character of the source of the quotation is predominatingly in mind it tends to be quoted with the simple φησί or λέγει, with the implication that it is God that says it: this is most richly exhibited in Philo, and, within the limits of the New Testament, most prevailingly in the Epistle to the Hebrews. Where and when, on the other hand, the consciousness that it is from a written source that the authoritative words are drawn is predominant in the mind, it tends to be quoted with the simple γέγραπται or the more formal ἡ γραφὴ λέγει: this is the mode in which it is most commonly cited in the epistles that bear the name of Paul. Both modes of citation rest on the common consciousness of the Divine authority of the matter cited, and have no tendency to exclude one another: they appear side by side in the same writer, and must be held to predominate variously in different writers only according to their prevailing habits of speaking of Scripture, and at different times in the same writer according as the circumstances under which he was writing threw the emphasis in his mind temporarily upon the Scriptures as written *oracles* or as *written* oracles.

From this point of view we may estimate Dr. Westcott's remark: "Nor can it be maintained that the difference of usage is to be explained by the difference of readers, as being [in Hebrews] Jews, for in the Gospels γέγραπται is the common formula (nine times in St. Matthew)." This remark, like his whole treatment of the subject, seems conceived in a spirit which is too hard and narrow, too drily statistical. No one, doubtless, would contend that the difference of readers directly produced the difference of usage, as if the Scriptures *must* be quoted to Jews as "oracles of God," and to Gentiles as "written documents." But it is far from obvious that the difference of readers may not, after all, have had very much to do with the prevalence of the one mode of citation in the Epistle to the Hebrews and of the other in the epistles that bear the name of Paul. The Jews were certainly accustomed to the current citation of the Scriptures as the living voice of God in oracular deliverances—

as the usage of Philo sufficiently indicates: and it may be that this was subtly felt the most impressive method of adducing the words of the Holy Book when addressing Jews. On the other hand, the heathen were accustomed to authoritative documents, cited currently, with an implication of their authority, by the formula γέγραπται: [29] and it may well be that this subtly suggested itself as the most telling way of adducing Scripture as authoritative law to the Gentiles. We need not ride such a notion too hard: but it at least seems far from inconceivable that the selfsame writer, addressing, on the one hand, a body of devout Jews, and, on the other, a body of law-loving Romans, might find himself using almost unconsciously modes of adducing Scripture suggestive, in the one case, of loving awe in its presence and, in the other, of its binding authority over the conscience. Be this as it may, however, it is quite clear that the fact that Paul ordinarily adduces Scripture with "the forms ($καθὼς$) γέγραπται (sixteen times in the Epistle to the Romans), ἡ γραφὴ λέγει, and the like, which never occur in the Epistle to the Hebrews," implies no far-reaching difference of conception on his part from that exhibited by that Epistle, as to the fundamental character of the Scriptures as an oracular book — which, on the contrary, is just what he calls them (Rom. iii. 2) — and certainly raises no presumption against his occasionally quoting them as an oracular book with the formula so characteristic of the Epistle to the Hebrews, ὁ θεὸς λέγει, or its equivalents. And the fact that "Paul not unfrequently quotes the words of God as 'Scripture' simply (e. g., Rom. ix. 17)" so far from raising a presumption that he would not quote "Scripture" as "words of God," actually demonstrates the contrary, as it only in another way indicates the identification on his part of the written word with the voice of the speaking God.

If we approach the study of such texts as Eph. iv. 8, v.

---

[29] Cf. Deissmann, "Bibelstudien," 109; "Neue Bibelstudien," 77: and also for the implications, Kuyper, "Encyclopædia of Sacred Theology," pp. 433–435 and 444–445.

14, therefore, from the point of view of the Pauline conception of Scripture, there is no reason why they should not be understood as adducing Scripture with a high "God says." To say that "we have reason to believe" that such a formula "could not be used by Paul," is as wide of the mark as could well be. To say that it is a formula more in accordance with the point of view of the Epistle to the Hebrews, is to confound mere occasional differences in usage with fundamental differences in conception. To Paul, too, the Scriptures are a book of oracles, and though he cites them ordinarily as *written* oracles there is no reason why he should not occasionally cite them merely as *oracles*. And in any case, whether we take the *subauditum* in such passages as "God," or "Scripture," or prefer to render simply by "it," from Paul's point of view the meaning is all one: in any case, Scripture is to him the authoritative dictum of God and what it says is adduced as the authoritative word that ends all strife.

In seeking to estimate the likelihoods as to the meaning of such a locution as the διὸ λέγει of Eph. iv. 8, v. 14, we should not lose from sight, on the other hand, the fact that the Greek language was not partial to true "impersonals," that is, absolutely indefinite uses of its verbs. Says Jelf:

" Of impersonal verbs (in English, verbs with the indefinite *it*) the Greek language has but few." [30]

Says Kühner:

" Impersonal verbs, by which we understand a verb agreeing with the indefinite pronoun *it*, are not known to the Greek language: for expressions like δεῖ, χρή . . . λέγεται, etc. . . . . the Greek always conceived as personal, in that the infinitive or subjoined sentence was considered the subject of these verbs." [31]

No doubt, the subject often suffers ellipsis — especially when it may be counted upon readily to suggest itself, either out

[30] § 373, 1. obs., 1.
[31] "Ausführ. ram.," ii. 30 (§ 352).

of the predicate itself, or out of the context, or out of the knowledge of the reader: and no doubt this implied subject is sometimes the indefinite τις. But it remains true that as yet there has turned up no single instance in all Greek literature of λέγει in the purely indefinite sense of "someone says," equivalent to "it is said" in the meaning of general rumor, or of a common proverb, or a current saying; and though there have been pointed out instances of something like this in the case of the kindred word φησί, it still remains somewhat doubtful precisely how they are to be interpreted. The forms commonly used to express this idea are either the expressed τις, or the third person plural, as λέγουσι, φασί, ὀνομάζουσιν, or the third person singular passive, as λέγεται, or the second person singular optative or indicative of the historical tenses, as φαίης ἄν, = *dicas*, or the like.[32]

We find it, indeed, occasionally asserted that φησί is used sometimes or frequently as a pure impersonal, in the sense of "it is said." The passage from Bernhardy, to be sure, to which reference has been made in support of this assertion, by more than one of the commentators adduced above, has its primary interest not in this point, but in the different one of the use of the singular φησί for the plural — like the Latin *inquit*, and the English "says" in that vulgar colloquial locution in which it is made to do duty not only in the form "he says," but also in such forms as "I says" and "you says," and even "they says" and "we says." What Bernhardy remarks is:[33]

" *The rhetorical employment of the singular* for the plural rests on the Greek peculiarity (K. 3, 5; 6, 13c.) of clearly conceiving and representing the multitude by means of the individual. A ready instance of this is supplied by the formula φησί, like the Latin *inquit* an expression for all persons and numbers for designating an indefinite speaker (den beliebigen Redner) — 'heisst es'; and by the more classic εἰπέ μοι in appeal to the multitude in Attic life, Arist. (as *Pac.*, 385, εἰπέ μοι τί

---

[32] Jelf, § 373, 7: Kühner, *l.c.*: Jannaris ("A Historical Greek Grammar," 1161 *seq.*), treats the omitted subject no otherwise than Kühner.

[33] "Syntax.," 419.

πάσχετ’ ὦνδρες; coll. *Eccl.*, 741), Plat. (clearly in a turn like εἰπέ μοι, ὦ Σώκρατές τε καὶ ὑμεῖς οἱ ἄλλοι), Demosth., *Phil.* i, p. 45; *Chers.*, p. 108; *Timocr.*, p. 718.” [34]

The usage of φησί here more particularly adverted to — for all numbers and persons — seems a not uncommon one. Instances may possibly be found in the “Discourses” of Epictetus i. 29, 34 (Schenkl, p. 95). “Even athletes are dissatisfied with slight young men: ‘He cannot lift me,’ φησί,” where φησί might perhaps be rendered by our vernacular, “says they,” referring to “the athletes.” Again, iv. 9, 15 (Schenkl, p. 383): “But learn from what the trainers of boys do. The boy has fallen: ‘Rise,’ φησί, ‘wrestle again, till you become strong!’” where we may possibly have another ‘says they,’ viz., the trainers. Possibly again ii. 10, 20 (Schenkl, p. 133), “But consider, if you refer everything to a small coin, not even he who loses his nose is in your opinion damaged. ‘Yes,’ φησί, ‘for he is mutilated in his body,’” where possibly φησί is “says you,” referring to the collocutor, addressed in the preceding context in the second person — though, no doubt, another explanation is here possible. Indeed, in no one of the instances cited is it impossible to conceive a singular subject derived from the contextual plural as specially in mind. If φησί were genuine in Wisdom xv. 12,[35] II Cor. x. 10,[36] these might well supply other instances — the “says they” in each case continuing the contextual or implicated plural. But in none of these instances, it is to be observed, would the subject be conceived as in the strict sense “indefinite.” It is a

[34] These references are added in a note: “Von φησί in späten manche nach Bentley, wie Dav. ad Cic. Tus. i. 39; Wytt. ad Plut., T. vi, p. 791. Von εἰπέ μοι, Heind. ad Euthyd., 29.”

[35] Cf. Grimm’s note, given above, p. 289.

[36] Meyer, *in loc.*, continues to read φησί. He says, “*It is said*, impersonal, as often with the Greeks. See Bernhardy, p. 419. The reading φασίν (Lachmann, following B. Vulg.), is a rash correction. Comp. Fritzsche, *ad Thesmoph.*, p. 189; Buttmann, *Neut. Gram.*, p. 119 [English translation, 136].” So in essence most commentators, including Flatt, Storr, Krause, De Wette, Kling, Waite. Rückert more warily comments: “φησίν is here properly recognized as a formula of adduction, without reference to the number of those speaking. See Winer (304).” Cf. above, p. 289.

perfectly definite subject that is present to the mind of the writer, given either in the immediate context or in the thorough understanding that exists between the writer and reader. There is in them nothing whatever of the vagueness that attaches to the French "on dit," or the German "man sagt," or the English "it is said." The Greeks had other locutions for expressing this idea, and if it was ever expressed by the simple φησί, only the slightest traces of it remain in their extant literature.

In the seventh edition of the Greek Lexicon of Liddell & Scott,[37] nevertheless, this usage is expressly assigned to φησί. We read:

"φασί parenthetically, *they say, it is said*, Il. 5, 638, Od. 6, 42 and Att.; but in prose also φησί, like French *on dit*, Dem. 650, 13, Plut. 2, 112 C., etc. (so Lat. *inquit, ait*, Gronov, Liv. 34, 3, Bent. Hor. 1 Sat. 4, 79; — especially in urging an objection or counter-argument, v. Interpp. Pers. Sat. 1, 40);—so also ἔφη, c. acc. et inf., Xen. An. i, 6, 6."

It is far from obvious, however, that the passages here adduced will justify precisely the usage which they are cited to illustrate. In the passage from Demosthenes — ἔστω, φησὶν, ὑπὲρ αὐτοῦ ἡ αὐτὴ τιμωρία, etc. — it seems to be quite clear, as the previous sentence suggests and the editors recognize,[38] that the subject of the φησί is ἕκαστος τῶν γεγραφότων, and is far from a purely indefinite τις. The passage from Plutarch ("Consolatio ad Apollonium," xxi) is more specious. It runs: ἀλλ' οὐ γὰρ ἤλπιζον, φησί, ταῦτα πείσεσθαι, οὐδὲ προσεδόκων; and is translated in the Latin version, "At, inquiunt, præter spem mihi hic casus et expectationem evenit"; and in Holland's old English version, "But haply you will say, I never thought that this would have befallen unto me, neither did I so much as doubt any such thing." A glance at the context, however, is enough to show that there is no purely indefinite φησί here, though it may be that we have here another instance of its usage without regard to number and person. In

---

[37] P. 1665a (Oxford, 1883).        [38] Whiston, Reiske, Weber.

any case, the subject is the quite definitely conceived inter-
locutor of the passage. That the ἔφη adduced at the end of
the note as in some degree of the same sort is not an indefinite
ἔφη, but has the Clearchus of the immediately preceding context as its subject, is too obvious for remark. Clearchus was
present by the request of Cyrus at the trial of Orontes, and
when he came out he reported to his friends the manner in
which the trial was conducted: "He said (ἔφη) that Cyrus
began to speak as follows." It is not by such instances as
these that the occurrence of a purely indefinite φησί can be
established.[39]

The subjectless φησί, to be sure, does occur very thickly
scattered over the face of Greek literature, introducing or
emphasizing quotations, or adducing objections, or the like:
but the "it" that is to be supplied to it is, ordinarily at least,
a quite definite one with its own definite reference perfectly
clear. A characteristic instance, often referred to, is that in
Demosth., "Leptin," § 56:[40] καὶ γάρ τοι μόνῳ τῶν πάντων αὐτῷ
τοῦτ' ἐν τῇ στήλῃ γέγραπται, ἐπειδὴ Κόνων, φησίν, ἠλευθέρωσε
τοὺς Ἀθηναίων συμμάχους. — Ἔστι δὲ τοῦτο τὸ γράμμα. . . . ."
Here F. A. Wolf comments: "Absolute ibi interjectum est
φησίν, aut, si mavis, subaudi ὁ γράψας"; and Schaefer adds:
"Subaudi ἡ στήλη." [41] It does not appear why we should not
render simply "it says": but this "it" is so far from an
"'indefinite' it" that it has its clear reference to the inscription just mentioned. Perhaps even more instructive is a passage in the third Philippic [42] of Demosthenes, which runs as
follows:

"That such is our present state, you yourselves are witnesses, and
need not any testimony from me. That our state in former times was
quite opposite to this, I shall now convince you, not by any arguments of mine, but by a decree of your ancestors (γράμματα τῶν

[39] We are indebted to Prof. S. S. Orris, of Princeton University, for suggestions in preparing this paragraph. He permits us to add that, in his opinion,
"φησί is never equivalent to the general, indefinite *they say* or *it is said*."

[40] Reiske, p. 477; Dindorf, ii. 23.      [41] Reiske and Schaefer, vi. 162.

[42] iii. §§ 41, 42 (p. 122); "Oratores Attici," v. 214.

προγόνων), which they inscribed upon a brazen column (στήλην) erected in the citadel. . . . What, then, says the decree (τί οὖν λέγει τὰ γράμματα)? 'Let Arithmius,' it says (φησίν), 'of Zelia, the son of Pythonax, be accounted infamous and an enemy to the Athenians and their allies, both he and all his race.' . . . The sentence imported somewhat more, for, in the laws importing capital cases, it is enacted (γέγραπται) that 'when the legal punishment of a man's crime cannot be inflicted he may be put to death,' and it was accounted meritorious to kill him. 'Let not the infamous man,' saith the law, 'be permitted to live' (καὶ ἄτιμος, φησί, τεθνάτω), intimating that he is free from guilt who executes this sentence (τοῦτο δὴ λέγει, καθαρὸν τὸν τούτων τινὰ ἀποκτείναντα εἶναι)."

In both cases it is doubtless enough to render φησί, "it says," its function being in each case to call pointed attention to the words quoted: but the "it" is by no means "indefinite" in the sense that its reference was not very definitely conceived. On the second instance of its occurrence Wolf comments: "s. ὁ φονικὸς νόμος," [43] while Schaefer says: [44]

"Pleonastice positum cum γέγραπται praecesserit. Verumtamen h. l. sensum paulo magis juvat quam ubi post εἶπον, εἶπε, continuo sequitur ἔφην, ἔφη. Ad φησί subaudi ὁ νομοθέτης."

These instances will supply us with typical examples of the "absolute" φησί; and, in this sense, "subjectless φησί" is of very common occurrence indeed in Greek literature.

But really "subjectless φησί," i. e., φησί without any implied subject in context or common knowledge, which therefore we must take quite indefinitely, is very rare indeed, if not non-existent. Perhaps one of the most likely instances of such a usage is offered us by a passage in Plutarch's "Consolatio ad Apollonium," 34.[45] Holland's old version of it runs thus: [46]

"And verily in regard of him who is now in a blessed estate, it has not been naturall for him to remaine in this life longer than the terme prefixed and limited unto him; but after he had honestly performed

---

[43] Reiske-Schaefer, v. 579.      [44] Op. cit., p. 581.
[45] P. 119 F (Wyttenbach, I. ii. 470).      [46] P. 530 (20–30).

the course of his time, it was needfull and requisit for him to take the way for to returne unto his destinie that called for him to come unto her."

From this we may at least learn that φησίν here presented some difficulty, as Holland passes it by unrendered. The common Latin version restores it, reading the last clause thus: "Sed ita postulabit natura ut hoc expleto *fatale* quod aiunt *iter* conficeret, revocante eum jam ad se natura"; the Greek running thus: "ἀλλ' εὐτάκτως τοῦτον ἐκπλήσαντι πρὸς τὴν εἱμαρμένην ἐπανάγειν πορείαν, καλούσης αὐτῆς, φησίν, ἤδη πρὸς ἑαυτήν." The theory of the Latin version obviously is that φησίν here is to be taken indefinitely, that is as an index hand pointing to a current designation of death as an entering upon the "fated journey" — ἡ εἱμαρμένη πορεία. This is explained to us by Wyttenbach's note: [47]

"φησίν] non debebat offendere viros doctos. Est *ut ait poeta ille unde hoc sumptum est.* Videt hoc et Reiskius. Correxi versionem. De Tragici dicto in Animadversibus dicetur."

Accordingly, in the Animadversions,[48] he addresses himself first to showing that the expression here signalized was a current poetical saying — appealing to Plato,[49] Julian, Philo; and then adds:

"Cæterum φησίν ita elliptice usitatum est: v. c. Plutarcho, p. 135 B.,[50] 817 D., Dion. Chrys., p. 493 D., 532 A., 562 B. Notavit et Uptonus ad Epict. in Indice. In annotatoribus ad Lambertum Bosium de Ellipsibus unus Schoettgenius, idque ex uno Paulo Apostolo hunc usum annotavit, p. 74. Et. Latine ita dicitur *inquit,*

[47] I, ii. 470.    [48] VI, ii. 791.

[49] Phaedo, 401 B. (115): "in these arrayed, [the soul] is ready to go on her journey to the world below, when her time comes. You, Simmias and Cebes, and all other men, will depart at some time or other. Me already, as the tragic poet would say, the voice of fate calls (ἐμὲ δὲ νῦν ἤδη καλεῖ, φαίη ἂν ἀνὴρ τραγικὸς, ἡ εἱμαρμένη)." The other passages adduced witness only to the currency of the phrase ἡ εἱμαρμένη πορεία. But the language of both Plutarch and Plato would seem to imply that the "calling" is certainly a part of the quotation.

[50] *Præcepta Sanit. Tuend.*, 135 B., οὐ κατά γε τὴν ἐμὴν, ἔφη, γνώμην. Wytt.: "ἔφη notat alterius dictum ut alibi φησί, de quo diximus, p. 119 F."

quod monuerunt J. F. Gronovius et A. Drakenborch. ad Livium
xxxiv. 3, J. A. Ernestus in Clav. Cic. voce *Inquit*."

It does not seem, however, that Wyttenbach would have us
read the φησί here quite indefinitely, as adducing for example a current saying: judging from his own paraphrase
this might appear to him as a certain exaggeration of its
implication. Its office would seem rather to be to call attention to the words, to which it is adjoined, as quoted, and
thus, in the good understanding implied to exist between
the writer and his readers, to point definitely to its source:
so that it might be a proper note to it to say, "subaudi ὁ
τραγικός, vel ὁ ποιητής" — and this might be done with a
considerable emphasis on the ὁ; nay, the actual name of the
poet, well known to both writer and reader, though now lost
to us, might equally well be the *subauditum*, and such, indeed, may be the implication of the *subauditum* suggested
by Wyttenbach: *ut ait poeta ille unde hoc scriptum est*. Surely,
an instance like this is far from a clear case of the absolutely
indefinite or even generally undefining use of φησί.

Among the references with which Wyttenbach supports
his note, the most promising sends us to Epictetus, whose
"Discourses" abound in the most varied use of φησί, and
offer us at the same time one of our most valuable sources of
knowledge of the Greek in common use near the times of the
apostles.[51] We meet with many instances here which it has
been customary to explain as cases of φησί in a wholly indefinite reference. But the matter is somewhat complicated
by the facts that we are not reading here Epictetus' "Discourses" pure and simple, but Arrian's report of them; and
that Arrian may exercise his undoubted right to slip in a
φησί of his own whenever he specially wishes to keep his
readers' attention fixed upon the fact that they are his
master's words he is setting down, or perhaps even merely
out of the abiding sense, on his own part, that he is report-
ing Epictetus and not writing out of his own mind. When

[51] Cf. Heinrici as above, p. 481; and Blass, "Gram. of New Testament
Greek," English translation, p. 2.

word must have been interjected into Greek conversation, but does not greatly alter the impression of its essential implication which we derive from the general use of the word. Take a single instance of its current use in the "Discourses" in its relation to kindred words:

"So also Diogenes somewhere says ($\pi o u$ $\lambda \epsilon \gamma \epsilon \iota$) that there exists but one means of obtaining freedom — to die contentedly, and he writes ($\gamma \rho \acute{a} \phi \epsilon \iota$) to the king of the Persians, 'You cannot enslave the city of the Athenians, any more,' says he ($\phi \eta \sigma \iota \nu$), 'than fishes.' 'How? Can I not catch them?' 'If you catch them,' says he ($\phi \eta \sigma \iota \nu$), 'they will immediately leave you and be gone, just like fishes: for whatever one of them you catch dies, and if these men die when they are caught, what good will your preparations do you?'" (iv, 1, 30).

The lively effect given by such unexpected interpositions of $\phi \eta \sigma \iota \nu$ is lost in our decorous translation of the New Testament examples: but it exists in them too. Thus: "But she, being urged on by her mother, 'Give me,' says she, 'here upon a charger, the head of John the Baptist'" (Matt. xiv. 8); "But he, 'Master, speak,' says he" (Luke vii. 40); "But Peter to them, 'Repent,' says he, 'and be baptized each one of you'" (Acts ii. 38); "'Let those among you,' says he, 'that are able, go down with me'" (Acts xxv. 5); "'To-morrow,' says he, 'thou shalt hear him'" (Acts xxv. 22); "But Paul, 'I am not mad,' says he, 'most noble Festus'" (Acts xxvi. 25).[54] The main function of $\phi \eta \sigma \iota$ then would appear to be to keep the consciousness of the speaker reported clearly before the mind of the reader. It is therefore often used to mark the transition from indirect to direct quotation [55]: and it lent itself readily, therefore, to mark the adduction both

[54] The matter of this interposition is investigated for Plato by Stallbaum, p. 472 D., 580 D. — where he seems to have collected all the instances of interposed $\phi a \mu \acute{e} \nu$ in Plato. Cf. also Bornemann and Sauppe on Xenophon's *Memorab.*, iii. 5, 13, and the indices of Schenkl on Arrian-Epictetus and Thieme-Sturz on Xenophon (sub. voc. $\phi \acute{a} \nu a \iota$).

[55] On Acts xxv. 5, Blass has this note: "5 fit transitus ex or. obliqua in rectam, ut I. 4 al; hinc $\phi \eta \sigma \iota \nu$ interpositum ut I. 4 $\beta$.," i. e., in the *Western* text of I, 4, which reads: "'Which ye heard,' says he, 'from my mouth.'" The interposition of a "he says," or some similar phrase, to keep the consciousness of the

of objections and of literary citations. But, one would imagine, it did not very readily lend itself to vague and indefinite references.

If we desire to find cases of "subjectless λέγει" in any way similar to those of φησί, we must apparently turn our back on profane Greek altogether.[56] We have fortunately in Philo, however, an author, the circumstances of whose writing made literary quotation as frequent with him as oral is in the lively pages of Epictetus' "Discourses." And in Philo's treatises λέγει takes its place by the side of its more common kinsman φησί, and is used in much the same way, though naturally somewhat less frequently. In harmony with his fundamental viewpoint — which looked on the Scriptures as a body of oracular sayings — Philo adduces Scripture commonly with verbs of "saying" — φησί, λέγεται, λέγει, εἶπεν (γέγραπται falling into the background). Passages so adduced are often woven into the fabric of his discussion of the contents of Scripture; and where the words adduced are words of a speaker in the Biblical narrative, the subject of the φησί or λέγει which introduces them naturally is often this speaker — whether God or some other person. Equally often, however, the subject given immediately or indirectly in the context is something outside of the narrative that is dealt with: in this case it is sometimes Moses, or "the prophet," or "the lawgiver" — at other times, "the Holy Word," or "the sacred Word," or "the Oracle," or "the Oracles" (ὁ θεῖος λόγος, ὁ ἱερὸς λόγος, ὁ χρησμός, τὸ λόγιον, οἱ χρησμοί, τὰ λόγια) — at other times still it is "God," under various designations. Often, however, the verb — φησί or λέγει — stands not only without expressed subject, but equally without indicated subject. The rendering of these cases has given students of Philo some trouble, arising out

hearer or reader bright on the fact that the words before him are *quoted* words is, of course, a general linguistic and not a specifically Greek usage. It is found in all languages. A Hebrew instance, for example, may be found in I Kgs. ii. 4.

[56] Schenkl catalogues in the "Discourses" of Epictetus two cases of interposited λέγει, quite in the style of φησί — iii. 19, 1 and "Fragment," xxi. 10 — but in both cases the subject is expressed.

of the apparent confusion, when the subject is expressed, of the reference of the verb, — now to a speaker in the text of Scripture and now to the author of the particular Scripture, to God as the author of all Scripture, or to Scripture itself conceived as a living Word. This apparent confusion is due solely to Philo's fundamental conception of Scripture as an oracular book, which leads him to deal with its text as itself the Word of God: he has himself fully explained the matter,[57] and we should be able to steer clear of serious difficulties with his explanation in our hands.

Nevertheless, a somewhat mechanical mode of dealing with his citations has produced, on more than one occasion, certain odd results. Prof. Ryle says:[58]

"The commonest forms of quotation employed by Philo are φησί, εἶπεν, λέγει, λέγεται, γέγραπται γάρ. Whether the subject of φησί be Moses or Scripture personified cannot in many cases be determined."

In no case is the subject strictly indeterminate, however, and the failure to determine it aright may introduce confusion. Thus, for example, in "De Confus. Ling.," § 26 (Mangey, i. 424), Philo mentions the Book of Judges, and cites it with the subjectless φησί. Prof. Ryle comments thus:[59]

"He does not mention any opinion as to authorship, and introduces his quotation with his usual formula φησίν. We are hardly justified in assuming that Philo intended Moses as the subject of φησίν, and regarded him as the author of Judges (so Dr. Pick, *Journal of Biblical Literature*, 1884). Moses is doubtless often spoken of by Philo as if he were the personification of the Inspired Word; but we cannot safely extend this idea beyond the range of the Pentateuch. All that we can say is that φησίν, used in this quotation from Judges, refers either to the unknown writer of this book or to the personification of Holy Scripture."

Or else, we may add, to God, the real author, in Philo's conception, of every word of Scripture. Prof. Ryle, however, has

---

[57] In "De Vita Mosis," iii. 23.     [58] "Philo and Holy Scripture," p. xlv.
[59] *Op. cit.*, p. xxv.

not caught precisely Dr. Pick's meaning: Dr. Pick does not commit himself to the extravagant view that wherever subjectless φησί occurs in Philo the *subauditum* "Moses" is implied: he only says, in direct words, that here — in this special passage — "Moses is introduced as speaking." It would seem obvious that he had a text before him which read "Moses says," and not simply "says," at this place. This text was doubtless nothing other than Yonge's English translation, which reads Moses here, as often elsewhere with as little warrant: "'For,' says Moses, 'Gideon swore, etc.'" [60] The incident illustrates the evil of mechanically supplying a supplement to these subjectless verbs — which cannot indeed be understood except on the basis of Philo's primary principle, that it is all one to say "Moses says," "the Scripture says," or "God says." The simple fact here is that Philo quotes Judges, as he does the rest of Scripture, with the subjectless "says," and with the same implication, viz., that Judges is to him a part of the Word of God.

As has been already hinted, by all means the commonest verb used by Philo thus, — without expressed or obviously indicated subject, — to introduce a Scripture passage, is φησί. Perhaps, however, the one instance to which we have incidentally adverted will suffice to illustrate the usage — other instances of which may be seen on nearly every page of Philo's treatises. It is of more interest for us to note that λέγει seems also to be used in the same subjectless way — examples of which may be seen, for instance, in the following places, "Legg. Allegor.," i, 15; ii, 4; iii, 8; "Quod Det. Pot. Insid.," 48; "De Posterit. Caini," 9; 22; 52; "De Gigant.," 11; 12; "De Confus. Ling.," 32; "De Migrat. Abrah.," 11; "Fragment. ex Joh. Monast." (ii, 668). In "Legg. Allegor.," i, 15, for instance, we have a string of quotations without obvious subject, introduced, the first by the subjectless φησίν, the next by the equally subjectless ἐπιφέρει πάλιν, and the third (from Exod. xx. 23) by λέγει δὲ καὶ ἐν ἑτέροις. In "Legg. Allegor.," ii, 4, we have Gen. ii. 19 intro-

[60] Vol. ii. p. 27.

duced by λέγει γάρ without any obvious subject. Yonge translates this too by "For Moses says": but to obtain warrant for this we should have to go back two pages and a half (of Richter's text), quite to the beginning of the treatise, where we find an apostrophe to the "prophet." In "De Posterit. Caini," 22, λέγει ἐπὶ μὲν 'Αβραὰμ οὕτως (Gen. xi. 29), though Yonge supplies "Moses" again, that would seem to be demonstrably absurd, as the passage proceeds to place "Moses," in parallelism with Abraham, in the *object.* Similarly the passages adduced from "De Gigant.," 11 and 12 (Num. xiv. 44 and Deut. xxxiv. 6) are *about* Moses, and it would scarcely do to fill out the ellipsis of subject with his name. Examples need not, however, be multiplied.

It would seem quite clear that both the subjectless φησί frequently, and the subjectless λέγει less often, occur in Philo after a fashion quite similar to the instances adduced from the New Testament. And it would seem to be equally clear that the lack of a subject in their case is not indicative of indefiniteness, but rather of definiteness in their reference. Philo does not adduce passages of Scripture with the bare φησί or λέγει because he knows or cares very little whence they come or with what authority; but because he and his readers alike both know so well the source whence they are derived, and yield so unquestionably to its authority, that it is unnecessary to pause to indicate either. The use of the bare φησί or λέγει in citations from Scripture is in his case, obviously, the outgrowth and the culminating sign of his absolute confidence in Scripture as the living voice of God, fully recognized as such both by himself and his readers. In the same sense in which to the dying Sir Walter Scott there was but one "Book," to him and his readers there was but one authoritative divine Word, and all that was necessary in adducing it was to indicate the fact of adduction. The φησί or λέγει serves thus primarily the function of "quotation marks" in modern usage: but under such circumstances and with such implications that bare quotation marks carry with them the assurance that the words adduced are divine words.

It would seem to be very easy, in these circumstances, to give ourselves more uneasiness than is at all necessary as to the precise *subauditum* which we are to assume with these verbs. It may serve very well to render them simply, "It says," with the implication that Philo is using the *codex* of Scripture as the living voice of God speaking to him and his readers. The case, in a word, would seem to be very similar to that of the common New Testament formula of quotation γέγραπται — meaning not that what is adduced is somewhere written, but that it is the authoritative law that is being adduced. Just so, "It says," in such a case would mean not that somebody or something says what is adduced, but that the Word of God says it. As the one usage is the natural outgrowth of the conception of the Scriptures as a written authoritative law, the other is the equally natural outgrowth of the conception of Scripture as the living voice of God. How very natural a development this usage is, may be illustrated by the fact that something very similar to it may be met with in colloquial English. In the same circles where we may hear God spoken of as simply "He," as if it were dangerous to name His name too freely, we may also occasionally hear the Bible quoted with a simple "It says," or even with an elision of the "it," as "'Tsays": and yet the "it," though treated thus cavalierly, is in reality a very emphatic "It" indeed — the phrase being the product of awe in the presence of "the Book," and importing that there is but one "It" that could be thought of in the case. Somewhat similarly, in the case of Philo, the Scriptures are cited with the bare φησί, λέγει, because, in his mind and in the circles which he addressed, there stood out so far above all other voices this one Voice of God embodied in His Scriptures, that none other would be thought of in the case. The phrase is the outgrowth of reverence for the Word and of unquestioning submission to it: and the fundamental fact is that no special subject is expressed simply because none was needed and it would be all one whether we understood as subject, Moses, the prophet and lawgiver — the holy or sacred Word or the oracle — or finally, God Himself. In any case, and with any *subauditum*, the real subject conceived as speaking is God.[61]

If now, in the light of the facts we have thus brought to our recollection, we turn back to the New Testament passages in which the Old Testament is cited with a simple φησί or λέγει, it may not be impossible for us to perceive their real character and meaning. There would seem to be absolutely no warrant in Greek usage for taking λέγει, and but very little, if any, for taking φησί really indefinitely: and even if there were, it would be inconceivable that the New Testament writers, from their high conception of "Scripture," should have adduced Scripture with a simple "it is said" — somewhere, by some one — without implication of reverence toward the quoted words or recognition of the authority inherent in them. It is rather in the usage of Philo that we find the true analogue of these examples. Like Philo, the author of the Epistle to the Hebrews looks upon Scripture as an oracular book, and all that it says, God says to him: and accordingly, like Philo, he adduces its words with a simple "it says," with the full implication that this "it says" is a "God says" also. Whenever the same locution occurs elsewhere in the New Testament, it bears naturally the same implication. There is no reason why we should recognize the Philonic φησί in Heb. viii. 5, and deny it in I Cor. vi. 16: or why we should recognize the Philonic λέγει in Heb. viii. 8 and deny it in Acts xiii. 35, Rom. ix. 15, xv. 10, II Cor. vi. 2, Gal. iii. 16, or in Eph. iv. 8, v. 14. Only in case it were very clear that Paul did not share the high conception of Scripture as the living voice of God which underlies this usage in

[61] The reverent use of an indefinite may be illustrated from the mode of citation adopted in Heb. ii. 6 — "one hath somewhere testified" — a mode of citation not uncommon in Philo [as, for example, *de Temul.* (ed. Mang., i. 365), εἶπε γάρ πού τις (i. e., Abraham, Gen. xx. 12), and other examples in Bleek, II, i. 239]. Delitzsch correctly explains: "The citation is thus introduced with a special solemnity, the author naming neither the place whence he takes it nor the original speaker, but making use (as Philo frequently) of the vague term πού τις, so that the important testimony itself becomes only the more conspicuous, like a grand pictured figure in the plainest, narrowest frame."

Philo and the Epistle to the Hebrews, could we hesitate to understand this phrase in him as we understand it in them. But we have seen that such is not the case: and his use in adducing Scripture of the subjectless φησί and λέγει quite in their manner is, rightly viewed, only another indication, among many, that his conception of Scripture was fundamentally the same with theirs, and it cannot be explained away on the assumption that it was fundamentally different.

It does not indeed follow that on every occasion when a Scripture passage is introduced by a φησί or a λέγει it is to be explained as an instance of this subjectless usage — even though a subject for it is given or plainly implied in the immediate context. That is not possible even in Philo, where the introductory formula often finds its appropriate subject expressed in the preceding context. But it does follow that we need not and ought not resort to unnatural expedients to find a subject for such a φησί or λέγει in the context, or that acquiescing, whenever that seems more natural, in its subjectlessness, we should seek to explain away its high implications.[62] Men may differ as to the number of clear

---

[62] The matter is approached in a sensible and helpful way by Viteau, in his "Étude sur le Grec du N. T.: sujet, complement et attribute" (1896), p. 61. He is treating of the subject to be mentally supplied, i. e., of the case where the reader may be fairly counted upon to supply the subject, and he remarks (inter alia): "76 (9). There is a kind of mental subject peculiar to the New Testament. When events of the Old Testament are spoken of, these events are supposed to be known to the reader or the hearer, who is invited to supply the subject of the verb mentally. . . . 77 (10). There is still another kind of mental subject peculiar to the New Testament and kindred to the preceding. In the citations made by the New Testament the subject is often lacking, as well for the verb which announces the citation as for the verb in the citation itself. The reader is supposed to recognize the passage and is invited to supply the subject. (a) For the verbs which announce the citation there occur as subjects: ὁ θεός, Acts ii. 17; ὁ προφήτης, Acts vii. 48; Δαυείδ, Rom. iv. 6; Μωϋσῆς, Rom. x. 19; Ἡσαίας, Rom. xv. 12; ἡ γραφή, Gal. iv. 30. When the verb has no subject, the reader is to supply it mentally: Acts xiii. 34, 35, εἴρηκεν and λέγει, the subject is ὁ θεός, according to the LXX., Es. lv. 3, and Ps. xv. 10; Rom. xv. 10, πάλιν λέγει (ὁ Μωϋσῆς), according to Deut. xxxii. 43; Eph. iv. 8, λέγει (ὁ θεός or Δαυείδ), according to Ps. lxvii. 19; Eph. v. 14, διὸ λέγει, those who regard the passage as imitated or partially cited from the Old Testament give Ἡσαίας as the subject of λέγει, according to Isa. lx. 1, 2, but if we regard this passage as containing some κῶλα of an early hymn (in imitation of

instances of such a usage, that may be counted in the New Testament. But most will doubtless agree that some may be counted: and will doubtless place among them Eph. iv. 8 and v. 14. Some will contend, no doubt, that in the latter of these texts, the passage adduced is not derived from the Old Testament at all. That, however, is "another story," on which we cannot enter now, but on which we must be content to differ. We pause only to say that we reckon among the reasons why we should think the citation here is derived from the Old Testament, just its adduction by διὸ λέγει — which would seem to advise us that Paul intended to quote the oracular Word.

There may be room for difference of opinion again as to the precise *subauditum* which it will be most natural to assume with these subjectless verbs: whether ὁ θεός or ἡ γραφή. In our view it makes no real difference in their implication: for, in our view, the very essence of the case is, that, under the force of their conception of the Scriptures as an oracular book, it was all one to the New Testament writers whether they said "God says" or "Scripture says." This is made very clear, as their real standpoint, by their double identification of Scripture with God and God with Scripture, to which we adverted at the beginning of this paper, and by which Paul, for example, could say alike "the *Scripture* saith to Pharaoh" (Rom. ix. 17) and "*God* . . . . saith, Thou wilt not give thy Holy One to see corruption" (Acts xiii. 34). We may well be content in the New Testament as in Philo to translate the phrase wherever it occurs, "It says" — with the implication that *this* "It says" is the same as "Scripture says," and that this "Scripture says" is the same as "God says." It is this implication that is really the fundamental fact in the case.

Isaiah) we must supply as the subject τις, 'it is said,' 'it is sung' (96a); Heb. viii. 5, φησίν (ὁ θεός), according to Ex. xxv. 40." We do not accord, of course, with the remark on Eph. v. 14; and we miss in Viteau's remarks the expected reference to the deeper fact in the case.

# VIII

## "THE ORACLES OF GOD"

a comprehensive view of it may help to correct some long-standing errors concerning its exact meaning, and may, indeed, point not obscurely to its true connotation — which is not without interesting implications. Upheld by this hope we shall essay to pass in rapid review the usage of the term in Classic, Hellenistic and Patristic Greek, and then to ask what, in the light of this usage, the word is likely to have meant to the writers of the New Testament.

I. It may be just as well at the outset to disabuse our minds of any presumption that a diminutive sense is inherent in the term λόγιον, as a result of its very form.[2] Whether we explain it with Meyer-Weiss [3] as the neuter of λόγιος and point to λογίδιον [4] as the proper diminutive of this stem; or look upon it with Sanday-Headlam [5] as originally the diminutive of λόγος, whose place as such was subsequently, viz., when it acquired the special sense of "oracle," taken by the strengthened diminutive λογίδιον — it remains true that no trace of a diminutive sense attaches to it as we meet it on the pages of Greek literature.[6]

We are pointed, to be sure, to a scholium on the "Frogs" of Aristophanes (line 942) as indicating the contrary. The passage is the well-known one in which Euripides is made to

[2] So very commonly: as, e. g., by Grimm ("Lexicon in N. T.," s. v.), Bleek ("Der Brief an die Hebräer," ii. 2, 114, on Heb. v. 12), Philippi ("Com. on Romans," E. T., i. 105, on Rom. iii. 2), Morrison ("Expos. of 3d Chap. of Rom.," p. 14).          [3] "Com. on Romans," on Rom. iii. 2 (E. T., i. 140, note 1).

[4] Plato, "Eryx.," 401, E.: ἐτάραττέ γε αὐτὸν . . . τὸ λογίδιον; Isocrates, "Contra Sophistas," 295 B. (Didot, 191): τοσούτῳ δὲ χείρους ἐγένοντο τῶν περὶ τὰς ἔριδας καλινδουμένων, ὅσον οὗτοι μὲν τοιαῦτα λογίδια διεξιόντες . . .; Aristophanes, "Vesp.," 64: ἀλλ' ἔστιν ἡμῖν λογίδιον γνώμην ἔχον | ὑμῶν μὲν αὐτῶν οὐχὶ δεξιώτερον. Cf. Blaydes on the passage in Aristophanes.

[5] "Com. on Rom.," on Rom. iii. 2: "The old account of λόγιον as a diminutive of λόγος is probably correct, though Mey.-W. make it neuter of λόγιος on the ground that λογίδιον is the proper diminutive. The form λογίδιον is rather a strengthened diminutive which, by a process common in language, took the place of λόγιον when it acquired the sense of 'oracle.'" When they add that it was as "a brief condensed saying" that the oracle was called λόγιον, they have no support in the literature.

[6] Jelf, who looks upon it as a diminutive, cites it as an extreme example of the fact that many simple diminutives in -ιον have lost their diminutive force — such as θηρίον, βιβλίον: λόγιον, he says, "has assumed a peculiar meaning." In any event, thus, no diminutive meaning clings to λόγιον.

respond to Æschylus' inquiry as to what things he manufactured. "Not winged horses," is the reply (as Wheelwright
translates it), "By Jupiter, nor goat-stags, such as thou, Like
paintings on the Median tapestry, But as from thee I first
received the art, Swelling with boastful pomp and heavy
words, I paréd it straight and took away its substance, *With
little words*, and walking dialogues,[7] And white beet mingled,
straining from the books A juice of pleasant sayings, — then
I fed him With monodies, mixing Ctesiphon." It is upon the
word here translated "with little words," but really meaning "verselets" (Blaydes: *versiculis*) — ἐπυλλίοις — that the
scholium occurs. It runs: ᾿Αντὶ τοῦ λογίοις μικροῖς· ὡς δὲ βρέφος
βρεφύλλιον, καὶ εἶδος εἰδύλλιον· οὕτω καὶ ἔπος ἐπύλλιον.[8] That is
to say, ἐπύλλιον is a diminutive of the same class as βρεφύλλιον
and εἰδύλλιον,[9] and means λόγιον μικρόν. Since the idea of
smallness is explicit in the adjective attached to λόγιον here,
surely it is not necessary to discover it also in the noun,[10]
especially when what the scholiast is obviously striving to
say is not that ἐπυλλίοις means "little wordlets," but "little
verses." The presence of μικροῖς here, rather is conclusive evidence that λογίοις by itself did not convey a diminutive
meaning to the scholiast. If we are to give λόγιον an unexampled sense here, we might be tempted to take it, therefore, as intended to express the idea "verses" rather than
the tautological one of "little words" or even "little maxims"
or "little sayings." And it might fairly be pleaded in favor of
so doing that λόγιον in its current sense of "oracle" not only
lies close to one of the ordinary meanings of ἔπος ("Od.," 12,
266; Herod., 1, 13, and often in the Tragedians), but also,
because oracles were commonly couched in verse, might
easily come to suggest in popular speech the idea of "verse,"

---

[7] ἐπυλλίοις καὶ περιπάτοις καὶ τευτλίοισι λευκοῖς.

[8] Dindorf, iv. ii. p. 113, on line 973.

[9] Blaydes adds some other instances: "Ejusdem formæ diminutiva sunt
εἰδύλλιον, βρεφύλλιον, μειρακύλλιον, ζωΰλλιον, κρεΰλλιον, ξενύλλιον."

[10] With this λόγιον μικρόν compare the βραχέα λόγια of Justin Martyr, "Contra
Tryph.," c. 18. When the idea of *brevity* needed to be conveyed, it would seem
that an adjective expressive of this idea was required to be added.

so that a λόγιον μ ι κ ρ ό ν would easily obtrude itself as the exact synonym of ἐπύλλιον, in Euripides' sense, i. e., in the sense of short broken verses. There is no reason apparent on the other hand why we should find a diminutive implication in the word as here used, and in any case, if this is intended, it is a sense unillustrated by a single instance of usage.

And the unquestionable learning of Eustathius seems to assure us that to Greek ears λόγιον did not suggest a diminutive sense at all. He is commenting on line 339 of the Second Book of the " Iliad," which runs,

πῆ δὴ συνθεσίαι τε καὶ ὅρκια βήσεται ἡμῖν,

and he tells us that ὅρκιον in Homer is not a diminutive, but is a formation similar to λόγιον, which means "an oracle": Οὐχ ὑποκοριστικὸν δὲ παρ' Ὁμήρῳ οὐδὲ . . . τὸ ἴχνιον. Ὥσπερ δὲ τὰ ὅρκια παρωνόμασται ἐκ τοῦ ὅρκου, οὕτω καὶ ἐκ τοῦ λόγου τὰ λόγια ἤγουν οἱ χρησμοί.[11] There is no direct statement here, to be sure, that λόγιον is not a diminutive; that statement is made — with entire accuracy — only of ὅρκιον and ἴχνιον:[12] nor is the derivation suggested for λόγιον, as if it came directly from λόγος, perhaps scientifically accurate. But there is every indication of clearness of perception in the statement: and it could scarcely be given the form it has, had λόγιον stood in Eustathius' mind as the diminutive of λόγος. It obviously represented to him not a diminutive synonym of λόγος, but an equal synonym of χρησμός. What λόγιον stood for, in his mind, is very clearly exhibited, further, in a comment which he makes on the 416th line of the First Book of the "Odyssey," where Telemachus declares that he does not "care for divinations such as my mother seeks, summoning a diviner to the hall":

οὔτε θεοπροπίης ἐμπάζομαι, ἥν τινα μήτηρ
ἐς μέγαρον καλέσασα θεοπρόπον ἐξερέηται.

---

[11] Ed. Bas., i. 177; Rom. i. 233: Weigel's Leipzig ed. (here used), i. 189.

[12] Liddell and Scott say, s. v.: "ὅρκιον is not with Buttm., "Lexil.," s. v., to be regarded as a dim. of ὅρκος, but rather as neuter of ὅρκιος, with which ἱερόν or ἱερά may be supplied"; "Dim. of ἴχνος only in form (v. Chandler, "Accent.," § 340)." Cf. in general Jelf, "Grammar," §§ 56, 2, and 335, c (Vol. i. pp. 53, 337).

Eustathius wishes us to note that θεοπρόπος means the μάντις, θεοπροπία his art, and θεοπρόπιον the message he delivers, which Eustathius calls the χρησμῷδημα, and informs us is denominated by the Attics also λόγιον. He says: Ἰστέον δὲ ὅτι θεοπρόπος μὲν ἄλλως, ὁ μάντις. θεοπροπία δὲ, ἡ τέχνη αὐτοῦ. θεοπρόπιον δὲ, τὸ χρησμῷδημα, ὃ καὶ λόγιον ἔλεγον οἱ Ἀττικοί.[13] To Eustathius, thus λόγιον was simply the exact synonym of the highest words in use to express a divine communication to men — θεοπρόπιον,[14] χρησμῷδημα, χρησμός. Similarly Hesychius' definition runs: Λόγια: θέσφατα, μαντεύματα, (προ)φητεύματα, φῆμαι, χρησμοί. In a word, λόγιον differs from λόγος not as expressing something smaller than it, but as expressing something more sacred.

The Greek synonymy of the notion "oracle" is at once extraordinarily full and very obscure. It is easy to draw up a long list of terms — μαντεῖα, μαντεύματα, πρόφαντα, θεοπρόπια, ἐπιθεσπισμοί θέσφατα, θεσπίσματα, λόγια, and the like; but exceedingly difficult, we do not say to lay down hard and fast lines between them, but even to establish any shades of difference among them which are consistently reflected in usage. M. Bouché-Leclercq, after commenting on the poverty of the Latin nomenclature, continues as to the Greek:[15]

" The Greek terminology is richer and allows analysis of the different senses, but it is even more confused than abundant. The Greeks, possessors of a flexible tongue, capable of rendering all the shades of thought, often squandered their treasures, broadening the meaning of

[13] Ed. Bas., pp. 1426, 1427; ed. Rom., p. 69; ed. Leipzig, i. p. 72.

[14] A scholium on the passage in the "Odyssey" brings out the meaning of θεοπρόπιον, to wit: τὸ ἐκ θεοῦ λεγόμενον, ἐξ οὗ καὶ θεοπρόπος ὁ τὰ τοῦ θεοῦ λέγων. Cf. also the Homeric Lexicons on the word: e. g., Ebeling, s. v. θεοπροπίη et θεοπρόπιον: "Sententia deorum, judicium quod dii (Juppiter potissimum et Appollo) cum vate (vel cum deo) communicant, vates cum aliis hominibus, oraculum. Cf. Nægelsb., H[omerische] Th[eologie], 187. Ap. 87, 4 μάντευμα τὸ ἐκ θεοῦ προλεγόμενον. Cf. Suid, i. 2, 1144 Hes."; and Capelle under same heading: "Alles was von den Göttern (bes[onders] Apollon und Zeus) angezeigt und durch den θεοπρόπος gedeutet wird, 'die von den Göttern eingegebenen Offenbarungen' (Nægelsb. zu A. 385. Cf. 'Hom. Th.,' S. 187), also Weissagung, Göttergebot, Götterbescheid, Orakel."

[15] "Histoire de la Divination dans l'Antiquité" (Paris, Leroux, 1879), Vol. ii. pp. 229, 230.

words at pleasure, multiplying synonyms without distinguishing between them, and thus disdaining the precision to which they could attain without effort. We shall seek in vain for terms especially appropriated to divination by oracles. From the verb χρῆσθαι, which signifies in Homer 'to reveal' in a general way, come the derivatives χρησμός and χρηστήριον. The latter, which dates from Hesiod and the Homerides, designates the place where prophecies are dispensed and, later, the responses themselves, or the instrument by which they are obtained. Χρησμός, which comes into current usage from the time of Solon, is applied without ambiguity to inspired and versified prophecies, but belongs equally to the responses of the oracles and those of free prophets. The word μαντεῖον in the singular designates ordinarily the place of consultation; but in the plural it is applied to the prophecies themselves of whatever origin. In the last sense it has a crowd of synonyms of indeterminate and changeable shades of meaning. The grammarians themselves have been obliged to renounce imposing rules on the capricious usage and seeking recognition for their artificial distinctions. We learn once more the impossibility of erecting precise definitions for terms which lack precision."

Among the distinctions which have been proposed but which usage will not sustain is the discrimination erected by the scholiast on Euripides, "Phœniss.," 907,[16] which would reserve θέσφατα, θεσπίσματα, χρησμοί for oracles directly from the gods, and assign μαντεῦαι and μαντεύματα to the responses of the diviners. The grain of truth in this is that in μάντις, μαντεύεσθαι, μαντεία, etymologically, what is most prominent is the idea of a special unwonted capacity, attention being directed by these words to the strong spiritual elevation which begets new powers in us. While, on the other hand, in θεσπίζειν the reference is directly to the divine inspiration, which, because it is normally delivered in song, is referred to by such forms as θεσπιῳδός, θεσπιῴδειν. Χρησμός, on the other hand, seems an expression which in itself has little direct reference either to the source whence or the form in which the oracle comes, but describes the oracle from the point of view of what it is in itself — viz., a "communication" —

---

[16] The scholium runs: θέσφατα, θεσπίσματα, χρησμοὶ τὸ αὐτό, ἐλέγοντο δὲ ἐπὶ θεῶν· μαντεῦαι δὲ καὶ μαντεύματα ἐπὶ μάντεων ἀνθρώπων.

going back, as it does, to χρῆν, the original sense of which
seems to be "to bestow," "to communicate." [17] Λόγιον doubtless may be classed with χρησμός in this respect — it is *par
excellence* the "utterance," the "saying." It would seem to be
distinguished from χρησμός by having even less reference than
it to the source whence — something as "a declaration" is
distinguished from "a message." If we suppose a herald coming with the cry, "A communication from the Lord," and
then, after delivering the message, adding: "This is His
utterance," it might fairly be contended that in strict precision the former should be χρησμός and the latter λόγιον, in
so far as the former term may keep faintly before the mind
the *source* of the message as a thing given, while the latter
may direct the attention to its *content* as *the very thing* received, doubtless with a further connotation of its fitness to
its high origin. Such subtlety of distinction, however, is not
sure to stamp itself on current use, so that by such etymological considerations we are not much advanced in determining the ordinary connotation of the words in usage.

A much more famous discrimination, and one which much
more nearly concerns us at present, has been erected on what
seems to be a misapprehension of a construction in Thucydides. In a passage which has received the compliment of
imitation by a number of his successors,[18] the historian is
describing the agitation caused by the outbreak of the Pe-

---

[17] The above is abstracted from J. H. Heinr. Schmidt in his "Handbuch der
Lateinischen und Griechischen Synonymik" (1889), § 21, pp. 77–82. The original
meaning assigned to χρῆν (*darreichen, ertheilen*) is supported by a reference to
Vaniček, p. 250. Surely it is a much more reasonable determination than that
of Bouché-Leclercq ("Hist. de la Divination," i. 192), who would derive it from a
cleromantic idea, as if χράω signified first of all "entailler." So he conceives
ἀναιρεῖν to refer to the lot, as we say to "draw lots," as if the Pythoness "drew
her revelations as we draw lots." Schmidt refers the use of this word to the early
idea that the words came up out of the depths of the earth.

[18] E. g., Polybius, 3, 112, 8: "All the oracles preserved in Rome were in every-
body's mouth (πάντα δ᾽ ἦν τὰ παρ᾽ αὐτοῖς λόγια πᾶσι τότε διὰ στόματος) and every
temple and house was full of prodigies and miracles: in consequence of which the
city was one scene of vows, sacrifices, supplicatory processions and prayers"
(Schuchburgh's translation). Appian, 2, 115, δείματα τὰ γὰρ ἄλογα πολλοῖς ἐνέπιπτε
περὶ ὅλην Ἰταλίαν. Καὶ μαντευμάτων παλαιῶν ἐπιφοβωτέρων ἐμνημόνευον. Dionys. Hal.,

loponnesian war, one symptom of which was the passion for oracles which was developed. "All Hellas," he says,[19] "was excited by the coming conflict between the two cities. Many were the prophecies circulated, and many the oracles chanted by diviners (καὶ πολλὰ μὲν λόγια ἐλέγοντο, πολλὰ δὲ χρησμολόγοι ᾖδον), not only in the cities about to engage in the struggle, but throughout Hellas." And again, as the Lacedæmonians approached the city, one of the marks he, at a later point, notes of the increasing excitement is that "soothsayers (χρησμολόγοι) were repeating oracles (ᾖδον χρησμούς) of the most different kinds, which all found in some one or other enthusiastic listeners." [20] On a casual glance the distinction appears to lie on the surface of the former passage that λόγια are oracles in prose and χρησμοί oracles in verse: and so the scholiast [21] on the passage, followed by Suidas [22] defines. But it is immediately obvious on the most cursory glance into Greek literature that the distinction thus suggested will not hold. The χρησμοί are, to be sure, commonly spoken of as sung; and the group of words χρησμῳδός, χρησμῳδέω, χρησμῳδία, χρησμῴδημα, χρησμῴδης, χρησμῳδικός, witnesses to the intimate connection of the two ideas. But this arises out of the nature of the case, rather than out of any special sense attached to the word χρησμός: and accordingly, by the side of this group of words, we have others which, on the one hand, compound χρησμός with terms not implicative of singing (χρησμηγορέω, χρησμαγόρης — χρησμοδοτέω, χρησμοδότης, χρησμοδότημα — χρησμολογέω, χρησμολόγος, χρησμολογία, χρησμολόγιον, χρησμολογική, χρησμολέσχης — χρησμοποιός), and, on the other hand, compound other words for oracles with words denoting singing (θεσπιῳδέω, θεσπιῴδημα, θεσπιῳδός). The fact

"Ant.," vii. 68: χρησμοί τ᾽ ᾔδοντο ἐν πολλοῖς χωρίοις κτλ. Dio Cassius, 431, 66 and 273, 64, where we read of λόγια παντοῖα ᾔδετο.

[19] ii. 8, Jowett's translation (i. p. 99).

[20] ii. 21, Jowett's translation (i. 109).

[21] In Didot's appendix, p. 416: Λόγιά ἐστι τὰ παρὰ τοῦ θεοῦ λεγόμενα καταλογάδην· χρησμοὶ δὲ οἵτινες ἐμμέτρως λέγονται, θεοφορουμένων τῶν λεγόντων.

[22] Ed. Bekker, p. 666: λόγια τὰ παρὰ θεοῦ λεγόμενα καταλογάδην, χρησμοὶ δὲ οἵτινες ἐμμέτρως λέγοντα᾽ θεοφορουμένων τῶν λεγόντων.

is that, as J. H. Heinr. Schmidt [23] points out in an interesting discussion, the natural expression of elevated feeling was originally in song: so that the singer comes before the poet and the poet before the speaker. It was thus as natural for the ancients to say vati-*cinium* as it is for moderns to say Weis-*sagung* or sooth-*saying:* but as the custom of written literature gradually transformed the consciousness of men, their thought became more logical and less pictorial until even the Pythia ceased at last to speak in verse. Meanwhile, old custom dominated the oracles. They were chanted: they were couched in verse: and the terms which had been framed to describe them continued to bear this implication. Even when called λόγια, they prove to be ordinarily [24] in verse; and these also are said to be sung, as we read, for example, in Dio Cassius (431, 66 and 273, 64): λόγια παντοῖα ᾔδετο. What appears to be a somewhat constant equivalence in usage of the two terms χρησμός and λόγιον, spread broadly over the face of Greek literature, seems in any event to negative the proposed distinction. Nor does the passage in Thucydides when more closely examined afford any real ground for it. After all, λόγια and χρησμοί are not contrasted in this passage: the word χρησμοί does not even occur in it. The stress of the distinction falls, indeed, not on the nouns, but on the verbs, the point of the remark being that oracles were scattered among the people by every possible method.[25] If we add that

[23] In his "Handbuch der Lateinischen und Griechischen Synonymik" (Leipzig, 1889), § 21 (pp. 77–82).

[24] So for example in Aristophanes' "Knights" *passim* (see below) and in Porphyry's collection of Oracles.

[25] This is the explanation of Croiset in the very sensible brief note he gives on the passage in his attractive edition of Thucydides (Paris, Hachette & Cie., 1886): He says: "λόγια, oracles: according to the scholiast, oracles in prose in contrast with χρησμοί or oracles in verse; but it may be seen in Aristophanes ("Knights," 999–1002), that the two expressions were synonyms: the distinction bears here only on the manner in which these oracles were spread among the people; ἐλέγοντο signifies: they were hawked about from mouth to mouth, without the intervention of the diviners (ἐλέγοντο in the plural, despite the neuter subject, because it is the idea of *diversity* that dominates, rather than an idea of *collectivity;* cf. Curtius "Gr. gr.," § 363, Rem. 1); ᾖδον is the appropriate word in speaking of χρησμολόγοι or oracle-deliverers whose business was to *recite* the prophecies in verse."

the second πολλά is probably not to be resolved into πολλοὺς χρησμούς,[26] the χρησμούς being derived from the χρησμῳλόγοι, but is to have λόγια supplied with it from the preceding clause, the assumed distinction between λόγια and χρησμοί goes up at once in smoke. Λόγια alone are spoken of: and these λόγια are said to be both spoken and sung.[27]

So easy and frequent is the interchange between the two terms that it seems difficult to allow even the more wary attempts of modern commentators to discriminate between them. These ordinarily turn on the idea that λόγια is the more general and χρησμός the more specific word, and go back to the careful study of the Baron de Locella,[28] in his comment on a passage in (the later) Xenophon's "Ephesiaca." Locella's note does indeed practically cover the ground. He begins by noting the interchange of the two words in the text before him. Then he offers the definition that *oraculorum responsa* are generically λόγια, whether in prose or verse, adducing the λόγια παλαιά of Eurip., "Heracl.," 406, and the λόγιον πυθόχρηστον of Plutarch, "Thes.," i. 55, as instances of λόγια undoubtedly couched in verse; while versified oracles,

---

[26] So still Franz Müller in his handy edition of this second book (Paderborn, 1886).

[27] So Steup-Classen in the fourth edition of Classen's "Second Book of Thucydides," brought out by Steup (Berlin, 1889). They say: "ἐλέγοντο : the unusual plural doubtless on account of the variety and diffusion of the λόγια : cf. 5, 26, 2; 6, 62, 4. Λόγια, according to the usage of the anaphora, is to be understood with πολλά in both instances (B. supposes the anaphora would require the prepositing of the noun, as I. 3; but there νεότης is emphasized by καί, which is not the case here with λόγια). Ἐλέγοντο : circulated by the mouth of the people, without fixed or metrical form, which would be given them or preserved for them by the χρησμολόγοι who were occupied professionally in the collection (hence — λόγοι) and interpretation of transmitted prophecies (cf. Herod. 7, 6, 142; Schömann, *Gr. Alt.*, 2³, 304). The distinction is between ἐλέγοντο and ᾖδον, not the object of the λόγια."

[28] Pp. 152, 153 of his edition of the piece (Vienna, 1796). It is reprinted entire in Peerlkamp's edition (Haarlem, 1818) with this addition by the later editor: "λόγια Latinis interdum *dictiones, dicta, sermones,* et *logia;* cf. Heins. ad *Ovid*, Her. v. 33 et Observ. Misc. V. I. T. I., p. 276. *Apollodorus* in Biblioth. saepe permutat λόγια et χρησμούς, qui quum scribit I, vi. § 1, τοῖς δὲ θεοῖς λόγιον ἦν mireris interpretem reddentem *rumor erat inter deos.* De discrimine λόγια inter et χρησμούς eadem jam ex *Aristophane* ejusque Schol. notarat *Tresling.* Adv. pag. 46, 47, addens *L. Bos* ad Rom. iii. 2 et *Alberti* Obs. Phil. pag. 298 *seq.*"

originally in hexameters and later in iambic trimeters are,
specifically, χρησμοί — whence χρησμῳδέω is *vaticinor*, χρησμῳδία, *vaticinium*, and χρησμῳδός, *vates*. As thus the difference
between the two words is that of genus and species, they
may be used promiscuously for the same oracle. It is worth
the trouble, he then remarks, to inspect how often λόγιον and
χρησμός are interchanged in the "Knights" of Aristophanes
between verses 109 and 1224, from which the error of the
scholiast on Thucydides, ii. 8, is clear and of Suidas following
him, in making λόγιον specifically an oracle in prose, and χρησμός one in verse. He then quotes Eustathius on the "Iliad,"
ii. ver. 233, and on the "Odyssey," i. ver. 1426; adduces the
gloss, λόγιον, ὁ χρησμός; and asks his readers to note what
Stephens adduces from Camerarius against this distinction.[29]
The continued designation by Greek writers of the prose
Pythian oracles as χρησμοί is adverted to, Plutarch's testimony being dwelt on: and relevant scholia on Aristophanes'
"Av"., 960, and "Nub.," 144, are referred to. It is not strange
that Locella's finding, based on so exhaustive a survey of the
relevant facts, should have dominated later commentators,
who differ from it ordinarily more by way of slight modification than of any real revision — suggesting that λόγια,
being the more general word, is somewhat less sacred;[30] or
somewhat less precise;[31] or somewhat less ancient.[32] The
common difficulty with all these efforts to distinguish the
two words is that there is no usage to sustain them. When
the two words occur together it is not in contrast but in

[29] Stephens (ed. Dindorf-Hase) merely adduces Camerarius' testimony: "So
Cam., adding that the discrimination of the grammarians is a false one, although
the passage in Thucydides, i (*sic.*) [8] seems to agree with it."

[30] This seems to be what Haack (on Thucyd., ii. 8) means when he defines
λόγια as *auguria, præsagia vatum*, and χρησμοί as *oracula deorum*.

[31] This seems the gist of Bredow's view (on Thucyd., ii. 8): "χρησμός cum
verbis χρᾶν et χρεῖσθαι oraculorum propriis cohaerens definite oraculum divinum
vocatur; λόγιον autem aperte generalius vocabulorum est, sermo ominosus,
verbum faticidium quod non interrogatus vel deus, vel vates elocutus est." Poppo
and Gœller *ad loc.* quote these views but add nothing of value to them.

[32] Bouché-Leclercq seems almost inclined to revert to Eustathius' statement
and look upon λόγιον as "an expression peculiar to the Attic dialect, as πρόφαντα
(Herod., v. 63; ix. 93) is an Ionic expression" (*op. cit.*, ii. 130, note 4).

apparently complete equivalence, and when λόγιον appears apart from χρησμός it is in a sense which seems in no way to be distinguishable from it. The only qualification to which this statement seems liable, arises from a faintly-felt suspicion that, in accordance with their etymological implications already suggested, χρησμός has a tendency to appear when the mind of the speaker is more upon the source of the "oracle" and λόγιον when his mind is more upon its substance.

Even in such a rare passage as Eurip., "Heracl.," 406, where the two words occur in quasi-contrast, we find no further ground for an intelligible distinction between them:

> "Yet all my preparations well are laid:
> Athens is all in arms, the victims ready
> Stand for the gods for whom they must be slain.
> By seers the city is filled with sacrifice
> For the foes' rout and saving of the state.
> All prophecy-chanters have I caused to meet,
> Into old public oracles have searched,
> And secret, for salvation of this land.[33]
> And mid their manifest diversities,
> In one thing glares the sense of all the same —
> They bid me to Demeter's daughter slay,
> A maiden of a high-born father sprung." [34]

And ordinarily they display an interchangeability which seems almost studied, it is so complete and, as it were, iterant. Certainly, at all events, it is good advice to follow, to go to Aristophanes' "Knights" to learn their usage. In that biting play Demos — the Athenian people — is pictured as "a Sibyllianizing old man" with whom Cleon curries favor by plying him with oracles,

ᾄδει δὲ χρησμούς· ὁ δὲ γέρων σιβυλλιᾷ.[35]

---

[33] χρησμῶν δ' ἀοιδοὺς πάντας εἰς ἓν ἁλίσας | ἤλεγξα καὶ βέβηλα καὶ κεκρυμμένα λόγια παλαιὰ τῇ δὲ γῇ σωτήρια.

[34] Way's translation, 398 seq.

[35] Line 61. Blaydes says: "sensus est, senes enim oracula amat."

Nicias steals τοὺς χρησμούς from Cleon, and brings τὸν ἱερὸν χρησμόν to Demosthenes, who immediately on reading it exclaims, ὦ λόγια ![36] "DEM.: Ὦ λόγια. Give me quick the cup! NIC.: Behold, what says the χρησμός? DEM.: Pour on! NIC.: Is it so stated in the λογίοις? DEM.: O Bacis!" To cap the climax, the scholiast remarks on ὦ λόγια: "(μαντεύματα): he wonders when he reads τὸν χρησμόν." Only a little later,[37] Demosthenes is counseling the Sausage Vender not to "slight what the gods by τοῖς λογίοισι have given" him and receives the answer: "What then says ὁ χρησμός?" and after the contents of it are explained the declaration, "I am flattered by τὰ λόγια." As the dénouement approaches, Cleon and the Sausage Vender plead that their oracles may at least be heard (lines 960–961: οἱ χρησμοί). They are brought, and this absurd scene is the result: "CLEON: Behold, look here — and yet I've not got all. S. V.: Ah, me! I burst — 'and yet I've not got all!' DEM.: What are these? CLEON: Oracles (λόγια). DEM.: All! CLEON: Do you wonder? By Jupiter, I've still a chestful left. S. V.: And I an upper with two dwelling rooms. DEM.: Come, let us see whose oracles (οἱ χρησμοί) are these? CLEON: Mine are of Bacis. DEM.: Whose are thine? S. V.: Of Glamis, his elder brother." And when they are read they are all alike in heroic measure.

It is not in Aristophanes alone, however, that this equivalence meets us: the easy interchange of the two words is, we may say, constant throughout Greek literature. Thus, for example, in the "Corinthiaca" of Pausanias (ii. 20, 10) an oracle is introduced as τὸ λόγιον, and commented on as ὁ χρησμός.[38] In Diodorus Siculus, ii. 14,[39] Semiramis is said to have gone

---

[36] Line 120. Wheelwright's translation is used throughout.      [37] Line 194.

[38] πρότερον δὲ ἔτι τὸν ἀγῶνα τοῦτον προεσήμηνεν ἡ Πυθία, καὶ τὸ λόγιον εἴτε ἄλλως εἴτε καὶ ὡς συνεὶς ἐδήλωσεν Ἡρόδοτος·

'Αλλ' ὅταν ἡ θήλεια τὸν ἄρρενα νικήσασα
ἐξελάσῃ καὶ κῦδος ἐν 'Αργείοισιν ἄρηται
πολλὰς 'Αργείων ἀμφιδρυφέας τότε θήσει.

Τὰ μὲν ἐς τὸ ἔργον τῶν γυναικῶν ἔχοντα τοῦ χρησμοῦ ταῦτα ἦν. In. v. 3, 1; iv. 9, 4; ix. 37, 4 in like manner χρησμός is identified with μάντευμα.

[39] Bekker, i. 150.

to Ammon χρησομένη τῷ θεῷ περὶ τῆς ἰδίας τελευτῆς, and, the narrative continues, λέγεται αὐτῇ γενέσθαι λόγιον. Similarly in Plutarch's "De Defectu Orac.," v.[40] we have the three terms τὸ χρηστηρίον, τὸ λόγιον and τὰ μαντεῖα ταῦτα equated: in "De Mul. Virt.," viii.[41] the λόγια are explained by what was ἐχρήσθη: in "Quæstiones Romanæ," xxi.[42] λόγια came by way of a χρησμῳδεῖν. In the "Ephesiaca" of the later Xenophon metrical μαντεύματα are received, the recipients of which are in doubt what τὰ τοῦ θεοῦ λόγια can mean, until, on consideration, they discover a likely interpretation for the χρησμόν that seems to meet the wish of the God who ἐμαντεύσατο.[43]

How little anything can be derived from the separate use of λόγιον to throw doubt on its equivalence with χρησμός as thus exhibited, may be observed from the following instances of its usage, gathered together somewhat at random: [44]

Herodotus, i. 64: "He purified the island of Delos, according to the injunctions of an oracle (ἐκ τῶν λογίων)"; i. 120: "We have found even oracles sometimes fulfilled in unimportant ways (τῶν λογίων ἔνια)"; iv. 178: "Here in this lake is an island called Phla, which it is said the Lacedæmonians were to have colonized according to an oracle (τὴν νῆσον Λακεδαιμονίοισί φασι λόγιον εἶναι κτίσαι)"; viii. 60: "Where an oracle has said that we are to overcome our enemies (καὶ λόγιόν ἐστι τῶν ἐχθρῶν κατύπερθε)"; viii. 62: "which the prophecies declare we are to colonize (τὰ λόγια λέγει)." Aristophanes, "Vesp.," 799: ὅρα τὸ χρῆμα, τὰ λόγι' ὡς περαίνεται; "Knights," 1050, ταυτὶ τελεῖσθαι τὰ λόγι' ἤδη μοι δοκεῖ. Polybius, viii. 30, 6: "For the eastern quarter of Tarentum is full of monuments, because those who die there are to this day all buried within the walls, in obedience to an ancient oracle (κατά τι λόγιον ἀρχαῖον)." Diodorus Siculus ap. Geog. Sync., p. 194 D ("Corpus Scriptorum Historiæ Byzantinæ," i. 366), "Fabius says an oracle came to Æneas (Αἰνείᾳ γενέσθαι λόγιον), that a quadruped should direct him

[40] ii. 412 D.
[41] ii. 247 D. ἀποπειρώμενοι τῶν λογίων. Ἐχρήσθη γὰρ αὐτοῖς· . . .
[42] ii. 268 E. ἀποφθέγγεσθαι λόγια, καὶ χρησμῳδεῖν τοῖς ἐρωτῶσιν· . . .
[43] i. 6.
[44] The word, as will be seen, is as old as Herodotus: on the other hand — if we may trust the indices — it does not seem to occur in Homer (Dunbar's "Concordance" [to Odyssey], Gehring's "Index"), Hesiod (Paulsen's "Index"), Plato (Ast's "Lexicon") or Aristotle, Xenophon or Sophocles.

to the founding of a city." Ælian, "Var. Hist.," ii. 41: "Moreover Mycerinus the Egyptian, when there was brought to him the prophecy from Budo (τὸ ἐκ Βούτης μαντεῖον), predicting a short life, and he wished to escape the oracle (τὸ λόγιον) . . ." Arrian, "Expedit. Alex.," ii. 3, 14 (Ellendt., i. 151): ὡς τοῦ λογίου τοῦ ἐπὶ τῇ λύσει τοῦ δεσμοῦ ξυμβεβηκότος; vii. 16, 7 (Ellendt., ii. 419), "But when Alexander had crossed the river Tigris with his army, pushing on to Babylon, the wise men of the Chaldeans (Χαλδαίων οἱ λόγιοι) met him and separating him from his companions asked him to check the march to Babylon. For they had an oracle from their God Belus (λόγιον ἐκ τοῦ θεοῦ τοῦ Βήλου) that entrance into Babylon at that time would not be for his good. But he answered them with a verse (ἔπος) of the poet Euripides, which runs thus: 'The best μάντις is he whose conclusion is good.'" Plutarch, "Non posse suaviter vivi," etc., 24 (1103 F.): "What of that? (quoth Zeuxippus). Shall the present discourse be left imperfect and unfinished because of it? and feare we to alledge the oracle of the gods (τὸ λόγιον πρὸς Ἐπίκουρον λέγοντες) when we dispute against the Epicureans? No (quoth I againe) in any wise, for according to the sentence of Empedocles, 'A good tale twice a man may tell, and heare it told as oft full well';" "Life of Theseus," § 26 (p. 12 C, Didot, p. 14), "He applied to himself a certain oracle of Apollo's (λόγιόν τι πυθόχρηστον)" § 27 (p. 12 E, Didot, p. 14): "At length Theseus, having sacrificed to Fear, according to the oracle (κατά τι λόγιον)"; "Life of Fabius," § 4 (Didot, p. 210), Ἐκινήθησαν δὲ τότε πολλαὶ καὶ τῶν ἀπορρήτων καὶ χρησίμων αὐτοῖς βίβλων, ἃς Σιβυλλείους καλοῦσι· καὶ λέγεται συνδραμεῖν ἔνια τῶν ἀποκειμένων ἐν αὐταῖς λογίων πρὸς τὰς τύχας καὶ τὰς πράξεις ἐκείνας. Pausanias, "Attica" [I. 44, 9] (taken unverified from Wetstein): θύσαντος Αἰακοῦ κατὰ δή τι λόγιον τῷ Πανελληνίῳ Διΐ. Polyænus, p. 37 (Wetstein) [I, 18]: ὁ θεὸς ἔχρησε — οἱ πολέμιοι τὸ λόγιον εἰδότες — τοῦ λογίου πεπληρωμένου; p. 347 [IV, 3, 27], ἦν δὲ λόγιον Ἀπόλλωνος. Aristeas, p. 119 (Wetstein): εὐχαριστῶ μὲν, ἄνδρες, ὑμῖν, τῷ δὲ ἀποστείλαντι μᾶλλον· μέγιστον δὲ τῷ θεῷ, οὗτινός ἐστι τὰ λόγια ταῦτα.

A survey of this somewhat miscellaneous collection of passages will certainly only strengthen the impression we derived from those in which λόγιον and χρησμός occur together — that in λόγιον we have a term expressive, in common usage at least, of the simple notion of a divine revelation, an oracle, and that independently of any accompanying implication of length or brevity, poetical or prose form, directness or indirectness of delivery. This is the meaning of λόγιον in the mass of profane Greek literature. As we have already suggested, the matter of the derivation of the word is of no great importance to our inquiry: [45] but we may be permitted to add that the usage seems distinctly favorable to the view that it is to be regarded rather as, in origin, the neuter of λόγιος used substantively, than the diminutive of λόγος. No implication of brevity seems to attach to the word in usage; and its exclusive application to "oracles" may perhaps be most easily explained on the supposition that it connotes fundamentally "a wise saying," and implies at all times something above the ordinary run of "words." [46]

II. It was with this fixed significance, therefore, that the word presented itself to the Jews of the later centuries before Christ, when the changed conditions were forcing them to give a clothing in Greek speech to their conceptions, derived from the revelation of the old covenant; and thus to prepare the way for the language of the new covenant. The oldest monument of Hellenistic Greek — the Septuagint Version of the Sacred Books, made probably in the century that stretched between 250 and 150 B.C. — is, however, peculiarly ill-adapted to witness to the Hellenistic usage of this word. As lay in the nature of the case, and, as we shall see later, was the actual fact, to these Jewish writers there were no "oracles" except what stood written in these sacred books themselves, and all that stood written in them were "oracles of God." In a translation of the books themselves, naturally this, the most significant Hellenistic application of the word

---

[45] See above, p. 336.

[46] Dr. Addison Alexander, with his usual clearness, posits the alternative admirably (on Acts vii. 38): "The Greek word (λόγια) has been variously explained as a diminutive of (λόγος) *word*, meaning a brief, condensed and frequent utterance; or as the neuter of an adjective (λόγιος) meaning rational, profound, wise, and as a substantive, a wise saying." It would seem difficult to rise from a survey of the classical usage without an impression that it justifies the latter derivation. This usage is stated with perfect accuracy by DeMoor ("Com. in Marckii Compend.," i. 13): τὸ λόγιον "when used substantively may be considered as more emphatic than τὸ ῥῆμα or even ὁ λόγος: for this term means with the Greeks not any kind of word, but specifically an *oracle*, a *divine response*."

"oracles," could find little place. And though the term might be employed within the sacred books to translate such a phrase as, say, "the word of God," in one form or another not infrequently met with in their pages, the way even here was clogged by the fact that the Hebrew words used in these phrases only imperfectly corresponded to the Greek word λόγιον, and were not very naturally represented by it. Though the ordinary Hebrew verb for "*saying*" — אָמַר [47] — to which etymologically certain high implications might be thought to be natural, had substantival derivatives, yet these were fairly effectually set aside by a term of lower origin — דָּבָר [48] — which absorbed very much the whole field of the conception "word." [49] The derivatives of מַאֲמָר, אֵמֶר, אִמְרָה, אֹמֶר–אָמַר — in accordance with their etymological impress of loftiness or authority, are relegated to poetic speech (except מַאֲמָר, which occurs only in Esther i. 15, ii. 20, ix. 32, and has the sense of *commandment*) and are used comparatively seldom. [50] Nevertheless, it was to one of these that the Septuagint translators fitted the word λόγιον. To דָּבָר they naturally consecrated the general terms λόγος, ῥῆμα, πρᾶγμα: while

[47] It occurs, according to the Brown-Gesenius "Lexicon," no less than 5287 times; according to Girdlestone ("Synonyms of the O. T.," ed. 2, p. 205), it "is generally rendered in the LXX. ἔπω and λέγω." There seems to be inherent in the word an undertone of loftiness or authoritativeness due possibly to its etymological implication of "prominence." Its derivations are accordingly mostly poetical words designating a lofty speech or authoritative speech.

[48] The verb, of doubtful origin, occurs according to Brown-Gesenius, 1142 times, and is generally rendered in the LXX. (Girdlestone, *loc. cit.*) λαλέω. The noun occurs 1439 times and is rendered "generally λόγος, sometimes ῥῆμα, and in 35 passages, πρᾶγμα."

[49] There is also the poetic word מָלַל and its derivative noun מִלָּה — a word "used in 30 passages, 19 of which are in Job and 7 in Daniel," and rendered in the LXX. λόγος and ῥῆμα (Girdlestone).

[50] אֹמֶר, "except in Josh. xxiv. 27 (E) used exclusively in poetry, 48 times, of which 22 are in Proverbs and 11 in Job" (Driver on Deut. xxxii. 1). אִמְרָה "only found in poetry (36 times, of which 19 are in Ps. cxix.)" (Driver on Deut. xxxii. 2). אֶמְרָה, Lam. ii. 17 only. מַאֲמָר, Esth. i. 15, ii. 20, ix. 32 only. On the general subject of their poetic usage see Green, "General Introduction to the O. T.: The Text," p. 19; Bleek, "Introduction to the O. T.," E. T., i. 98; Hävernick, "Einleitung," i. 172; Gesenius, "Geschichte der hebräischen Sprache," p. 22, and "Lehrgebäude," Register, p. 892; Vogel, "De Dialecto Poetica."

they adjusted λόγιον as well as might be to אִמְרָה, and left to one side meanwhile its classical synonyms [51] — except μαντεία and its cognates, which they assigned, chiefly, of course, in a bad sense, to the Hebrew קסם in the sense of "divination."

אִמְרָה is, to be sure, in no sense an exact synonym of λόγιον. It is simply a poetical word of high implications, prevailingly, though not exclusively, used of the "utterances" of God, and apparently felt by the Septuagint translators to bear in its bosom a special hint of the authoritativeness or awesomeness of the "word" it designates. It is used only some thirty-six times in the entire Old Testament (of which no less than nineteen are in Ps. cxix.), and designates the solemn words of men (Gen. iv. 23, cf. Isa. xxix. 4 bis., xxviii. 23, xxxii. 9; Ps. xvii. 6; Deut. xxxii. 2) as well as, more prevailingly, those of God. In adjusting λόγιον to it the instances of its application to human words are, of course, passed by and translated either by λόγος (Gen. iv. 23; Isa. xxix. 4 bis.; Isa. xxviii. 23, xxxii. 9), or ῥῆμα (Deut. xxxii. 2; Ps. xvii. 6). In a few other instances, although the term is applied to "words of God," it is translated by Greek words other than λόγιον (II Sam. xxii. 31, LXX. ῥῆμα, and its close parallel, Prov. xxx. 5, LXX. λόγοι, though in the other parallels, Ps. xii. 7, xviii. 31, the LXX. has λόγια; Ps. cxix. [41][52], 154, where the LXX. has λόγος; in Ps. cxxxviii. 2, the LXX. reads τὸ ἅγιόν σου, on which Bæthgen remarks, in loc., that "ἅγιον seems to be a corruption for λόγιον," which is read here by Aquila and the Quinta). In the remaining instances of its occurrences, however — and that is in the large majority of its occurrences — the word is uniformly rendered by λόγιον

---

[51] χρησμός, for example, which we have found the constant accompaniment of λόγιον in the classics and shall find always by its side in Philo, does not occur in the LXX. at all. The cognates χρηματίζω (Jer. xxxii. (25) 30, xxxiii. (26) 2, xxxvi. (29) 23, xxxvii. (30) 2, χρηματισμός (Prov. xxiv. 69 (xxxi. 1), II Macc. ii. 4), χρηματιστηρί (I Kgs. viii. 6), are, however, found, and in their high sense. It is somewhat overstrained for Delitzsch (on Heb. viii. 5, E. T., Vol. ii. 32) to say: "The Septuagint word for the deliverance of a divine oracle or injunction is χρηματίζειν (τοὺς λόγους) τινί or πρός τινα:" χρηματίζειν is found in this sense only in the LXX.

(Deut. xxxiii. 9; Ps. xii. 7 *bis.*, xviii. 31, cv. 19, cxix. 11, 38
[41],[52] 50, 58, 67, 76, 82, 103, 116, 123, 133, 140, 148, 158,
162, 170, 172, cxlvii. 15; Isa. v. 24). If there is a fringe of
usage of אִמְרָה thus standing outside of the use made of
λόγιον, there is, on the other side, a corresponding stretch-
ing of the use made of λόγιον beyond the range of אִמְרָה — to
cover a few passages judged by the translators of similar import. Thus it translates אֹמֶר in Num. xxiv. 4, 16; Ps. xviii.
15 [xix. 15], cvi. [cvii.] 11, and דָּבָר in Ps. cxviii. [cxix.] 25,
65, 107, 169, [cxlvii. 8]; Isa. xxviii. 13; and it represents
in a few passages λόγον, a variation from the Hebrew,
viz., Ps. cxviii. [cxix.]; Isa. xxx. 11, 27 *bis.* In twenty-five
instances of its thirty-nine occurrences, however, it is the
rendering of אִמְרָה.[53] It is also used twice in the Greek apocrypha (Wis. xvi. 11; Sir. xxxvi. 19 [16]), in quite the same
sense. In all the forty-one instances of its usage, it is needless
to say, it is employed in its native and only current sense, of
"oracle," a sacred utterance of the Divine Being, the only
apparent exception to this uniformity of usage (Ps. xviii. 15
[xix. 15]) being really no exception, but, in truth, significant
of the attitude of the translators to the text they were translating — as we shall see presently.

What led the LXX. translators to fix upon אִמְרָה as the
nearest Hebrew equivalent to λόγιον,[54] we have scanty material for judging. Certainly, in Psalm cxix, where the word
most frequently occurs, it is difficult to erect a distinction
between its implications and those of דָּבָר with which it
seems to be freely interchanged, but which the LXX. trans-

Jeremiah. A very rich body of illustrations for the New Testament usages (Luke
ii. 26, Acts x. 22, Heb. viii. 5) might, however, be culled from Philo.

[52] In some codd. but in the edd. we read, κατὰ τὸ ἔλεός σου.

[53] The passages are already enumerated just above.

[54] The other versions add nothing of importance. At Ps. cxix. 41 the אִמְרָה
rendered ἔλεος by LXX. is rendered λόγιον by Aq. and Th. In Ps. cxxxvii. (cxxxviii).
2 the אִמְרָה rendered by LXX. ἅγιον (though Bæthgen remarks that this seems
merely a corruption of λόγιον) is rendered λόγιον by Aq. and Quinta. In Isa. xxxii. 9,
the אִמְרָה rendered in LXX. by λόγοι is given as λόγιον by Aq., a case quite parallel
with Ps. xviii. 15 (xix. 15) in LXX. In Jer. viii. 9 the phrase בִּדְבַר־יְהֹוָה is rendered in Aq. by λόγιον.

lators keep reasonably distinct from it by rendering it prevailingly by λόγος,[55] while equally prevailingly reserving
λόγιον for אִמְרָה.[56] Perhaps the reader may faintly feel even
in this Psalm, that אִמְרָה was to the writer the more sacred
and solemn word, and was used, in his rhetorical variation of
his terms, especially whenever the sense of the awesomeness
of God's words or the unity of the whole revelation of God [57]
more prominently occupied his mind; and this impression is
slightly increased, perhaps, in the case of the interchange of
λόγιον and λόγος in the Greek translation. When we look beyond this Psalm we certainly feel that something more requires to be said of אִמְרָה than merely that it is poetic.[58] It is
very seldom applied to human words and then only to the
most solemn forms of human speech — Gen. xxiv. 23 (LXX.,
λόγοι); Deut. xxxii. 2 (LXX., ῥῆμα); Ps. xxvii. (LXX., ῥῆμα);
cf. Isa. xxix. 4 *bis* (LXX., λόγοι) where the speaker is Jerusalem whose speech is compared to the murmuring of familiar
spirits or of the dead,[59] and Isa. xxviii. 23, xxxii. 9, where the
prophet's word is in question. It appears to suggest itself
naturally when God's word is to receive its highest praises

[55] The statistics of this Psalm are: אִמְרָה is used 19 times: being translated by
λόγιον 17 times, viz., at verses 11, 38, 50, 58, 67, 76, 82, 103, 115, 123, 133, 140,
148, 158, 162, 170, 172; at v. 41 it is translated τὸ ἔλεος, though some codices read
τὸν λόγον and some τὸ λόγιον; at v. 154 it is translated by λόγον. דָּבָר is used 23 times:
being translated by λόγος 15 times, viz., at verses 9, 16, 17, 28, 42, 43, 49, 74, 81,
89, 101, 130, 147, 160, 161; by λόγιον 4 times, viz., at verses 25, 65, 107, 109; by
ἐντολή twice, viz., at verses 57, 139; by νόμος at v. 105, and by λαός at v. 114 (though
some cod. read λόγοι or λόγος). Λόγιον is used 23 times: being the translation of אִמְרָה
17 times, viz., at verses 11, 38, 50, 58, 67, 76, 82, 103, 115, 123, 133, 140, 148, 158,
162, 170, 172; of דָּבָר 4 times (25, 65, 107, 169); of חֶסֶד once (124) and of משׁפט
once (149). Λόγος is used 17 times: being the translation of דָּבָר 15 times, viz.,
at verses 9, 16, 17, 28, 42, 43, 49, 74, 81, 89, 101, 130, 147, 160, 161 and of אִמְרָה
once (154, cf. 41), while once (42a) it is inserted without warrant from the Hebrew.

[56] Delitzsch on v. 9 *seq.*: "The old classic (e. g., xviii. 31), אִמְרָתֶךָ alternates
throughout with דְּבָרֶךָ; both are intended collectively." Perowne on v. 11: "WORD,
or rather 'saying,' 'speech,' distinct from the word employed, for instance, in v. 9.
Both words are constantly interchanged throughout the Psalm."

[57] Delitzsch on v. 145–152: "אִמְרָה is here as in verses 140, 158, the whole
Word of God, whether in its requirements or its promises."

[58] Driver on Deut. xxxii. 2: "Only found in poetry (36 times, of which 19 are
in Ps. 119); cf. Isa. xxviii. 23, xxxii. 9."

[59] On this passage cf. König, "Offenbarungsbegriff," ii. 149, 150.

(II Sam. xxii. 31; Ps. xii. 7, xviii. 31; Prov. xxx. 5; Ps. cxxxviii. 2), or when the word of Jehovah is conceived as power or adduced in a peculiarly solemn way (Ps. cxlvii. 18 [60]; Isa. v. 24). Perhaps the most significant passage is that in Psalm cv. 19, where the writer would appear to contrast man's word with God's word, using for the former דָּבָר (LXX., λόγος) and for the latter אִמְרָה (LXX., λόγιον): Joseph was tried by the word of the Lord until his own words came to pass.[61] Whatever implications of superior solemnity attached to the Hebrew word אִמְרָה, however, were not only preserved, but emphasized by the employment of the Greek term λόγιον to translate it — a term which was inapplicable, in the nature of the case, to human words, and designated whatever it was applied to as the utterance of God. We may see its lofty implications in the application given to it outside the usage of אִמְרָה — in Num. xxiv. 4, for example, where the very solemn description of Balaam's deliverances — "oracle of the hearer of the words of God" (אִמְרֵי־אֵל) — is rendered most naturally φησὶν ἀκούων λόγια ἰσχυροῦ. Here, one would say, we have the very essence of the word, as developed in its classical usage, applied to Biblical conceptions: and it is essentially this conception of the "unspeakable oracles of God" (Sir., xxxvi. 19, [16]) that is conveyed by the word in every instance of its occurrence.

An exception has been sometimes found, to be sure, in Ps. xviii. 15 (xix. 14), inasmuch as in this passage we have the words of the Psalmist designated as τὰ λόγια: "And the words (τὰ λόγια) of my mouth and the meditation of my heart shall be continually before thee for approval, O Lord, my help and my redeemer." In this passage, however — and

---

[60] "The God of Israel is the Almighty Governor of nature. It is He who sends His fiat (אִמְרָתוֹ after the manner of the וַיֹּאמֶר of the history of creation, cf. xxxiii. 9), earthward. . . . The word is His messenger (cf. in cvii. 20), etc." Delitzsch, *in loc.*

[61] It seems certainly inadequate to render אִמְרָה by "saying," as is very frequently done, e. g., by Dr. John DeWitt in his "Praise Songs of Israel" (we have only the first edition at hand), by Dr. Maclaren in the cxix. Psalm ("Expositor's Bible") and by Dr. Driver at Ps. cv. 19; cf. cxlvii. 15 *seq.* This English word suggests nothing of the lofty implications which seem to have attached to the Hebrew term.

in Isa. xxxii. 9 as rendered by Aquila, which is similar — we would seem to have not so much an exception to the usage of τὰ λόγια as otherwise known, as an extension of it. The translators have by no means used it here of the words of a human speaker, but of words deemed by them to be the words of God, and called τὰ λόγια just because considered the "tried words of God." This has always been perceived by the more careful expositors. Thus Philippi [62] writes:

"Psalm xix. 14 supplies only an apparent exception, since τὰ λόγια τοῦ στόματός μου there, as spoken through the Holy Spirit, may be regarded as at the same time, λόγια θεοῦ."

And Morrison: [63]

"In Psalm xix. 15 (14) the term thus occurs: 'let the words of my mouth (τὰ λόγια τοῦ στόματός μου = אִמְרֵי־פִּי, from אָמַר), and the meditation of my heart, be acceptable in thy sight, O Lord, my strength and my Redeemer.' But even here the term may be fitly regarded as having its otherwise invariable reference. The Septuagint translator looked upon the sacred writer as giving utterance in his Psalm — *the words of his mouth* — to diviner thoughts than his own, to the thoughts of God Himself. He regarded him as 'moved' in what he said, 'by the Holy Ghost.'" [64]

In a word, we have here an early instance of what proves to be the standing application of τὰ λόγια on Hellenistic lips — its application to the Scripture word as such, as the special word of God that had come to them. The only ground of surprise that can emerge with reference to its use here, therefore, is that in this instance it occurs within the limits of the Scriptures themselves: and this is only significant of the customary employment of the term in this application — for, we may well argue, it was only in sequence to such a customary employment of it that this usage could intrude itself thus, unobserved as it were, into the Biblical text itself.

[62] On Rom. iii. 2.
[63] On Rom. iii. 2 (pp. 14, 15).
[64] Possibly Bleek *in loc.* Heb. v. 12 means the same thing when he says the word stands here of "the inspired religious song of the poet."

It is scarcely necessary to do more than incidentally advert to the occasional occurrence of λόγιον = λογεῖον in the Septuagint narrative, as the rendering of the Hebrew חֹשֶׁן, that is, to designate the breastplate of the high priest, which he wore when he consulted Jehovah.[65] Bleek writes, to be sure, as follows:[66]

"How fully the notion of an utterance of God attended the word according to the usage of the Alexandrians too is shown by the circumstance that the LXX. employed it for the oracular breastplate of the High Priest (חֹשֶׁן), Ex. xxviii. 15, 22 seq., xxix. 5, xxxix. 8 seq.; Lev. viii. 8; Sir. xlv. 12, for which λογεῖον, although found in Codd. Vat. and Alex., is apparently a later reading; λόγιον, to which the Latin translation rationale goes back, has also Josephus, "Ant.," iii. 7, 5, for it: ἐσσήνης (חֹשֶׁן) μὲν καλεῖται, σημαίνει δὲ τοῦτο κατὰ τὴν Ἑλλήνων γλῶτταν λόγιον; c. 8, 9: ὅθεν Ἕλληνες . . . τὸν ἐσσήνην λόγιον καλοῦσιν; viii. 3, 8. And similarly apparently Philo, as may be inferred from his expositions, in that he brings it into connection with λόγος, reason, although with him too the reading varies between the two forms: see "Legg. Allegor.," iii. 40, p. 83, A. B.; § 43, p. 84, C. "Vit. Mos.," iii. 11, p. 670 C.; § 12, p. 672 B.; § 13, p. 673 A. "De Monarch.," ii. 5, p. 824 A."

It is much more probable, however, that we have here an itacistic confusion by the copyists, than an application by the Septuagint translators of λόγιον to a new meaning. This confusion may have had its influence on the readers of the LXX., and may have affected in some degree their usage of the word: but it can have no significance for the study of the use of the word by the LXX. itself.

III. Among the readers of the Septuagint it is naturally to Philo that we will turn with the highest expectations of light on the Hellenistic usage of the word: and we have already seen Bleek pointing out the influence upon him of the

[65] Ex. xxviii. 15, 22, 23, 24, 24, 26, xxix. 5, 5 A. R., xxxv. 27, xxxvi. 15, 16, 22, 24, 25, 27, 29, 29; Lev. viii. 8, 8; Sir. xlv. 10. Also in Aq.: Ex. xxv. 6 (7), xxviii. 4, xxxv. 9. In Sm.: Ex. xxviii. 4, 28. In Th.: Ex. xxv. 6 (7), xxviii. 4, 23, 23, xxviii. 24, 26, 28, xxxv. 9.

[66] Hebrews, pp. 115, 116, note.

LXX. use of λόγιον = λογεῖον. Whatever minor influence of this kind the usage of the Septuagint may have had on him, however, Philo's own general employment of the word carries on distinctly that of the profane authors. In him, too, the two words χρησμός and λόγιον appear as exact synonyms, interchanging repeatedly with each other, to express what is in the highest sense the word of God, an oracle from heaven. The only real distinction between his usage of these words and that of profane authors arises from the fact that to Philo nothing is an oracle from heaven, a direct word of God, except what he found within the sacred books of Israel.[67] And the only confusing element in his usage springs

---

[67] It is not intended to deny that Philo recognized a certain divine influence working beyond the limits of Scripture: but he does this without prejudice to his supreme regard for the Scriptures as the only proper oracles of God. At the opening of the tractate "Quod Omn. Prob. Lib." (§ 1, M. 444, 445), he gives expression in the most exalted terms to his appreciation of the value of Greek thought: the Pythagoreans are a most sacred brotherhood (ἱερώτατος θίασος) whose teachings are κάλα, and all men who have genuinely embraced philosophy (φιλοσοφίαν γνησίως ἠσπάσαντο) have found one of their λόγοι a θεσμὸν ἰσούμενον χρησμῷ. Elsewhere he speaks of Parmenides, Empedocles, Zeno and Cleanthes and their like as "divi homines" constituting a "sacer coetus" ("De Prov.," § 48), who did not cast their teachings in verse only because it was fitting that they should not be quite gods ("De Prov.," § 42). But even here the χρησμός is the standard to which their teaching is only likened: with all their wisdom they fall short of deity; and it is the utterance of deity alone which is "oracular" — and this utterance is discernible only in the Scriptures of the Jews. We venture to quote here the statements of Prof. James Drummond ("Philo Judæus," i. pp. 13 seq.): The Scriptures "were the 'oracles,' the 'sacred' or 'divine word,' whose inspiration extended to the most minute particulars. Philo distinguishes indeed different kinds of inspiration, but the distinction did not affect its divine authority. . . . Communion between God and man is among the permanent possibilities of our race; and Philo goes so far as to say that every good and wise man has the gift of prophecy, while it is impossible for the wicked man to become an interpreter of God ("Quis rer. div. heres." 52 [i. 510]). It is true that he is referring here primarily to the good men in the Scriptures, but he seems to regard them as representatives of a general law. He did not look upon himself as a stranger to this blessed influence, but sometimes 'a more solemn word' spoke from his own soul, and he ventured to write down what it said to him ("Cherubim," 9 [i. 143]). In one passage he fully records his experience ("Migrat. Abrah.," 7 [i. 441]). . . . Elsewhere he refers to the suggestions of the Spirit which was accustomed to commune with him unseen ("De Somniis," ii. 38 [i. 692]). . . . But he ascribed to the Biblical writers a fullness of this divine enthusiasm, and consequent infallibility of utterance, which he claimed for no others."

from the fact that the whole contents of the Jewish sacred
books are to him "oracles," the word of God; so that he has
no nomenclature by which the oracles recorded in the Scriptures may be distinguished from the oracles which the
Scriptures as such are. He has no higher words than λόγιον
and χρησμός by which to designate the words of God which
are recorded in the course of the Biblical narrative: he can
use no lower words than these to designate the several passages of Scripture he adduces, each one of which is to him a
direct word of God. Both of these uses of the words may be
illustrated from his writings almost without limit. A few instances will suffice.

In the following, the "oracle" is a "word of God" recorded in the Scriptures [68]:

"For he inquires whether the man is still coming hither, and the
sacred oracle answers (ἀποκρίνεται τὸ λόγιον), 'He is hidden among the
stuff' (I Sam. x. 22)" ("De Migrat. Abrah.," § 36, pp. 418 E). "For
after the wise man heard the oracle which being divinely given said
(θεσπισθέντος λογίου τοιούτου) 'Thy reward is exceeding great' (Gen. xv.
1), he inquired, saying. . . . And yet who would not have been amazed
at the dignity and greatness of him who delivered this oracle (τοῦ
χρησμῷ δούντος)?" ("Quis rer. div. her.," § 1, pp. 481 D). "And he
(God) mentions the ministrations and services by which Abraham displayed his love to his master in the last sentence of the divine oracle
given to his son (ἀκροτελεύτιον λογίου τοῦ χρησθέντος αὐτοῦ τῷ υἱεῖ) ("Quis
rer. div. her.," § 2, pp. 482 E). "To him (Abraham), then. being conscious of such a disposition, an oracular command suddenly comes
(θεσπίζεται λόγιον), which was never expected (Gen. xxii. 1) . . . and
without mentioning the oracular command (τὸ λόγιον) to anyone . . ."
("De Abrah.," § 32, P., p. 373 E). "[Moses] had appointed his
brother high-priest in accordance with the will of God that had been
declared unto him (κατὰ τὰ χρησθέντα λόγια") ("De Vita Moysis," iii.

[68] Yonge's translation (in Bohn's Ecclesiastical Library) is made use of in
these citations. The paging of Mangey is often given and sometimes that of the
Paris edition: but the edition of Richter is the one that has been actually used.
The shortcomings of Yonge's translation (cf. Edersheim's article, "Philo," in
Smith and Wace's "Dictionary of Christian Biography," iv. 367 A, note o), will
be evident to the reader; but when important for our purpose will be correctable
from the Greek clauses inserted.

**21**, P., p. 569 D). "Moses . . . being perplexed . . . besought God to decide the question and to announce his decision to him by an oracular command (χρησμῷ). And God listened to his entreaty and gave him an oracle (λόγιον θεσπίζει). . . . We must proceed to relate the oracular commands (λόγια χρησθέντα). He says . . . (Num. ix. 10)" ("De Vita Moysis," iii. 30, P., p. 687 D). "And Balaam replied, All that I have hitherto uttered have been oracles and words of God (λόγια καὶ χρησμοί), but what I am going to say are merely the suggestions of my own mind. . . . Why do you give counsel suggesting things contrary to the oracles of God (τοῖς χρησμοῖς) unless indeed that your counsels are more powerful than his decrees (λογίων)?" ("De Vita Moysis," i. 53, P., p. 647 D). "Was it not on this account that when Cain fancied he had offered up a blameless sacrifice an oracle (λόγιον) came to him? . . . And the oracle is as follows (τὸ δὲ λόγιόν ἐστι τοιόνδε) (Gen. iv. 7)" ("De Agricult.," § 29, M. i. 319). "And a proof of this may be found in the oracular answer given by God (τὸ θεσπισθὲν λόγιον) to the person who asked what name he had: 'I am that I am'" ("De Somniis," i. § 40, M. 1, 655). "But when he became improved and was about to have his name changed, he then became a man born of God (ἄνθρωπος θεοῦ) according to the oracle that was delivered to him (κατὰ τὸ χρησθὲν αὐτῷ λόγιον), 'I am thy God'" ("De Gigant.," § 14, M. 1, 271). "For which reason, a sacred injunction to the following purport (διὸ καὶ λόγιον ἐχρήσθη τῷ σοφῷ τοιόνδε) 'Go thou up to the Lord, thou and Aaron,' etc. (Gen. xxiv. i.). And the meaning of this injunction is as follows: 'Go thou up, O soul'" ("De Migrat. Abrah.," § 31, M. 1, 462). "For which account an oracle of the all-merciful God has been given (λόγιον τοῦ ἵλεω θεοῦ μεστὸν ἡμερότητος) full of gentleness, which shadows forth good hopes to those who love instruction in these times, 'I will never leave thee nor forsake thee' (Jos. i. 5)" ("De Confus. Ling.," § 32, M. i. 430). "Do you not recollect the case of the sooth-sayer Balaam? He is represented as hearing the oracles of God (λόγια θεοῦ) and as having received knowledge from the Most High, but what advantage did he reap from such hearing, and what good accrued to him from such knowledge?" ("De Mutat. Nominum," § 37). "There are then a countless number of things well worthy of being displayed and demonstrated; and among them one which was mentioned a little while ago; for the oracle (τὸ λόγιον) calls the person who was really his grandfather, the father of the practiser of virtue, and to him who was really his father it has not given any such title; for it says, 'I am the Lord God of Abraham, thy Father' (Gen. xxviii. 13), and in reality he was his grandfather, and, again, 'the God of Isaac,' not adding this time, 'thy Father' ('De Somniis,' i. § 27)." "And there is something closely resembling this in the passage of Scripture (*lit.* the oracle: τὸ χρησθὲν λόγιον) concerning the High Priest (Lev. xvi. 17)" ("De Somniis," ii. § 34).

On the other hand, in the following instances, the reference is distinctly to Scripture as such:

"And the following oracle given with respect to Enoch (τὸ χρησθὲν ἐπὶ 'Ενὼχ λόγιον) proves this: 'Enoch pleased God and he was not found' (Gen. v. 24)" ("De Mutat. Nom.," § 4).

It is a portion of the narrative Scriptures which is thus adduced.

"But let us stick to the subject before us and follow the Scripture (ἀκολουθήσαντες τῷ λογίῳ) and say that there is such a thing as wisdom existing, and that he who loves wisdom is wise" (*do*).

Here τὸ λόγιον is either Scripture in general, or, perhaps more probably, the passage previously under discussion and still in mind (Gen. v. 24).

"Μαρτυρεῖ δέ μοι λόγιον τὸ χρησθὲν ἐπὶ τοῦ 'Αβραάμ τόδε, 'He came into the place of which the Lord God had told him; and having looked up with his eyes, he saw the place afar off (Gen. xxii. 9)'" ("De Somniis," i. 11).

This narrative passage of Scripture is here cited as λόγιον τὸ χρησθέν.

"This is a boast of a great and magnanimous soul, to rise above all creation, and to overleap its boundaries and to cling to the great uncreated God above, according to his sacred commands (κατὰ τὰς ἱερὰς ὑψηγήσεις) in which we are expressly enjoined 'to cleave unto him' (Deut. xxx. 20). Therefore he in requital bestows himself as their inheritance upon those who do cleave unto him and who serve him without intermission; and the sacred Scripture (λόγιον) bears its testimony in behalf of these, when it says, 'The Lord himself is his inheritance' (Deut. x. 9)" ("De Congressu erud. grat.," § 24, p. 443).

Here the anarthrous λόγιον is probably to be understood of "a passage of Scripture" — viz., that about to be cited.

"Moreover she (Consideration) confirmed this opinion of hers by the sacred scriptures (χρησμοῖς), one of which ran in this form (ἑνὶ μὲν τοιῷδε — without verb) (Deut. iv. 4). . . . She also confirmed her statement by another passage in Scripture of the following purport (ἑτέρῳ τοιῷδε χρησμῷ) (Deut. xxx. 15) . . . and in another passage we read (καὶ ἐν ἑτέροις) (Deut. xxx. 20). And again this is what the Lord himself hath said . . . (Lev. x. 3) . . . as it is also said in the Psalms (Ps. cxiii. 25) . . . but Cain, that shameless man, that parricide, is nowhere spoken of in the Law (οὐδαμοῦ τῆς νομοθεσίας) as dying: but there is an oracle delivered respecting him in such words as these (ἀλλὰ καὶ λόγιον ἔστιν ἐπ' αὐτῷ χρησθὲν τοιοῦτον): 'The Lord God put a mark upon Cain' (Gen. iv. 15)" ("De Profug.," § 11, M. i. 555).

Here it is questionable whether "the Law" (ἡ νομοθεσία) is not broad enough to include all the passages mentioned — from Genesis, Leviticus and the Psalms — as it is elsewhere made to include Joshua ("De Migrat. Abrah.," § 32, M. i, 464. See Ryle: p. xix). At all events, whatever is in this νομοθεσία is a χρησθὲν λόγιον: the passage more particularly adduced being a narrative one.

"After the person who loves virtue seeks a goat by reason of his sins, but does not find one; for already as the sacred Scripture tells us (ὡς δηλοῖ τὸ λόγιον), 'It hath been burnt' (Lev. x. 16) . . . Accordingly the Scripture says (φησὶν οὖν ὁ χρησμός) that Moses 'sought and sought again,' a reason for repentance for his sins in mortal life . . . on which account it is said in the Scripture (διὸ λέγεται) (Lev. xvi. 20)" ("De Profug.," § 28, M. i. 569).

Here τὸ λόγιον seems to mean not so much a passage in Scripture as "Scripture" in the abstract: Lev. x. 16 not being previously quoted in this context. The same may be said of the reference of ὁ χρησμός in the next clause and of the simple λέγεται lower down — the interest of the passage turning on the entire equivalence of the three modes of adducing Scripture.

"This then is the beginning and preface of the prophecies of Moses under the influence of inspiration (τῆς κατ' ἐνθουσιασμὸν προφητείας Μωϋσέως). After this he prophesied (θεσπίζει) . . . about food . . . being full of inspiration (ἐπιθειάσας). . . . Some thinking, perhaps, that what was said to them was not an oracle (οὐ χρησμούς). . . . But the father established the oracle by his prophet (τὸ λόγιον τοῦ προφήτου). . . . He gave a second instance of his prophetical inspiration in the oracle (λόγιον, anarthrous) which he delivered about the seventh day" ("De Vit. Moysis," iii. 35 and 36).

"And the holy oracle that has been given (τὸ χρησθὲν λόγιον = 'the delivered oracle'; Ryle, 'the utterance of the oracle') will bear witness, which expressly says that he cried out loudly and betrayed clearly by his cries what he had suffered from the concrete evil, that is from the body" ("Quod det. pot. insid.," § 14, M. I., 200).

Here the narrative in Gen. iv, somewhat broadly taken, including vers. 8 and 10, is called τὸ χρησθὲν λόγιον.

"There is also something like this in the sacred scriptures where the account of the creation of the universe is given and it is expressed more distinctly (τὸ παραπλήσιον καὶ ἐν τοῖς περὶ τῆς τοῦ παντὸς γενέσεως χρησθεῖσι λογίοις περιέχεται σημειωδέστερον). For it is said to the wicked man, 'O thou man, that hast sinned; cease to sin' (Gen. iv. 7)" ("De Sobriet.," § 10, M. 1, 400).

Here there is a formal citation of a portion of Scripture, viz., the portion "concerning the creation of the universe," which means, probably, the Book of Genesis (see Ryle's "Philo and Holy Scripture," p. xx); and this is cited as made up of "declared oracles," ἐν τοῖς χρησθεῖσι λογίοις. The Book of Genesis is thus to Philo a body of χρησθέντα λόγια.

"And this is the meaning of the oracle recorded in Deuteronomy (παρ' ὃ καὶ λόγιον ἔστι τοιοῦτον ἀναγεγραμμένον ἐν Δευτερονομίῳ), 'Behold I have put before thy face life and death, good and evil'" ("Quod Deus Immut.," § 10, M. i. 280).

Here the "oracle" is a "written" thing; and it is written in a well-known book of oracles, viz., in "Deuteronomy," the second book of the Law. This book, and of course the others like it, consists of written oracles.

"And the words of scripture show this, in which (δηλοῖ δὲ τὸ λόγιον ἐν ᾧ) it is distinctly stated that 'they both of them went together, and came to the plain which God had mentioned to them (Gen. xxii. 3)" ("De Migrat. Abrah." § 30, M. i. 462).

"And for this reason the following scripture has been given to men (διὸ λόγιον ἐχρήσθη τοιόνδε), 'Return to the land of thy father and to thy family, and I will be with thee' (Gen. xxxi. 3)" ("De Migrat. Abrah.," § 6, M. i. 440).

Here, though the words are spoken in the person of God, the generalized use of them seems to point to their Scriptural expression as the main point.

"Moses chose to deliver each of the ten commandments (ἕκαστον θεσπίζειν τῶν δέκα λογίων) in such a form as if they were addressed not to many persons but to one" ("De. Decem Oracul.," περὶ τῶν Δέκα Λογίων, § 10).

"And the sacred scripture (λόγιον, anarthrous) bears its testimony in behalf of this assertion, when it says: 'The Lord himself is his inheritance' (Deut. x. 9)" ("De Congr. Erud. Grat.," § 24, M. i. 538).

"For there is a passage in the word of God (λόγιον γὰρ ἐστιν) that . . . (Lev. xxvi. 3)" ("De praem. et poen.," § 17, M. ii. 424).

Both classes of passages thus exist in Philo's text in the greatest abundance — no more those which speak of words of God recorded in Scripture as λόγια than those which speak of the words of Scripture as such as equally λόγια. Nor are we left to accord the two classes of passages for ourselves. Philo himself, in what we may call an even overstrained attempt at systematization, elaborately explains how he distinguishes the several kinds of matter which confront him in Scripture. The fullest statement is probably that in the "De Vita Moysis," iii, 23 (Mangey, ii, 163). Here he somewhat artificially separates three classes of "oracles," all having equal right to the name. It is worth while to transcribe enough of the passage to set its essential contents clearly before us. He is naturally in this place speaking directly of Moses — as indeed commonly in his tracts, which are confined, generally speaking, to an exposition of the Pentateuch: but his words will apply also to the rest of the "sacred books," which he uniformly treats as the oracles of God alike with the Pentateuch.[69] He writes:

[69] Cf. on this matter Edersheim in Smith and Wace's "Dictionary of Christian Biography," art. "Philo" (Vol. iv. pp. 386, 387): The only books "of which

"Having shown that Moses was a most excellent king and law-giver and high priest, I come in the last place to show that he was also the most illustrious of the prophets (προφητῶν). I am not unaware, then, that all the things that are written in the sacred books are oracles delivered by him (ὡς πάντα εἰσὶ χρησμοὶ ὅσα ἐν ταῖς ἱεραῖς βίβλοις ἀναγέγραπται χρησθέντες δι' αὐτοῦ): and I will set forth what more particularly concerns him, when I have first mentioned this one point, namely, that of the sacred oracles (τῶν λογίων) some are represented as delivered in the person of God by His interpreter, the divine prophet (ἐκ προσώπου τοῦ θεοῦ δι' ἑρμηνέως τοῦ θείου προφήτου), while others are put in the form of question and answer (ἐκ πεύσεως καὶ ἀποκρίσεως ἐθεσπίσθη), and others are delivered by Moses in his own character, as a divinely prompted lawgiver possessed by divine inspiration (ἐκ προσώπου Μωϋσέως ἐπιθειάσαντος καὶ ἐξ αὐτοῦ κατασχεθέντος).

"Therefore all the earliest [Gr. πρῶτα = the first of the three classes enumerated] oracles are manifestations of the whole of the divine virtues and especially of that merciful and boundless character by means of which He trains all men to virtue, and especially the race which is devoted to His service, to which He lays open the road leading to happiness. The second class have a sort of mixture and communication (μίξιν καὶ κοινωνίαν) in them, the prophet asking information on the subjects as to which he is in difficulty and God answering him and instructing him. The third sort are attributed to the lawgiver, God having given him a share in His prescient power by means of which he is enabled to foretell the future.

"Therefore we must for the present pass by the first; for they are too great to be adequately praised by any man, as indeed they could

it may with certainty be said that they are not referred to by Philo, are Esther and the Song of Solomon. The reference to Ecclesiastes is very doubtful, much more so than that to Daniel (p. 387 a)." Cf. also Ryle, "Philo and Holy Scripture," pp. 16–35: "It is abundantly clear that to Philo the Pentateuch was a Bible within a Bible, and that he only occasionally referred to other books, whose sanctity he acknowledged, as opportunity chanced to present itself" (p. 27). Cf. also Ewald, "History of Israel," E. T., vii. 204, 205: "Although he uses, and generally in the order in which they are now found in the Hebrew Canon, the other books much less gradatim than the Pentateuch, their authors are, nevertheless, considered by him as of equal holiness and divinity with Moses, and inasmuch as from his whole view and treatment of the Scriptures, he can attribute but little importance to their authors as authors, or to their names and temporal circumstances, he likes to call them all simply friends, or associates, or disciples of Moses, or prefers still more to quote the passage to which he refers simply as a sacred song, sacred word, etc." "It is only the books which we now find collected in the scarcely be panegyrized worthily by the heaven itself and the nature of the universe; and they are also uttered by the mouth, as it were, of an interpreter (καὶ ἄλλως λέγεται ὡσανεὶ δι' ἑρμηνέως). But (δὲ) interpretation and prophecy differ from one another. And concerning the second kind I will at once endeavor to explain the truth, connecting with them the third species also, in which the inspired character (ἐνθουσιῶδες) of the speaker is shown, according to which he is most especially and appropriately looked upon as a prophet." [70]

A somewhat different distribution of material — now from the point of view, not of mode of oracular delivery, but of nature of contents — is given at the opening of the tract "De præm. et poen." (§ 1, init.):

"We find then that in the sacred oracles delivered by the prophet Moses (τῶν διὰ τοῦ προφήτου Μωϋσέως λογίων) there are three separate characters: for a portion of them relates to the creation of the world, a portion is historical, and the third portion is legislative."

Hebrew Canon which he regarded as holy, and he was both sufficiently learned and careful not to rank all the others which were at that time gradually appended to the Greek Bible upon an equality with them." Cf. also Lee, "The Inspiration of Holy Scripture," pp. 69, 70.

[70] Compare Ewald, "The History of Israel," E. T., vii. 203, 204: "The sacred Scriptures are to Philo so immediately divine and holy, that he consistently finds in them simply the divine word rather than Scripture, and therefore really everywhere speaks less of the *Sacred Scriptures* than of divine oracles [χρησμοί, λόγια] of which they were wholly composed, or, when he desires to designate them briefly as a whole, of *the sacred* and *divine Word*, as if the same Logos, of whom he speaks so much elsewhere, were symbolized and incorporated in them for all time, as far as that is possible in a book [ὁ ἱερὸς, more rarely ὁ θεῖος λόγος, likewise ὁ ὀρθὸς λόγος (e. g., i. 308, 27; 681, 17; cf. esp., ii. 163, 44) is the expression which he constantly uses in this case; cf. esp. i. 676, 37 *seq.*; 677, 12]. It is true that in the case of the general subject matter, of the Pentateuch for instance, he makes a certain distinction, inasmuch as some of the oracles come to the prophet, as a mere interpreter directly as from the presence and voice of God alone, while others are revealed to him by God in answer to his interrogations, and again others have their origin in himself when in an inspired state of mind. But he makes this threefold distinction simply because he found it in reading particular passages of the Bible, and not with a view of further reflecting upon it and drawing references from it. On the contrary, he regards and treats all the sentences and words of the Scripture as on a perfect equality and teaches expressly that sacred Scripture must be interpreted and applied, as forming even to its smallest particles, one inseparable whole [cf. esp. "Auch.," ii. 170, 212 *seq.*; in other respects, cf. i. 554, 14, and many other passages of a similar character]."

Accordingly in the tract "De Legat. ad Caium," § 31 (Mangey, ii. 577), we are told of the high esteem the Jews put on their laws:

"For looking upon their laws as oracles directly given to them by God Himself (θεόχρηστα γὰρ λόγια τοὺς νόμους ἔιναι ὑπολαμβάνοντες) and having been instructed in this doctrine from their earliest infancy, they bear in their souls the images of the commandments contained in these laws as sacred."

By the side of this passage should be placed doubtless another from the "De Vita Contemplativa," §3, since it appears that we may still look on this tract as Philo's:

"And in every house there is a sacred shrine . . . Studying in that place the laws and sacred oracles of God enunciated by the holy prophets (νόμους καὶ λόγια δεσπισθέντα διὰ προφητῶν) and hymns and psalms and all kinds of other things by reason of which knowledge and piety are increased and brought to perfection."

It is not strange that out of such a view of Scripture Philo should adduce every part of it alike as a λόγιον. Sometimes, to be sure, his discrimination of its contents into classes shows itself in the formulæ of citation; and we should guard ourselves from being misled by this. Thus, for example, he occasionally quotes a λόγιον "from the mouth (or 'person') of God" — which does not mean that Scriptures other than these portions thus directly ascribed to God as speaking, are less oracular than these, but only that these are oracles of his first class — those that "are represented as delivered from the person of God (ἐκ προσώπου τοῦ θεοῦ) by his interpreter, the divine prophet." A single instance or two will suffice for examples:

"And the sacred oracle which is delivered as" [dele "as"] "from the mouth" [or "person"] "of the ruler of the universe (λόγιον ἐκ προσώπου θεσπισθὲν τοῦ τῶν ὅλων ἡγεμόνος) speaks of the proper name of God as never having been revealed to anyone [71] when God is repre-

[71] The translation here is unusually expanded: the Greek runs Δηλοῖ δὲ καὶ λ. ε. π. θ. τ. τ. δ. ἡ. περὶ τοῦ μεδενὶ δεδηλῶσθαι ὄνομά τι αὐτοῦ κύριον, κτλ.

sented as saying, 'For I have not shown them my name' (Gen. vi. 3)" ("De Mutat. Nom.," § 2). "And the oracles" (οἱ χρησμοί which is a standing term for 'the Scriptures' in Philo) "bear testimony, in which it is said to Abraham ἐκ προσώπου τοῦ θεοῦ (Gen. xvii. 1)" (ditto, § 5). "And he (Jeremiah the prophet) like a man very much under the influence of inspiration (ἅτε τὰ πολλὰ ἐνθουσιῶν) uttered an oracle in the character of God (χρησμόν τινα ἐξεῖπεν ἐκ προσώπου τοῦ θεοῦ) speaking in this manner to most peaceful virtue: 'Hast thou not called me as thy house' etc. (Jer. iii. 4)" ("De Cherub.," § 14, M. i. 148).

The other oracles, delivered not ἐκ προσώπου τοῦ θεοῦ but in dialogue or in the person of the prophet, are, however, no less oracular or authoritative. To Philo all that is in Scripture is oracular, every passage is a λόγιον, of whatever character or length; and the whole, as constituted of these oracles, is τὰ λόγια, or perhaps even τὸ λόγιον — the mass of logia or one continuous logion.

It is not said, be it observed, that Philo's sole mode of designating Scripture, or even his most customary mode, is as τὰ λόγια. As has already been stated, he used χρησμός equally freely with λόγιον for passages of Scripture, and οἱ χρησμοί apparently even more frequently than τὰ λόγια for the body of Scripture. Instances of the use of the two terms interchangeably in the same passage have already been incidentally given.[72] A very few passages will suffice to illustrate his constant use of χρησμός and οἱ χρησμοί separately.

In the following instances he adduces passages of Scripture, each as a χρησμός:

"On this account also the oracle (ὁ χρησμός) which bears testimony against the pretended simplicity of Cain says, 'You do not think as you say' (Gen. iv. 15)" ("Quod det. potiori insid.," § 45, M. i. 223). "And of the supreme authority of the living God, the sacred scripture is a true witness (ὁ χρησμὸς ἀληθὴς μάρτυς) which speaks thus (Lev. xxv. 23)" ("De Cherub.," § 31, M. i. 158). "For a man will come forth, says the word of God (φησὶν ὁ χρησμός) leading a host and warring furiously, etc. (Num. xxiv. 7)" ("De Praem. et Poen.," § 16, M. ii. 423). "And the sacred scripture bears witness to this fact

[72] "De Profug.," §§ 11 and 28; "De Vita Moysis," i. 53; iii. 23, 30, 35, 36.

(μαρτυρεῖ δὲ ὁ περὶ τούτων χρησμός): for it says (Num. xxiii. 19)" ("De Migrat. Abrah.," § 20, M. i. 454). "For though there was a sacred scripture (χρησμοῦ γὰρ ὄντος) that 'There should be no harlot among the daughters of the seer, Israel' (Deut. xxiii. 17)" ("De Migrat. Abrah.," § 39, M. i. 472). "And witness is borne to this assertion by the scripture (μάρτυς δὲ καὶ χρησμός) in which it is said: 'I will cause to live,' etc. (Deut. xxxii. 39)" ("De Somniis," ii. 44, M. i. 698). "The oracle (ὁ χρησμός) given to the all-wise Moses, in which these words are contained" ("Quod det. pot. insid.," § 34, M. i. 215). "Which also the oracle (ὁ χρησμός) said to Cain" (do., § 21). "And I know that this illustrious oracle was formerly delivered from the mouth of the prophet (στόματι δ' οἶδά ποτε προφητικῷ θεσπισθέντα διάπυρον τοιόνδε χρησμόν), 'Thy fruit,' etc., (Hos. xiv. 9)" ("De Mutat. Nom.," § 24, M. ii. 599). In this last case it is to be noticed that the "oracle" is taken from Hosea: the corresponding passage in "De Plant. Noe.," § 33, M. 1, 350, should be compared: "And with this assertion, this oracle delivered by one of the prophets is consistent, etc. (Hos. xiv. 9) (τούτῳ καὶ παρά τινι τῶν προφητῶν χρησθὲν συνᾴδει τόδε)."

Two other passages may be adduced for their inherent interest. The first from " De Profug.," §32 (M. i. 573), where we read:

"There are passages written in the sacred scriptures (οἱ ἀναγραφέντες χρησμοί) which give proof of these things. What they are we must now consider. Now in the very beginning of the history of the law there is a passage to the following effect (Gen. ii. 6) (αἴδεταί τις ἐν ἀρχῇ τῆς νομοθεσίας μετὰ τὴν κοσμοποιΐαν εὐθὺς τοιόσδε)."

Here there is a precise designation where, among " the written χρησμοί," a certain one (τις) of them may be found, viz., in the beginning of "The Legislation" immediately after "The Creation" (cf. Ryle, p. xxi, note 1). The other is from the first book of the " De Somniis," § 27 (M. i. 646):

"These things are not my myth, but an oracle (χρησμός) written on the sacred tables (ἐν ταῖς ἱεραῖς ἀναγεγραμμένος στήλαις), For it says (Gen. xlvi. 1)."

This passage in Genesis is thus an oracle "written in the sacred tablets" — and thus this phrase emerges as one of

Philo's names for the Scriptures. Elsewhere we read some-what more precisely:

"Now these are those men who have lived irreproachably and ad-mirably, whose virtues are durably and permanently recorded as on pillars in the sacred scriptures (ὧν τὰς ἀρετὰς ἐν ταῖς ἱερωτάταις ἐστηλι-τεῦσθαι γραφαῖς συμβέβηκεν)" ("De Abrah.," § 1, M. ii. 2). "There is also in another place the following sentence (γράμμα) deeply engraven (ἐστηλιτευμένον), (Deut. xxxii. 8)" ("De Congr. Erud. Grat.," § 12, M. i. 527).

The "Scriptures" thus bear to Philo a monumental charac-ter: they are a body of oracles written, and more — a body of oracles permanently engraved to be a lasting testimony forever.

The designations for Scripture in Philo are, indeed, some-what various — such as ἱεραὶ γραφαί ("Quis rerum div. heres," § 32 M. i. 495); ἱεραὶ βίβλοι ("Quod det. pot. insid.," § 44, M. i. 222); τοῖς ἱεροῖς γράμμασιν ("Legat. ad Caium.," § 29, M. ii. 574). But probably none are used so frequently as, on the one hand, λόγος, with various adjectival enhancements — such as ὁ προφητικὸς λόγος ("De Plantat. Noe," § 28, M. i. 437), ὁ θεῖος λόγος ("Legg. Alleg.," iii, § 3, M. i. 89; "De Mutat. Nom.," § 20; "De Somniis," i. 33, ii. 37), and ὁ ἱερὸς λόγος ("De Ebriet.," § 36, M. i. 379; "De Mut. Nom-inum," § 38; "De Somniis," i. 14, 22, 33, 35, 37, 39, 42; ii. 4, 9, 37, etc.); and especially, on the other hand, οἱ χρησμοί, occurring at times with extraordinary frequency.[73] Some passages illustrative of this last usage are the following:

"For the sacred Scriptures (οἱ χρησμοί) say that he entered into the darkness" ("De Mutat. Nom.," § 2). "But the sacred oracles (οἱ χρησμοί) are witnesses of that in which Abraham is addressed (the words being put in the mouth of God), (ἐν οἷς λέγεται τῷ 'Αβραὰμ ἐκ προσώπου τοῦ θεοῦ) (Gen. xvii. 1)" (do. § 5). "And these are not my

---

[73] Philo's designations of Scripture have been collected by Cl. Frees Horne-mann, in his "Observationes ad illustr. doctr. de Can. V. T. ex. Philone" (1775); more briefly by Eichhorn in his "Einl. in d. A. Test."; and in a not alto-gether complete or exact list by Ryle, "Philo and Holy Scripture."

words only but those of the most holy scriptures (χρησμῶν τῶν ἱερω
τάτων, —anarthrous to bring out the quality in contrast to ἐμὸς μῦθος),
in which certain persons are introduced as saying . . ." (do. § 28). Of
Isaiah xlviii. 22 it is said in do. § 31: λόγος γὰρ ὄντως καὶ χρησμός ἐστι
θεῖος. "Accordingly the holy scriptures (οἱ χρησμοί) tell us that . . ."
(do. § 36). "Therefore the sacred scriptures (οἱ χρησμοί) represent Leah
as hated" (do. § 44) "For she is represented by the sacred oracles (διὰ
τῶν χρησμῶν) as having left off all womanly ways (Gen. xviii. 12)"
("De Ebrietat.," § 14, M. i. 365). "On which account the holy scripture (οἱ χρησμοί) very beautifully represent it as 'a little city and yet
not a little one'" ("De Abrah.," § 31, M. ii. 25). "Therefore the
sacred scriptures (οἱ χρησμοί) say (Gen. xxiv. 1)" ("De Sobriet.," § 4,
M. i. 395). "According as the sacred scriptures (οἱ χρησμοί) testify, in
which it is said (Ex. viii. 1)" ("De Confus. Ling.," § 20, M. i. 419).
"On which account it is said in the sacred scriptures (ἐν χρησμοῖς)
(Deut. vii. 7)" ("De Migrat. Abrah.," § 11, M. i. 445). "God having
drawn up and confirmed the proposition, as the Scriptures (οἱ χρησμοί)
show, in which it is expressly stated that (Deut. xxx. 4)" ("De Confus.
Ling.," § 38, M. i. 435).

When we combine these passages with those in which
λόγιον occurs it will probably not seem too much to say that
the dominant method of conceiving the Bible in Philo's mind
was as a book of oracles. Whether he uses the word λόγιον or
χρησμός, it is, of course, all one to him. Indeed, that nothing
should be lacking he occasionally uses also other synonyms.
For example, here is an instance of the Homeric word θεοπρό
πιον cropping out: "For there is extant an oracle delivered to
the wise man in which it is said (Lev. xxvi. 12), (καὶ γάρ ἐστι
χρησθὲν τῷ σοφῷ θεοπρόπιον ἐν ᾧ λέγεται)" ("De Somniis," i,
§ 23). And this oracular conception of Scripture is doubtless
the reason why it is so frequently quoted in Philo by the subjectless φησί, λέγει, λέγεται (instead of, say, γέγραπται). There
are in general, speaking broadly, three ways in which one
fully accepting the divine origin and direct divine authority
of Scripture may habitually look upon it. He may think of
it as a library of volumes and then each volume is likely to
be spoken of by him as a γραφή and the whole, because the
collection of volumes, as αἱ γραφαί, or, when the idea of its

unity is prominently in mind, as itself ἡ γραφή. On the other hand, the sense of its composite character may be somewhat lost out of habitual thought, swallowed up in the idea of its divine unity, and then its several sentences or passages are apt to be thought and spoken of as each a γράμμα, and the whole, because made up of these sentences or passages, as τὰ γράμματα. Or, finally, the sense of the direct divine utterance of the whole to the soul, and of its immediate divine authority, may overshadow all else and the several sentences or passages of the book be each conceived as an unmediated divine word coming directly to the soul — and then each passage is likely to be called a λόγιον or χρησμός, and the whole volume, because the sum of these passages, τὰ λόγια or οἱ χρησμοί — or occasionally, when its unity is prominently in mind, one great τὸ λόγιον or ὁ χρησμός. Each of these three ways of looking at the Scriptures of the Old Testament finds expression in Philo,[74] in Josephus and in the New Testament. But it is the last that is most characteristic of the thought of Philo, and the first possibly of the writers of the New Testament: [75] while perhaps we may suspect that the intermediate

[74] As to γραφαί, see "Quis rerum div. heres," § 32 (Mangey, i. 495), παρ' ὃ καὶ ἐν ἱεραῖς γραφαῖς λέγεται; "De Abrah.," § 1 (M. ii. 2), "Now these are those men who have lived irreproachably . . . whose virtues are durably and permanently recorded as on pillars, ἐν ταῖς ἱερωτάταις γραφαῖς." As to γράμμα, γράμματα, see "De Congr. Erud. Grat.," § 12 (M. i. 527), Ἔστι δὲ καὶ ἑτέρωθι τὸ γράμμα τοῦτο ἐστηλιτευμένον (Deut. xxxii. 8)"; "Quod Deus Immut.," § 2 (M. i. 273), "For in the first book of Kings (= I Sam. i. 20), she (Hannah) speaks in this manner: 'I give him (Samuel) unto thee freely,' the expression here used being equivalent to 'I give him unto thee whom thou hast given unto me,' κατὰ τὸ ἱερώτατον Μωϋσέως γράμμα τοῦτο, 'My gifts and my offerings, and my firstfruits, ye shall observe to offer unto me'"; "Legat. ad Caium," § 29 (M. ii. 574), "You have never been trained in the knowledge of the sacred Scriptures (τοῖς ἱεροῖς γράμμασιν"; "De Vita M.," iii. 39; etc.

[75] In the New Testament γράμμα does not occur in the sense of a passage of Scripture — as indeed τὰ γράμματα occurs of Scripture only in II Tim. iii. 15, cf. John v. 47. The place of γράμμα in this sense is taken in the New Testament by γραφή, though it is extreme to say with Lightfoot on Gal. iii. 22 (cf. Westcott on John ii. 22) that γραφή, always in the New Testament refers to a particular passage. On the other hand this use of γραφή is far from peculiar to the New Testament as seems to be implied by Stephens ("Thes." sub. voc.). Not only does it occur familiarly in the Fathers, as e. g. (from Sophocles): Clems. Rom., ii. 2; Justin

one was most congenial to the thought of Josephus, who, as a man of affairs and letters rather than of religion, would naturally envisage the writings of the Old Testament rather as documents than as oracles.

From this survey we may be able to apprehend with some accuracy Philo's place in the development of the usage of the word λόγιον. He has received it directly from profane Greek as one of a series of synonyms — λόγιον, χρησμός, θεοπρόπιον, etc. — denoting a direct word from God, an "oracle." He has in no way modified its meaning except in so far as a heightening of its connotation was inseparable from the transference of it from the frivolous and ambiguous oracles of heathendom to the revelations of the God of Israel, a heightening which was, no doubt, aided by the constant use of the word in the Septuagint — Philo's Bible — to translate the Hebrew אָמְרָה with all its high suggestions. But in this transference he has nevertheless given it a wholly new significance, in so far as he has applied it to a fixed written revelation and thus impressed on it entirely new implications. In his hands, λόγιον becomes, by this means, a synonym of γράμμα, and imports "a passage of Scripture" — conceived, of course, as a direct oracle from God. And the plural becomes a synonym of τὰ γράμματα, αἱ γραφαί, οἱ βίβλοι, ὁ λόγος — or whatever other terms are used to express the idea of "the Holy Scriptures" — and imports what we call "the Bible," of course with the implication that this Bible is but a congeries of "oracles," or

Mart., "Advs. Tryph.," cc. 56, 65 (a very instructive case), 69, 71 (cf. Otto's note here) and elsewhere; Clems. Alex., "Cohort ad Gentes.," ix. ad init.: but also in Philo, as e. g., "De Praem. et Poen.," § 11 near the end (M. ii. 418): "Being continually devoted to the study of the Holy Scriptures both in their literal sense and also in the allegories figuratively contained in them (ἐν ταῖς ῥηταῖς γραφαῖς καὶ ἐν ταῖς ὑπόνοιαν ἀλληγορίαις)," and "Quis rerum div. her.," § 53 (M. i. 511): "And the historian connects with his preceding account what follows in consistency with it, saying . . . (τὸ δὲ ἀκόλουθον προσυφαίνει τῇ γραφῇ φάσκων)." Of course Philo sometimes uses ἡ γραφή in the non-technical sense also, of a human treatise: thus at the opening of "De Somniis" he refers to what was contained in the preceding treatise ἡ μὲν οὖν πρὸ ταύτης γραφὴ περιεῖχε). What is said in the text is not intended to traverse such facts as these, indicating other usages; but is meant only to suggest in a broad way what seems to be the primary distinction between the three usages; the subsequent development undergone by them is another story.

direct utterances of God, or even in its whole extent one great "oracle" or utterance of God — that it is, in a word, the pure and absolute "Word of God." But when we say that λόγιον is in Philo's hands the equivalent of "a passage of Scripture," we must guard against supposing that there is any implication of brevity attaching to it: its implication is that of direct divine utterance, not of brevity; and "the passage" in mind and designated by λόγιον may be of any length, conceived for the time and the purpose in hand as a unitary deliverance from God, up to the whole body of Scripture itself.[76] Similarly τὰ λόγια in Philo has not yet hardened into a simple synonym of "Scripture," but designates any body of the "oracles" of which the whole Scripture is composed — now the "ten commandments," now the Book of Genesis, now the Pentateuch, now the Jewish Law in general.[77]

There is little trace in Philo of the application made in the LXX. of λόγιον to the high priestly breastplate, by which it came to mean, not only the oracular deliverance, but the place or instrument of divination — though, quoting the LXX. as freely as he does, Philo could not help occasionally incorporating such a passage in his writings. We read, for example, in the "Legg. Allegor.," iii, § 40 (M. i. 111):

"At all events the Holy Scripture (ὁ ἱερὸς λόγος), being well aware how great is the power of the impetuosity of each passion, anger and appetite, puts a bridle in the mouth of each, having appointed reason (τὸν λόγον) as their charioteer and pilot. And first of all it speaks thus of anger, in the hope of pacifying and curing it, 'And you shall put manifestation and truth' [the Urim and Thummim] 'in the oracle of judgment (ἐπὶ τὸ λόγιον τῶν κρίσεων) and it shall be on the breast of Aaron, when he comes into the Holy Place before the Lord' (Ex.

---

[76] Thus of the passage cited above: in "Quod det. pot. insid.," § 14, the reference is to the narrative of Gen. iv; in "De Vita Moysis," iii. 35, to the whole legislation concerning food; in "De Profug.," § 28, and "De Mutat. Nom.," § 4, apparently to the whole Bible.

[77] "De Decem Oraculis," title and § 10; "De Sobrietate," § 10; "De Praem. et Poen.," § 1; "De Vita Moysis," iii. § 23; "De Legat. ad Caium," § 31; "De Vita Contemplativa," § 3.

xxviii. 30). Nor by the oracle (λόγιον) is here meant the organs of speech which exist in us. . . . For Moses here speaks not of a random, spurious oracle (λόγιον) but of the oracle of judgment, which is equivalent to saying a well-judged and carefully examined oracle."

Thus Philo gradually transmutes the λόγιον = λογεῖον of his text into the λόγιον = χρησμός of his exposition: and it is a little remarkable how little influence this LXX. usage has on his own use of the word. With him λόγιον is distinctively a passage of Scripture, and the congeries of these passages make τὰ λόγια.

That this usage is not, however, a *peculium* of Philo's merely, is evidenced by a striking passage from Josephus, in which it appears in full development. For example, we read:

"The Jews, by demolishing the tower of Antonia, had made their temple square, though they had it written in their sacred oracles (ἀναγεγραμμένον ἐν τοῖς λογίοις) that their city and sanctuary should be taken when their temple should become square. But what most stirred them up was an ambiguous oracle (χρησμός) that was found also in their sacred writings (ἐν τοῖς ἱεροῖς εὑρημένος γράμμασιν) that about that time one from their country should become ruler of the world. The Jews took this prediction to belong to themselves, and many wise men were thereby deceived in their judgment. Now this oracle (τὸ λόγιον) certainly denoted the rule of Vespasian" ("De Bello Jud.," vi. 5, 4).

In this short passage we have most of the characteristics of the Philonean usage repeated: here is the interchangeable usage of λόγιον and χρησμός, on the one hand, and of τὰ λόγια and τὰ γράμματα, on the other: the sacred writings of the Jews are made up of "oracles," so that each portion of them is a λόγιον and the whole τὰ λόγια. [78]

IV. That this employment of τὰ λόγια as a synonym of αἱ γραφαί was carried over from the Jewish writers to the early Fathers, Dr. Lightfoot has sufficiently shown in a brief but effective passage in his brilliant papers in reply to the

[78] Cf. the echo of Josephus' language in Tacitus, "Hist.," v. 13: "Pluribus persuasio inerat, *antiquis sacerdotum litteris* ( = ἐν τοῖς ἱεροῖς γράμμασι) contineri, eo ipso tempore fore ut valesceret Oriens profectique Judæa rerum potirentur. Quae *ambages* ( = χρησμὸς ἀμφίβολος = τὸ λόγιον) Vespasianum et Titum praedixerant."

author of "Supernatural Religion." [79] It is not necessary to go over the ground afresh which Dr. Lightfoot has covered. But, for the sake of a general completeness in the presentation of the history of the word, it may be proper to set down here some of the instances of its usage in this sense among the earlier Fathers. Clement of Rome, after having quoted examples from the Scriptures at length, sums up the lesson thus: "The humility, therefore, and the submissiveness of so many great men, who have thus obtained a good report, hath through obedience made better not only us, but also the generations which were before us, even them that received his oracles in fear and truth" (c. 19); again (c. 53), "For ye know, and know well the sacred Scriptures (τὰς ἱερὰς γραφάς), dearly beloved, and ye have searched into the oracles of God (τὰ λόγια τοῦ θεοῦ)"; and still again (c. 62), "And we have put you in mind of these things the more gladly, since we knew well that we were writing to men who are faithful and highly accounted and have diligently searched into the oracles of the teaching of God (τὰ λόγια τῆς παιδείας τοῦ θεοῦ)." The same phenomenon obviously meets us here as in Philo: and Harnack [80] and Lightfoot [81] both naturally comment to this effect on the middle instance — the former calling especially attention to the equation drawn between the two phrases for Scripture, and the latter to the fact, as shown by the Scriptures immediately adduced, that the mind of the writer in so designating Scripture was not on "any divine precept or prediction, but *the example of Moses*." Equally strikingly, we read in II Clem., xiii, "For the Gentiles when they hear from our mouth the oracles of God, marvel at them for their beauty and greatness. . . . . For when they hear from us that God saith, 'It is no thank unto you, if ye love them that love you, but this is thank unto you, if you love your enemies and them that hate you [Luke vi. 32]' — when they hear these things, I say, they marvel at their exceeding goodness."

[79] *The Contemporary Review*, August, 1875, p. 400; "Essays on the Work entitled Supernatural Religion" (1889), p. 173.
[80] *In loc.*                                    [81] *Loc. cit.*

"The point to be observed," says Lightfoot,[82] "is that the expression here refers to an *evangelical* record." Similarly Polycarp, c. vii, writes: "For every one 'who will not confess that Jesus Christ is come in the flesh is antichrist' (I John iv. 2, 3); and whosoever shall not confess the testimony of the cross is of the devil; and whosoever shall pervert the oracles of the Lord (τὰ λόγια τοῦ κυρίου) to his own lusts and say there is neither resurrection nor judgment, that man is the firstborn of Satan." On this passage Zahn, followed by Lightfoot, very appropriately adduces the parallel in the Preface to Irenæus' great work, "Against Heresies," where he complains of the Gnostics "falsifying the oracles of the Lord (τὰ λόγια Κυρίου), becoming bad exegetes of what is well said": while later ("Hær.," i. 8, 1) the same writer speaks of the Gnostics' art in adapting the dominical oracles (τὰ κυριακὰ λόγια) to their opinions, a phrase he equates with "the oracles of God," and uses in a context which shows that he has the whole complex of Scripture in mind. In precisely similar wise, Clement of Alexandria is found calling the Scriptures the "oracles of truth" ("Coh. ad Gent.," p. 84 ed. Potter), the "oracles of God" ("Quis Div. Sal.," 3) and the "inspired oracles" ("Strom.," i. 392); and Origen, "the oracles," "the oracles of God" "De Prin.," iv. 11; in Matt., x. § 6): and Basil, the "sacred oracles," "the oracles of the Spirit" ("Hom.," xi. 5; xii. 1). The Pseudo-Ignatius ("ad Smyr.," iii) writes: "For the oracles (τὰ λόγια) say: 'This Jesus who was taken up from you into heaven,' etc. [Acts i. 11]" — where the term certainly is just the equivalent of ἡ γραφή.[83] And Photius tells us ("Bibl.," 228) that the Scriptures recognized by Ephraem, Patriarch of Antioch (*circa* 525–545 A.D.), consisted of the Old Testament, the Dominical Oracles (τὰ κυριακὰ λόγια) and the Preaching of the Apostles" — where the adjective κυριακά is obviously intended to limit the broad τὰ λόγια, so that the phrase means just "the Gospels."

[82] *In loc.*
[83] Cf. what Prof. Ropes says of this passage in *The American Journal of Theology*, October, 1899 (iii. 698) and his strictures on Resch's use of it.

Dr. Lightfoot's object in bringing together such passages, it will be remembered, was to fix the sense of λόγια in the description which Eusebius gives of the work of Papias and in his quotations from Papias' remarks about the Gospels of Matthew and Mark. Papias' book, we are told by Eusebius ("H. E.," iii, 39), was entitled Λογίων κυριακῶν ἐξηγήσεις — that is, obviously, from the usage of the words, it was a commentary on the Gospels, or less likely, on the New Testament: and he is quoted as explaining that Matthew wrote τὰ λόγια in the Hebrew language and that Mark made no attempt to frame a σύνταξιν τῶν κυριακῶν λογίων,[84] or, as is explained in the previous clause, of τὰ ὑπὸ τοῦ Χριστοῦ ἢ λεχθέντα ἢ πραχθέντα — that is, as would seem again to be obvious, each wrote his section of the "Scriptures" in the manner described. The temptation to adjust these Papian phrases to current theories of the origin of the Gospels has proved too strong, however, to be withstood even by the demonstration of the more natural meaning of the words provided by Dr. Lightfoot's trenchant treatment: and we still hear of Papias' treatise on the "Discourses of the Lord," and of the "Book of Discourses" which Papias ascribes to Matthew and which may well be identified (we are told) with the "Collection of Sayings of Jesus," which criticism has unearthed as lying behind our present Gospels.[85] Indeed, as time has run on,

[84] Or λόγων, as is read by both Schwegler and Heinichen: contra Routh, Lightfoot and Gebhardt-Harnack.

[85] If there ever was such a "Collection of Sayings of Jesus," the natural title of it would certainly not be τὰ κυριακὰ λόγια, but something like the ἡ σύνταξις τῶν κυριακῶν λόγων which Papias says (if we adopt the reading λόγων) Mark did not write. We observe with astonishment, the venerable Prof. Godet saying, in his recent volume on the Gospels, that the existence of such collections of λόγια is now put beyond doubt by the discovery of the Oxyrhynchus fragment. The last word has doubtless not been said as to the nature and origin of this fragment: but that it was a collection of ΛΟΓΙΑ rests solely on the ascription of that title to it by its editors — a proceeding which in turn rests solely on their traditional misunderstanding of the Papian phrase. And that Matthew's "Logia" were "Logia" like these is scarcely a supposable case to a critic of Prof. Godet's views. Meanwhile we cannot but account it unfortunate that Messrs. Grenfell and Hunt should have attached so misleading a title to their valuable discovery: to which it is suitable only in one aspect, viz., as describing these "sayings" of Jesus as (in

there seems in some quarters even a growing disposition to neglect altogether the hard facts of usage marshaled by Dr. Lightfoot, and to give such rein to speculation as to the meaning of the term λόγια as employed by Papias, that the last end of the matter would appear to threaten to be worse than the first. We are led to use this language by a recent construction of Alfred Resch's, published in the "Theologische Studien" dedicated to Bernhard Weiss on his seventieth birthday. Let us, however, permit Resch to speak for himself. He is remarking on the identification of the assumed fundamental gospel (*Urevangelium*) with the work of Matthew mentioned by Papias. He says:

"Thus the name — λόγια — and the author — Matthew — seemed to be found for this *Quellenschrift*. In the way of this assumption there stood only the circumstance that the name 'λόγια' did not seem to fit the *Quellenschrift* as it had been drawn out by study of the Gospels, made wholly independently of the notice of Papias — since it yielded a treatise of mixed narrative and discourses. This circumstance led some to characterize the *Quellenschrift*, in correspondence with the name λόγια, as a mere collection of discourses; while others found in it a reason for sharply opposing the identification of the Logia of Matthew and the fundamental gospel (*Urevangelium*), or even for discrediting the whole notice of Papias as worthless and of no use to scholars. No one, however, thought of looking behind the λόγια for the hidden Hebrew name, although it was certainly obvious that a treatise written in Hebrew could not fail to have a Hebrew title. And I must myself confess that only in 1895, while the third volume of my 'Aussercanonischen Paralleltexte' was passing through the press, did it occur to me to ask after the Hebrew name of the λόγια. But with the question the answer was self-evidently at once given: הַדְּבָרִים,[86] therefore דִּבְרֵי יֵשׁוּעַ. To this answer attached itself at once, however, the reminiscence of titles ascribed in the Old Testament to a whole series of *Quellenschriften*: דִּבְרֵי שְׁמוּאֵל, דִּבְרֵי גָד הַחֹזֶה (הָרֹאֶה), דִּבְרֵי נָתָן הַנָּבִיא, דִּבְרֵי דָוִיד הַמֶּלֶךְ (cf. I Chron. xxix. 29); דִּבְרֵי שְׁלֹמֹה סֵפֶר (I Kings xi. 41); דִּבְרֵי מְנַשֶּׁה, דִּבְרֵי מַלְכֵי יִשְׂרָאֵל (II

the conception of the compiler, as the constant λέγει shows) "oracular utterances" of present and continuous authority.

[86] Why should Resch, we may ask, think of דבר instead of אמרה as the Hebrew original of λόγιον? Cf. above p. 353.

Chron. xxxiii. 18). As, then, there in the Old Testament, it is just historical *Quellenschriften* of biographical contents that bear the name of דְּבָרִים, so this New Testament *Quellenschrift*, the title דִּבְרֵי יֵשׁוּעַ. It contained therefore the history of Him of whom the prophets had prophesied, Who was greater than Solomon, David's Son and David's Lord and the King of Israel. And as the LXX. had translated the title דִּבְרֵי, certainly unskillfully enough by λόγοι, so Papias or his sponsor (*Gewährsmann*) by λόγια. The sense, however, of the Hebrew דְּבָרִים is, as Luther very correctly renders it — 'Histories.' Cf. Heft iii. 812. By this discovery of the original title, the New Testament *Quellenschrift* which from an unknown had already become a known thing, has now become from an unnamed a named thing. The desiderated *x* has been completely found." [87]

Criticism like this certainly scorns all facts. The Hebrew word דבר, meaning a "word," passed by a very readily understood process into the sense of "thing." In defining the term as used in the titles which Resch adduces, Dr. Driver says: [88] "*words:* hence *affairs, things* — in so far as they are done, 'acts'; in so far as they are narrated, 'history.'" The word דבר thus readily lent itself, in combinations like those adduced by Resch, to a double meaning: and it is apparently found in both these senses. In instances like דִּבְרֵי קֹהֶלֶת (Eccl. i. 1, cf. Prov. xxx. 1, xxxi. 5; Jer. i. 1; Am. i. 1; Neh. i. 1) it doubtless means "words of Koheleth," and the like. In the instances adduced by Resch, it is doubtless used in the secondary sense of "history." The Greek word λόγος, by which דבר was ordinarily translated in the LXX., while naturally not running through a development of meaning exactly parallel to that of דבר, yet oddly enough presented a fair Greek equivalent for both of these senses of דִּבְרֵי, used in titles: and why Resch should speak of λόγοι as unskillfully used in the titles he adduces, does not appear on the surface of things. Certainly, from Herodotus down, οἱ λόγοι bore the specific meaning of just "Histories," as afterwards it bore the sense of "prose writings": and the early Greek historians

[87] *Op. cit.*, p. 121 *seq.*
[88] "Introduction," last ed., 527, note 1.

were called accordingly οἱ λογογράφοι.[89] The LXX. translators, in a word, could scarcely have found a happier Greek rendering for the titles of the *Quellenschriften* enumerated in I Chron. xxix. 29, 30, etc. Who, however, could estimate the unskillfulness of translating דברי in such titles by λόγια — a word which had no such usage and indeed did not readily lend itself to an application to human "words?" Papias (or his sponsor) must have been (as Eusebius calls him) a man of mean capacity indeed, so to have garbled Matthew's Hebrew. It should be noted, further, that Papias does not declare, as Resch seems to think, that Matthew wrote τὰ λόγια τοῦ 'Ιησοῦ, or even τὰ κυριακὰ λόγια — it is Papias' own book whose title contains this phrase; and it will be hard to suppose that Papias (or his sponsor) was a man of such mean capacity as to fancy the simple τὰ λόγια a fair equivalent for the Hebrew דברי ישוע in the sense of "The History of Jesus." If he did so, one does not wonder that he has had to wait two thousand years for a reader to catch his meaning. Such speculations, in truth, serve no other good purpose than to exhibit how far a-sea one must drift who, leaving the moorings of actual usage, seeks an unnatural meaning for these phrases. Their obvious meaning is that Papias wrote an "Exposition of the Gospels," and that he speaks of Matthew's and Mark's books as themselves sections of those "Scriptures" which he was expounding. Under the guidance of the usage of the word, this would seem the only tenable opinion.[90]

It is not intended, of course, to imply that there is no trace among the Fathers of any other sense attaching to the

[89] See Liddell and Scott, *sub. voc.*, iv. and v.

[90] We must account it, then, as only another instance of that excess of caution which characterizes his application of the "apologetical" results of investigation, when Dr. Sanday still holds back from this conclusion and writes thus: "The word λόγια, indeed, means 'oracles' and not 'discourses.' But while the term 'the oracles' might well from the first have been applied to our Lord's words it is hardly likely that it should so early have been applied to a writing of the New Testament as such. Moreover, even when the inspiration of the New Testament had come to be as clearly recognized as that of the Old Testament, the term 'the oracles' would not have been a fitting one for a single work, simply on the ground that it formed part of the collection" (Hastings' "Bible Dictionary," ii. p. 235 a).

words τὸ λόγιον, τὰ λόγια, than "the Scriptures" as a whole. Other applications of the words were found standing side by side with this in Philo, and they are found also among the Fathers. Τὸ λόγιον, used of a specific text of Scripture, for example, is not uncommon in the Fathers. It is found, for instance, in Justin Martyr, "Apol.," i. 32: "And Jesse was his forefather κατὰ τὸ λόγιον" — to wit, Isa. xi. 1, just quoted. It is found in Clement of Alexandria ("Strom.," ii. Migne, i. 949a), where Isa. vii. 9 is quoted and it is added: "It was this λόγιον that Heraclitus of Ephesus paraphrased when he said . . . ." It is found repeatedly in Eusebius' "Ecclesiastical History," in which the Papian passages are preserved, as, e. g., ix. 7, ad fin., "So that, according to that divine (θεῖον) λόγιον," viz., Matt. xxiv. 24; x. 1, 4, "the λόγιον thus enjoining us," viz., Ps. xcvii. (xcviii.) 1; x. 4, 7, "concerning which a certain other divine λόγιον thus proclaims," viz., Ps. lxxxvi. (lxxxvii.) 3. Τὰ λόγια is also used in the Fathers, as in Philo, for any body of these Scriptural λόγια, however small or large (i. e., for any given section of Scripture) — as, e. g., for the Ten Commandments. It is so used, for instance, in the "Apostolical Constitutions," ii. 26: "Keep the fear of God before your eyes, always remembering τῶν δέκα τοῦ θεοῦ λογίων"; and also in Eusebius (H. E., ii. 18, 5). So, again, we have seen it, modified by qualifying adjectives, used for the Gospels — and indeed it seems to be employed without qualifications in this sense in Pseudo-Justin's "Epistola ad Zeram et Serenum" (Otto, i.

Apart altogether from the fact that these caveats are founded on a demonstrably mistaken conception of the origin of the New Testament Canon, they are in themselves invalid. The term λόγια was contemporaneously applied to writings of the New Testament as such — as a glance at II Clem. xiii. and Polycarp vii. will show — and as Lightfoot's note on the former passage, correcting his less careful earlier note on the latter passage, points out. And that τὰ λόγια could easily refer to any definite portion of the congeries of "oracles" known also as "Scripture," Philo's usage as indicated above (p. 374) sufficiently exhibits. For the rest, it cannot be doubted that Papias was understood by all his early readers to mean by his τὰ λόγια of Matthew, just Matthew's Gospel. This has been sufficiently shown ("Einleitung," ii. 265) by Zahn, who in his rich and fundamentally right remarks on the subject both here and elsewhere (e. g., pp. 254 seq. and "Geschichte d. Kanons," i. 857 seq., ii. 790 seq.) supplies another instance of how near a great scholar can come to the truth of a matter without precisely adopting it.

70*b*). It is further sometimes used apparently not of the Scripture text as such, but of certain oracular utterances recorded in it — as, for example, when Justin says to Trypho (c. 18): "For since you have read, O Trypho, as you yourself admitted, the doctrines taught by our Saviour, I do not think that I have done foolishly in adding some short utterances of his (βραχέα τοῦ ἐκείνου λόγια) to the prophetic statements" — to wit, words of Jesus recorded in Matt. xxi, xxiii and Luke xi, here put on a level with the oracles of the prophets, but apparently envisaged as spoken. All these are usages that have met us before.

But there are lower usages also discoverable in the later Patristic writers at least. There is an appearance now and then indeed as if the word was, in popular speech, losing something of its high implication of "solemn oracular utterances of God," and coming to be applied as well to the words of mere men [91] — possibly in sequence to its application to the words of prophets and apostles as such and the gradual wearing down, in the careless popular consciousness, of the distinction between their words as prophets and apostles and their words as men; possibly, on the other hand, in sequence to the freer use of the word in profane speech and the wearing away of its high import with the loss of reverence for the

[91] In the thirty-fifth chapter of the fourth book of Origen's "Against Celsus," there is a passage which is given this appearance in Dr. Crombie's excellent English translation, printed in the "Ante-Nicene Library" (Am. Ed., iv. 512): "And yet if Celsus had wished honestly to overturn the genealogy which he deemed the Jews to have so shamelessly arrogated, in boasting of Abraham and his descendants (as their progenitors), he ought to have quoted all the passages bearing on the subject; and, in the first place, to have advocated his cause with such arguments as he thought likely to be convincing, and in the next to have bravely refuted, by means of what appeared to him to be the true meaning, and by arguments in its favor, the errors existing on the subject (καὶ τοῖς ὑπὲρ αὐτῆς λογίοις τὰ κατὰ τὸν τόπον)." The rendering of λογίοις here by "arguments," however, is certainly wrong. The whole context is speaking of Celsus' misrepresentation of the teaching of the Hebrew Scriptures; and what Origen would have him do is to point out the *passages in them* which will bear out his allegations. According to Koetschau's index the word occurs but twice elsewhere in the treatise "Against Celsus," viz., V. xxix. *ad fin.*, and VI. lxxvii. near the end (inserted by Koetschau from Philoc. 85, 16): and in both of these cases the high meaning of the word is unmistakable.

thing designated. Thus we read as early as in the "Acts of Xanthippe and Polyxena," edited by Prof. James for the "Cambridge Texts and Studies," and assigned by him to the middle of the third century (c. 28, p. 78), the following dialogue, in the course of a conversation between Polyxena and Andrew, "the apostle of the Lord": "Andrew saith: 'Draw not near me, child, but tell me who thou art and whence.' Then saith Polyxena: 'I am a great friend of these here (ξένη τῶν ἐνταῦθα), but I see thy gracious countenance and thy logia are as the logia of Paul and I presume thee, too, to belong to his God.'" If we may assume this to mark a transition stage in the usage, we may look upon a curious passage in John of Damascus as marking almost the completion of the sinking of the word to an equivalence to ῥήματα. It occurs in his "Disput. Christiani et Saraceni" (Migne, i. 1588, iii. 1344). The Saracenic disputant is represented as eager to obtain an acknowledgment that the Word of God, that is Christ, is a mere creature, and as plying the Christian with a juggle on the word λόγια. He asks whether the λόγια of God are create or increate. If the reply is "create," the rejoinder is to be: "Then they are not gods, and you have confessed that Christ, who is the Word (λόγος) of God is not God." If, on the other hand, the reply is "increate," the rejoinder apparently is to be that the λόγια of God nevertheless are not properly gods, and so again Christ the λόγος is not God. Accordingly John instructs the Christian disputant to refuse to say either that they are create or that they are increate, but declining the dilemma, to reply merely: "I confess one only Λόγος of God that is increate, but my whole Scripture (γραφή) I do not call λόγια, but ῥήματα θεοῦ." On the Saracen retorting that David certainly says τὰ λόγια (not ῥήματα) of the Lord are pure λόγια, the Christian is to reply that the prophet speaks here τροπολογικῶς, and not κυριολογικῶς, that is to say, not by way of a direct declaration, but by way of an indirect characterization. It is a remarkable logomachy that we are thus treated to: and it seems to imply that in John's day λόγια had sunk to a mere synonym of ῥήματα.

That men had then ceased to speak of the whole γραφή as τὰ θεῖα λόγια we know not to have been the case: but apparently this language was now made use of with no more pregnancy of meaning than if they had said τὰ θεῖα ῥήματα.[92] This process seems to have continued, and in the following passage from a work of the opening of the eleventh century — the "Life of Nilus the Younger," published in the 120th volume of Migne's "Pat. Græc." (p. 97 D), — we have an instance of the extreme extension of the application of the word: "Then saith the Father to him: 'It is not fitting that thou, a man of wisdom and high-learning, should think or speak τὰ τῶν κοινῶν ἀνθρώπων λόγια.'"[93] And accordingly we cannot be surprised ιο find that in modern Greek the word is employed quite freely of human speech. Jannaris tells us that it is used in the sense of "maxim," and that in colloquial usage τὰ λόγια may mean "promise" — in both of which employments there may remain a trace of its original higher import.[94] While Kontopoulos gives as the English equivalents of λόγιον, the follow-

---

[92] Dr. F. W. Farrar, with his fatal facility for quoting phrases in senses far other than those attached to them by their authors (other instances meet us in his dealing with the formula "*Scriptura complectitur Verbum Dei*" and with the word "Inspiration" in the same context, — see pp. 369, 370 of work cited) makes a thoroughly wrong use of this passage ("Hist. of Interpretation," p. 374, note 2). He says: "But as far back as the eighth century the eminently orthodox Father, St. John of Damascus, had said, 'We apply not to the written word of Scripture the title due to the Incarnate Word of God.' He says that when the Scriptures are called λόγια θεοῦ the phrase is only figurative, 'Disput. Christiani et Saraceni' (see Lupton, St. John of Damascus, p. 95)." But John says the Scriptures *are* called without figure ῥήματα τοῦ θεοῦ: he only means to say they are not God's Word *in the same sense* that the Logos is: in comparison with Him who is the only incarnate Word of God, they are only figuratively words of God, but they are real words of God, nevertheless, His ῥήματα, by which designation, rather than λόγια, John would have them called, not to avoid confessing them to be God's utterances, but to escape a Moslem jibe.

[93] An instance of the secular use of the word in this lowered meaning, is found doubtless in the Scholium on the "Frogs" of Aristophanes adduced above, p. 336. The date of this Scholium is uncertain, but it seems to belong to the later strata of the Scholia. It is not found in the "Ravenna MS.," which Rutherford is publishing; nor in the "Venetus" (Marc. 474), cf. Blaydes, "Ranae," p. 391; nor indeed in four out of the six MSS. used by Dindorf (iv. 2, p. 113).

[94] In his "Concise Dictionary of English and Modern Greek," *sub. vocc.* "word" and "saying."

ing list: "A saying, a word; a maxim; a motto, an oracle; τὰ θεῖα λόγια, the divine oracles, the sacred Scriptures." [95]

Thus not only all the usages of the word found, say, in Philo, are continued in the Fathers, but there is an obvious development to be traced. But this development itself is founded on and is a witness to the characteristic usage of the word among the Fathers — that, to wit, in which it is applied to the inspired words of prophets and apostles. And by far the most frequent use of the word in the Patristic writings seems to be that in which it designates just the Holy Scriptures. Their prevailing usage is very well illustrated by that of Eusebius. We have already quoted a number of passages from his "Ecclesiastical History" in which he seems to adduce special passages of Scripture, each as a λόγιον. More common is it for him to refer to the whole Scriptures as τὰ λόγια, or rather (for this is his favorite formula) τὰ θεῖα λόγια — and that whether he means the Old Testament (which in the "Præp. Evang.," ii. 6 [Migne, iii. 140 A], he calls τὰ Ἑβραίων λόγια), or the New Testament, or refers to the prophetic or the narrative portions. Instances may be found in "H. E.," v., 17, 5, where we are told that Miltiades left monuments of his study of the θεῖα λόγια; vi. 23, 2, where the zeal of Origen's friend Ambrose for the study of the θεῖα λόγια is mentioned as enabling Origen to write his commentaries on the θεῖαι γραφαί; ix. 9, 8, where a sentence from Ex. xv. 1 is quoted as from the θεῖα λόγια; x. 4, 28, where Ps. lvii. (lviii.), 7 is quoted from the θεῖα λόγια; "Palestinian Martyrs," xi. 2, where the devotion of the Palestinian martyrs to the θεῖα λόγια is adverted to. Even the singular — τὸ λόγιον — seems occasionally used by Eusebius (as by Philo) as a designation of the whole Scripture fabric. We may suspect this to be the case in "H. E.," x. 4, 43, when we read of "the costly cedar of Lebanon of which τὸ θεῖον λόγιον has not been unmindful, saying, 'The forests of the Lord shall rejoice and the cedars of Lebanon which he planted' (Ps. cv. [civ.] 16)." And we cannot doubt it at "H. E.," ii. 10, 1, where we read concerning Herod Agrippa,

[95] In his "New Lexicon of Modern Greek and English," *sub voc.*

that "as ἡ τῶν πράξεων γραφή relates, he proceeded to Cæsarea and . . . . τὸ λόγιον relates 'that the angel of the Lord smote him'" — in which account it is worth while to observe the coincidence of Josephus' narrative with τὴν θείαν γραφήν. Here, of course, τὸ λόγιον is primarily the Book of Acts — but as the subsequent context shows, it represents that book only as part of the sacred Scriptures, so that τὸ λόγιον emerges as a complete synonym of ἡ θεία γραφή. Whatever other usage may from time to time emerge in the pages of the Fathers, the Patristic usage of the term, κατ᾽ ἐξοχήν, is as a designation of the "Scriptures" conceived as the Word of God.[96]

In the light of these broad facts of usage, certain lines may very reasonably be laid down within which our interpretation of [τὰ] λόγια in the New Testament instances of its occurrence should move. It would seem quite certain, for example, that no lower sense can be attached to it in these instances, than that which it bears uniformly in its classical and Hellenistic usage: it means, not "words" barely, simple "utterances," but distinctively "oracular utterances," divinely authoritative communications, before which men stand in awe and to which they bow in humility: and this high meaning is not merely implicit, but is explicit in the term. It would seem clear again that there are no implications of brevity in the term: it means not short, pithy, pregnant sayings, but high, authoritative, sacred utterances; and it may be applied equally well to long as to short utterances — even though they extend to pages and books and treatises. It would seem to be clear once more that there are no implications in the term of what may be called the literary nature of the utterances to which it is applied: it characterizes the utterances to which it is applied as emanations from God, but whether they be prophetic or narrative or legal, parenetic or promissory in character, is entirely indifferent: its whole

---

[96] Sophocles, in his "Lexicon," gives also the following references for this sense: Titus of Bostra (Migne, xviii. 1253 B); Serapion of Egypt (Migne, xl. 908 C, 909 B). References might be added, apparently, indefinitely.

function is exhausted in declaring them to be God's own utterances.[97] And still further, it would seem to be clear that it is equally indifferent to the term whether the utterances so designated be oral or written communications: whether oral or written it declares them to be God's own Word, and it had become customary to designate the written Word of God by this term as one that was felt fitly to describe the Scriptures as an oracular book — either a body of oracles, or one continuous oracular deliverance from God's own lips.

This last usage is so strikingly characteristic of the Hellenistic adaptation of the term that a certain presumption lies in favor of so understanding it in Hellenistic writings, when the Scriptural revelation is in question: though this presumption is, of course, liable to correction by the obvious implications of the passages as wholes. In such a passage as Rom. iii. 2 this presumption rises very high indeed, and it would seem as if the word here must be read as a designation of the "Scriptures" as such, unless very compelling reasons to the contrary may be adduced from the context. That the mind of the writer may seem to some to be particularly dwelling upon this or that element in the contents of the Scriptures cannot be taken as such a compelling reason to the contrary: for nothing is more common than for a writer to be thinking more particularly of one portion of what he is formally adducing as a whole. The paraphrase of Wetstein appears in this aspect, therefore, very judicious: "They have the Sacred Books, in which are contained the oracles and especially the prophecies of the advent of the Messiah and the calling of the Gentiles; and by these their minds should be prepared"; though, so far as this paraphrase may seem to separate between the Sacred Books and the Oracles they contain, it is unfortunate. The very point of this use of the word is that it *identifies* the Sacred Books with the Oracles;

[97] It is therefore a perfectly blind comment that we meet with in Gerhard Heine's recent " Synonymik des N. T. Griechisch " (1898), p. 157 — when in contrast to λόγος as the " reasonable expression " of the νοῦς, τὸ λόγιον is said to be "more the separate utterance, with the (occasional?) accessory notion of promise (Rom. iii. 2)."

and in this aspect of it Dr. David Brown's comment is more satisfactory: "That remarkable expression, denoting 'Divine Communications' in general, is transferred to the sacred Scriptures to express their oracular, divinely authoritative character." The case is not quite so simple in Heb. v. 12: but here, too, the well-balanced comment of Dr. Westcott appears to us to carry conviction with it: "The phrase might refer to the new revelation given by Christ to His apostles (comp. c. i. 2); but it seems more natural to refer it to the collective writings of the Old Testament which the Hebrew Christians failed to understand." In Acts vii. 38 the absence of the article introduces no real complication: it merely emphasizes the qualitative aspect of the matter; what Moses received was emphatically *oracles* — which is further enhanced by calling them "lively," i. e., they were not merely dead, but living, effective, operative oracles. The speaker's eye is obviously on Moses as the recipient of these oracles, and on the oracles as given by God to Moses, as is recorded in the Pentateuch: but the oracles his eye is on are those recorded in the Pentateuch, and that came to Moses, not for himself, but for the Church of all ages — "to give *to us*." Here we may hesitate to say, indeed, that λόγια means just the "Scriptures"; but what it means stands in a very express relation to the Scriptures, and possibly was not very sharply distinguished from the Scriptures by the speaker. With the analogies in Philo clearly in our mind, we should scarcely go far wrong if we conceived of λόγια here as meaning to the speaker those portions of Scripture in which Moses recorded the revelations vouchsafed to him by God — conceived as themselves these revelations recorded. In I Peter iv. 11 the interpretation is complicated by the question that arises concerning the charisma that is intended, as well as by the casting of the phrase into the form of a comparison: "let him speak *as it were* oracles of God." It is not clear that the Divine Scriptures as such are meant here; but the term, in any case, retains all its force as a designation of sacred, solemn divine utterances: the speaker is to speak as becomes one whose words are not his own, but the very words of God — oracles proclaimed through his mouth. Whether it is the exercise of the prophetic gift in the strict sense that is adverted to, so that Peter's exhortation is that the prophet should comport himself in his prophesying as becomes one made the vehicle of the awful words of revelation; or only the gift of teaching that is is question, so that Peter's exhortation is that he who proclaims the word of God, even in this lower sense, shall bear himself as befits one to whom are committed the Divine oracles for explanation and enforcement — must be left here without investigation. In either case the term is obviously used in its highest sense and implies that the λόγια of God are His own words, His awesome utterances.

What has thus been said in reference to these New Testament passages is intended to go no further in their explanation than to throw the light of the usage of the word upon their interpretation. Into their detailed exegesis we cannot now enter. We cannot pass by the general subject, however, without emphasizing the bearing these passages have on the New Testament doctrine of Holy Scripture. It will probably seem reasonable to most to interpret Rom. iii. 2 as certainly, Heb. v. 12 as probably, and Acts vii. 38 as very likely making reference to the written Scriptures; and as bearing witness to the conception of them on the part of the New Testament writers as "the oracles of God." That is to say, we have unobtrusive and convincing evidence here that the Old Testament Scriptures, as such, were esteemed by the writers of the New Testament as an oracular book, which in itself not merely contains, but is the "utterance," the very Word of God; and is to be appealed to as such and as such deferred to, because nothing other than the crystallized speech of God. We merely advert to this fact here without stopping to develop its implications or to show how consonant this designation of the Scriptures as the "Oracles of God" is with the conception of the Holy Scriptures entertained by the New Testament writers as otherwise made known to us. We have lately had occasion to point out in this *Review* some of the other ways in which this conception expresses itself in the New Testament writings.[98] He who cares to look for it will find it in many ways written largely and clearly and indelibly on the pages of the New Testament. We content ourselves at this time, however, with merely pointing out that the designation of the Scriptures as τὰ λόγια τοῦ θεοῦ fairly shouts to us out of the pages of the New Testament, that to its writers the Scriptures of the Old Testament were the very Word of God in the highest and strictest sense that term can bear — the express utterance, in all their parts and each and every of their words, of the Most High — the "oracles of God." Let him that thinks them something other and less than this, reckon, then, with the apostles and prophets of the New Covenant — to whose trustworthiness as witnesses to doctrinal truth he owes all he knows about the New Covenant itself, and therefore all he hopes for through this New Covenant.

[98] See Chapters VI and VII of this volume.

# APPENDIX I

## THE CANON OF THE NEW TESTAMENT: HOW AND WHEN FORMED

# THE FORMATION OF THE CANON OF THE NEW TESTAMENT[1]

In order to obtain a correct understanding of what is called the formation of the Canon of the New Testament, it is necessary to begin by fixing very firmly in our minds one fact which is obvious enough when attention is once called to it. That is, that the Christian church did not require to form for itself the idea of a " canon," — or, as we should more commonly call it, of a " Bible," — that is, of a collection of books given of God to be the authoritative rule of faith and practice. It inherited this idea from the Jewish church, along with the thing itself, the Jewish Scriptures, or the " Canon of the Old Testament." The church did not grow up by natural law: it was founded. And the authoritative teachers sent forth by Christ to found His church, carried with them, as their most precious possession, a body of divine Scriptures, which they imposed on the church that they founded as its code of law. No reader of the New Testament can need proof of this; on every page of that book is spread the evidence that from the very beginning the Old Testament was as cordially recognized as law by the Chirstian as by the Jew. The Christian church thus was never without a " Bible " or a " canon."

But the Old Testament books were not the only ones which the apostles (by Christ's own appointment the authoritative founders of the church) imposed upon the infant churches, as their authoritative rule of faith and practice. No more authority dwelt in the prophets of the old covenant than in themselves, the apostles, who had been " made sufficient as ministers of a new covenant "; for (as one of themselves argued) " if that which passeth away was with glory, much more that which remaineth is in glory." Accordingly not only was the gospel they delivered, in their own estimation, itself a divine revelation, but it was also preached " in the Holy Ghost " (I Pet. i. 12) ; not merely the matter of it, but the very words in which it was clothed were " of the Holy Spirit " (I Cor. ii. 13). Their own commands were, therefore, of divine authority (I Thess. iv. 2), and their writings were the depository of these commands (II Thess. ii. 15). " If any man obeyeth not our word by this epistle," says Paul to one church (II Thess. iii. 14), " note that man, that ye have no company with him." To another he makes it the test of a Spirit-led man to

[1] Pub. 1892, by the American Sunday School Union, Philadelphia, Pa.

411

recognize that what he was writing to them was "the commandments of the Lord" (I Cor. xiv. 37). Inevitably, such writings, making so awful a claim on their acceptance, were received by the infant churches as of a quality equal to that of the old "Bible"; placed alongside of its older books as an additional part of the one law of God; and read as such in their meetings for worship — a practice which moreover was required by the apostles (I Thess. v. 27; Col. iv. 16; Rev. i. 3). In the apprehension, therefore, of the earliest churches, the "Scriptures" were not a *closed* but an *increasing* "canon." Such they had been from the beginning, as they gradually grew in number from Moses to Malachi; and such they were to continue as long as there should remain among the churches "men of God who spake as they were moved by the Holy Ghost."

We say that this immediate placing of the new books — given the church under the seal of apostolic authority — among the Scriptures already established as such, was inevitable. It is also historically evinced from the very beginning. Thus the apostle Peter, writing in A.D. 68, speaks of Paul's numerous letters not in contrast with the Scriptures, but as among the Scriptures and in contrast with "the *other* Scriptures" (II Pet. iii. 16) — that is, of course, those of the Old Testament. In like manner the apostle Paul combines, as if it were the most natural thing in the world, the book of Deuteronomy and the Gospel of Luke under the common head of "Scripture" (I Tim. v. 18): "For the Scripture saith, 'Thou shalt not muzzle the ox when he treadeth out the corn' [Deut. xxv. 4]; and, 'The laborer is worthy of his hire'" (Luke x. 7). The line of such quotations is never broken in Christian literature. Polycarp (c. 12) in A.D. 115 unites the Psalms and Ephesians in exactly similar manner: "In the sacred books, . . . as it is said in these Scriptures, 'Be ye angry and sin not,' and 'Let not the sun go down upon your wrath.'" So, a few years later, the so-called second letter of Clement, after quoting Isaiah, adds (ii. 4): "And another Scripture, however, says, 'I came not to call the righteous, but sinners'" — quoting from Matthew, a book which Barnabas (*circa* 97–106 A.D.) had already adduced as Scripture. After this such quotations are common.

What needs emphasis at present about these facts is that they obviously are not evidences of a gradually-heightening estimate of the New Testament books, originally received on a lower level and just beginning to be tentatively accounted Scripture; they are conclusive evidences rather of the estimation of the New Testament books from the very beginning as Scripture, and of their attachment as Scripture to the other Scriptures already in hand. The early Christians did not, then, first form a rival "canon" of "new books" which came only gradually to be accounted as of equal divinity and authority with the " old books "; they received new book after new book from the apostolical circle, as equally " Scripture " with the old books, and added them one by one to the collection of old books as additional Scriptures, until at length the new books thus added were numerous enough to be looked upon as another *section* of the Scriptures.

The earliest name given to this new section of Scripture was framed on the model of the name by which what we know as the Old Testament was then known. Just as it was called " The Law and the Prophets and the Psalms " (or " the Hagiographa "), or more briefly " The Law and the Prophets," or even more briefly still " The Law "; so the enlarged Bible was called " The Law and the Prophets, with the Gospels and the Apostles " (so Clement of Alexandria, " Strom." vi. 11, 88; Tertullian, " De Præs. Hær." 36), or most briefly " The Law and the Gospel " (so Claudius Apolinaris, Irenæus) ; while the new books apart were called " The Gospel and the Apostles," or most briefly of all " The Gospel." This earliest name for the new Bible, with all that it involves as to its relation to the old and briefer Bible, is traceable as far back as Ignatius (A.D. 115), who makes use of it repeatedly (e. g., " ad Philad." 5; " ad Smyrn." 7). In one passage he gives us a hint of the controversies which the enlarged Bible of the Christians aroused among the Judaizers (" ad Philad." 6). " When I heard some saying," he writes, " ' Unless I find it in the *Old* [Books] I will not believe the *Gospel*,' on my saying, ' It is written,' they answered, ' That is the question.' To me, however, Jesus Christ *is* the Old [Books] ; his cross and death and resurrection, and the faith which is by him, the undefiled Old [Books] — by which I wish, by your prayers, to be justified. The priests indeed are good, but the High Priest better," etc. Here Ignatius appeals to the "Gospel " as Scripture, and the Judaizers object, receiving from him the answer in effect which Augustine afterward formulated in the well-known saying that the New Testament lies hidden in the Old and the Old Testament is first made clear in the New. What we need now to observe, however, is that to Ignatius the New Testament was not a different book from the Old Testament, but part of the one body of Scripture with it; an *accretion*, so to speak, which had grown upon it.

This is the testimony of all the early witnesses — even those which speak for the distinctively Jewish-Christian church. For example, that curious Jewish-Christian writing, " The Testaments of the XII. Patriarchs " (Benj. 11), tells us, under the cover of an *ex post facto* prophecy, that the " work and word " of Paul, i.e., confessedly the book of Acts and Paul's Epistles, " shall be written in the Holy Books," i.e., as is understood by all, made a part of the existent Bible. So even in the Talmud, in a scene intended to ridicule a " bishop " of the first century, he is represented as finding Galatians by "sinking himself deeper " into the same " Book " which contained the Law of Moses (" Babl. Shabbath," 116 a and b). The details cannot be entered into here. Let it suffice to say that, from the evidence of the fragments which alone have been preserved to us of the Christian writings of that very early time, it appears that from the beginning of the second century (and that is from the end of the apostolic age) a collection (Ignatius, II Clement) of " New Books " (Ignatius), called the " Gospel and Apostles " (Ignatius, Marcion), was already a part of the " Oracles " of God (Polycarp, Papias, II Clement), or " Scriptures " (I Tim., II Pet., Barn., Polycarp, II Clement), or the " Holy Books " or " Bible " (Testt. XII. Patt.).

The number of books included in this added body of New Books, at the opening of the second century, cannot be satisfactorily determined by the evidence of these fragments alone. The section of it called the " Gospel " included Gospels written by " the apostles and their companions " (Justin), which beyond legitimate question were our four Gospels now received. The section called " the Apostles " contained the book of Acts (The Testt. XII. Patt.) and epistles of Paul, John, Peter and James. The evidence from various quarters is indeed enough to show that the collection in general use contained all the books which we at present receive, with the possible exceptions of Jude, II and III John and Philemon. And it is more natural to suppose that failure of very early evidence for these brief booklets is due to their insignificant size rather than to their non-acceptance.

It is to be borne in mind, however, that the extent of the collection may have — and indeed is historically shown actually to have — varied in different localities. The Bible was circulated only in hand-copies, slowly and painfully made; and an incomplete copy, obtained say at Ephesus in A.D. 68, would be likely to remain for many years the Bible of the church to which it was conveyed; and might indeed become the parent of other copies, incomplete like itself, and thus the means of providing a whole district with incomplete Bibles. Thus, when we inquire after the history of the New Testament Canon we need to distinguish such questions as these: (1) When was the New Testament Canon completed? (2) When did any one church acquire a completed canon? (3) When did the completed canon — the complete Bible — obtain universal circulation and acceptance? (4) On what ground and evidence did the churches with incomplete Bibles accept the remaining books when they were made known to them?

The Canon of the New Testament was completed when the last authoritative book was given to any church by the apostles, and that was when John wrote the Apocalypse, about A.D. 98. Whether the church of Ephesus, however, had a completed Canon when it received the Apocalypse, or not, would depend on whether there was any epistle, say that of Jude, which had not yet reached it with authenticating proof of its apostolicity. There is room for historical investigation here. Certainly the whole Canon was not universally received by the churches till somewhat later. The Latin church of the second and third centuries did not quite know what to do with the Epistle to the Hebrews. The Syrian churches for some centuries may have lacked the lesser of the Catholic Epistles and Revelation. But from the time of Irenæus down, the church at large had the whole Canon as we now possess it. And though a section of the church may not yet have been satisfied of the apostolicity of a certain book or of certain books; and though afterwards doubts may have arisen in sections of the church as to the apostolicity of certain books (as e. g. of Revelation): yet in no case was it more than a respectable minority of the church which was slow in receiving, or which came afterward to doubt, the credentials of any of the books that then as now constituted the Canon of the New Testament accepted by the church at large. And in every case the principle on which a book was accepted, or doubts against it laid aside, was the historical tradition of apostolicity.

Let it, however, be clearly understood that it was not exactly apostolic *authorship* which in the estimation of the earliest churches, constituted a book a portion of the " canon." Apostolic authorship was, indeed, early confounded with canonicity. It was doubt as to the apostolic authorship of Hebrews, in the West, and of James and Jude, apparently, which underlay the slowness of the inclusion of these books in the " canon " of certain churches. But from the beginning it was not so. The principle of canonicity was not apostolic authorship, but *imposition by the apostles as " law."* Hence Tertullian's name for the " canon " is " *instrumentum* "; and he speaks of the Old and New *Instrument* as we would of the Old and New Testament. That the apostles so imposed the Old Testament on the churches which they founded — as their " Instrument," or "Law," or " Canon " — can be denied by none. And in imposing new books on the same churches, by the same apostolical authority, they did not confine themselves to books of their own composition. It is the Gospel according to Luke, a man who was not an apostle, which Paul parallels in I Tim. v. 18 with Deuteronomy as equally " Scripture " with it, in the first extant quotation of a New Testament book as

Scripture. The Gospels which constituted the first division of the New Books, — of " The Gospel and the Apostles," — Justin tells us, were " written by the apostles and their companions." The authority of the apostles, as by divine appointment founders of the church, was embodied in whatever books they imposed on the church as law, not merely in those they themselves had written.

The early churches, in short, received, as we receive, into their New Testament all the books historically evinced to them as given by the apostles to the churches as their code of law; and we must not mistake the historical evidences of the slow circulation and authentication of these books over the widely-extended church, for evidence of slowness of " canonization " of books by the authority or the taste of the church itself.

# APPENDIX II

## INSPIRATION AND CRITICISM

have thought I could not do better than to take up one of our precious old doctrines, much attacked of late, and ask the simple question: What seems the result of the attack? The doctrine I have chosen, is that of " Verbal Inspiration." But for obvious reasons I have been forced to narrow the discussion to a consideration of the inspiration of the New Testament only; and that solely as assaulted in the name of criticism. I wish to ask your attention, then, to a brief attempt to supply an answer to the question:

### Is the Church Doctrine of the Plenary Inspiration of the New Testament Endangered by the Assured Results of Modern Biblical Criticism?

At the very outset, that our inquiry may not be a mere beating of the air, we must briefly, indeed, but clearly, state what we mean by the Church Doctrine. For, unhappily, there are almost as many theories of inspiration held by individuals as there are possible stages imaginable between the slightest and the greatest influence God could exercise on man. It is with the traditional doctrine of the Reformed Churches, however, that we are concerned; and that we understand to be simply this: — *Inspiration is that extraordinary, supernatural influence (or, passively, the result of it,) exerted by the Holy Ghost on the writers of our Sacred Books, by which their words were rendered also the words of God, and, therefore, perfectly infallible.* In this definition, it is to be noted: 1st. That this influence is a supernatural one — something different from the inspiration of the poet or man of genius. Luke's accuracy is not left by it with only the safeguards which " the diligent and accurate Suetonius " had. 2d. That it is an extraordinary influence — something different from the ordinary action of the Spirit in the conversion and sanctifying guidance of believers. Paul had some more prevalent safeguard against false-teaching than Luther or even the saintly Rutherford. 3d. That it is such an influence as makes the words written under its guidance, the words of God; by which is meant to be affirmed an absolute infallibility (as alone fitted to divine words), admitting no degrees whatever — extending to the very word, and to all the words. So that every part of Holy Writ is thus held alike infallibly true in all its statements, of whatever kind.

Fencing around and explaining this definition, it is to be remarked further:

1st. That it purposely declares nothing as to the mode of inspiration. The Reformed Churches admit that this is inscrutable. They content themselves with defining carefully and holding fast the effects of the divine influence, leaving the mode of divine action by which it is brought about draped in mystery.

2d. It is purposely so framed as to distinguish it from revelation; — seeing that it has to do with the communication of truth not its acquirement.

3d. It is by no means to be imagined that it is meant to proclaim a mechanical theory of inspiration. The Reformed Churches have never held such a theory: [3] though dishonest, careless, ignorant or over eager controverters of its doctrine have often brought the charge. Even those special theologians in whose teeth such an accusation has been oftenest thrown (e. g., Gaussen) are explicit in teaching that the human element is never absent.[4] The Reformed Churches hold, indeed, that every word of the Scriptures, without exception, is the word of God; but, alongside of that, they hold equally explicitly that every word is the word of man. And, therefore, though strong and uncompromising in resisting the attribution to the Scriptures of any failure in absolute truth and infallibility, they are before all others in seeking, and finding, and gazing on in loving rapture, the marks of the fervid impetuosity of a Paul — the tender saintliness of a John — the practical genius of a James, in the writ-

[3] See Dr. C. Hodge's " Systematic Theology," page 157, Vol. I.

[4] Cf. Gaussen's " Theopneusty," New York, 1842; pp. 34, 36, 44 *seq. et passim.* In these passages he explicitly declares that the human element is never absent. Yet he has been constantly misunderstood: thus, Van Oosterzee (" Dog.," i. p. 202), Dorner (" Protestant Theo.," ii. 477) and even late English and American writers who, if no others, should have found it impossible to ascribe a mechanical theory to a man who had abhorrently repudiated it in an English journal and in a note prefixed to the subsequent English editions of his work. (See: " It is Written," London: Bagster & Sons, 3d edition, pp. i–iv.) In that notice he declares that he wishes " loudly to disavow " this theory, " that he feels the greatest repugnance to it," " that it is gratuitously attributed to him," " that he has never, for a single moment, entertained the idea of keeping it," etc. Yet so late a writer as President Bartlett, of Dartmouth (*Princeton Review,* January, 1880, p. 34), can still use Gaussen as an example of the mechanical theory. Gaussen's book ought never to have been misunderstood; it is plain and simple. The cause of the constant misunderstanding, however, is doubtless to be found in the fact that his one object is to give a proof of the existence of an everywhere present divine element in the Scriptures, — not to give a rounded statement of the doctrine of inspiration. He has, therefore, dwelt on the divinity, and only incidentally adverted to the humanity exhibited in its pages. Gaussen may serve us here as sufficient example of the statement in the text. The doctrine stated in the text is the doctrine taught by all the representative theologians in our own church.

ings which through them the Holy Ghost has given for our guidance. Though strong and uncompromising in resisting all effort to separate the human and divine, they distance all competitors in giving honor alike to both by proclaiming in one breath that all is divine and all is human. As Gaussen so well expresses it, " We all hold that every verse, without exception, is from men, and every verse, without exception, is from God "; " every word of the Bible is as really from man as it is from God."

4th. Nor is this a mysterious doctrine — except, indeed, in the sense in which everything supernatural is mysterious. We are not dealing in puzzles, but in the plainest facts of spiritual experience. How close, indeed, is the analogy here with all that we know of the Spirit's action in other spheres! Just as the first act of loving faith by which the regenerated soul flows out of itself to its Saviour, is at once the consciously-chosen act of that soul and the direct work of the Holy Ghost; so, every word indited under the analogous influence of inspiration was at one and the same time the consciously self-chosen word of the writer and the divinely-inspired word of the Spirit. I cannot help thinking that it is through failure to note and assimilate this fact, that the doctrine of verbal inspiration is so summarily set aside and so unthinkingly inveighed against by divines otherwise cautious and reverent. Once grasp this idea, and how impossible is it to separate in any measure the human and divine. It is all human — every word, and all divine. The human characteristics are to be noted and exhibited; the divine perfection and infallibility, no less.

This, then, is what we understand by the church doctrine: — a doctrine which claims that by a special, supernatural, extraordinary influence of the Holy Ghost, the sacred writers have been guided in their writing in such a way, as while their humanity was not superseded, it was yet so dominated that their words became at the same time the words of God, and thus, in every case and all alike, absolutely infallible.

I do not purpose now to undertake the proof of this doctrine. I purpose rather to ask whether, assuming it to have been accepted by the Church as apparently the true one, modern biblical criticism has in any of its results reached conclusions which should shake our previously won confidence in it. It is plain, however, that biblical criticism could endanger such a doctrine only by undermining it — by shaking the foundation on which it rests — in other words by attacking the proof which is relied on to establish it. We have, then, so far to deal with the proofs of the doctrine. It is evident, now, that such a doctrine must rest primarily on the claims of the sacred writers. In the very nature of the case, the writers themselves are the prime witnesses of the fact and nature of their inspiration. Nor does this argument run in a vicious circle. We do not assume inspiration in order to prove inspiration. We assume only honesty and sobriety. If a sober and honest writer claims to be inspired by God, then here, at least, is a phenomenon to be accounted for. It follows, however, that besides their claims, there are also secondary bases on which the doctrine of the plenary inspiration of the Scriptures rests, and by the shaking of which it can be shaken. These are: — first, the allowance of their claims by the contemporaries of the writers, — by those of their contemporaries, that is, who were in a position to judge of the truth of such claims. In the case of the New Testament writers this means the contemporary church, who had the test of truth in its hands: " Was God visibly with the Apostles, and did He seal their claims with His blessing on their work?" And, secondly, the absence of all contradictory phenomena in or about the writings themselves. If the New Testament writers, being sober and honest men, claim verbal inspiration, and this claim was allowed by the contemporary church, and their writings in no respect in their character or details negative it, then it seems idle to object to the doctrine of verbal inspiration on any critical grounds.

In order, therefore, to shake this doctrine, biblical criticism must show: either, that the New Testament writers do not claim inspiration; or, that this claim was rejected by the contemporary church; or, that it is palpably negatived by the fact that the books containing it are forgeries; or, equally clearly negatived by the fact that they contain along with the claim, errors of fact or contradictions of statement. The important question before us to-day, then, is: Has biblical criticism proved any one of these positions?

I. Note, then, in the first place, that modern biblical criticism does not in any way weaken the evidence that the New Testament writers claim full, even verbal, inspiration. Quite the contrary. The careful revision of the text of the New Testament and the application to it of scientific principles of historico-grammatical exegesis, place this claim beyond the possibility of a doubt. This is so clearly the case, that even those writers who cannot bring themselves to admit the truth of the doctrines, yet not infrequently begin by admitting that the New Testament writers claim such an inspiration as is in it presupposed. Take, for instance, the twin statements of Richard Rothe: " To wish to maintain the inspiration of the subject-matter, without that of the words, is a folly; for everywhere are thoughts and words inseparable," and " It is clear that the orthodox theory of inspiration [by which he means the very strictest] is countenanced by the authors of the New Testament." If we approach the study of the New Testament under the guidance of and in the use of the methods of modern biblical science, more clearly than ever before is it seen that its authors make such a claim. Not only does our Lord promise a supernatural guidance to his Apostles, both at the beginning of their ministry (Matthew x. 19, 20) and at the close of his life (Mark xii. 11; Luke xxi. 12, cf. John xiv and xvi) but the New Testament writers distinctly claim divine authority. With what assurance do they speak — exhibiting the height of delirium, if not the height of authority. The historians betray no shadow of a doubt as to the exact truth of their every word, — a phenomenon hard to parallel elsewhere among accurate and truth-loving historians who commonly betray less and less assurance in proportion as they exhibit more and more painstaking care. The didactic writers claim an absolute authority in their teaching, and betray as little shadow of doubt as to the perfectly binding character of their words (II Cor. x. 7, 8). If opposed by an angel from heaven, the angel is indubitably wrong and accursed (Gal. i. 7, 8). Therefore, how freely they deal in commands (I Thes. iv. 2, 11; II Thes. iii. 6–14); commands, too, which they hold to be absolutely binding on all; so binding that it is the test of a Spirit-led man to recognize them as the commandments of God (I Cor. xiv. 37), and no Christian ought to company with those who reject them (II Thes. iii. 6–14). Nor is it doubtful that this authority is claimed specifically for the written word. In I Cor. xiv. 37, it is specifically " the things which I am writing " that must be recognized as the commands of the Lord; and so in II Thes. ii. 15; iii. 6–14, it is the teaching transmitted by letter as well as by word of mouth that is to be immediately and unquestionably received.

Now, on what is this immense claim of authority grounded? If a mere human claim, it is most astounding impudence. But that it is not a mere human claim, is specifically witnessed to. Paul claims to be but the transmitter of this teaching (II Thes. iii. 6; παρά ); it is, indeed, his own (II Thes. iii. 14, ἡμῶν ), but still, the transmitted word is God's word (I Thes. ii. 13). He speaks, indeed, and issues commands, but they are not his commands, but Christ's, in virtue of the fact that they are given through him by Christ (I Thes. iv. 2). The other writers exhibit the same phenomena. Peter distinctly claims that the Gospel was preached in ( ἐν) the Holy Spirit (I Peter, i. 12); and John calls down a curse on those who would in any way alter his writing (Rev. xxii. 18, 19; cf. I John, v. 10). These, we submit, are strange phenomena if we are to judge that these writers professed no inspiration.

" But," we are asked, " is this all?" We answer, that we have but just begun. All that we have said is but a cushion for the specific proof to rest easily on. For here we wish to make two remarks:

1. *The inspiration which is implied in these passages, is directly claimed elsewhere.* We will now appeal, however, to but two passages. Look at I Cor. vii. 40, where the best and most scientific modern exegesis proves that Paul claimed for his " opinion " expressed in this letter direct divine inspiration, saying, " this is my opinion," and adding, not in modesty, or doubt, but in meiotic irony, " and it seems to me that I have the Spirit of God." If this interpretation be correct, and with the " it seems to me " and the very emphatic " I " staring us in the face, drawing the contrast so sharply between Paul and the impugners of his authority, it seems indubitably so; then it is clear that Paul claims here a direct divine inspiration in the expression of even his " opinion " in his letters. Again look for an instant at I Cor. ii. 13. " Which things, also we utter not in words taught by human wisdom, but in those taught by the Spirit; joining spiritual things with spiritual things "; where modern science, more clearly even than ancient faith, sees it stated that both the matter and the manner of this teaching are from the Holy Ghost — both the thoughts and the words — yes, the words themselves. " It is not meet," says the Apostle, " that the things taught by the Holy Ghost should be expressed in merely human words; there must be Spirit-given words to clothe the Spirit-given doctrines. Therefore, I utter these things not in the words taught by human wisdom — not even in the most wisely-chosen human words — but in those taught by the Spirit, joining thus with Spirit-given things (as was fit) only Spirit-given words." It is impossible to deny that here there is clearly taught a *suggestio verborum.* Nor will it do to say that this does not bear on the point at issue, seeing that λόγος and not ῥῆμα is the term used. Not only is even this subterfuge useless in the face of what we will have still to urge, but it is even meaningless here. No one supposes that the mere grammatical forms separately considered are inspired: the claim concerns words in their ordered sequence — in their living flow in the sentences — and this is just what is expressed by λόγοι. This passage thus stands before us distinctly claiming verbal inspiration. The two together seem reconcilable with nothing less far reaching than the church doctrine.

2. But we must turn to our second remark. It is this: *The New Testament writers distinctly place each other's writings in the same lofty category in which they place the writings of the Old Testament; and as they indubitably hold to the full — even verbal — inspiration of the Old Testament, it follows that they claim the same verbal*

*inspiration for the New.* Is it doubted that the New Testament writers ascribe full inspiration to the Old Testament? Modern science does not doubt it; nor can anyone doubt it who will but listen to the words of the New Testament writers in the matter. The whole New Testament is based on the divinity of the Old, and its inspiration is assumed on every page. The full strength of the case, then, cannot be exhibited. It may be called to our remembrance, however, that not only do the New Testament writers deal with the Old as divine, but that they directly quote it as divine. Those very lofty titles, " Scripture," " The Scriptures," " The Oracles of God," which they give it, and the common formula of quotation, " It is written," by which they cite its words, alone imply their full belief in its inspiration. And this is the more apparent that it is evident that for them to say, " Scripture says," is equivalent to their saying, " God says," (Romans ix. 17; x. 19; Galatians iii. 8.) Consequently, they distinctly declare that its writers wrote in the Spirit (Matthew xxii. 43; cf. Luke xx. 42; and Acts ii. 24); the meaning of which is made clear by their further statement that God speaks their words (Matthew i. 22; ii. 15, etc.), even those not ascribed to God in the Old Testament itself (Acts xiii. 35; Hebrews viii. 8; i. 6, 7, 8; v. 5; Eph. iv. 8), thereby evincing the fact that what the human authors speak God speaks through their mouths (Acts iv. 25). Still more narrowly defining the doctrine, it is specifically stated that it is the Holy Ghost who speaks the written words of Scripture (Hebrews iii. 7) — yea, even in the narrative parts (Hebrews iv. 4). In direct accordance with these statements, the New Testament writers use the very words of the Old Testament as authoritative and " not to be broken." Christ, himself, so deals with a tense in Matthew xxii. 32, and twice elsewhere founds an argument on the words (John x. 34; Matthew xxii. 43); and it is in connection with one of these word arguments that his divine lips declare " the Scriptures cannot be broken." His Apostles follow his example (Galatians iii: 16). Still, further, we have, at least, two didactic statements in the New Testament, directly affirming the inspiration of the Old (II Timothy iii. 16, and II Peter i. 21). In one of these it is declared that every Scripture is God-inspired; in the other, that no prophecy ever came by the will of man, but borne along by the Holy Ghost it was that holy men of God spoke. It is, following the best results of modern critical exegesis, therefore, quite certain that the New Testament writers held the full verbal inspiration of the Old Testament. Now, they plainly place the New Testament books in the same category. The same Paul, who wrote in II Timothy, " Every Scripture is God-inspired," quotes in its twin letter, 1 Timothy, **a** passage from Luke's Gospel calling it "Scripture" (I Timothy, v. 18), — nay, more, — parallelizing it as equally Scripture with a passage from the Old Testament. And the same Peter, who gave us our other didactic statements, and in the same letter, does the same for Paul that Paul did for Luke, and that even more broadly, declaring (II Peter iii. 16) that all Paul's Epistles are to be considered as occupying the same level as the rest of the Scriptures. It is quite indisputable, then, that the New Testament writers claim full inspiration for the New Testament books.

Now none of these points are weakened in either meaning or reference by the application of the principles of critical exegesis. In every regard they are strengthened. We can be quite bold, therefore, in declaring that modern criticism does not set aside the fact that the New Testament writers claim the very fullest inspiration.

II. We must ask, then, secondly, if modern critical investigation has shown that this claim of inspiration was disallowed by the contemporaries of the New Testament writers. Here again our answer must be in the negative. The New Testament writings themselves bristle with the evidences that they expected and received a docile hearing; parties may have opposed them, but only parties. And again, all the evidence that exists coming down to us from the sub-apostolic church — be it more or less voluminous, yet such as it is admitted to be by the various schools of criticism — points to a very complete reception of the New Testament claims. No church writer of the time can be pointed out who made a distinction derogatory to the New Testament, between it and the Old Testament, the Divine authority of which latter, it is admitted, was fully recognized in the church. On the contrary, all of them treat the New Testament with the greatest respect, hold its teachings in the highest honor, and run the statement of their theology into its forms of words as if they held even the forms of its statements authoritative. They all know the difference between the authority exercised by the New Testament writers and that which they can lawfully claim. They even call the New Testament books, and that, as is now pretty well admitted, with the fullest meaning, "Scripture." Take a few examples: No result of modern criticism is more sure than that Clement of Rome, himself a pupil of Apostles, wrote a letter to the Corinthians in the latter years of the first century; and that we now possess that letter, its text witnessed to by three independent authorities and therefore to be depended on. That epistle exhibits all the above-mentioned characteristics, except that it does not happen to quote any New Testament text specifically as Scripture. It treats the New Testament with the greatest respect, it teaches for doctrines only what it teaches, it runs its statements into New Testament forms, it imitates the New Testament style, it draws a broad distinction between the authority with which Paul wrote and that which it can claim, it declares distinctly that Paul wrote " most certainly in a spirit-led way " ( ἐπ' ἀληθείας πνευματικῶς. c. 47.) Again, even the most sceptical of schools place the Epistle of Barnabas in the first or at the very beginning of the second century, and it again exhibits these same phenomena, — moreover quoting Matthew definitely as Scripture. One of the latest triumphs of a most acute criticism has been the vindication of the genuineness of the seven short Greek letters of Ignatius, which are thus proved to belong to the very first years of the second century and to be the production again of one who knew Apostles. In them again we meet with the same phenomena. Ignatius even knows of a collected New Testament equal in authority to the Divinely inspired Old Testament. But we need not multiply detailed evidence; every piece of Christian writing which is even probably to be assigned to one who knew or might have known the Apostles, bears like testimony. This is absolutely without exception. They all treat the New Testament books as differentiated from all other writings, and no single voice can be adduced as raised against them. The very heretics bear witness to the same effect; anxious as they are to be rid of the teaching of these writings they yet hold them authoritative and so endeavor to twist their words into conformity with their errors. And if we follow the stream further down its course, the evidence becomes more and more abundant in direct proportion to the increasing abundance of the literary remains and their change from purely practical epistles or addresses to Jews and heathen to controversial treatises between Christian parties. It is exceedingly clear, then, that modern criticism has not proved that the contemporary church resisted the assumption of the New Testament writers or withstood their claim to inspiration: directly the contrary. Every particle of evidence in the case exhibits the apostolic church, not as disallowing, but as distinctly recognizing the absolute authority of the New Testament writings. In the brief compass of the extant fragments of the Christian literature of the first two decades of the second century we have Matthew and Ephesians distinctly quoted as Scripture, the Acts and Pauline Epistles specifically named as part of the Holy Bible, and the New Testament consisting of evangelic records and apostolic writings clearly made part of one sacred collection of books with the Old Testament.[5] Let us bear in mind that the belief of the early church in the inspiration of the Old

[5] See Barn, 4, Poly. 12. Test. xii., Patt. Benj. 10. Ign. Phil. 5, 8, etc.

Testament is beyond dispute, and we will see that the meaning of all this is simply this: The apostolic church certainly accepted the New Testament books as inspired by God. Such are the results of critical enquiry into the opinions on this subject of the church writers standing next to the Apostles.

III. If then, the New Testament writers clearly claim verbal inspiration and the apostolic church plainly allowed that claim, any objection to this doctrine must proceed by attempting to undermine the claim itself. From a critical standpoint this can be done only in two ways: It may be shown that the books making it are not genuine and therefore not authentic, in which case they are certainly not trustworthy and their lofty claims must be set aside as part of the impudence of forgery. Or it may be shown that the books, as a matter of fact, fall into the same errors and contain examples of the same mistakes which uninspired writings are guilty of, — exhibit the same phenomena of inaccuracy and contradiction as they, — and therefore, of course, as being palpably fallible by their very character disprove their claims to infallibility. It is in these two points that the main strength of the opposition to the doctrine of verbal inspiration lies, — the first being urged by unbelievers, who object to any doctrine of inspiration, the second by believers, who object to the doctrine of plenary and universal inspiration. The question is: Has either point been made good?

1. In opposition to the first, then, we risk nothing in declaring that *modern biblical criticism has not disproved the authenticity of a single book of our New Testament.* It is a most assured result of biblical criticism that every one of the twenty-seven books which now constitute our New Testament is assuredly genuine and authentic. There is, indeed, much that arrogates to itself the name of criticism and has that honorable title carelessly accorded to it, which does claim to arrive at such results as set aside the authenticity of even the major part of the New Testament. One school would save five books only from the universal ruin. To this, however, true criticism opposes itself directly, and boldly proclaims every New Testament book authentic. But, thus two claimants to the name of criticism appear, and the question arises, before what court can the rival claims be adjudicated? Before the court of simple common sense, it may be quickly answered. Nor is it impossible to settle once for all the whole dispute. By criticism is meant an investigation with three essential characteristics: (1) a fearless, honest mental abandonment, apart from presuppositions, to the facts of the case, (2) a most careful, complete and unprejudiced collection and examination of the facts, and (3) the most cautious care in founding

inferences upon them. The absence of any one of these characteristics throws grave doubts on the results; while the acme of the uncritical is reached when in the place of these critical graces we find guiding the investigation that other trio, — bondage to preconceived opinion, — careless, incomplete or prejudiced collection and examination of the facts, — and rashness of inference. Now, it may well be asked, is that true criticism which starts with the presupposition that the supernatural is impossible, proceeds by a sustained effort to do violence to the facts, and ends by erecting a gigantic historical chimera — overturning all established history — on the appropriate basis of airy nothing? And, is not this a fair picture of the negative criticism of the day? Look at its history, — see its series of wild dreams, — note how each new school has to begin by executing justice on its predecessor. So Paulus goes down before Strauss, Strauss falls before Baur, and Baur before the resistless logic of his own negative successors. Take the grandest of them all, — the acutest critic that ever turned his learning against the Christian Scriptures, and it will require but little searching to discover that Baur has ruthlessly violated every canon of genuine criticism. And if this is true of him, what is to be said of the school of Kuenen which now seems to be in the ascendant? We cannot now follow theories like this into details. But on a basis of a study of those details we can remark without fear of successful contradiction that the history of modern negative criticism is blotted all over and every page stained black with the proofs of work undertaken with its conclusion already foregone and prosecuted in a spirit that was blind to all adverse evidence.[6] Who does not know, for example, of the sustained attempts made to pack the witness box against the Christian Scriptures? — the wild denials of evidence the most undeniable, — the wilder dragging into court of evidence the most palpably manufactured? Who does not remember the remarkable attempt to set aside the evidence arising from Barnabas' quotation

[6] We hear much of " apologists " undertaking critical study with such preconceived theories as render the conclusion foregone. Perhaps this is sometimes true, but it is not so necessarily. A Theist, believing that there is a personal God, is open to the proof as to whether any particular message claiming to be a revelation is really from him or not, and according to the proof, he decides. A Pantheist or Materialist begins by denying the existence of a personal God, and hence the possibility of the supernatural. If he begins the study of an asserted revelation, his conclusion is *necessarily* foregone. An honest Theist, thus, is open to evidence either way; an honest Pantheist or Materialist is not open to any evidence for the supernatural. See some fine remarks on this subject by Dr. Westcott, *Contemporary Review*, xxx. p. 1070.

of Matthew as Scripture, on the ground that the part of the epistle which contained it was extant only in an otherwise confessedly accurate Latin version; and when Tischendorf dragged an ancient Greek copy out of an Eastern monastery and vindicated the reading, who does not remember the astounding efforts then made to deny that the quotation was from Matthew, or to throw doubt on the early date of the epistle itself? Who does not know the disgraceful attempt made to manufacture, — yes simply to manufacture, — evidence against John's gospel, persevered in in the face of all anner of refutation until it seems at last to have received its death ow through one stroke of Dr. Lightfoot's trenchant pen on "the lence of Eusebius?"[7] In every way, then, this criticism evinces self as false.

But false as it is, its attacks must be tested and the opposition of true criticism to its results exhibited. The attack, then, proceeds on the double ground of internal and external evidence. It is claimed that the books exhibit such contradictions among themselves and errors in historical fact, as evince that they cannot be authentic. It is claimed, moreover, that external evidence such as would prove them to have existed in the Apostolic times is lacking. How does true criticism meet these attacks?

Joining issue first with the latter statement, sober criticism meets it with a categorical denial. It exhibits the fact that every New Testament book, except only the mites Jude, II and III John, Philemon and possibly II Peter, are quoted by the generation of writers immediately succeeding the Apostles, and are thereby proved to have existed in the apostolic times; and that even these four brief books which are not quoted by those earliest authors in the few and brief writings which have come down from them to us, are so authenticated afterwards as to leave no rational ground of doubt as to their authenticity.

It is admitted on all hands that there is less evidence for II Peter than for any other of our books. If the early date of II Peter then can be made good, the early date of all the rest follows *a fortiori;* and there can be no doubt but that sober criticism fails to find adequate grounds for rejecting II Peter from the circle of apostolic writings. It is an outstanding fact that at the beginning of the third century this epistle was well known; it is during the early years of that century that we meet with the first explicit mention of it, and then it is quoted in such a way as to exhibit the facts that it was believed to be Peter's and was at that time most certainly in the canon. What has to be accounted for, then, is how came it in the

[7] *Contemporary Review,* xxv. p. 169.

canon of the early third century? It was certainly not put there by
those third century writers; their notices utterly forbid this. Then,
it must have been already in it in the second century. But when in
that century did it acquire this position? Can we believe that critics
like Irenaeus, or Melito, or Dionysius would have allowed it to
be foisted before their eyes into a collection they held all-holy?
It could not, then, have first attained that entrance during the latter
years of the second century; and that it must have been already in
the New Testament, received and used by the great writers of the
fourth quarter of the second century, seems scarcely open to doubt.
Apart from this reasoning, indeed, this seems established; Clement
of Alexandria certainly had the book, Irenaeus also in all probability possessed it. If, now, the book formed a part of the canon
current in the fourth quarter of the second century, there can be
little doubt but that it came from the bosom of the Apostolic circle.
One has but to catch from Irenaeus, for instance, the grounds on
which he received any book as scripture, to be convinced of this.
The one and all-important *sine-qua-non* was that it should have
been handed down from the fathers, the pupils of the Apostles, as
the work of the Apostolic circle. And Irenaeus was an adequate
judge as to whether this was the case; his immediate predecessor
in the Episcopal office at Lyons was Pothinus, whose long life
spanned the whole intervening time from the Apostles, and his
teacher was Polycarp, who was the pupil of John. That a book
formed a part of the New Testament of this period, therefore au-
thenticates it as coming down from those elders who could bear
personal witness to its authorship. This is one of the facts of criticism apart from noting which it cannot proceed. The question,
then, is not: do we possess independently of this, sufficient evidence
of the Petrine authorship of the book to place it in the canon?
but: do we possess sufficient evidence against its Petrine authorship, to reject it from the canon of the fourth quarter of the second
century authenticated as that canon as a whole is? The answer to
the question cannot be doubtful when we remember that we have
absolutely no evidence against the book; but, on the contrary, that
all the evidence of whatever kind which is in existence goes to establish it. There is some slight reason to believe, for instance, that
Clement of Rome had the letter, more that Hermas had it and
much that Justin had it. There is also a good probability that the
early author of the Testaments of the XII. Patriarchs had and used
it. Any one of these references, independently of all the rest, would,
if made good, throw the writing of the book back into the first
century. Each supports the others, and the sum of the probabilities

raised by all, is all in direct support of the inference drawn from the reception of the book by later generations, so that there seems to be really no room for reasonable doubt but that the book rightly retains its position in our New Testament. This conclusion gains greatly in strength when we compare the data on which it rests, with what is deemed sufficient to authenticate any other ancient writing. We find at least two most probable allusions to II Peter within a hundred years after its composition, and before the next century passes away we find it possessed by the whole church and that as a book with a secured position in a collection super-authenticated as a whole. Now, Herodotus, for instance, is but once quoted in the century which followed its composition, but once in the next, not at all in the next, only twice in the next, and not until the fifth century after its composition is it as fully quoted as II Peter during its second century. Yet who doubts the genuineness of the histories of Herodotus? Again the first distinct quotation from Thucydides does not occur until quite two centuries after its composition; while Tacitus is first cited nearly a century after his death, by Tertullian. Yet no one can reasonably doubt the genuineness of the histories of either Thucydides or Tacitus.[8] We hazard nothing then, in declaring that no one can reasonably doubt the authenticity of the better authenticated II Peter.

If now such a conclusion is critically tenable in the case of II Peter, what is to be said of the rest of the canon? There are some six writings which have come down to us, which were written within twenty years after the death of John; these six brief pieces alone, as we have said, prove the prior existence of the whole New Testament, with the exception of Jude, II and III John, Philemon and (possibly) II Peter, and the writers of the succeeding years vouch for and multiply their evidence. In the face of such contemporary testimony as this, negative criticism cannot possibly deny the authenticity of our books. A strenuous effort has consequently been made to break the force of this testimony. The genuineness of these witnessing documents themselves has been attacked or else an attempt has been made to deny that their quotations are from the New Testament books. Neither the one effort nor the other, however, has been or can be successful. And yet with what energy have they been prosecuted! We have already seen what wild strivings were wasted in an attempt to get rid of Barnabas' quotation of Matthew. That whole question is now given up; it is admitted that the quotation is from Matthew; and it is admitted that Barnabas was written in the immediately sub-apostolic times. But Barnabas

[8] See Rawlinson's " Hist. Evid.," p. 370 f.

quotes not only Matthew, but I Corinthians and Ephesians, and in Keim's opinion witnesses also to the prior existence of John. This may be taken as a type of the whole controversy. The references to the New Testament books in the Apostolic fathers are too plain to be disputed and it is simply the despair of criticism that is exhibited by the invention of elaborate theories of accidental coincidences or of endless series of hypothetical books to which to assign them. The quotations are too numerous, too close, and glide too imperceptibly and regularly from mere adoption of phrases into accurate citations of authorities, to be explained away. They therefore stand, and prove that the authors of these writings already knew the New Testament books and esteemed them authoritative.

Nor has the attempt to deny the early date of these witnessing writers fared any better. The mere necessity of the attempt is indeed fatal to the theory it is meant to support; if to exhibit the unauthenticity of the New Testament books, we must hold all subsequent writings unauthentic too, it seems plain that we are on a false path. And what violence is done in the attempt! For instance, the Epistle of Polycarp witnesses to the prior existence of Matthew, Luke, Acts, eleven Epistles of Paul, I Peter and I John; and as Polycarp was a pupil of John, his testimony is very strong. It must then be got rid of at all hazards. But Irenaeus was Polycarp's pupil, and Irenaeus explicitly cites this letter and declares it to be Polycarp's genuine production; and no one from his time to ours has found cause to dispute his statement until it has become necessary to be rid of the testimony of the letter to our canon. But if Polycarp's letter be genuine, it sets its own date and witnesses in turn to the letters of Ignatius, which themselves bear internal testimony to their own early date; and these letters of Ignatius testify not only to the prior individual existence of Matthew, John, Romans, I Corinthians, Ephesians, Philippians, I Thessalonians and I John; but also to the prior existence of an authoritative Divinely-inspired New Testament. This is but a specimen of the linked character of our testimony. Not only is it fairly abundant, but it is so connected by evidently undesigned, indeed, but yet indetachable articulations, that to set aside any one important piece of it usually necessitates such a wholesale attack on the literature of the second century as to amount to a *reductio ad absurdum*. We may, then, boldly formulate as our conclusion that external evidence imperiously forbids the dethronement of any New Testament book from its place in our canon.

What, then, are we to do with the internal evidence that is relied upon by the negative school? What, but set it summarily aside also?

It amounts to a twofold claim: (1.) The sacred writers are hopelessly inconsistent with one another, and (2.) they are at variance with contemporary history. Of course, disharmony between the four gospels, and between Acts and the Epistles is what is mainly relied on under the first point, and it must be admitted that much learning and acuteness has been expended on the effort to make out this disharmony. But it is to be noted: (1.) That even were it admitted up to the full extent claimed, it would be no proof of unauthenticity; it would be no more than that found between secular historians admitted to be authentic, when narrating the same actions from different points of view. And (2.) in no case has it been shown that disharmony must be admitted. No case can be adduced where a natural mode of harmonizing cannot be supplied, and it is a reasonable principle, recognized among critics of secular historians, that two writers must not be held to be contradictory where any natural mode of harmonizing can be imagined. Otherwise it amounts to holding that we know fully and thoroughly all the facts of the case, — better even than eye-witnesses seem ever to know them. In order to gain any force at all, therefore, for this objection, both the extent and degree of the disharmony has been grossly exaggerated. Take an example: It is asserted that the two accounts (in Matthew and Luke) of the events accompanying our Lord's birth are mutually exclusive. But even a cursory examination will show that there is not a single contradiction between them. How then is the charge of disharmony supported? In two ways: First, by erecting silence into contradiction. Since Matthew does not mention the visit of the shepherds, he is said to contradict Luke who does. Since Luke does not mention the flight into Egypt he is said to contradict Matthew who does. And secondly, by a still more astounding method which proceeds by first confounding two distinct transactions and then finding irreconcilable contradictions between them. Thus Strauss calmly enumerates no less than five discrepancies between Matthew's account of the visit of the angel to Joseph and Luke's account of the visit of the angel to Mary. On the same principle we might prove both Motley's " Dutch Republic " and Kingslake's " Crimean War " to be unbelievable histories by gravely setting ourselves to find " discrepancies " between the account in the one of the brilliant charges of Egmont at St. Quentin and the account in the other of the great charge of the six hundred at Balaclava. This is not an unfair example of the way in which the New Testament is dealt with in order to exhibit its internal disharmony. We are content, however, that it should pass for an extreme case. For it will suffice for our present purpose to be able to say that if the New Testament books are to be proved unauthentic by their internal contradictions, by parity of reasoning the world has never yet seen an authentic writing. In fact so marvelously are our books at one that, leaving the defensive, the harmonist may take the offensive and claim this unwonted harmony as one of the chief evidences of Christianity. Paley has done this for the Acts and Epistles; and it can be done also for the Gospels.

Perhaps we ought to content ourselves with merely repeating this same remark in reference to the charge that the New Testament writers are at variance with contemporary history. So far is this from being true that one of the strongest evidences for Christianity is the utter accord with the minute details of contemporary history which is exhibited in its records. There has been no lack indeed of "instances" of disaccord confidently put forth; but in every case the charge has recoiled on the head of its maker. Thus, the mention of Lysanias in Luke iii. 1 was long held the test case of such inaccuracy and sceptics were never weary of dwelling upon it; until it was pointed out that the whole "error" was not Luke's but — the sceptic's. Josephus mentions this Lysanias and in such a way that he should not have been confounded with his older namesake; and inscriptions have been brought to light which explicitly assign him to just Luke's date. And so this stock example vanishes into the air from which it was made. The others have met a like fate. The detailed accuracy of the New Testament writers in historical matters is indeed wonderful, and is more and more evinced by every fresh investigation. Every now and then a monument is dug up, touching on some point adverted to in the New Testament; and in every case only to corroborate the New Testament. Thus not only has Luke long ago been proved accurate in calling the ruler of Cyprus a "proconsul," but Mr. Cesnola has lately brought to light a Cyprian inscription which mentions that same Proconsul Paulus whom Luke represents Paul as finding on the island. — ("Cyprus," p. 425.) Let us but consider the unspeakable complication of the political history of those times; — the frequent changes of provinces from senatorial to imperial and *vice versa*, — the many alterations of boundaries and vacillations of relation to the central power at Rome, —which made it the most complicated period the world has ever seen, and renders it the most dangerous ground possible for a forger to enter upon; — and how impossible is it to suppose that a book whose every most incidental notice of historical circumstances is found after most searching criticism to be minutely correct, — which has threaded all this labyrinth with firm and unfaltering step, — was the work of unlearned forgers, writing some hundred years after the facts they record. Confessedly accurate Roman historians have not escaped error here; even Tacitus himself has slipped.[9] To think that a second century forger could have walked scathless among all the pitfalls that gaped around him, is like believing a blind man could thread a row of a hundred cambric needles at a thrust. If we merely apply the doctrine of probabilities to the accuracy of these New Testament writers they are proved to be the work of eye-witnesses and wholly authentic.[10]

We can, then, at the end, but repeat the statement with which we began: Modern negative criticism neither on internal nor on external grounds has been able to throw any doubt on the authenticity of a single book of our New Testament. Their authenticity, accuracy and honesty are super-vindicated by every new investigation. They are thus proved to be the productions of sober, honest, accurate men; they claim verbal inspiration; their claim was allowed by the contemporary church. So far modern criticism has gone step by step with traditional faith. There remains but one critical ground on which the doctrine we are considering can be disputed. Do these books in their internal character negative their claim? Are the phenomena of the writings in conflict with the claim they put forth? We must, then, in conclusion consider this last refuge of objection.

2. Much has been already said incidentally which bears on this point; but something more is needed. An amount of accuracy which will triumphantly prove a book to be genuine and surely authentic, careful and honest, may fall short of proving it to be the very word of God. The question now before us is: Granting the books to be in the main accurate, are they found on the application of a searching criticism to bear such a character as will throw destructive objection in the way of the dogma that they are verbally from God? This inquiry opens a broad — almost illimitable — field, utterly impossible to treat fully here. It may be narrowed somewhat, however, by a few natural observations. (1). It is to be remembered that we are not defending a mechanical theory of inspiration. Every word of the Bible is the word of God according to the doctrine we are discussing; but also and just as truly, every word is the word of a man. This at once sets aside as irrelevant a large number of the objections usually brought from the phenomena of the New Testament against its verbal inspiration. No finding of traces of human influence in the style, wording or forms of statement or argumentation touches

[9] Cf. " Annal," xi. p. 23.
[10] See this slightly touched on by Dr. Peabody, *Princeton Rev.*, March, 1880.

the question. The book is throughout the work of human writers and is filled with the signs of their handiwork. This we admit on the threshold; we ask what is found inconsistent with its absolute accuracy and truth. (2). It is to be remembered, again, that no objection touches the question, that is obtained by pressing the primary sense of phrases or idioms. These are often false; but they are a necessary part of human speech. And the Holy Ghost in using human speech, used it as He found it. It cannot be argued then that the Holy Spirit could not speak of the sun setting, or call the Roman world " the whole world." The current sense of a phrase is alone to be considered; and if men so spoke and were understood correctly in so speaking, the Holy Ghost, speaking their speech would also so speak. No objection then is in point which turns on a pressure of language. Inspiration is a means to an end and not an end in itself; if the truth is conveyed accurately to the ear that listens to it, its full end is obtained. (3). And we must remember again that no objection is valid which is gained by overlooking the prime question of the intentions and professions of the writer. Inspiration, securing absolute truth, secures that the writer shall do what he professes to do; not what he does not profess. If the author does not profess to be quoting the Old Testament *verbatim*, — unless it can be proved that he professes to give the *ipsissima verba*, — then no objection arises against his verbal inspiration from the fact that he does not give the exact words. If an author does not profess to report the exact words of a discourse or a document — if he professes to give, or it is enough for his purposes to give, an abstract or general account of the sense or the wording, as the case may be, — then it is not opposed to his claim to inspiration that he does not give the exact words. This remark sets aside a vast number of objections brought against verbal inspiration by men who seem to fancy that the doctrine supposes men to be false instead of true to their professed or implied intention. It sets aside, for instance, all objection against the verbal inspiration of the Gospels, drawn from the diversity of their accounts of words spoken by Christ or others, written over the cross, etc. It sets aside also all objection raised from the freedom with which the Old Testament is quoted, so long as it cannot be proved that the New Testament writers quote the Old Testament in a different sense from that in which it was written, in cases where the use of the quotation turns on this change of sense. This cannot be proved in a single case.

The great majority of the usual objections brought against the verbal inspiration of the Sacred Scriptures from their phenomena, being thus set aside, the way is open to remarking further, that no single argument can be brought from this source against the church doctrine which does not begin by *proving* an error in statement or contradiction in doctrine or fact to exist in these sacred pages. I say, that does not begin by *proving* this. For if the inaccuracies are apparent only, — if they are not indubitably inaccuracies, — they do not raise the slightest presumption against the full, verbal inspiration of the book. Have such errors been pointed out? That seems the sole question before us now. And any sober criticism must answer categorically to it, No! It is not enough to point to passages *difficult* to harmonize; they cannot militate against verbal inspiration unless it is not only *impossible* for us to harmonize them, but also unless they are of such a character that they are clearly contradictory, so that if one be true the other cannot by any possibility be true. No such case has as yet been pointed out. Why should the New Testament harmonics be dealt with on other principles than those which govern men in dealing with like cases among profane writers? There, it is a first principle of historical science that any solution which affords a possible method of harmonizing any two statements is preferable to the assumption of inaccuracy or error — whether those statements are found in the same or different writers. To act on any other basis, it is clearly acknowledged, is to assume, not prove, error. We ask only that this recognized principle be applied to the New Testament. Who believes that the historians who record the date of Alexander's death — some giving the 28th, some the 30th of the month — are in contradiction? [11] And if means can be found to harmonize them, why should not like cases in the New Testament be dealt with on like principles? If the New Testament writers are held to be independent and accurate writers, — as they are by both parties in this part of our argument, — this is the only rational rule to apply to their writings; and the application of it removes every argument against verbal inspiration drawn from assumed disharmony. Not a single case of disharmony can be proved.

The same principle, and with the same results, may be applied to the cases wherein it is claimed that the New Testament is in disharmony with the profane writers of the times, or other contemporary historical sources. But it is hardly necessary to do so. At the most, only three cases of even possible errors in this sphere can be now even plausibly claimed: the statements regarding the taxing under Quirinius, the revolt under Theudas, and the lordship of Aretas over Damascus. But Zumpt's proof that Quirinius was twice governor of Syria, the first time just after our Lord's birth,

[11] For methods by which these are harmonized, see Lee " Inspiration," p. 350.

sets the first of these aside; whereas the other two, while not corroborated by distinct statements from other sources, yet are not excluded either. Room is found for the insignificant revolt of this Theudas — who is not to be confounded with his later and more important namesake — in Josephus' statement that at this time there were " ten thousand " revolts not mentioned by him. And the lordship of Aretas over Damascus is rendered very probable by what we know from other sources of the posture of affairs in that region, as well as by the significant absence of Roman-Damascene coinage for just this period. Even were the New Testament writers in direct conflict in these or in other statements, with profane sources, it would still not be proven that the New Testament was in error. There would still be an equal chance, to say the least (much too little as it is), that the other sources were in error. But it is never in such conflict; and, therefore, cannot be charged with having fallen into historical error, unless we are prepared to hold that the New Testament writers are not to be believed in any statement which cannot be independently of it proved true; in other words, unless it be assumed beforehand to be untrustworthy. This, again, is to assume, not prove error. Not a single case of error can be proved.

We cannot stop to mention even the fact that no doctrinal contradictions, or scientific errors can be proved. The case stands or falls confessedly on the one question: Are the New Testament writers contradictory to each other or to other sources of information in their record of historical or geographical facts? This settled, indubitably all is settled. We repeat, then, that all the fierce light of criticism which has so long been beating upon their open pages has not yet been able to settle one indubitable error on the New Testament writers. This being so, no argument against their claim to write under a verbal inspiration from God can be drawn from the phenomena of their writings. No phenomena can be pled against verbal inspiration except errors, — no error can be proved to exist within the sacred pages; that is the argument in a nut-shell. Such being the result of the strife which has raged all along the line for decades of years, it cannot be presumptuous to formulate our conclusion here as boldly as after the former heads of discourse: — Modern criticism has absolutely no valid argument to bring against the church doctrine of verbal inspiration, drawn from the phenomena of Scripture. This seems indubitably true.

It is, indeed, well for Christianity that it is. For, if the phenomena of the writings were such as to negative their distinct claim to full inspiration, we cannot conceal from ourselves that much more than their verbal inspiration would have to be given up. If the sacred writers were not trustworthy in such a witness-bearing, where would they be trustworthy? If they, by their performance, disproved their own assertions, it is plain that not only would these assertions be thus proven false, but, also, by the same stroke the makers of the assertions convicted of either fanaticism or dishonesty. It seems very evident, then, that there is no standing ground between the two theories of full verbal inspiration and no inspiration at all. Gaussen is consistent; Strauss is consistent: but those who try to stand between! It is by a divinely permitted inconsistency that they can stand at all. Let us know our position. If the New Testament, claiming full inspiration, did exhibit such internal characteristics as should set aside this claim, it would not be a trustworthy guide to salvation. But on the contrary, since all the efforts of the enemies of Christianity — eager to discover error by which they might convict the precious word of life of falsehood — have proved utterly vain, the Scriptures stand before us authenticated as from God. They are, then, just what they profess to be; and criticism only secures to them the more firmly the position they claim. Claiming to be verbally inspired, that claim was allowed by the church which received them, — their writers approve themselves sober and honest men, and evince the truth of their claim, by the wonder of their performance. So, then, gathering all that we have attempted to say into one point, we may say that modern biblical criticism has nothing valid to urge against the church doctrine of verbal inspiration, but that on the contrary it puts that doctrine on a new and firmer basis and secures to the church Scriptures which are truly divine. Thus, although nothing has been urged formally as a proof of the doctrine, we have arrived at such results as amount to a proof of it. If the sacred writers clearly claim verbal inspiration and every phenomenon supports that claim, and all critical objections break down by their own weight, how can we escape admitting its truth? What further proof do we need?

With this conclusion I may fitly close. But how can I close without expression of thanks to Him who has so loved us as to give us so pure a record of His will, — God-given in all its parts, even though cast in the forms of human speech, — infallible in all its statements, — divine even to its smallest particle! I am far from contending that without such an inspiration there could be no Christianity. Without any inspiration we could have had Christianity; yea, and men could still have heard the truth, and through it been awakened, and justified, and sanctified and glorified. The verities of our faith would remain historically proven true to us — so bountiful has God been in his fostering care — even had we no

Bible; and through those verities, salvation. But to what uncertainties and doubts would we be the prey! — to what errors, constantly begetting worse errors, exposed! —to what refuges, all of them refuges of lies, driven! Look but at those who have lost the knowledge of this infallible guide: see them evincing man's most pressing need by inventing for themselves an infallible church, or even an infallible Pope. Revelation is but half revelation unless it be infallibly communicated; it is but half communicated unless it be infallibly recorded. The heathen in their blindness are our witnesses of what becomes of an unrecorded revelation. Let us bless God, then, for His inspired word! And may He grant that we may always cherish, love and venerate it, and conform all our life and thinking to it! So may we find safety for our feet, and peaceful security for our souls.

INDEX

# INDEX